T0354702

OUTBURSTS OF A PRETENTIOUS HYPOCRITE;

THOUGHTS OF AN ENLISTED SLAVE
(YEAR THREE)

BAETHAN BALOR

OUTBURSTS OF A PRETENTIOUS HYPOCRITE; THOUGHTS OF AN ENLISTED SLAVE (YEAR THREE)

iUniverse books may be ordered through booksellers or by contacting:

iUniverse
1663 Liberty Drive
Bloomington, IN 47403
www.iuniverse.com
844-349-9409

ISBN: 978-1-6632-0626-8 (sc)
ISBN: 978-1-6632-0623-7 (e)

Library of Congress Control Number: 2020915705

Print information available on the last page.

iUniverse rev. date: 09/24/2020

CONTENTS

DEDICATION

Dedicated to my Ego, Self, and I.

"He is at last made free, and presently having nowhere to eat he seeks whom he may flatter, with whom he may sup. He then either submits to prostitution and endures the most infamous degradation, and if he can obtain admission to some great man's table, falls into slavery much worse than the former; or perhaps, if the ignorant fellow should grow rich, he dotes upon some girl, laments, and is unhappy, and wishes for slavery again."

- Epictetus, *The Discourses*

ACKNOWLEDGMENT

Entities are accounted to the best of my
truth. Errors in spelling, punctuation, grammar, and
syntax are fundamental. The reader is a fool.

NOVEMBER

1:57 PM

Journals are self-indulgent.

I begin a new document (to my embittered satisfaction) with irreverent vulgarity:[1]

Two Old Men Sitting on Chairs on a Backyard Patio in Suburban America Engaged in Conversation

The first man is an ascetic.

The second man is a child rapist.

The child rapist said, "I never liked you."

The ascetic laughed and said, "You think I give a shit what *you*, of all people, think of me?"

"I think you do."

"Fuck you Jeff, that's what I think of you."

The child rapist leaned forward in his seat, raised his arms out in front of him, and said, "Why do people call each other by name when trying to sound sincere, I mean—what determines if someone greets you with, 'Hey *man*,' or 'Hey *Paulie*,' I really want to know. What are they playing at?"

The ascetic frowned and said, "Don't call me Paulie, you know I hate that."

"Please."

"No—no fucking 'please.' Just don't."

The child rapist slapped the inner of his sweat-laden thighs and said, "See, there you go—always no fun to be around. Why the fuck do I even come out here?"

"I'm your only friend."

The child rapist sipped his beer and eyed the grill. He said, "Yeah, don't remind me," and leaned back in his chair.

The ascetic said, "Why not?"

---

[1] The accompanying story incited the severance of an amorous relationship with a previous employer (Chloe), my gift to her one evening on her request for an example of my writing; she wept two-thirds through the read, finished, and said, "Why? I hate *it*. I'm going to bed. I hate *it*; there are absolutely no redeemable qualities in that story at all."

"You aren't exactly pleasant company."

"Then get the fuck outta' here."

"No, I like *it* here."

Chicken flesh sizzled; the child rapist licked his lips and tapped his foot on a stone patio; he said, "Awesome weather we're havin' lately, blue skies, not a cloud up there."

"Don't start with the weather."

"Alright then—what—what the fuck would be acceptable dialogue for you, what can you tolerate?"

"Have you taken up any new hobbies?" muttered the ascetic.

"Besides the one I already have—no, why?"

"What's that, watching football all day?"

The child rapist leaned to his right, farted, and said, "I don't watch football all day, only the team I care about."

"Why do you care about a specific football team?"

"Why the fuck do you care?" snorted the child rapist.

The ascetic crossed his right leg over his left leg and said, "Why do you watch so much football? Go outside and play football—look at yourself Jeff—you fat fucking pig."

The child rapist chortled and said, "I'm sixty-four years old; did you forget—you fucking idiot?"

"I'm fifty-nine and I'm not a slovenly heap of shit like you."

"Sure, let me call all my buddies up and arrange a game of football on Sunday evenings. Bring the kids—bring the whole fucking family!" yelled the child rapist; he smiled and sniffed at two bubbles of foam on the rim of his beer can.

"That'd be something."

"What the fuck do *you* even do all day?"

The ascetic smiled, tilted a glass of water up to his lips, sipped, swallowed, looked up towards the sky, and said, "This."

"Fuck you."

"Go home then if you don't like what I do."

"I don't give a fuck about what you do; *it's* the matter that I don't like being judged."

The ascetic turned to the child rapist, raised an eyebrow, and said, "Holy shit. You *are* upset."

"Yeah? Did you expect a different reaction? I don't judge you for your lifestyle, why judge me then? I don't care how long I've known you—*Paulie*."

"We've talked about this before; everybody judges everyone, don't deny *it*."

"I don't judge you *Paulie*—look, I'm not askin' for much here. Be a fucking friend and don't shame me for how I live my life—alright?"

"If you feel ashamed of my observations of you, that should tell you something. You are in control of-"

"Fuck you Paul. *Fuck* you."

The ascetic nodded towards the grill and said, "Wings smell done."

"Want me to check?"

"Yeah."

The child rapist grunted, lurched to the edge of his seat, stood, murmured to himself, hobbled to the grill, stopped halfway, placed his right hand over his left thigh, bent forward, grimaced, and said, "Knee is fuckin' killin' me."

"Probably because you sit on your ass watching football and drinking beer instead of exercising for an hour every day."

The child rapist grinned and said, "You know watching football isn't all I do."

The ascetic locked eyes with the child rapist and said, "Yes—I know."

The child rapist lifted the grill cover and sniffed; he picked up a pair of tongs on an adjacent table, prodded three of the eighteen wings on the rack, and said, "Oh yeah baby—lookin' good."

"What the hell are you doing? Leave them be."

A fire alarm for the town resounded from a distant street.

The child rapist said, "Relax will ya'. Just giving a little love to these bad boys."

"Don't push them around, *pick* them up and flip them. That's how tongs are used you idiot."

The child rapist said, "Oh?" and poked two more wings with the tongs.

The ascetic stared at the child rapist's back, the rolls of fat around his waist, the wisps of frayed hair on the lower region of his neck, the whitened nubs of chafed elbows, and said, "You still in that cult?"

"Oh here we go, gonna' judge me on that too?"

"I'll take that as a 'yes.'"

"Yeah—I enjoy *it*."

The ascetic rattled the ice in his glass and said, "I thought I'd let you know that the local nursery in this neighborhood is looking for volunteers."

The child rapist gazed over his shoulder at the ascetic and said, "Do we have plates out here or what?"

"Second to the last shelf."

"Real funny by the way. Do you plan to mock me all evening or are we gonna' eat some fuckin' chicken wings and discuss business as we intended?"

The ascetic sighed and said, "Always business with you. Why don't you find yourself a wife."

"After four of them I decided to take matters into my own hands."

"Yes—you certainly have."

The child rapist fumbled with the drawer and said, "Second to last?"

"Yeah."

"*It*'s locked."

"No *it*'s not."

The child rapist tugged harder and the drawer eased open; he pulled two silver plates from the compartment, slammed the shelf closed, and said, "Silver? Why not gold?"

The ascetic sneered at him and said, "Those were gifts."

"I have gold."

"Of course you do."

The child rapist inspected each wing; his head hovered inches above the grill; he said, "Oh, yeah baby—look at that. Damn."

The ascetic cleared his throat and said, "What business, then?"

"Funny you mention the *cult*, as you like to call *it*. We'd like to extend an invitation to you."

"I can't afford *it*."

The child rapist chuckled and said, "Don't worry about that; I got you covered."

"Oh?"

"You've no idea, Paulie, of what I have—what I've done."

"What's *it* like from way up there, surrounded by enemies, yet your brothers by oath. Are you ever scared for your life?"

The child rapist straightened, his gaze fixed ahead at the forest's edge several meters out from the patio; he said, "No."

"What about your family?"

"What fucking family—my divorced wives and my kids who don't even know me?"

The ascetic cocked his head and said, "You don't care for them at all?"

"Why the hell should—no, why the hell *would* I? Are you interested in joining or not—christ."

"You really are a slovenly bastard. Sit around with all your money watching football, no care in the world other than yourself."

"Is that supposed to hurt my feelings?" quipped the child rapist.

The ascetic narrowed his eyes and said, "No."

"How many wings do you want?"

"Eight, well—I'll take seven."

"Ten *it* is."

"I don't want *ten;* I want seven."

The child rapist mock-blubbered and said, "Want—want—want, listen to yourself, you big baby. Take what you get."

The ascetic accepted the plateful of wings extended to him and said, "I don't think I'd join even if you covered the expenses."

"Think. If. You sound awfully fickle."

"I'm contemplating the option," whispered the ascetic.

"Good. We'd like to have you. At least I know I would."

"I'm flattered."

The child rapist said, "You should be," and transferred the remainder of the fourteen chicken wings from the grill to his plate; he shuffled towards his seat, looked down at the ascetic, gestured an outstretched hand to his left, and said, "What the hell did you take most-the food for Paulie?"

The ascetic peeled the skin off a wing, opened his mouth to form a word, closed his mouth, and shook his downcast head.

The child rapist said, "Skins' the best part."

"Unhealthy."

"We're all gonna' die someday."

"Sooner you than me."

The child rapist fell back into his chair, outstretched his legs, moaned, and said, "Yeah baby, but first, I'm gonna' eat me some of these *damn fine* chicken wings—skin and all."

"You'd eat the bone too if you could."

"I *can,* but I won't."A squirrel emerged from the forest, ran across the lawn, and hid behind a wooden shed. The child rapist said, "Look at that little fucker. What do you think squirrels do all day?"

"Climb trees, collect nuts, fuck each other and run around."

"Sounds like a great life to me."

"I thought that *it is* your life."

The child rapist flexed and said, "I do *it* all besides climb trees."

The ascetic smiled and peeled the skin off another wing; he said, "I'd like to see you try to climb a tree."

"I used to climb many back in my prime."

"Did you play a lot of football too?"

The child rapist dropped a half-eaten chicken wing onto his plate and said, "What the fuck do you have against football?"

"You sit around watching football—staring at a T.V.—subjecting yourself to all the advertisements that run between sessions."

"Yeah—so what?"

"Your mind is numbed and you end up the way you are now."

The child rapist grinned and said, "And what way would that be?"

"Dissipated."

"What the fuck do you mean by that?"

"You're a useless degenerate focused entirely on the pursuit of pleasure."

The child rapist gnawed at a different chicken wing, tore a large chunk of flesh from the bone, and said, "Oh—and you're focused entirely on the pursuit of, displeasure, or just being a haughty *douche*bag?"

"Health and contentment."

"A douchebag then."

The ascetic fingered the wings on his plate, pushed them around, lifted one by the tip, and said, "I don't want all these. Take three."

"You might sin if you eat more than *exactly* seven."

The ascetic lifted the plate off his lap and leaned towards the child rapist. "Take three of them."

"No, a growing boy like yourself needs the extra protein."

"They'll go to waste—just take them."

"Weren't you the one who told me that 'there is nothing lost or wasted in this life'? Where'd you read that, a self-help book?"

The ascetic returned the plate to his lap, peeled the skin off a third wing, and said, "I figured you'd be happy to have them."

The child rapist gasped and said, "*Oh!* You thought I'd be *happy?* You're such a sweetheart."

"Remind me why I invited you over."

"You wanted to join our merry band of men and I'm the guy to talk to."

The ascetic stared down at his plate and closed his eyes; he opened them, turned his chest towards the child rapist, and said, "I have no interest in ass-fucking kids."

"You don't know what you're missing."

"You're right."

The child rapist picked at a piece of meat between his teeth; orange hot sauce outlined his lips; he said, *"It*'s good for your health—physical and mental. Enlightening, I'd say."

"Enlightening?"

"It stimulates the pineal gland."

"You believe that?"

"Hell—of course I do, I've experienced *it.*"

The ascetic watched the squirrel peek out from behind the shed, sniff the air, and disappear back into the forest. "How many times?"

The child rapist laughed, slurped his beer, and sucked chicken grease off the nail of his right index finger. "Hundreds, brother. Done me *wonders.*"

"Wonders. Fucking kids in the ass has 'done you *wonders.*' I think I've heard enough."

"Thinking does you no good. Better to have experiences."

"Thinking is unfamiliar territory for you."

"Thinking didn't make me rich, Paulie. Action did."

The ascetic poked at the wings on his plate and slid whitened bones against a heap of skin. "You disgust me."

The child rapist sighed, chewed harder, tucked his feet under the space of his chair, and said, "Who are you to judge me?"

"Paulie."

The child rapist chortled and winked. "My old friend *Paulie.*"

A patch of clouds rolled in from beyond the horizon where treetops rimmed the sky and concealed an afternoon sun.

The ascetic said, "I think you should go."

"What? I just got here; I'm not even finished eating; we've hardly spoken of business."

"I don't care about *business,* haven't I made that clear?"

"What's wrong with you? I haven't done fuck-all to deserve this."

The ascetic grimaced and said, "This is my home, and I'm ready for you to go."

The child rapist set his plate of wings on the patio and wiped the sauce stained on his hands along the sides of his cargo shorts. He groaned, burped, turned full-body towards the ascetic and said, "Listen to me— what I'm offering you is a one-time deal; opportunities like this don't come every day, you know this Paulie, c'mon." He paused and examined the ascetic's face:

Vacant.

The child rapist coughed twice and said, "We're a group of highly esteemed and respectable gentleman that-"

"*Esteemed* and *respectable?* You fuck toddlers in the ass."

"But you know *why*—Paulie, you *know* of the otherworldly."

"Only what you've told me."

"That's not all we do."

The ascetic peeled the skin off a fifth wing. "What else do you do Jeff?"

"We eat them after."

"You eat the kids *after* you fuck them?"

The child rapist smiled and cocked his head. "Well we clean them first of course; a long hose attachment gets the job done. All jokes aside, we only eat the parts that matter."

"What parts would those be?"

"Well, *it's* more of a conglomeration, a blend—spirit cooking as we dubbed *it.*" The child rapist slurped on the rim of his beer, drained the remnants, crunched the can in his fist, and continued, "We mix swine blood, human semen, and fresh breast milk from our very own Abigail in a large vat. After that, we divvy up the portions in wine glasses and roll out the kid on one of those fancy restaurant serving trays. Most times they're baked; sometimes we have em' raw, slit down the middle so we can reach in and take what we want—most times they're baked, though. When they're baked, we're told in advance and we let the cook know—usually Frank—what we want."

The ascetic watched a small plume of smoke circle upwards from the coals in the basin of the grill. "So, what parts do *you* eat?"

"I always go for the brain but usually that bastard Howard always gets *it*—fucking cunt. If not the brain… the heart and liver. A few of the guys tell me the consumption of brains makes you crazy; explains Howard's behavior, I think he paid them to tell me that."

"Does *it* taste any good?"

"What, brains? You ever had roe?"

"Once, many years ago."

"Well, the brain tastes like fish roe, without the fishiness."

"I don't remember what roe tastes like."

The child rapist scratched his head and said, "They taste like eggs—a scrambled egg, closest comparison to your civilian food I can think of."

The ascetic smirked and said, *"Civilian* food? You pompous lot."

"Pompous for a reason brother, I've never felt better in my life since I started six—no." The child rapist squinted his eyes, "Seven months ago—I think. Somewhere between six and seven, but man—I'm telling you Paulie, you gotta' put morality aside and consider the deal I'm offering you."

"I think you're a sick fuck—and you should leave."

The child rapist fidgeted and shifted in his seat; plastic chair legs scraped against stone. "I figured you'd say that, but please—*Paulie*, look at who's asking you right now. Fuck, I'm *begging* you, I'll pay the fees. C'mon buddy, humor an old pal and *experience* something rather than… sitting around all day in this rundown shit hole with nothing but thoughts and your hand in the wee hours of the night."

"You're dense."

The child rapist giggled, leaned back in his chair, relaxed, and said, "If you would-"

A man in a soiled white clown suit emerged from the forest's edge and stood motionless next to the shed. Three large balls adorned the front of the suit: orange, fuzzy, and frayed. A blue cone-shaped hat framed the forehead of his monochrome-painted face.

The child rapist said, "What in the *fuck,*" and pointed at the clown.

The ascetic peered up from his sixth wing and said, "What?" He saw the man by the forest's edge. "Oh—what the hell, is that a *clown?*"

"Yeah. What the fuck."

The ascetic scrutinized the clown for six seconds, set his plate on the patio to his left, stood, and said, "Get the fuck off my property!"

The clown sprinted towards the patio; a machete swung in large vertical arcs at his side.

The child rapist said, *"Holy fuck!"*

The ascetic's eyes widened; he stumbled on the leg of his chair in an attempt to flee.

The clown rounded the grill and shrieked a low, guttural, masculine cry; he hammered the machete down into the ascetic's neck. Blood spurted from the gash across the patio stone and arched upwards onto the child rapist's lap. The clown raised his right leg, kicked a slippered foot at the ascetic's left shoulder, and wrenched the machete free. The ascetic clawed at the wound, sputtered, convulsed, and collapsed face-first onto the patio.

Transfixed by the spectacle, the child rapist remained seated, stupefied.

The clown swung the bloodstained machete against the child rapist's left arm, split bone, released the machete handle, and lurched onto the child rapist's lap. The plastic chair tilted back, destabilized, and slipped out from underneath both.

The clown wedged both knees against the child rapist's bloated abdomen; he gripped the bald temples of the child rapist's head and slammed the rear of the skull against the stone patio with nine, forceful, consecutive movements. All quieted. The clown scurried up from the moribund body, retrieved the machete, and bounded back into the forest.

9:33 PM

Another late-night bound through the boneyard, clear skies reveal a bright oval moon slanted against a starless sky. My muscles ache from moderate calisthenics. Deadlifts and squats would be far more effective.

My father gifted me an old shoebox wrapped in yellow smiley face wrapping paper for my birthday. Written in black permanent marker on the box cover: **"First aid supplies."** Eight cans of sardines, three cans of tuna, and three cans of anchovies met my eyes on the removal of the lid; a suitable gift for one of my tastes. He said, "I'm worried about you."

I stared at the corner of the shoebox, the blurred contours of a dessert tray full of wrapped candies, an old trash removal bill positioned upright against a square tote, and said, "Why," as a rhetorical statement.

"You seem despondent."

I stretched my arms over the kitchen table and said, "Yes. I'll be going now."

We hugged: an exchange of oxytocin.

In my unheated attic apartment, Bulgarian orthodox church music plays from my writing device stationed on top of my podium. Aristotle's *Nicomachean Ethics* is splayed open and balanced on the corner. An empty bottle inherited from the nursing home is set to my right. A few pens. A flashlight. Several copies of my first published book, a folded burlap bank bag. Three copies of Epictetus' *The Enchiridion* stacked on the kitchen counter. Merino wool gloves tucked inside of cut resistant gloves bestowed to me from the medical facility. A row of spices and a bottle of apple cider vinegar. A compact umbrella. A skeletal-hand goblet. A roll of paper towels.

I spy with my little eye… a dead fly upturned on the windowsill.

Oh!—I see *it!*

November 21st, 2018

10:57 AM

Thirty-nine days until homelessness. I have many plans in motion.

November 22nd, 2018

8:21 PM

An unexpected Thanksgiving spent with Chloe in a galley full of strangers; we dined on cold turkey and exchanged life sentiments over obnoxious chatter and song. Afterward, I returned to her suburban villa and watched *Frontline* videos in condemnation of neo-nazi practitioners with her. Thereafter, we descended to her basement and smashed clay pots wrapped in towels in preparation for a mannequin decoration project I intend to never see to fruition.

On our return upstairs, we partook in reheated chicken noodle soup, and I commented on my listlessness, disassociation with the "self" and cited Chloe's previous statement half a year ago of "cognitive dissonance" as a reference for her to associate with. Chloe commented on my potential depression and considers me to be autistic[2]—*intelligent*, though… always the supposed *intelligence*.

We watched the first episode of a show titled, *The Good Doctor,* I presume as a sympathetic demonstration of the merits of autistic people. I didn't relate. What merit is an autistic man bestowed with a keen emotional intelligence?

Chloe gifted me one-third of a block of cheddar cheese, a pack of raspberries, and a windbreaker jacket. More items would have been gifted to me if I hadn't protested and proclaimed my disgruntled reluctance.

I assisted Chloe with a late-night after-dinner digital documentation transference: a reboot of a computer and a copy of photos from one harddrive to another. On her bookshelf, Eckhart Tolle's *A New Earth; Awakening to your Life's Purpose,"* seized my attention.

---

[2] Chloe's beliefs of my autism are new conceptions of her perceptions of my character due to our recent interaction. My conduct is void of pretenses I once practiced when with her; my once-proud, animated, arrogant, and downright pompous character diminished to a reactive wretch. There is no care.

Tolle's philosophy is a vacuous head bobble accompanied with a contented smile.

A brief flip through the book revealed a bottom-left page folded inward. I began to read the passages printed on the two pages—marked by Chloe—splayed open in my hands, and marveled on the oscillations of archetypes, the happenstance occurrence of my compulsion:

"*It* is important to recognize here that the story and the thought forms that make up the story, whether people agree with *it* or not, have absolutely nothing to do with who you are. Even if people agree with *it*, *it* is ultimately a fiction. Many people don't realize until they are on their deathbed and everything external falls away that nothing ever had anything to do with who they are. In the proximity of death, the whole concept of ownership stands revealed as ultimately meaningless. In the last moments of their life, they then also realize that while they were looking throughout their lives for a more complete sense of self, what they were really looking for, their Being, had actually always already been there, but had been largely obscured by their identification with things, which ultimately means identification with their mind.

"'Blessed are the poor in spirit,' Jesus said, 'for theirs will be the kingdom of heaven.' What does 'poor in spirit' mean? No inner baggage, no identifications. Not with things, nor with any mental concepts that have a sense of self in them. And what is the 'kingdom of heaven' The simple but profound joy of Being that is there when you let go of identifications and so become 'poor in spirit'.

"This is why renouncing all possessions has been an ancient spiritual practice in both East and West. Renunciation of possessions, however, will not automatically free you of the ego. *It* will attempt to ensure *it*s survival by finding something else to identify with, for example, a mental image of yourself as someone who has transcended all interest in material possessions and is therefore superior, is more spiritual than others. There are people who have renounced all possessions but have a bigger ego than some millionaires. If you take away one kind of identification, the ego will quickly find another. *It* ultimately doesn't mind what *it* identifies with as long as *it* has an identity. Anti-consumerism or anti-private ownership would be another thought form, another mental position, that can replace identification with possessions. Through *it* you could make yourself right and others wrong. As we shall see later, making yourself right and others wrong is one of the principal egoic mind patterns, one of the main forms of unconsciousness. In other words, the content of the ego may change; the mind structure that keeps *it* alive does not."[3]

Eckhart Tolle's conviction of his belief that the ego will always seek a new identification is *his* identification with his own ego; he tells the story of his own experiences and supposed comprehension of consciousness.

Though I *do* agree, the ego is what compels us to become something other than what we are. If the majority of the human population were "poor in spirit," civilization would collapse and tyrants would reign; is this the vision of *a new earth?* To write a book with "A New Earth" as a title is an egoic identification—*to write a book*—is to imply that others are in need of corrective information in order to transform human affairs (The book is issued as "self-help").

"Jesus wept."

- The Bible, Gospel of John, 11:35

Why did Jesus weep: An unparalleled ego.

November 23rd, 2018

11:12 AM

"When I first met him, he swept me off my feet with his cleverness and wit!" said a far-gone woman; her pensive stare pierced the visage of the man with whom she spoke.

The man nodded and said, "Oh yeah."

"Charming and handsome—and so well-kept—the bastard never cared for me."

"Uh-huh."

"I don't know why I even bother talking about him with you."

"Hm."

"You don't even care about me either. I'm so sick of men."

---
[3] Eckhart Tolle's *A New Earth; Awakening to your Life's Purpose*

"Ah…" the man tugged at a fishing rod and said, "Why do you say that?"

The woman huffed, turned away, and said, "You care more about catching some dumb fish than you do about listening to me."

The man observed the slow encroachment of a low tide lap against a pebbled shoreline and said, "Why do you think that?"

An exasperated sigh from the woman split the prolonged period of silence between the man's question and her answer into two vexing segments; she fiddled with a hairbrush pressed tight between her two reddened palms with intent to crush the wooden handle and said, "I don't care anymore."

"Huh," said the man.

November 24th, 2018

5:07 PM

I've sent an email to Chloe stating reasons for severance of our relationship, and grieved on behalf of humanity.

I ascended a mountain with two work acquaintances one late winter night. Our flashlights guided the way; impermeable darkness enclosed around narrow beams of three erratic rays. We emerged from a steep trail at the mountain summit and clambered onto a rocky pinnacle layered with snowy striations. Frigid winds lashed over our hats and face masks—chilled to the bone. The three of us paused and admired a starry sky laced with thin rows of dusky clouds and the expanse of civilization far below us. Veritable kings—little "big" boys on the mountaintop—we roared together, an ephemeral triumph, an escape from the reality of responsibility. I removed my overburdened pack from my back and withdrew a large rectangular black loudspeaker from the main compartment. My associates gazed down at my activity, bewildered and amused with my antics.

J. S. Bach's *Mass in B Minor* began, a glorious outburst of harmonics carried away by thirty mile-per-hour winds. Laughter ensued behind me. I stepped forward to the edge of the outcrop, limbs spread-eagled—arms stretched to the sky, and boots braced against the smooth, flat expanse of the mountain's apex. Icy gusts whipped crystallized tears out from the contours of my eyes. I smiled: a great, toothy beam behind my face mask—prepared to die—pushed over the edge by my two fickle relations—a moment I embraced the "thought" of—ready for, a moment which (obviously) never transpired.

My companions veered away and left me at the peak, absorbed in my morbid fantasies, a soul whisked out of a body through the ethereal resonance of the choir surged up and out of an electronic component; the reality of my imagination dawned on me then. Soon after the music began, the youthful magic ebbed. To my right, my companions snapped and gathered suitable twigs, tree bark, and foliage for a fire. I joined them, and we started a meager blaze in a hollowed quasi cave of stone where they recounted the women they once claimed as their own.

I listened.

November 26th, 2018

7:56 PM

Canned Fish

Greasy lips drip oil
Onto the contours of my chin.
Tuna, sardines, anchovies and kippers;
Mercury-laden treats prompt
Salivary glands to excrete.
Headless morsels impaled on
Prongs of plastic forks.

The family below me love each other. My presence is a faded red ember compared to the radiant blue flame of activity shared between all members. The grandmother occupies the bottom apartment while the stepfather/father occupies the one below mine. In the mother's absence, due to her jail sentence, family bonds have amplified.

I hear, to my dismay, the activities and conversations of the three children, the father, and the grandmother: dishwashing, food preparation, jovial outbursts, bounds up and down the stairwell. Most often I hear the children shout, "I love you!" directed at the grandmother, accompanied by a door slam.

Above the tribe, I lurk, and appreciate the dynamics from a ceiling/floor away.

I imagine late-night secrets whispered between the two youngest of the three, tucked into respective beds within a shared room:

"A strange man lives in the attic," whispered an adolescent girl to her younger brother.

The boy pulled a massive green sheet up to his neck and said, "He's nice to us; he wrote us stories."

"He's creepy though," muttered the girl. "Sometimes I don't even think he's there, and then he walks and I get kinda scared."

The boy flared his nose, lifted his chin, and said, "Daddy doesn't like him."

"I know."

"Daddy says there's something not right about him."

November 27th, 2018

2:44 PM

At the age of twenty, I volunteered to inherit a Betta fish from a previous lover's friend. This fish swam in a small glass bowl mounted on top of a square wooden stand beside my desk in an empty apartment I once shared with the aforementioned lover. The fish came to me with a pineapple ornament inspired from the cartoon show *Spongebob Squarepants*, erect in the center of the bowl, wedged into a layer of brown pebbles.

I visited the local pet store and browsed various ornamentations for fish and settled on a miniature mountain themed with three grey skulls; slackened jaws and angry sockets served as entry and exit points. The mountain supplanted the pineapple and I also implemented a three-inch double-sided mirror suspended by a small floatation device.

The Betta fish, whose name I fail to recall (I believe I renamed him/ her *it* "Fish"), attacked the reflection of *it*self. This exercise of illusory futility amused me for two days. On the third day, I pitied Fish, and removed the mirror. However, soon after the mirror's removal, Fish began to float with listless intent around the contours of the bowl at a pace akin to a snail—enough to oxygenate *it*self. I reinstalled the mirror, and to my quizzical satisfaction, Fish's vigor restored; sustained attacks began anew.

Despite my cleaning of the bowl, pebbles, and miniature mountain twice within the first week of my inheritance, Fish developed fin rot due to the uncouth conditions and frigid temperatures of the water on account of the previous owner. I attempted every known remedy to cure Fish of the corruption and watched the creature degrade into a zombified vessel. My efforts failed; the research of the most humane ways to end the life of a fish was my only recourse:

I dumped Fish outside near a trash and recycling bin behind the apartment and struck Fish's skull with a hammer. The single strike exacted a quick death, to my satisfaction. I dropped the lifeless body into the trash bin.

5:53 PM

I've passed the preliminary qualification test for entry into the United States Navy with what my two recruiters inform me is an "excellent score"; my interest in nuclear engineering has been questioned; my interest is null.

Journalism is a volunteer occupation aboard a vessel.

Counterintelligence, mechanical engineer, and research psychology were a few options dangled before me with intent to entice.

My recruiter disclosed a "Chaplain Assistant" role in response to my query of a sociological opportunity during the ride back to my apartment.

I said, "Oh—a *bodyguard*… For a *priest!*"

My recruiter grinned and said, "Yes. Depending on the sector you're assigned, you could be presented opportunities to assist with creative writing."

I smiled (acknowledged the humor), braced my hands on my thighs, and said, "That's just the icing on the cake."

Tomorrow and Sunday are further lectures on my opportunities. Monday is my vocational aptitude test and four-hour medical examination. I've requested immediate deployment and have been guaranteed a ship date January; if circumstances proceed per "perfection": late December.

November 28th, 2018

8:26 AM

New research "reveals" there is no difference in the benefits of caloric restriction or intermittent fasting; there is no difference between a low carbohydrate and high-fat intake diet than there is from a high carbohydrate and low-fat diet; a diet with a balance of "healthier" fats and carbohydrates is crucial.

New research "reveals" data masqueraded as information and interpreted as knowledge.

4:42 PM

One chilly twilight, an earthworm bored up from the warm depths of the earth. Minuscule muscles contracted and coiled against a layer of frozen topsoil. Pebbles shifted; the worm emerged, drained and lifeless, out onto a patch of withered grass alongside a suburban sidewalk.

"Ah," thought the worm, "Now I shall fleet this body and end the eternal turmoil of my accursed flesh; enough damnation and anguish— take me, sweet wintry winds and crystalline grass blades, and pass me through the nether, beyond the infinite expanse of all I will ever know and cease to-"

A crow swooped down and initiated a voracious series of nine consecutive pecks. The worm thrashed and ripped into four flaccid segments, each swallowed by the crow in seven seconds. The crow turned to an author seated on a nearby bench and said, *"If twenty worms writhed on the ground, and I pecked seventy-two times, how many worm segments could I swallow?"* and cawed.

The author said, "I'm no mathematician, now fly away so I may observe your stride."

"At least try."

The author shifted straight against the bench, aligned his pencil with the spiral binding of a moleskine notebook, and murmured, "Well that'd be… Seventy-two you said?—multiplied by four…" he counted on his fingers, hesitated, and announced, "two-hundred and eight."

"You forgot to divide by the rate at which I swallow."

"Oh come on now—first of all, you're a crow, what do you know more about mathematics than I—and second, I haven't performed a dividing calculation in years, and I can already tell that two-hundred and eight divided by four—eight, no, I don't even *know* the rate at which you swallow for you haven't specified—and third, you've broken my train of thought; such a wonderful scene, watching you eat that morsel, and you tarnish the moment with your theoretical challenge of how much you *could* eat if twenty worms lay sprawled out across the lane, *as if* that would ever happen."

"I'm disappointed by you."

"I have-"

The crow surged up from the cold earth and flew behind a slanted rooftop.

November 29th, 2018

8:24 PM

All people lie.

November 30th, 2018

6:25 PM

A month to train before boot camp revitalizes my *desire*. I've signed up for a local gym and begin anew with strength training. Now, a run.

7:50 PM

There will be no pretense, no variable style of clothes, no mating dance.

There will be superiors, equals, and inferiors.

"*It* is better to live with one free man and to be without fear and free, than to be a slave with many."

-Enchiridion, Fragments of Epictetus

Ah, and if freedom entails destitution and a night-time sprawl out in a frozen gutter, or being a veritable leech among others who failed to help themselves in a ~~welfare distribution center~~ homeless shelter, what is *better?*

Who is a once-crippled-now-dead slave to judge on what is better when his limited condition is all he ever knew? Epictetus, on his freedom, "escaped" to a home with a wife and raised *her* brood. Hypocrisy? Contentment?

"If you seek the truth, you will not seek by every means to gain a victory; and if you have found truth, you will have the gain of not being defeated."

- Enchiridion, Fragments of Epictetus

And if there *is no truth* (there isn't), you will have the loss of perpetual defeat.

What then, if truth *is* victory, and you pursue all means to seek truth despite the cruel ~~fact~~ opinion that there is ~~none~~ god?

Oh—yes, *scientific* and *mathematical* ~~facts~~ theories—paradigms—a sham, a scry into the infinite unknown, a means to an inconceivable end. The number of religious doctrines is on par with the multitudinous languages of the world.

Stumble into a decrepit wooden shack nestled inside a shadowy canopy of tangled vines deep within the jungles of Brazil and you'll encounter an altar dedicated to a monstrous deity worshipped through the utilization of petrified wooden blocks inscribed with symbolic anomalies.

DECEMBER

December 1st, 2018

8:01 AM

Spontaneous messages received and reciprocated from Dick, my expelled roommate:

Dick: Remember this. You will see me again. You are a fruitcake and everyone you work with says this. Remember I know people you work with nutcase.
Baethan: I'll remember that.
Dick: You will when I see you. And I will. You were lucky you were not there when I 'seen' my stuff.
Baethan: Why?
Dick: Use that thing you wanna' call a brain child.
Baethan: You would behave as the intemperate man you are and yell insults?
Dick: You will have to wait and see. Cannot insult someone like you anyways. The fact you were born is insult enough to society.
Baethan: I'm impervious to being insulted yet you insult me.
Dick: One day you will see. Now lose my number ya' tard. Not gonna' deal with a child.
Baethan: Somewhere... Over the rainbow...
Dick: Like I said, lose my number child.

10:44 PM

I lay for two hours on the floor in an attempt to sleep and listen to the incessant low-pitched murmur of a paper mill.
I'm too young to die... I'm too old to cry...

December 2nd, 2018

7:58 AM

"Amor Fati-"
Love of one's fate.
I don't believe in either. Emotional states are transient, inconsequential

reminders to function. Wake up beside a sultry woman; stroke your palms down her bare thigh, up a hip, to the defined inner curvature of her waist, to the flattened flesh of a breast against her sternum. A sensual moan slips out from between her lustrous lips. What an elegant, slender neck. What immaculate skin, devoid of blemishes. Ah, and her face... Oh... That *feeling* of love between your legs arises. Pursue your fate.

Love of one's children is the quintessential love of one's fate.

An inscrutable reality of sensory inputs and bizarre occurrences, of energy exchange, of infinite reasons to fear with no cause, of symbiotic reciprocations and mutual perspectives, of circles and angles.

Strung up by broken limbs and confined to a hospital bed; life is a gift.

Skewered by a pike and suspended over a cooking fire; life is a gift.

Shot by a hollow-point .50 caliber round on account of your beliefs; life is a gift.

Cuddle up with your family and think *it* all away; life is a gift.

6:13 PM

I'm in a hotel room and have consumed a large, colorful chicken salad. My roommate: a nervous, vexed, eighteen-year-old-enlisted-marine-infantryman, struggles to defecate in the bathroom. Prior to our shared dinner, I gave him a copy of *The Enchiridion* despite his disinterest in literature. He hopes to kill "evil people" and believes his meaning of life is the defense of the country. The initial motivation for his decision to join the military is the video game, *Call of Duty*. He achieved an above average-score on the qualification test and admitted to me that he guessed on the majority of the questions. I'll never see him again after tonight.

8:16 PM

The void in my heart swells; to be aware of the body—a piece of meat to be tossed to a machine, is absolution. All ordeals meet at a culmination, and I hope to find my end stained in blood or reduced to a pulp. My spirit yearns to be broken; my body, to be mangled and abused. A marine may have been the better calling. The one I room with reads through the fragments of *The Enchiridion* and sighs aloud. I know he is grateful, and I, too, am grateful for the feelings he shares with me, for being among the presence of one who is youthful and vibrant with fear.

26

To be one with a unit, shamed, humiliated, defaced, and destroyed—I yearn for the subjugation, dejection, the ridicule, the abrasive atrocity of being human among a clan of fellow rejects, fearless and fearful, shameful and shameless—is there a difference between flesh when the soul—whatever *that* is—may gleam with a vibrancy despite the external conditions perceived to be lamentable?

Epictetus may have brought solace to a kindred spirit in need of guidance… love, whatever *it* is. The youngster devours the words of the ancient stoic behind me while together we listen to the glorious cantatas of J.S. Bach; he prepares for departure to boot camp the following morning, whereas I await the full test of my aptitudes, physical condition, and *mental* integrity.

Lies.

Peter bounced an inflated red ball into a street.

"Peter!" yelled Peter's mother, and the young boy trounced along, unaware of a-

"Look at the duck!" yelled Peter's mother.

Peter glanced at the duck on a sidewalk and smiled.

December 3rd, 2018

4:37 PM

I passed my exam with opportunities for any (rating) job except aviation due to poor depth perception. Failure to swear an oath for enlistment occurred due to my pending results of an STD test.[4] One of my three recruiters and I stormed into the hospital and retrieved the records right before closing hours; he pledged to have me sworn in with a chosen job by this Thursday or next Monday.

One young Irish man I sat with on my way to the facility, two years younger than myself, failed to enlist due to poor hearing; his dreams were crushed and visions wiped away. I offered him a cookie and potato chips provided as tertiary nourishment to my sandwich and salad; he refused, defeated and crestfallen, and exited the facility to never return, family

---

[4] Intercourse with Shelly from last year disturbed me and I (finally) purchased a full spectrum blood work exam from my local hospital; the results tested negative and needed to be faxed to the military facility in order for my enlistment process to finalize.

in-tow. The other young man I sat with failed due to below-average test scores.

One man, in particular, a nineteen-year-old with the body of a darkened Adonis, stripped down in front of myself and three other young men; his age astounded us due to his physique *and* (false) humility. He spoke with me afterward in the waiting room on the matter of how "not all things are as they seem."

I inquired if he wished people saw his mind before his body.

His low (false) self-esteem compelled him to answer in a disjointed, ambiguous manner that concluded neither "yes" or "no." A nineteen-year-old Clark Kent in the flesh, thick-rimmed glasses and mesomorph build. 5 '6 and one-hundred and fifty-seven pounds of solid muscle and bone; he crushed the egotistical enthusiasm of the others with his aspect alone. We spoke of mind and body being united—the body being a representation of what the mind is capable of.

My mind preoccupied with the serious nature of my emprise, and the condition of a temporary prohibition of my voice recorder caused me to fail in the retention of the conversation in-depth. I wished the primed youth luck in life with the assumption that we'd never see each other again. The youth's mien implied we would meet again later that day. We didn't.

December 4th, 2018

12:01 PM

Wind chimes outside resonate from chill winds. Sunlight warms my legs through a diagonal rooftop window. Pigeons rustle and coo on slanted shingles overhead.

Five pigeons mingled on a slanted rooftop, braced against each other for warmth. The smartest pigeon eyed the smallest; the smallest brushed a wing against the largest; the largest defecated on the talons of the prettiest, and the prettiest pecked the oldest.

"A creature knelt beside a fiery chasm with a meal. Long ashen hair adhered to the contours of a reddened, sinewy spine warped with coiled muscles defined from eons of repetitive movement. The cre-"

A young girl tucked between a firm mattress and a thin blanket said, *"Eons* of labor? How old is this thing?"

An old blind woman said, "Are you going to let me tell the story or not?"

The girl sighed and said, "Sorry grandma."

"Eons of repetitive labor defined the... Oh, no, I already said that. Hm. Where was I?"

"The part that was about to come after."

"The part after what?"

"... The part you *just* said."

"Ah... The creature, ah..."

"Forget *it* grandma."

The woman giggled and said, "I already have."

"What's the point of some dumb story about something eating something—probably a human or a *young girl* like usual." The girl groaned and pulled the blanket over her head.

"And... *just like that*... the creature crawled up Ashleigh's bed and..." A prolonged pause prompted the girl to lower the blanket and peek with a single eye; the woman yelled, "Tickled her to *death!*" and followed with a stiff-fingered-two-handed series of prods to the girl's ribs.

Ashleigh's mother stood silent, stared straight forward, and listened to the charged laughter with her back braced to the wall outside of the room.

December 7th, 2018

8:45 AM

Two-hundred and three dollars to my name. Rent is paid for December. After my last round of bills for electricity, phone, internet, and gym membership, I'll be down to seventy dollars: cash for food.

This condition is the poorest I've ever been since I *began* paid labor throughout my teenage years—yet I'm content with my *freedom.* Even if a stroke of ill-fated happenstance disqualifies me from admission into the military-industrial complex, my contentment will persist. I'd be better off, in *my* reality, if I *were* to be rejected; otherwise I will bloat with unwarranted pride, the strength of comradeship, and financial security.

My father has relocated from an apartment building he owned and has now relinquished responsibility of on account of an unpaid mortgage, to live at his other apartment building a few blocks down the road; he informs me that without my help throughout the past two weeks, his move wouldn't have been (immediately) possible.

My father's curiosity overcomes him concerning my ventures, and his ceaseless inquiries broke my silence. To my dismay, he began to praise and congratulate me of my choice to join the Navy. I've raised expectations. He opens his home to me and implores me to return to live with him if my "plan" fails, an offer I refuse on all facets of my character. I'd rather perish in a frozen gutter, destitute, with my integrity intact, than to live a shameful life alongside my progenitor.

9:19 AM

I lost my virginity at the age of thirteen one evening after school to a black-haired girl inside of a house located on "Main Street" of my hometown. Our intent for intercourse had been planned, an unspoken vow communicated through sly smirks and lustful glances into each other's eyes.

I penetrated a stiff quasi corpse atop a square bed fifteen minutes before the anticipated arrival of a maternal figure. The ordeal would have been mistaken for rape to a spectator. Two rigid knees bent at seventy-degree angles, toenails painted black, frilly red skirt and oversized hoodie. My kisses grazed a stiff neck and my circumspect thrusts elicited ambiguous moans. Fingernails painted red dug into a white linen blanket. Eyes shadowed purple and lined with thin black crescents shut tight. A pleased grimace gasped for air. She avoided contact with my lips.

A back door slammed and our intercourse ceased; an abrupt severance of our genitalia voided my climax.

The quasi corpse sprung to life, reeled away, touched her fist-sized ejaculation stain on the bedding with a forefinger, recoiled, and said, "Oh my god, is that mine?"

I said, *"It* isn't mine."

I'm questioned by my landlords on my activities; a disbelief of my acceptance and/or competence for a military role is noted.

On their departure down the stairwell, I said, "I know you're eager to prove my… authenticity."

Forced laughter from one and silence from the other validated my skepticism of *their* skepticism.

The beauty with writing is far removed from grace, enlightenment, nobility, courage, knowledge, or entertainment. Raw acknowledgment of a condition is understood by all. I'm disgusted by the disgust of others. Shamed by the shame of others, a scumbag, a heathen, a miscreant—*oh yes,* this merry-go-round of human feculence spins and paints the contours of a spherical enclosure brown—an allegory—for a cave? No, a cave is unnecessary. An allegory for a feigned smile, a pseudo nod of respect, a limp-wristed handshake, a quiver of an eyelid, a compliment spoken with feet pointed away, an insult spoken with a back turned, an embrace ceased at the first itch of discomfort.

December 8th, 2018

12:17 PM

I sneer at the beautiful: natural and artificial, from nubile youths to aged starlets, from an architectural marvel to a well-stocked grocer's shelf; all are destined and subject to entropic chaos.

Gaze in a reflection and think to a time prior when your face expressed a tidbit more of jovial glee, when the red vitals of life colored the lines of your visage with a shade brighter than now beheld.

Imagine yourself naked and hairless; what beauty is there? Do you possess a body toned and shaped from a particular labor which you are proud, or is the realm of your identity hidden in the self-described *nebulous* depths of your mind—a mind far too convoluted and profound for *anyone* to *ever* understand—eh?—is that *it?*—or rather, *all?*

December 9th, 2018

9:30 AM

A descent into an aperture to hell dismembers an angel's wings. Plumes of smoke spew from swollen angelic eyes and reduce the once resplendent orbs to beady flecks of blackened swill. Multifaceted layers of holy raiments fizzled and burned to reveal a sublime spectrum of ethereal energy—this too, is warped; a humanoid skeletal chassis manifests and is enveloped with viscera and sinew. Blisters and boils pulsated. Newfound claws groped at intangible walls. Blue flame spewed from an agape mouth. The flesh-cursed angel screamed ash.

A spiraled plummet downward through serpentine stone grottos, suspended pillars of fire, and tightened corridors of serrated bone—a collision, the angel is enveloped with a slab of liquified slag and upraised by a manifold force.

An inferno. Tendrils of blue embers swayed from superheated gusts expelled from endless rows of colossal furnaces. A black horizon spanned over expansive fields of molten decay and stygian fortresses.

4:53 PM

Food is tiresome. Eggs, oats, mushrooms, spinach, peppers, peanut butter, rice, sauerkraut, almonds, and milk. I'm weaker than ever before despite daily gym activities in preparation for military standards. Now that my strength and endurance *matters,* of course, I find myself back at square one.

To do—at all—is tiresome; energy is irrelevant—in surplus…the desire lacks. I enforce a routine of consumption, strength training, timed runs, and reading by my podium. This document spawns *it*self regardless of my innate being.

Prostration overtakes me often; naked, I brace my knees and forearms against the clean carpet of my empty home, stretched out beneath the rooftop window, and wonder at my animalistic nature in conjunction with the essence of existence—to even *be* is remarkable and I've remarked too much. Music has lost enchantment; taste is a byproduct of persistence; silent interactions with others bore and disappoint me. Frilly carpet fibers jut into the edges of my fingernails. I behold my miserable sack of flesh, my burden and salvation, my single friend, a true ally; my body never lies to me.

My mind… oh… what a fiend, a scoundrel.

Under the sunlight, my mind beholds my body and laments the condition. The body, sensitive to the mind's energy, roils from a negative onslaught.

Two creatures—mind and body; often, they work in tandem. Now, the body wishes I sit and the mind rejects. The mind wishes to forgo food and the body protests. A severance of body or mind from the other would result in a quandary, a paradox, a sterile science fiction tale.

My mind and body once conspired together to be attractive, i.e., fatuous, and have *always* succeeded in being meretricious.

Maturation is to assimilate and abide by the expectations of others.

December 10th, 2018

8:56 AM

A twenty-minute video recording of myself in the act of breakfast preparation through the utilization of my writing devices' built-in camera exposed my idle gloom. I consumed while I watched my old self prepare the meal.

4:19 PM

Lay on the floor, fixate and stare at a random element of the room, and have yourself a *good* cry—not *for* yourself… for everyone. All you've ever known and loved now gone; fragmented faces, memories of touch. Estimated to be of high or low caliber at varying degrees, personal opinion is based on the limited vantage of interactions at brief moments throughout each other's lives. Our personalities manifest due to the opinions of others. We are not who we think we are.

I shook hands with a man today; his bare hand clenched my gloved hand.

My father said, "I am damned if I do and damned if I don't with you. What do you want from me, Baethan? To leave you alone, forget about you? Not ask you questions? Stop loving you? Detest you? Tell you that you are hopeless, worthless? Lie to you? Not get excited about your accomplishments? Not be involved in your life?"

I said, "Yes—nailed *it*—everything."

"Why?"

"There is no simple answer for my brief lifetime of experiences."

"Well, you can't change how I feel; I love you."

I failed to say, "I love you too," despite my desire.

I stood in line at a convenience store and listened to a man my age correct his young daughter on the proper usage of the word "waste"; his impatience rippled into everyone around.

I approached the counter and paid for my product. A voluptuous woman engaged with stocking cigarette merchandise behind a counter *behind* the counter I stood at said, "Did you get your milk and your eggs?" in a voice one would use to address a familiar child. She wore reindeer antlers over a company hat.

My dejected frown met her amiable beaming; I looked her square in the eyes and said, "I did."

She looked away, fought to suppress a frown of her own, and said, "Have a good day."

"You too."

On my return home, I ascended the stairwell, placed my milk and eggs in the fridge, entered the bathroom, blew my nose, relieved my bladder, dripped a single tear into the toilet water, and turned to the mirror where I laughed—laughed at my salty cheeks, unwashed from the night before, and stared into my bleary, bloodshot eyes.

Time to eat.

December 12th, 2018

6:03 PM

I'm sick of this (writing)—nauseated, though I continue, and seal my self-adhered fate.

December 14th, 2018

11:02 AM

After many setbacks, tests, and deliberations, I've sworn my oath to the United States Navy and assume the position of a submarine Yeoman (YNS). I've requested to ship to the city of North Chicago in Illinois to attend "Boot Camp" at the soonest available date.

3:59 PM

Something Smells

Sordid pile of black clothes speckled with
Skin flakes encrusted on sweat-stained
Socks turned inside out alongside
Saturated underwear lined with
Streaks of diluted shit.

5:34 PM

My father's desperation to maintain correspondence with me prompts tears to well up in the corners of my eyes. I'm rendered emotional, vulnerable, and weakened whenever I meet with him due to my knowledge of his embittered state inflicted onto himself wrought by his misanthropy, traits I once assumed for feelings of my own.[5] I know he shifts from heartbreak, to apathy, to wrath, and wishes me dead and/or by his side. I've cried more for my father than for myself; in fact, the instances on which

---

[5] "Yes, and I'm responsible for world hunger too," said an indignant old man.

I cried for myself in this life, I could count on one hand, and pertained to my youthful relationships with girls I no longer care about.

In retrospect, I've been molded. There is a desire to attend my father's invitations to serve me dinner or engage in idle conversation for his sake— that is all. We've helped each other in equal proportion up to this point, granted each other sorrow and joy, shouldered burdens, endured a lifetime of happiness and sadness in similar strides.

6:53 PM

Lowered to a prostration on my standing mat at the base of my podium in my temporary attic domain, I engage in a silent prayer for my father, an active process of thought. Beethoven's *Symphony No. 3 in E-Flat Major, Op. 55 "Eroica": 2nd movement,* resonates at a quiet volume.

I flatten my hands against the standing mat and observe the gaunt contours of my fingers against the black material. Intransigent dictation of life and death; I find no recourse in the lunacy of my actions; to condemn myself to years of service to an establishment I've never identified with or supported… is *liberation* from myself.

My father's pain at the loss of his youthful son haunts me. Familiar tears bubble to the surface and are at once blinked away.

December 15th, 2018

11:19 PM

$112.34–numbers in my bank account—my net worth. Four books, *The Bhagavad Gita, Epictetus' Discourses, Nicomachean Ethics,* and *The Book of the Law* are my final possessions beyond clothing, foodstuffs/spices,[6] dozens of writing utensils, sheets of blank paper, two moleskin journals, a cup, one of each cutlery utensil, three Tupperware bowls, cleaning/ hygienic supplies, a towel, birth certificate, social security card, standing mat, podium, backpack, and writing device. In two weeks, all items except

---

[6] Two dozen eggs, a small container of portobello mushrooms, 3/4th gallon of whole milk, 1 ½ box of whole-grain pasta, 1/3rd bag of brown rice, 2 lbs of steel-cut oats, and 3 lbs of almonds. Salt, pepper, cinnamon, nutmeg, paprika, oregano, sage, garlic, cumin, cayenne pepper, and apple cider vinegar.

my backpack, writing device, journals, clothing, and hygienic supplies will be relinquished to designated receivers.

Declined for loans due to lack of credit experience despite an "excellent" credit score, I resign and prepare myself for a lifestyle among the homeless, to serve and live at shelters, churches, and soup kitchens until my undesignated ship date.

~~Generosity~~ Ego is the impetus for my ~~predicament~~ situation. I've donated funds and belongings *willy nilly* to acquaintances/projects and have, by effect, reduced my imminent social status to a destitute vagrant by New Years. My father lives a twenty minute walk away and has offered me to live with him, or in his now abandoned home of my youth, free of charge; I refuse. Many would take me in. I'd rather suffer and delight what I'm due; a martyr to folly, my nonexistent bed is made.

A fool? Oh—yes. A fool with integrity.

In the meantime, I edit yesteryear's journal (destined to be error-ridden) and create this unprofitable emprise.

December 16th, 2018

10:03 AM

I've finished a read of W.N.P. Barbellion's *Journal of a Disappointed Man,* and am horrified, haunted. I must process the content in full before I record sentiments…

11:15 AM

A letter sent to me by one of my father's recent ex-girlfriends, Carissa, a literary professor, compared me to Barbellion and commended the first installment of this expository tripe. My father had mailed her a copy of my first book with my name listed as the sender: a clandestine action.

Regardless, her comparison of Barbellion and I set me to rigorous digestion of the man's post mortem publication and has thereby opened new faculties of comprehension on the nature of humanity; I repeat: We are *all* the same-

No, no—spare me the label of liberal extremist, socialist, or activist of any kind; I scorn the misaligned agendas of everyone who feels *and* thinks low enough of their own character and thoughts to delve even lower and identify with a group/party of any devotion. Failure to acknowledge one has been deceived by an amalgamate convened for perfunctory distinction mortifies me.

We are the same in our humanity. Stand together a sunburnt shamanistic hermit from Madagascar next to a Portuguese hairdresser and I reckon two beings of equal merit in flesh and baseness.

Still experience difficulties?—a stout old woman in Comoros spends her afternoons engaged in the intensive labor of seashell collection, returns home at 8:30 PM on the *dot* every night, eats a slice of homemade apple pie cooked weeks in advance to ensure there is an abundance, proceeds to mount her imported adolescent transgender male consort, and moans out her agape circular window at a crescent moon; a wealthy CEO of a children's cancer charity is her equal.

Yes, ~~you~~ I *must* be disillusioned to believe such fancies. Forget *it*. You're hopeless.

9:21 PM

A mirror of myself, this Barbellion, bittersweet homage to my soul— to read his lifelong experiences and feelings encapsulated within a single manuscript. I've been altered by a phantasmal influence. The sentiment is equivalent to a photograph of yourself shown to you: a foreign entity is acknowledged, on the prolonged observation you see a distorted, or rather, *real* version of what you are.

Barbellion is a reflection of everyone. Circumstances and demeanor impelled him to write despite his hate and simultaneous love of what he had become—on realization his journal is the single, self-engrossed, egotistical, absurd, solitary hope he has *to "become"*... He died in misery and self-disgust. The hope of his journal trumped his family: wife and one-year-old daughter; both to him were whimsical, fugitive, intangible elements of a fickle, crystalline love equivalent to a half-inch sheet of ice spread over a darkened lake surface: one crack and the inscrutable depths are revealed and unknowable.

We are parallels because we are human. There is a coincidence of character. This life we feel that permeates all is a familiar flux; distinction and segregation is folly.

December 19th, 2018

7:52 AM

On the stage of a university talent show, a lanky, spray-tanned bodybuilder entered from the shadowed alcove of the rightmost lavender curtain. Rounded shoulder muscles the size of two tennis balls glistened under the glow of a harsh fluorescent stage light. He smiled to reveal browned teeth and strut to the center of the stage with a gaunt, emaciated, Mozambican infant underarm in the manner one carries a gym towel.

The audience's boisterous cheer stifled to a hushed reflection of awed whispers and sudden gasps.

The disproportionate bodybuilder turned to the rows of horrified faces and said, "This is my cousin Aderito"; he hoisted the skeletal infant up by one arm. Dissipated, apathetic, and bleary-eyed, the infant produced a blubbery noise redolent to a burp. "I'm Steve, and today, we're going to show you *our* talent. Ready Aderito?"

Aderito dangled from the end of Steve's outstretched arm and gestured a meaningless point of a cadaverous finger towards the domed ceiling.

Steve said, "Alright baby!" and drooped Aderito four inches above the wooden floor panels. Steve released his grip and Aderito landed on his bare feet, collapsed onto two bony knees, began to cry, and prostrated.

A silent audience observed Steve lurch onto the floor, roll to his back, lean to his left, seize Aderito in both hands, and balance the infant's skin-taut sternum in the palm of his extended right hand—striated arm extended towards the stage lighting. Steve lowered the nineteen-pound infant close to his face and pushed away; lowered, raised, lowered, raised. The infant's precarious balance in the bodybuilder's callous grip exasperated incessant sobs.

Steve muttered, "Oh yeah, *destroying it*," to himself, the audience an inconsequential element of his practiced routine. "Fucking killing *it*," he blurted. Aderito teetered, fell off the flattened pedestal of Steve's hand, and descended three feet onto the floor, whereupon he thrashed, wailed, and crawled onto Steve's distended pectorals. Steve recoiled at the touch of Aderito, flashed a disgusted grimace, jumped to his feet, thereby hurtling the infant seven feet across the length of the stage. The sobs and wails ceased.

A nameless voice in the audience screamed, *"You sick fuck!"*

Another shouted, *"Get down!"*
An old woman screamed.
Throngs of spectators stood.
"Boo!"
"You're terrible!"
"Call an ambulance!"
"I'm going to kick your ass!"
"Oh my God call the cops!"
"Boo!"
"Get off the fucking stage!"

Steve grinned, bowed his head, lunged towards Aderito, tucked the emaciated infant under his armpit and scampered into the shadowed alcove of the curtain to his left.

December 20th, 2018

2:28 PM

Day by day in this attic, I trek to the gym for strength training and a run along a forest trail every other day. The mind is a lonesome occupation, segregated between the recount of my past, the recording of the present, and the study of Aristotle's *Nicomachean Ethics.*

I've requested employment with over twenty establishments, three gig opportunities, and bide time.

Do I desire pity—no, with a downturned thumb, I snub and sneer at myself and all. Ten days remain in this space until I'm vomited into the unknown. I'm astonished at my complete disregard for everything.

I attempted to be magnanimous, though I am poor, and am therefore a fool. My rock bottom will sink lower than I thought possible—or am I elevated?

Loveless, childless, penniless, purposeless; I'm primed for the military and await a verdict on my use of CBD oil. Regardless, my "placeholder" contract is signed, enlisted as a cook with a ship date of May 5th— "Temporary," my recruiters assured me. "A guy like you with the scores on your test would be wasted talent as a cook."

Wasted *talent…* I laugh aloud, alone.

"So I set my mind to know wisdom and madness and folly;
I learned that this, too, is a pursuit of the wind." [7]

"Yet when I considered all the works that my hands had accomplished
and what I had toiled to achieve, I found everything to be futile, a
pursuit of the wind; there was nothing to be gained under the sun." [8]

"So I hated life, because the work that is done under the sun was
grievous to me. For everything is futile and a pursuit of the wind." [9]

"I saw that all labor and success spring from a man's envy of his
neighbor. This too is futile and a pursuit of the wind." [10]

"There is no limit to all the people who were before them,
yet those who come later will not rejoice in the successor.
This too is futile and a pursuit of the wind." [11]

"Better what the eye can see than the wandering of desire.
This too is futile and a pursuit of the wind." [12]

Wayward mortal, in your pursuit of knowledge, the desire of
entertainment, and the quest for progress, have you considered your God:
Entropy? I ~~command~~ implore you to avert your eyes, otherwise, loathe me.

December 21st, 2018

6:39 AM

I lay on the floor and can tolerate my thoughts no longer.
Two consecutive dreams, horrid and malevolent; the first:
Dog and squirrel torture and mutilation. Why?—I haven't the slightest
inclination; my inner psyche and subconscious concoct a fantasy for me

---

[7] Ecclesiastes 1:17
[8] Ecclesiastes 2:11
[9] Ecclesiastes 2:17
[10] Ecclesiastes 4:4
[11] Ecclesiastes 4:16
[12] Ecclesiastes 6:9

where I may stifle the movement of small animals and twist their jaws off. I'm sickened with… Could I even claim the fragmented unreality as my own? Some of the beasts are hybrids and scream unholy cries of dog yelps homogenized with squirrel calls. Affectionate canines held tight in my armpit scramble to escape from my inflicted torment. The snap of bone, pop of ligaments, and the muffled tear of flesh *excite* and prompts me to mangle jawbones and suffocate snouts—never to death, the pleasure my unknown self experiences is due to the pain I invoke. One after another, a new victim supplants the last. This recurrent dream, for years now, is my worst nightmare.

I wake in fright and listen to a downpour of rain batter the attic rooftop. Sleep subverts me soon after. The second:

A strange manor ramified with university halls, personal housing, and above-ground sewage lines. I brushed my teeth in a public bathroom and the mirror in front of me swung open to reveal *Jasmine*, an adolescent version of her I had never known. I gazed up, shocked; she reckoned my surprise, giggled, rolled her eyes, and slammed the mirror closed. I see my reflection… A younger version of myself, full of life and color, a head full of hair before I had shaved down to half an inch.[13] The sound of the tap water amplified with each moment passed at a rate that jarred me awake from the immensity of the noise… to the sound of reality—the downpour I hear against the rooftop.

I rose to recount the experience and will now proclaim my disdain for myself and everyone—for our yearnings, goals, ambitions and desires; I wish I could fly into the stratosphere and explode into a small-grained shower of blood.

7:59 PM

Irreverence, apathy, indifference, is this evil? Rather, is any other state a false pretense we cling to for the sake of relations and gain?

"Gaze in the mirror and be still my child," whispered a 6 '9 raven-haired naked woman. She spoke to herself and ogled her reflection; a wiry,

---

[13] Jasmine's mother, a hairdresser, deemed me a threat to her daughter's future. I shaved half of my once vainglorious shoulder-length hair off on a whim and progressively shaved off what remained over the course of a week to test the integrity of my newfound relationship. My bald head had no effect other than to reduce my effeminate attractiveness; I've maintained short hair since.

pale-skinned amalgamate of sharp curvature and protruded bone. "Gaze in the mirror…" she choked, "and be… *still*…." Two rounded breasts spasmed from the furious pump of a heart within the confines of a warped rib cage. *"Be still…"* the woman murmured and closed her eyes.

Woe betides the one who stands and listens.

December 22nd, 2018

7:52 AM

A relentless deluge woke me in the middle of the night. Discussions and discourses of the weather are my banes, though this storm… While I lay on the floor and contemplated everything I once wished for and the inanity of past desires, streets flooded and thunder rumbled in waves preceded by flashes of lightning, brief illuminations reckoned by me through a triangular window at my rear. I closed my eyes and listened to the torrential downpour for what could have been an hour with thoughts of each relationship I once sustained, now abandoned, relinquished, forsaken, at the forefront of my fancied qualms.

Others, too—the taxi driver, Jeremy, below me on his couch: I hear his pained smokers cough and daily preparation of meals. Neighbor activities are my unwanted distractions. Jeremy suffers in isolation despite an immediate family of three kids and mother-in-law. He bides his time for a year and awaits the release of his lover imprisoned due to opioid abuse; she will be different to his expectations on return: a betrayal of memories; he too will be an altered man.

I'm amazed by my distrust and abhorrent cynical conclusions about the true nature of others. This energy is a feedback loop; a social element of self-comparisons, judgments, and envy is the powerful facet of the human race which motivates scientists to "harness" quantum and "comprehend" dark energy—to develop breakthroughs in realms of science and philosophical/theological paradigms to "better" the world—to create artistic masterpieces, architectural marvels, and holistic infrastructure… All pursuits demand an unparalleled ego crystallized by resolute beliefs.

I'm amazed *and* sick of the grandiose notions and aggregated ambitions.

Yet, what do *I* do?

December 23rd, 2018

10:20 PM

A male ambulance driver will arrive at my attic tonight to perform oral sex and an oil massage on me. My shameful trepidation of the upcoming event has abated in favor of irreverent excitement.

Yes, I'm excited to engage in a sexual exploit with a stranger of the same sex. Bizarre. I'm *thrilled* to record the sentiment in this document; a questionable act—yet to unfold.

The voice recorder is invaluable.

Behold, reader: You are nothing to me.

"I desire."

December 24th, 2018

12:19 AM

-Fickle flesh reacts the same no matter the gender. Tender spots and stimuli respond per expectations.

Far from pleasant, I prefer a woman.

Out of all the self-disgust, shame, and hatred I've ever felt for myself, I imagined I'd be at my pinnacle with such feelings this moment; on the contrary, I am content, and enjoy a sated curiosity.

Regardless, I'm averse to both sexes and wish to remain in solitude. I've severed contact with the eager individual who wishes to repeat his performance and intend to revert to my disciplines. Eggs and broccoli in the morning.

11:23 AM

My "self" has become-

More open to the possibilities of chaos and retains the single conviction that nothing is true and nothing, in the full spectrum of an idea, can be known. "Schizophrenic" thoughts are a product of negative self-*anything* in conjunction with self-absorption, the diagnosis is a farce. I "know" the cure to all you schizo-loons with your sticky fingers in the welfare pot—be

44

bold; your timidity, self-doubt, and self-consciousness is the trident in your ass. No, you do not possess a sixth sense or magical powers.

"Consciousness gives no clue as to where the answer comes from; the processes that produce *it* are unconscious. *It* is the result of thinking, not the process of thinking, that appears spontaneously in consciousness."

- George A Miller's, Psychology: The Science of Mental Life [1962]

Therefore, by the near-sixty-year-old statement above which continues to serve as the fundamental understanding of consciousness to this day, the negative thoughts one may experience due to "schizophrenia" and *it*'s variations are a result of *thinking;* likewise, positive thoughts, etc.

Think further: Control your *feelings.*

Is the purpose of thought to *end* all thought? Would peace be achieved if thoughts were to end? I.e., Death. Is death a new beginning?—oh, *spooky* thoughts.

Do I have a hidden agenda?

Who cares?

There is no such thing as "mental illness," e.g., schizo-affective/phrenia, schizoid, dementia/Alzheimer's (natural [often diet-induced] brain decay), depression, bipolar, obsessive-compulsive, attention deficit, and the *four-hundred and fifty* additional diagnoses one may identify with. Investing in the research and study of entropic or genetically endowed neuronal, chemical, and biological processes is artful. The American Psychiatric Association (APA) is a self-fulling government-approved cult *of* identities.

"Doctor, I'm so happy to see you."

"Please enter your payment information on the screen, sign here, and tell me everything."

"Well I-"

"Yes well you're clearly ill and are unfit for productive work until we provide you relief."

"Oh—I had no idea I was so sick!"

"Yes, yes, I've concluded that we must relieve you of your psychosis so that you may get back to work. Your alcohol abuse is compounded by your PTSD from years of service in the armed forces."

"How did you know about any of this? This is my first-"

"Your breath smells of alcohol, you wear a veteran's cap, and you stepped into my office."

Thus everyone rose into the air hand-in-hand—spiritual freedom; clipboards dropped from the clenched grips of college graduates and electrodes detached from patient's heads. With accumulated knowledge of everyone feeling sorry for themselves, all was known.

1:54 PM

Receiver:

Your letter is well-received; a curious card that exudes praise on my behalf. I hadn't expected anything of this nature on account of my father being the one to have sent you an E-book stub using my name and address, unbeknownst to me; he informed me afterward. I'm uncertain why he did this without my consultation, though I'm thankful he did with consideration of how events transpired to which I now respond to your accolades and warm sentiments. I presume my father misses you and regrets how your relationship with him ended on an unfortunate note. As an outsider looking inward, I imagine the cause of your severance is multifaceted and involves more than the unfortunate scenario involving his ex-girlfriend and yourself.

Regardless, I am grateful you've set aside time to not only read my expulsion but to *also* purchase a copy of your own! I believe you are my first authentic sale. This factor in mind, I'm delighted to present to you my signed book; I recommend you offer the copy you bought to your closest enemy.

Your comparison of me to W.N.P. Barbellion incited me to cast aside all my current projects and immerse myself in the literature. I'm aghast, horrified, and *empowered* by what I've read. You have my genuine gratitude for the sincere comparison; I've been "enlightened" by a parallel of the human condition.

Thus, [Receiver], you have impacted my life with the power of your word, and by extension, the words of a disappointed dead man have breached barriers of my comprehension and illuminated nuances of the lunacy we all undergo. Your compliment of me being equivalent to Barbellion is sinister and heartfelt; I appreciate the deviousness of your benevolence.

I believe you'll be pleased to know I intend to write and publish my tripe until death, thereby I have already outpaced Barbellion in scope *and* ambition—his Achilles' heel. I yearn for an average death and become more foul, spiritless, and melancholic each passing night into morning.

I've included my three referential waypoints of philosophical dribble as an additional token of my respect that you may handle as you deem appropriate: *The Bhagavad Gita, Epictetus' Discourses,* and *The Book of the Law.* Enlistment in the U.S. Navy as a Yeoman renders these materials useless to me; I've retained and consolidated all beneficial information from each into a single mote of neurological/delusional expertise.

A remarkable difference between myself and Barbellion (and Marie Bashkirtseff), is that I loathe achieving fame and am eager to die: A fatuous fanatic.

I'm unaware of what my father wrote on the letter he addressed as from me to you; however, I *do* remember you fondly.

Merrily,
- Baethan

5:48 PM

When life *is* employment, there is no scarcity. Engrossed with my words, the sun rises and falls.

8:19 PM

Santa is coming to town…

December 25th, 2018

7:14 AM

Christmas mornings are any other except for the boisterous activity of the two children and joyful exclamations of adults below me. I imagine the woman convicted for opioid possession weeps for herself and is chastised by fellow inmates for her good fortune:
"I'm so sad—my family experiences Christmas without me!"
A disgruntled inmate responds, "Join the club."

47

Another replies, "At least you *have* a family."

A contemptuous one said, "How long have you been in for anyway?"

The woman said, "Ah, you're right, I'll see them all later today and I'm only in for nine more months."

The disgruntled one said, "*It's* been six Christmas mornings for me."

The contemptuous one said, "Stop fuckin' crying—you've no right."

The woman chuckled, wiped tears from her cheeks, and said, "Wow, you guys made me feel better about myself real fast!"

"Fuck you," said the disgruntled one.

This season, for the first time in my life, I haven't been exposed to a single Christmas song: the second-best gift of all (first being a decent book).

Out of all the Christmas songs, *"Santa Claus is Coming to Town,"* is by far the most terrible and disturbing due to a single verse:

"He sees you when you're sleeping; he knows when you're awake."

To know if you've been bad or good (based on Christian/Catholic dictations) is critical, but the aforementioned? Does this pertain to all-year-round, or is the invasive power exclusive to Christmas Eve?

Ho ho, ho!—jilted parents stifle outbursts of anger due to children's malcontent with Santa's generous offerings nationwide and take account of lost financial savings.

2:43 PM

In a few peculiar living rooms of America, estranged families gather 'round and discuss how "things" have been since last Christmas. Children play with new ~~toys~~ video games, phones, and handheld devices in front of television sets tuned to holiday movies and programs featuring a stationary camera fixed on bunnies and puppies converged in front of a hearth. Satisfied parents mingle, brownies and/or alcoholic beverage in-hand, perhaps a few indulgent servings of chips and dip. "Oh, I'll need to hit the gym later after today—oh!—ha ha!—ho ho!"

"Bah, the *gym*... When I go home tonight I'll have a few beers! Ha-he-ho-ha!"

"These cookies are delicious, who brought them?"

"Oh those are Charlotte's specialty—ho-ha!"

"Teehee—whose Charlotte?"

48

"David's new fiancé."

"Oh *man* I can't get enough of these—they're *so* good!"-

And so a majority of Americans consumed and celebrated what their overtime hours employed at jobs they hate reaped. Until next year.

December 26th, 2018

8:27 PM

I loath and loathe to write. At first I thought the act clever, cute, witty, intelligent, and splendid in the way of how thoughts may be summoned to "action" and "power" with all the nonsensical tripe of yesteryears ramblings and falsehoods—now I *know* of the vitriolic hate I expel through the format and pretense of *art*.

I stand in the kitchen of the vacant, abandoned home of my youth; my father's belongings have been cleared out through my assistance; I've helped him prepare his new home from a horrible downtrodden dingy hole to a revitalized retirement abode fit for slow death by indulgence.

Ah, my life is empty—a void of inconsequential nothings and trivial thoughts recorded to a printed book and digital screen—a waste of my mind's resources and labor, yet, *you*—you sadist—*you* read and must derive *some* entertainment from this assembly of despicable expressions. Watch a movie, play a video game, or read a self-help book you knave—yes— **yourself** included when you once more go back to edit this for clarity—*fool*. Go—away from these drab, meaningless, *panderings*.

Alright, I'll give you *something,* something I've learned that I may pass onto the eager learner, desperate and hopeful that *maybe* their time spent— seconds—minutes—hours—*days* invested in this so-called entertainment is worth your time; think this is humorous, do you?

Imagine meeting yourself.

Would either of you be embarrassed? To encounter another entity you wholly understand? Would you be attracted to one another or repulsed? Yes, I envision one of two scenarios if any individual—no exceptions—were to meet themselves:

1. Instantaneous sex.
2. Contempt.

Perhaps contemptuous sex or sex preceded *and* followed with contempt.

Yes, I endorse the same-sex relationships of the doppelgänger/clone for the egotistical facet, self engrossment with yourself!—after all, you'd both know what you enjoy best. Are you repulsed by the idea, you empty-headed cretin? Are you *that* close-minded to dispel the premise of absolute euphoria on the engagement of sex with yourself? What's better than simultaneous orgasm and mutual estrangement with full comprehension of one another's feelings thereafter?

Boring. Too *boring*? Oh, well, that's a shame.

Oh! Right! What I've learned—I almost *forgot!*

I've learned that I have transcended shame, for shame is learned; there is no truth.

What are you ashamed of this moment, reader? To read this?—you *should* be. See? I've taught you what I *"know!"*

December 27th, 2018

7:47 AM

There is nothing new.

Unemployed for two months, I engross myself with *this*, the absurd edit and refinement of the previous installment of *this*, continue to study Aristotle and Heraclitus, trek back and forth across town to train at a local gym as a prerequisite for an unknown ship date to boot camp (May 5th the latest and worst option), and now plan to transfer what little I own to my old, empty, abandoned home—where I stand now, writing device propped on top of three empty boxes atop a kitchen counter, and write of what I *do*, what I *think*, with angst and disgust permeated throughout every cell of my being—yes, if these words were to animate before your eyes, every letter would be imbued with noxious fumes and *writhe*.

Loneliness, depression, anxiety?—*no*, these are faults for the *unknowing*, those who fail to understand the innate nature of life—to suffer and be grateful for *it*. Instead, I am content with my mission, my purpose, my trivial activity of no consequence, regardless of the endeavor.

I break my forty-eight hour fast this morning with a morning walk to my father's new habitation to partake in a pickle, six eggs, a handful of nuts, and coffee. Afterward, I'll walk to my soon-to-be relinquished attic domain for a lunch of sautéed broccoli and peppers with a side of sauerkraut and a handful of cacao nibs. For dinner, I have consumed a refrigerated boiled sweet potato with a tablespoon of peanut butter. Reading, editing, perhaps revisit *this*, attend the gym for up to two hours in the evening, and walk back to where I stand now—to *live* and be *free!*

"Yet thro' all my nausea, here I remain happy to discuss myself and my little mishaps. I'm damned sick of myself and all my neurotic whimperings, and so I hereby and now intend to lead a new life and throw this Journal to the Devil. I want to mangle *it*, tear *it* to shreds. You smug, hypocritical readers! You'll get no more of me. All you say I know is true before you say *it* and I know now all the criticism you are going to launch. So please spare yourself the trouble. You cannot enlighten me upon myself. I know. I disgust myself—and you, and as for you, you can go to the Devil with this Journal."

- WNP Barbellion's The Journal of a Disappointed Man

7:44 PM

My confidence would benefit from a dose of unbearable suffering.

I grin at those proud of their flesh, acknowledge those elevated by status in a particular field with indifferent regard, and strut through my little pocket of society with absolute defiance. To shake the hand of a crack-addicted lecher in the manner one would an eminent "achiever" renders me disrespectful to the proud and merciful to the shameful.

I scoff at imposed hierarchies and return a suggestive gaze of a man or woman with a dissipated eyebrow raise.

Yes, a blow to my esteem would benefit my undue magnanimity. My gift of tolerance to others is often too much for the receiver to bear— indeed, to encounter one who is *averse* to judge another on failures *and* achievements must be awkward!

For what is justice other than settlements? Show me a paragon of virtue and I will show you my shaved anus.

"Oh—*oh*—I never expected this behavior from Baethan; the man is flagrant—this much I knew, but flagrant *and* gay?"

"Fool," I shout with an averted gaze and uplifted palm, "Sexuality in all forms is base and irrelevant to the condition of my abject disillusionment. Men and women alike are a tired prize to be won-over—I've had both now to experience the transcendental pathological abnormalities shared across genders."

"Baethan- *What?* What you speak is trashy malarkey. There is no validity to any statement you have ever made."

"Well, you interrupted me."

A head scratch. "Carry on then."

And so the curious man typed with frenetic strokes across his keyboard for the sake of progress and thereby his confidence amplified with each admission of behavior:

"This is my journal, you damned pissant. Are you ungrateful for what I've gifted you? Would you appreciate a scandalous admission of guilt and shame—for I have none—only ~~truths~~ truisms and affirmations."

The reader suppressed an irritated glower, failed, and said, "At this point, I'll take anything you give me; I'm invested in your literature."

"Thank you," said Baethan. "I'll do my best to appease you with my confession: I've been attracted to men who resemble women. Throughout early grade school, I sported long, blonde, luxurious hair, wore black eyeliner, black clothing, and spent an excessive portion of my time engrossed with my reflection—not out of vanity, but of awed intrigue of the *creature*. My face demanded a retort."

"Alright, I've read enough."

"Then refrain from reading, you impudent fleck of meaningless nothing. Now, I've decided Epictetus' philosophy is moot due to the infinite potentials of brain chemistry being altered by *externals*. We *are* external to ourselves, unknowing, lost, and estranged from purpose. What did you expect will happen if you are strapped down to a stretcher and forced to partake in mind-altering drugs—do you retain a *choice* of how you react then? Easy to say 'Go on then, cut off my head for I am not my body,' when a dull knife has yet to slide across your neck."

"Baethan, you *really* are a fool. Your ramblings depress me. If you persist, I believe I will, in fact, quit reading your… 'literature,' indefinitely."

"And what will happen then? Do you expect me to grovel or plead for your redemption, worm?"

"You're a despicable man," said a disappointed reader.

"Yes?"

"I'm done with you."

"Alright." Baethan waited and contemplated his next droll remark.

The reader said, "I admit, your writing *is* entertaining when your thought processes are conveyed through imagined conversations between you and me."

Well, too bad, I'm finished with that act for the moment and would rather expound on the baselessness of psychology, sociology, and philosophy, my three most revered and studied topics of the last three years of my life.

There is no social justice because there is no justice. There are settlements, agreements, resolutions, accommodations, and compromises. Justice is an impossible concept equivalent to the abstract idealism of a utopia. There will never be the fruition of either conception due to the will for life, e.g.,/i.e., power, consumption, and procreation.

Thrice, I've been called a fruity lunatic by my now forcibly evicted alcoholic roommate.

"Help!—Help!—I'm being oppressed!"[14]—by my*self!* This inexplicable, cyclical thought process of paradigms, beliefs, and fundamental "rights" and "wrongs" of self-imposed delusions, is oppressive!

I've been hired as a night shift dishwasher at a hectic social venue dead center of downtown, a now forty-minute walk away, which would have otherwise been a four-minute walk if I had retained the attic domain.

I forsook my vow of homelessness. ~~Shame on me.~~

What now—ah, yes… my Navy recruiter informed me there has been no update on the CBD oil verdict which will permit or deny me access to a submarine; "legislators" idle.

December 28th, 2018

10:12 AM

A nameless nobody said, "Baethan, what events in your life produced the disturbed and disillusioned individual that you are today?"

"Nothing extraordinary. In my youth, I searched for and studied violent videos and images on the internet with an intent to educate myself on the atrocities of humanity. There is also a plethora of literature written on and by practitioners of 'evil.' Being a youth holed up in my little suburban fantasy, there isn't much in the way of 'enlightenment' to the horrible potential of humanity other than seeking authentic experiences of 'evil' or the perpetuation of your own acts of 'evil.' Instead, the abundance of information shared by the invention of the internet allowed me to access men and women beheaded with knives, beaten to death, burned alive, raped and tortured, etc. These are isolated events captured on camera—a

---

[14] Monty Python's *The Holy Grail*

fractional snippet of the innate indifference to life experienced *by* life. This is by no means a determinant of my condition, rather, a causal element to my present awareness."

Yes, an imaginative response to a fictitious query is nonsensical sensationalist panderings compared to reality.

12:04 PM

With wanton abandonment, I write and engage my mind and body in labors of futile progress for the sake of personal confidence.

December 30th, 2018

5:40 AM

I awoke on my side, bodyweight pressed against my right arm, with my right ear flat against the attic floor, and listened to the fury of my downstairs neighbor masturbating; subtle gyrations discomfited me: quick, successive jerks. I heard the final groan of climatic pleasure from below.

This ceaseless discharge of sperm and excrement all around me is wearisome.

7:31 AM

Two nights of my favorite labor of dishwashing and my right wrist is reddened, raw, and uncooperative; a single pushup elicits extreme pain. My fingerprint is distorted and must be renewed for my writing device's fingerprint recognition software. Both hands are dried and chaffed, bleeding from four cuticles.

Dishes come in; dishes come out.

8:44 PM

At least three-hundred crows—no exaggeration—converged in a grand murder among the branches of seven enormous trees along the back parking lot perimeter of the city hospital. Enthralled by the spectacle of black wings strewn across the twilight horizon while I stood positioned at the zenith of a large hill overlooking the expansive bridge of a polluted river, I decided to engage with the multitudinous intelligent life.

A cacophony of caws heightened with urgency on my approach between two outdoor maintenance sheds; I emerged near the first closest tree, outspread my arms, and yelled, "Caw—damn you, verminous creatures—*caw!*" and compelled a majority of the branch's occupants to uplift in a surge. Fellow brethren remained idle and observed me with coal-black eyes nestled in oblong heads.

I retreated from between a narrow alley and descended the concrete path of the hill, my gaze held upward at the vast throngs of birds uttering signals for food, mating instructions, travel commands, and warnings against the impending humanoid nuisance. On my approach towards the incalculable hoard above, dozens of crows dispersed in a preemptive escape; I laughed aloud, grinned skyward, and despite my position in a public realm during final daylight hours, I tightened the straps of my pack, lurched towards the trees—and cried: "Devious rats with wings! Away! Be gone with you!" Ah, and a fraction of them dispensed into the sky—a panicked queue of misplaced sensibilities lodged within tiny skulls! "Feeble-minded fickle flesh-" I bellowed, "Just what are you but a heinous bunch of spineless scoundrels!" I chuckled—*giggled* at the absurdity of my behavior and launched myself into a frenzy of jovial histrionics for the benefit of gross self-satisfaction beneath the gnarled branches above and stood in expectancy of my demise…

The crows whispered amongst each other, disturbed and entertained in equal measure; many without a care for a foolish man; each in turn ventured forth and scouted distant venues.

At the base of the tree trunks, surrounded and overcome by the multilayered sound waves of *caws*, I yelled, "There is nothing to you! …" whereupon I continued to stand, expectant, impatient, hopeful for the murder to swoop down and devour me, to peck between the spaces of my bloodied fingers held over my eyes—a futile effort to ward off a hail of vicious beaks, to mount me with a hundred talons and tear through the soft fibrous material of my merino wool, to enjoy my flesh while I fought tooth and nail only to succumb beneath a black blanket of death…

And lo, I turned and departed the scene, across the bridge, away from the so-called "murder."

JANUARY

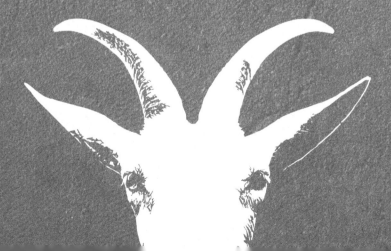

January 1st, 2019

1:19 AM

I believe I'm ready to die.

No—no, dearest journal, this isn't some fickle play with words.

Ten hours at a kitchen dish sink—oh *boo hoo;* a half-hour walk home to my father's abandoned house and contention with the intense pain of a swollen arm, wrist, and hand, conditions I can no longer ignore. I believe I work with a fractured arm; I'm uncertain and lack the funds for inspection. Amazed with what I tolerate in myself: how I type with a swollen right hand juxtaposed against the angular normalcy of my bony left.

Even my voices taunt me at work from passersby:

"He must masturbate often."

"This guy is working with a burned arm."

My self-consciousness? More bitch-tinted complaints of a feeble plebeian all-star?

Oh? Holocaust victims flagellated and tortured; plague victims hemorrhage and bleed out from infected orifices; men beaten with sticks as a drunken cretin would a dog—and *dogs,* also beaten to death with blunt cudgels and hunks of rebar.

"Life is pain," said a man to me today.

"Nay," I said, "Life is suffering."

There's no plausible explanation for my arm being fractured or broken—I slept on the damned forearm and now I hear the creak of a bone and/or inflamed muscle tissue—my diagnosis is null. Oh, entropy, do you prevent me from my ambition in the armed forces? Will this inconvenient pain persist and become a permanent handicap? How *exciting*—I'm thrilled to be among the vibrant thoughts of my active mind!

Yes, a can of tuna, some almonds, and a few spoonfuls of peanut butter to cap off my night. What a wonderful world!

I scrubbed a pan submerged in green coagulated water and listened to over fifty intoxicated bar and table patrons holler in delight for the sake of a sleazy night in the sack with a respective other, devoid of all ill-emotion. My maligned ape friends, dressed in your suits and slathered in makeup, I wonder, with my humble dejection hunched over a sink, what a twenty-three-year-old prisoner locked away for a life sentence feels when the year notches a single-digit higher through our curious sentimental custom of *time...* Yes—*it* all ebbs onward! Blast this arm to hell—I'm tired and stare at a screen! Foul reader, I hate you, though don't take *it* personally.

9:17 AM

In isolation, I hear nothing but the whispered sentiments of a man and woman—rational aspects of my psyche I wish to abide by for the sake of community and relationships, the true *"knowers"* of my condition—myself.

My condition of *reality*. I've been sober for *years*—since the imbibement of absinthe two years ago—I have *it* on record! The strings of Vivaldi's cello and violin tether me to this world—or am I *deluded* by this single well of entertainment I tap into when I am at my lowest? There is nothing— *always*—nothing special, to all and any, surrounded by egos vying for life and recognition, a little snippet of love and validation addressed through a chosen field of self-proclaimed expertise: P.H.D. holders, charlatans, hands-folded-in-front-of-the-pelvis-suit-wearers.

I asked a nineteen-year-old boy named Allen last night—a small-statured one-hundred-and-eight pound "pretty" boy with a full head of wild gelled hair streaked with red and purple colorations, undeveloped mustache, and snakebite piercings, what his meaning of life is...

"Uhhh, well I really have no idea man—I'm just burnt out from this place and working all the time I mean people are shoulder to shoulder out there bumping into each other! Crazy man! Peek your head out there and look."

"I'd rather not."

Allen stood close enough for me to observe every little pocket of youthful pores clogged by sebaceous fluids and every twinge of drug-induced glee towards the ceiling. Deadened eyes at such a young age, "burnt out," vapid; I listened:

"Yeah bro but I gotta' get back out there, *so* much stuff to do."

I continued to mop and reflected on this one instance of my assertion into the space around me throughout the entire day. If the question were to be reversed on me, I believe I'd say the same as Allen in a succinct, poignant manner:

"I don't know."

A tale of modern love:

A girl I work with expressed extreme interest in me through a series of inquiries throughout the last three days.

I answered with brief conceptions and marked disinterest.

Yesterday, she announced to me that she is a strong, independent woman, without provocation on my part, while I scrubbed a stack of pans, and she marched away.

I'm uncertain if the satire was intended.

11:24 AM

Called off from work.
Tendonitis.

4:54 PM

Hate.

Is this entertainment—I bet, *exquisite* joy, you reader—you've no idea how lucky you are to read the words wrought into existence by one who laments the whole grand *lack* of design of humanity to such a degree that whenever I perceive myself in the mirror I am overtaken with the supreme emotion of *hate*—abject hate on account for all life is.

Smirk and giggle, you feeble sham—we are the same; there is no differentiation between you and me; how much your flesh grows, or however occluded the contents of your mind are with the dribble of an arcane matter you believe is *known* only by you, is void of merit to the reality of inconsequential progress. The journey of a human overwrought with the weight of the world on a set of slumped shoulders is a subtle reflection—a transient reverb of empathetic sorrow of every tear you shed for yourself. Baseless cretins, you deem this fun, or are you set about educating yourself—a fool's errand, to analyze the nihilistic expulsion *of* a fool?

I depict myself in a manner far more wretched than I am; this journal is my shadow, my unholy confidante, my mission—and to whomever *you* may be—a leisure and pastime, *you imbecile.*

Music is but a fanciful flicker of sound waves passed in and out—akin to a romp in the sack with a sensuous mate—and food, oh, the act— spinach, mushrooms, and tuna play with my tongue this instant while

I waste away in the extraneous output of my embittered state of reckless loathing.

My body yearns to be worked and I am stymied due to the condition of my arm! Behold—entropy, oh yes, a whiny, infantile man bemoans and complains of a slight circumstance of the body while thousands are mutilated, disfigured, incapacitated—on the verge of death this moment— oh, a few died amidst the throes of agonal pain this *instant*-

And here I stand—the gall, the nerve, the audacity—and you—reader, I fail to think of an insult to encapsulate your esteem. If, by personal happenstance, *I* introduced *you* to this literature, you've been duped. If you decide to pursue this route and you've progressed this far, or if you fumbled through the pages of digital print and settled on this singular segment— perhaps a few other passages, you're a curious sort and I approve of your inquisitive nature—*confounded,* yet I approve. Damn your ego and mine. Hold hands with a loved one and plunge into a mutual void.

I'm enveloped by a mental cage, a metaphor of a rat within a multifaceted maze filled with cheese-rigged traps at every end; I know *you* are too, therein springs the pain.

8:17 PM

For the sake of my physiology, I chose to convert my madness and malcontent to a state of equanimity and contentment; healing of my arm depends on this factor, though the damage induced by my misanthropic outburst accelerated entropy throughout my framework.

January 2nd, 2019

5:56 PM

My first received "professional" review of "Year One" of *this* nonsense:

"Balor's debut memoir tells of his struggle to find his own identity and purpose in life. The author, a 25-year-old grocery store janitor somewhere in suburban America, tells readers that he set out to write a novel, but his focus soon shifted to the journal he was writing at the same time. This yearlong chronicle begins as a stream-of-consciousness narrative, filled with seemingly random observations on such subjects as the wonder of black holes; he refers to his journal entries as a 'cluster of ceaseless thoughts.' However, his quest for self-discovery ultimately becomes the book's driving force. He constantly questioned the meaning of his life, and he sought inspiration by inquiring about his co-workers' life-goals. Although he felt an attraction to women, he says, he had no discernible sex drive and also suffered from depression, apparently related to his parents' divorce when he was 2. Over the course of this book, he tells of a gradually developing fear that he could be a paranoid schizophrenic. For example, inside his home, he says, he often heard voices, and he wasn't sure whether they were from the tenants living upstairs or only in his head. He later suffered feelings of emptiness and moroseness, and although his interactions with others seemed to improve by the end of the memoir (he made some friends), he also seemed to need some more recovery time. Balor's memoir is long and occasionally verbose, which he acknowledges, but the prose is strong and engaging throughout. Poems and snippets of short stories offset the personal narrative; they initially seem like asides but they quickly provide further insight into the author: 'My aspirations are a ruse / To convince myself and acquire validation / From other plebs as lost as I.' Likewise, his worries about potential schizophrenia come across as earnest; at one point, for instance, he tells of being convinced that neighbors were listening to and regularly talking about him. The book is, at times, too metafictional, as the author sporadically discusses publishing his book, sifts through title possibilities, and even includes faux reviews from anonymous readers.

A sometimes-bizarre but undeniably intriguing self-examination. " [15]

Ah—the literary world, one of the biggest shams ever devised, the Bible being anachronistic/contemporary proof.

Now, a review of this review:

The reviewer, an entity paid to skim through my work and write a 352-word synopsis (*two* words over the *minimum* required), has written me and the public an injustice in regards to what the content of my work is:

Preface: I didn't make any *friends,* nor did I want to.

Oh yes, let's get right down to the nitty-gritty—*metafictional!* Metafictional implies the piece is a work of fiction despite the entire series thus far being an all-too-real reality. Rather, a *metanonfictional* delve into an obscure mind of a *pleb as lost as I.* What is this—'*too*' metafictional, eh?

---

[15] Kirkus Reviews

I address you now, reviewer, and condemn that your review is *too* placid. You fail to mention how I lambast and mock the intelligence of my reader. Is this review of your review *too* ~~metafictional~~ metanonfictional for your taste? You flatter me and thereby flatter yourself with statements such as *"Balor's memoir is long and occasionally verbose, which he acknowledges, but the prose is strong and engaging throughout,"* and *"A sometimes-bizarre but undeniably intriguing self-examination."* Yes, I'm also intrigued by long-winded reflections of mental duress and hopeless recounts. *You lie*—reviewer, with your 352-word review, for your thoughts are unthoughtful. Your tentative judgments of *"seemed"* and *"apparently"* are reminiscent of a high schooler's essay read aloud in front of a class on what he/she believed George Orwell's *Animal Farm* meant:

A self-conscious high school pretty boy held a page-and-a-half essay with arms skewed in front of him before an English class comprised of twenty-four students and read aloud, "The pigs seemed to be cruel and avaricious while the other animals were apparently subjugated-"

"-Very good, Timmy, please sit down," interjected a disinterested teacher; he clicked a laser-pointer mouse twice, stared at his computer screen, and entered "C+" on Timmy's slot on a twenty-six row spreadsheet.

Timmy nodded, uncertain and confused why—after his nineteen-minute labor the previous night composing his report, he had been dismissed with the utterance of a few sentences, though he hurried to his seat and set the paper flat on top of his desk, hands folded, and smiled, contented with the outcome.

Is this what I deserve, reviewer?—a C+? I'd rather you annihilate my **writing** with unabashed carelessness than psychoanalyze my character as if you *apparently seemed* to *unwittingly* disregard my contempt for the entire publishing industry and my disillusionment with creeds, beliefs, doctrines, and self-delusions—beyond my *own*.

No: I'm a morose-self-diagnosed-schizophrenic-janitor-man who is also depressed because my parents divorced at the age of two—*then* you spoil the ending!—*I made some friends!*—Oh—all is well and peachy-keen because I *made some friends* (I've yet to determine who), yet—the cliff hanger: I seem to need some recovery…

My verbose 427-word review of your review is a metanonfictional middle finger to your forced corporate expulsion.

Another male encounter with a stranger I met in passing on the street who desired to perform oral sex on me; I seem to attract effeminate men, yet, I failed to orgasm, though my companion had experienced sincere delight. Now I know what a dissipated slut who seeks emotional validation through spontaneous sexual encounters feels like—for I have become this ever-present trope. There will be no masturbation finale now or thereafter. I'd rather lose my sexual drive—for what will I reap other than perpetual labor of pretenses, extremes, and an abundance of lies?

No—I disappoint myself; indifferent and detached from relations, the constant is flesh. Bestial modes disgust me. No—I am far from ashamed… liberated from shame… I am sad and desire to cry yet fail to do so. There is an emptiness in relations without the bond of a family to solidify the development of mutual care, understanding, and empathy. I stand naked at the late hours of the night and reminisce about a time when I was happy, *true* happiness, for what the notion qualifies for; a hark back to the innocence of childhood when Santa Claus was real and pain a far-fetched scare tactic, when the body knew no defilement and glowed with the lustrous sheen of youth.

No… I am *merely* disgusted, aghast, and sad; I'm a sad little man who has experimented with the male form on multiple occasions and have rediscovered my immutable apathy.

Present me the finest female, and I will shun her beauty.

Present me the finest male, and I will shun his flattery.

For the sake of solace, I am disgusted.

Best to return to my studies and dispel any notion of sexual encounters.

The *Bhagavad Gita*… a doctrine which states, "There is nothing lost or wasted in this life"—I cling to the premise, my shredded vestiges of hope, my tattered scrawl of commandments, my immolated tome of null words—my *God*—my *mind;* my bulwark shatters and a single tear drips onto my bare chest. Self-pity? Perhaps. You love *it,* reader—*and* future self—*oh*—too much metanonficitonal exposition for you, for me to address myself and future entities in a time of enervated sadness on behalf of my estrangement from human bonding?

Yes, much like Barbellion, I sell my sorrow.

"This evening [I] went to the Library and read about her (Marie Bashkirtseff) in Mathilde Blind's introductory essay to her Journal. I

am simply astounded. *It* would be difficult in all the world's history to discover any two persons with temperaments so alike. She is the 'very spit of me!' I devoured Mathilde Blind's pages more and more astonished. We are identical! Oh, Marie Bashkirtseff! how we should have hated one another! She feels as I feel. We have the same self-absorption, the same vanity and corroding ambition. She is impressionable, volatile, passionate—ill! So am I. Her journal is my journal. All mine is stale reading now. She has written down all my thoughts and forestalled me! Already I have found some heart-rending parallels. To think I am only a replica: how humiliating for a human being to find himself merely a duplicate of another. Is there anything in the transmigration of souls? She died in 1886. I was born in 1889. "

— WNP Barbellion's The Journal of a Disappointed Man

January 3rd, 2018

8:14 PM

One quiet suburban morning, a fresh half-inch layer of snow coated the neighborhood.

A medium-sized english mastiff named Samson roused from his kennel, sniffed the air, sniffed the snow, sniffed a patch of dirt, sniffed his anus, sniffed his left hind leg, and barked thrice: a harsh, loud, bestial outcry. The ruler of a backyard domain.

From a distance, seven houses down at the corner of an intersection, a full-blooded german shepherd named Lars jarred against a three-foot chain tied around his neck and a two-foot diameter tree trunk; he replied with long-winded intermittent bark-howls:

"**Good morning, chap!**" barked Samson.

Lars howled, "Vhat time iz *it?*"

"**A time for a bit to eat, I hope!**"

"Ja, koot, I'fe already zampled a dazte of my fecez diz mornink—I'm schdarved, I dell joo!"

"**Yes, yes, breakfast this morning should be a fine bit of kibbles and maybe some leftover scrap from dinner last evening!**"

"Vhat'd dey have?"

"**Meatloaf over grits!**"

"Ja, dat sounds divine—ja—I'm hungry and cold, hungry and cold!"

"Didn't expect overnight snow!"

"Neizer did I!"

"Smelled dry last night!"

"Ja, ja!"

"Hey now, what!-" a shrill yowl resounded from the backyard of the mastiff; a once deep and resonant bark reduced to a pathetic whimper.

"Ja—jour mornink beatink! I vant mine doo! *God!* I'm hungry and cold!"

9:12 PM

When I write, "I killed someone," this is a lie; therefore, words are delimited from power. Thoughts are intangibles often aggrandized and manifested into what we call "technology." As a unified species throughout thousands of years, we harnessed and manipulated our world's matter, designed architectural marvels, practiced social policies, and invented a system(s) to "understand" the framework of the universe. The inexhaustible list of minutiae details of what humanity has "accomplished" is as ridiculous as a careless tromp into a bookstore where one beholds the immense shelves and wall of tomes, and stops to contemplate—to consider the desperate vie for validation and escape on behalf of both the writer *and* the reader respectively.

I'm a lunatic—really; I've no appreciation for sensibility. I act the part, oh yes, cultivated and established; however, I pace... and pace... read, write, eat, work the body, and proceed to fail on all accounts of every endeavor I undertake—though I write—and when *this* tidbit of information slips into the mind of another, the individual is *impressioned*.

Intelligent people glean through my ruse, and I theirs; we embarrass one another; I'll never be satisfied in a relationship due to this.

Well now, do I dare to be complacent in my development and acknowledge the incessant flattery and remarks of my intelligence I often receive? Intelligence is the singular accursed blessing of my character—*they* tell me *so:* "*so* intelligent," the fools haven't an idea of their own superior acumen in relation to mine. However, one who would witness me trudge through the snow with a backpack full of produce/canned fish/peanut butter/cacao/supplements, books, spare clothing, and miscellaneous equipment, would jeer and say, "*This* fucking moron..." from their vehicle, and I'm inclined to agree. *Just* like *you*, reader—yes, I lambast you once more and will persist: my recurrent theme.

"I killed someone"—no—no—this is a lie, you fool! Remove the thought and instead think of your next meal… Ah, what a comfort.

No, I refuse to lie to you, dearest reader, as much as I revile, contempt, loathe, and hate you; your variegated judgments are what validates me, and mine: you. Now that I address you with my *too* meta(non)fictional style, aren't you flattered to be referred to as a nameless entity of absolute importance?

I'm a crazed saint! I can perform no foul deed! Oh, pity—pity for us, for ever knowing the other.

January 4th, 2019

8:44 AM

A fellow of my esteem and mien would've been murdered and assimilated with the earth long ago if living amongst a primitive tribe; therefore shamanism would be my route: to claim I possess magical powers; however, I'd decry my own merit and be hunted regardless.

To revert back to my thinned frame and "underweight" aspect of 145 lbs has an allure of longevity and functional strength. Many brutes and overstuffed gargantuan graze akin to cattle and swell with pomp and pride from the result of swollen muscle tissue. This sick life is a theatre. Jettison me out.

11:12 PM

No reader, I could never lie to you—for if I did, I would lie to myself, and what good is a fallacious journal? For instance, I have two accounts to record:

I spoke to Alton for the first time, a cook, while we cleaned the kitchen during closing hours: "Hey, Alton."

Alton glanced at me and looked away towards the floor.

I said, "Do you believe there is an authentic self, or, in other words, that there are only pretenses of personality?"

Alton continued to stare at the floor, sidelong, away from me, and said, "I have *no* idea."

I stepped towards the dish pit and called back to him, "Neither do I!"

The old dishwasher woman who "trains" me, Halle, informed me that she has four children, the youngest being thirty-seven-years-old.

Halle has been married five times; all of her husbands died:

The first to a pneumatic machine malfunction: a giant roll of paper toppled loose and crushed him.

The second had a penchant for tequila and died from liver failure.

The third I don't recall.

The fourth in a motorcycle accident.

And the fifth suffers heart complications and undergoes surgery on the 22nd and 23rd of this month; thereby, Halle has requested me to fill in for her shift on those dates.

I said, "Sounds as though you have experienced much grief in life."

"Oh yeah—I've been around once or twice, Hunny!"

I've partaken in immoderate consumption of foodstuffs. My strength has stagnated for years—far too long. Engorgement on spoonfuls of peanut butter, handfuls of almonds, a half-gallon of milk, a scoop of whey, a can of sardines, and a cucumber... At a weight of 162 lbs, I intend to grow before basic training whittles me down.

This morning I condemned the glutton; now I become one.

"For what sense or understanding have they? They follow minstrels and take the multitude for a teacher, not knowing that many are bad and few good. For the best men choose one thing above all—immortal glory among mortals; but the masses stuff themselves like cattle."

- Heraclitus (c. 500 A.D.)

January 5th, 2019

11:44 AM

My father and I repel and attract; our idiosyncrasies synergize and rebound off of each other's hateful and malcontent existence: a codependent relationship. I'd enjoy a read of a journal full of his thoughts, a shame he's too engrossed in *Candy Crush* and ten to twenty-five-year-old television reruns, coffee, cigarettes, and bong rips to do anything *but* think. *What* he thinks… I hope not much, for his sake. "I'm fucking retired," he refutes; his averted gaze peers upward on the occasion to evaluate facial expressions and demeanor. Retirement is a cozy jingle, a sought-after word employed to excuse yourself.

January 6th, 2019

11:56 AM

I've attracted the self-proclaimed "Strong Independent Woman": a gregarious fellow kitchen slave, who, on my second discussion with her, disclosed innumerable tidbits of personal information about her tragic childhood. I had a hunch from the onset of the interactions of our subdued chemistry; her idle gawks at me while my back is turned and inquiries such as, "Baethan, do you have a significant other?" affirmed my suspicions. *Now* I am ashamed, for I *do* find this woman attractive; we wish to dominate one another with wanton genitalia rancor. Intelligent women desire to control stupid (productive) men. Intelligent men desire to dominate stupid (beautiful) women; we both believe we are more intelligent than the other: a formula for romance.

On my way through the neighborhood, I walked alongside the old lawn care specialist who lives on the corner of the street: Gary, the man who I've credited in the past for his impeccable handiwork with hedge trimming. I've dealt with him on many occasions, one instance in which he invited me into his home to sell me onto a pyramid scheme[16] for an electric company.

He heard my boot steps and waved.

I said, "Hello Gary. Do you believe there is a true authentic self, or that there is only pretense of the personality?"

Gary called back to me from twenty feet away, "Can you repeat that?"

We continued our walk and I repeated the question.

Gary scratched his head, stopped, and approached me, where we

---

[16] I've been invited to many "pyramid schemes" and have *almost* succumbed; however, to join another's paradigm would add an extra layer to the pyramid scheme I already play on behalf of being alive.

continued our discourse at the center of the street for forty minutes. Neighbors mulled about their yards and within garages while Gary and I probed the thin veneer of reality, faith, philosophy, and the manifestations of God—which to him, (God) was tantamount one morning when he awoke, forlorn and forsaken in an empty apartment room with nothing left to live for one lonesome night; the room became illuminated with a "divine glow," which compelled him to fall asleep with ease despite his previous months of restlessness.

A tale of interest, a conversation I wish I could have transcribed in full, though I destroyed my voice recorder in a washing machine due to negligence and am saddened to have filtered most of the conversation out of my mind due to Gary's flattery of my character: How "deep" I am, and my ability to, as he said, "Take a linear path with a single thought and go down that path until there is nothing else to think about." I presume he finds this supposed "ability" impressive. I think Gary's experience with the divine aspect of his own consciousness alone in an apartment room at night is also impressive; I'm a tad envious.

10:42 PM

On the owner of the bar's request to work at an adjacent tavern, I accepted and proceeded to succeed the expectations of social relations and work standards.

In social relations, I ignored everyone except my direct trainer and kitchen mates in order to learn the placement of dishware. Many who attempted to interact with me were left with feelings of animosity and revulsion of my apathy and indifference.

In work standards, I employed my numbed hands to scrub the entire station and removed grease accumulation I had been told would be "impossible to clean."

At closing, my trainer, a man who loathes himself and his job and blared bluegrass/hippie music from two water-stained speakers, said, "I'll leave you alone because you obviously know what you're doing."

Ah, so, more metanonfictional dribble for you—reader, you find this to be entertainment? To read of my dishwashing exploits, or rather, a corporate exploit *of* my character *to* dish-wash? Human dishwashers worldwide are the unsung heroes of the globe, elevated beyond the most talented of cooks and disciplined executive chefs. In your average household of bygone times there was a dishwasher—a wench, a peasant, a *pleb*—heroes. Even the most basic bowl of gruel demands a proper rinse after consumption. Now, most depend on machines to labor on their behalf, in *all* facets of life. Even now, the digital is my domain, the keyboard is my instrument, and Mozart's *Symphony No. 38 in D Major* is my current augmentation.

Are you weary of my verbose declamatory remarks on society and myself, my bitter ruminations and tired diatribes?—you sick, sorry fools, whatever you feel of my character, you feel for yourself—your shadow leers at you through my written word; my conduct and behavior is a veritable mirror for your own inner disharmony. Judge me childish, do you?—well, *who* reads this: You, entertainment seeker, you pompous ingrate, you *self-indulgent* hypocrite.

There's a bartender at my first post—at the "high-class" bar, that passes me while I labor and inquires of me to guess between two numbers. He glares at me and speaks something along the lines of, "Seventeen or twenty-three," to which I respond at random. The first instance I was "correct," and pleased him; the other two instances, I was *"wrong,"* and he jerked his head away and strutted into a different room. This evening he visited the adjacent tavern and saw me, to his surprise, and said, "Oh whoa!"

I passed by him, set my racks of dishware on the back counter, crossed back around the bar, and while I sped towards him, I said, "Five or six?"

His instantaneous outburst of "Five," was met by my immediate and affected response of-

"You're *right!*" Whereafter, I escaped into the kitchen. I wonder if he wonders as much as I wonder about the absurdity of life.

11:28 PM

By my bloodied hands and bloated belly, I swear, reader, you'd be unlucky to *know* me.

January 7th, 2019

11:08 PM

I encounter men each day who hate themselves worse than I do myself. I fantasize about the social scenarios these men engage in; "truths" play out in dialogues. My own thoughts are displaced by these imaginings.

"Merry Christmas Martha!"

Martha bounded down carpeted stairs; every painting, light fixture, and unsecured piece of furniture rattled: "Santa came! Santa came!"

The mother blushed, placed her hands along her hips, and said, "I thought you didn't believe in Santa."

Martha shouted, "I do *this* morning!" and darted for her stocking. Loud, petulant giggles echoed off a gift-littered floor. A corpulent hand reached into the stocking and ripped the soft white and red polyester fabric off from a loose nail hammered into a wallpapered slab of sheetrock. "Oh—my—God—oh—my... *God*... I'm *so!*-"

The mother fought to suppress tears of joy and watched Martha drop to her knees, pour the contents of the stocking onto the floor, and scream.

"Oh—my—God! *Mom! Mom!*-" Martha managed to say between a fit of high-pitched screeches. She fumbled through a pile of wrapped peanut butter cups and chocolate-coated wafers for a small white pill bottle labeled, "Live Tapeworm Eggs," rose to her feet, held the bottle to her chest with all eight of her fingers interlaced around the bottle, tilted her head towards a yellowed ceiling, and roared an open-mouthed triumph of ecstatic joy from between two red-hot cheeks.

"I know I said we couldn't afford liposuction but Santa brought you the next best thing!"

"Oh—my—God—mom—I—love—you! You!—You!—You! *Not* Santa!—Oh—my—God!" Martha bumbled over the pile of wrapped chocolates into her mother's arms and began to weep.

"You still have all your other presents to go, silly!"

"I know... I..." Martha coughed and continued, "I love you so much mom, where did you get these?"

"*Santa* is a resourceful ma—*lady!*"

Martha's laughter boomed throughout the house; she said, "You're *so* awesome mom! I wish dad were here."

The mother stiffened; her chin nestled on Martha's brown hair strewn over a broad shoulder; she pulled away, gripped her daughter by the forearms, and said, "Let's open the rest of your presents."

11:42 PM

I viewed my face in a mirror on the immediate finalization of the previous sentence of the above story and saw a visage of myself I'm unacquainted with, one of vileness. Yes, my furrowed brow accentuated hollowed blue eyes, and lines of my cheeks creased down into a wicked frown. I maintained this aspect even after the innate feeling which had inspired *it* fleeted, and inspected the profile from a variety of angles as one would a face of an ugly stranger.

A family tavern hosted six groups in a row of booths; four harlots and one stud sat at the bar. The stud addressed the bartender, a woman with low self-esteem: "Why are you so down tonight?"

The bartender leaned over the counter, enamored with the one-hundred and ninety-two-pound heap of flesh and bone, with immaculate skin, an effortless tuft of hair, two rows of whitened teeth, designer cologne, and apathetic eyes; she said, "Oh there's this one cute new guy who works in the kitchen who snubbed me the other day and made me feel like shit."

"You like him?"

"Well, I don't know, I *want* to get to know him," she giggled, frowned, leaned closer to the stud, and said, "but he won't even say hi to me when I say hi to him so—whatever, I guess."

The stud gazed over the bartender's head past a row of display shot glasses in front of a mirror and said, "How about I fuck you instead?"

The bartender quivered and said, "Are you serious?—like—*really*?"

"Yeah."

"Ohhh, uh—wow, oh, I mean, are you serious—you?"

"Yeah me, why not me?"

"Um, because you're fucking gorgeous and I'm just a little fat and dumpy thing, like, you're a dreamboat and—I'm getting *so* flustered right now."

"Alright, you're starting to turn me off now."

"No!—No!—I'm sorry, I'm sorry, I'll stop talking about *it.*"

"Cool."

The bartender turned to serve a new patron, turned back to the stud, and said, "So, when… do…"

"Tonight after I'm finished here."

"Are you sure—you aren't just playing with me? I mean, really, you're-"

"Yeah, I'm just a guy and you're just a girl so why not?"

"You're not just a guy; you're *Maverick;* you're like—so gorgeous and huge, a real man; are you sure you want me?"

"Okay—yeah, I'm not sure, forget *it.*"

"What? No!—whoa—wait—wait, I'm sorry—I'm sorry; I'm *so* sorry; are you serious? Are-"

The stud locked eyes with the bartender and said, "Yeah, forget *it*, you're acting pretty pathetic; you're practically groveling for me to fuck you so just forget about *it*."

"Maverick... " the bartender started, and instead, stormed away to a new patron and said, "What can I get you?"

The new patron ordered a beer. The bartender suppressed tears and poured a beer into a small circular glass.

A woman of similar stature and disposition as the bartender approached the aloof stud and sat at the barstool to his right. She said, "Yo."

The stud said, "Hey," and nodded his head.

"Don't you think what you did is fucked up?"

"What I did, what?"

"What you did to Jessica—got her all excited and then destroyed her like that?"

"She was too desperate, turned me off."

"Well you didn't need to be so mean about the whole thing."

"Do you want to fuck instead?"

The woman blushed and said, "Ummm, *no?* I have a boyfriend. This is why I don't like muscular men: you guys think you can have anyone just by looking at them."

"C'mon, I'll fuck you real good and he won't ever know."

The woman said-

January 8th, 2019

12:31 PM

In my first installment of this now-three-part series of shameless propositions, I detailed an article I read in *Scientific American* that examined the calorie expenditure of the sedentary American compared with one of the last contemporary hunter-gatherer tribes. I theorized that our brains utilized more calories, to which, I have discovered, I am wrong, due to narrowed "research" *permitted* by my lord and master *Google*, and have "learned" that even eight hours of intense thoughts devoted to mathematical processing demands *only*, at most, 100-150 calories... an amount of glucose which may be replenished by the consumption of a few jelly beans.

Alas, all thoughts are theories; there is no truth; I'm disillusioned with this tripe and fail to maintain serious conversation about what is "known"—by anyone—damned self-ascribed intellectuals, scholars—proponents of "progress"; how I once yearned to *be* a bearded sage at the top of an ivory tower is a travesty.

Alexander the Great, may you have burned *every* library in the world to ashes and occluded humanity with a perpetual fog of ignorance, how *negligible* of a difference your destructive actions would have wrought will never be *known*... I write to the wind.

10:45 PM

I enjoyed a multifaceted conversation spanned over the course of the night in the kitchen with a cook named Tyler. We discoursed truth, the self, idealism, and delusions. He is a well-spoken, college-educated dropout of three different degrees, two (of which I know) are computer engineering and accounting. Tyler's diverse cultural background, dyed and styled hair atop an Asian-contoured face, tall stature, and tattooed arms, make for an unassuming character, one who plays the role of an idiot to conceal his intelligence.

Tyler—this twenty-five-year-old man, has traveled to many provinces, his favorite among them being Hawaii (his state of origin). He claims to have spoken and assisted with the psyche of drug-dealers, murderers, and rapists, due to his claim of "making them feel at ease." We spoke of antiquated times: peasants subjugated by priests and corrupt governments, the merits of Adolf Hitler and Osama Bin Laden due to their *beliefs* that what they strived for was *good*—in their subjective truths.

My voice recorder would have proved to be an excellent tool in this encounter. I refuse to record an inaccurate dialogue; our discussion was far too manifold throughout the course of the night to commit the injustice of falsified quotations. Instead, a few points in brief:

We agreed, after extreme conjecture, that the singular truth is what we believe. Life is whatever you wish *it* to be dependent on your truth. Life is an illusion and we are deluded by our own beliefs.

Tyler dismissed my proposal of suffering being the singular truth, though he looked down at his feet, laughed, and smiled at my follow-up: "Entropy is god."

"Entropy is god..." he said; our conversation moved to the domain of

"Blood is thicker than water." Tyler asked if I knew what that meant in regards to truth.

I said, "No."

Tyler expounded on covenants being stronger than family ties, e.g., cults, governments, wartime comradeship, factions, political paradigms, religions, philosophies, and ideologies.

I enjoy Tyler; he cooks me delicious meals and has recipcorated my outrageous questions with an eagerness to answer with a profundity of thought I am unacquainted with. On his encouragement of me to ask him another loaded question, I said, "Do you think I'm a pompous intellectual?"

Tyler said, "No, you're not pompous at all, just a humble confidence, not arrogant or anything. I mean, you're tall, and I'm tall too, so-" he trailed off and smirked. A strange man.

On our night's closure, Tyler offered his hand to shake; I accepted. On his departure, he said, "If you ever want someone to talk to when you're feeling disgruntled with the world, I can help you out."

My incredulous grimace incited Tyler to grin: "That's a large claim to make."

"I think I can."

I'm curious if Tyler's truth is compatible with my truth; he has offered to save me from myself: a veritable Jesus.

January 9th, 2019

8:29 AM

I've performed many "bad" deeds in life and have yet to cross the threshold into "horrible" or "terrible."

I once wore a wolf mask and stood in the doorway of my younger brother's room one night while he watched cartoons from his bed. I observed the seven-year-old for several minutes—engrossed with a television, while I stood, statuesque; he noticed me and screamed a horrendous outburst of terror. I bounded away and returned without the mask, feigned concern in my countenance, and mock disbelief in the tonality of my reassurance.

I've severed relationships with many girls throughout middle school and high school with cold and callous deference due to my desire to be alone, engrossed with books, music, and videogames. The number of tearful faces I've elicited and half-hearted hugs I've given is a gross figure.

Ants, grasshoppers, beetles, moths, larvae, worms, and slugs, have met many gruesome ends within a spider's web due to my intervention.

I filmed a video in high school with a few friends with intent to mock one of our friends, who we thought—as a group, spent "too much time" with his new girlfriend and not enough time with us. I acted the role of our victim; he was my best friend at the time and my performance was, therefore, an accurate depiction of his character. This video became a school-wide sensation and was brought to the attention of the teachers, superintendent, and principal. I was ~~interviewed~~ interrogated, deemed a "cyberbully," accused of rape (a mock sex scene with my girlfriend was filmed), and suspended from school for two weeks. I never recovered the relationship with my "victimized" best friend, nor did I attempt to.

The worst deed I've ever committed, my final past confession which haunts me rare mid-mornings before the sun has arisen while I lay in a cold sweat:

At the age of eighteen, I enjoyed a video game one late night by my lonesome as many kids of suburbia do in the wee hours before bed when I was interrupted by a few knocks on my window. I opened the curtain and a beautiful young girl with a voluptuous body and coy face stood with a chessboard and two bottles of red wine.

Being the apathetic young man I was and ~~in some essence~~ still am, I raised an eyebrow, for I knew this girl—not well... on casual terms, the sister of a loose acquaintance. Her name was Brittany.

I allowed the curtain to fall, waltzed out into the living room, opened the front door, and allowed Brittany in. We exchanged minimal banter and she issued me a challenge to a game of chess. I accepted with grace and eagerness.

The bottles of alcohol were questionable, though I "knew" the insinuated suggestion; the fire in her eyes affirmed her true intentions. I played along, defeated her as though she hadn't attempted to win, and we imbibed. We played again, and once more, I won, thereby the chessboard was disregarded in favor of dissipated foreplay. Between us both, a full bottle of wine flowed through our bloodstreams. The rigors of passion caught me unaware and my titillation peaked when I pushed her down onto my pillow: a new body to explore, a domain of soft white flesh of this red-headed beauty *wanted* to be defiled.

I did so—yes, in the darkness, I probed, and due to gratuitous alcohol consumption (an instance reminiscent of my one night stand with Shelly), I suffered premature ejaculation. *However,* too embarrassed to tell Brittany,

I utilized the "pull-out method," climaxed onto my sheets in silence while I kissed her thighs, pushed myself back over her body where I hovered, feigned despair on account of her feelings, and whispered into her ear, "I'm sorry, I can't do this... You have a boyfriend."

Tears, sadness, despondency, and disbelief—on her part. We dressed and Brittany phoned her boyfriend to pick her up... a strange... harrowing event, for *his* sake; what excuse she conjured up for her presence with me is a mystery, for they are married now—the last I knew through the social grapevine. I consoled her concerning our "licentious" behavior on my front steps at four in the morning. The sun had crept up over the horizon and illuminated her lifeless, dejected face, similar to Jasmine's... Now that I think of this and confess, I realize the many repeated events of my "injustices" to the fragile sensibilities of young women (and alcohol-induced premature ejaculation). I continued to hold Brittany on the front steps of the porch while she cried somber tears. Brittany's silence spoke volumes. A white van pulled up and she flashed me one final grimace of hate—well deserved and everlasting.

9:16 AM

Now I stand in the same house where the aforementioned events transpired, only the house is a pilfered, gutted, empty shell of all the love that once dwelled within. I remain in this temporary station, standing among a kitchen with my writing device mounted on a cardboard box propped up on the kitchen counter. My foodstuffs to my left, clothing and backpack to my right... I've nothing else to account for. Leo Tolstoy's *The Death of Ivan Ilyich* is the single book I own: a recent gift from my father.

My confidence resides in the steady growth of my muscle tissue and this series of dreadful manuscripts—a detestable manifestation of a human mind; a reflection of the latent self within us all.

"What can we call our own except energy, strength, and will?"

- Johann Wolfgang Von Goethe

January 10th, 2019

1:01 AM

I consecrate my love for entropy with self-flagellation and feasting. Called into work, a nightlife of dishwashing, afterward a trip to the gym in the bitter cold, pack on my back, wrapped in merino wool, I veer around ice and over snowy sidewalks; culminated lifetime hours of walking is incalculable!

Saddened on all counts, no matter what venture I undergo, the intuitive hauntings of my ego persist and are my reality, a chemical imbalance, a multifaceted spectrum of variegated *shit* in my brain. I'm in love—with *being* disgruntled. I have become accustomed to a slight limp and persistent pain in my right foot due to incessant walking—to never sit, ah! I sled leg press four-hundred pounds, full-extension, slow reps of ten, for five sets, and stifle pained exhalations among my fellow gym-haters; yes, everyone at the gym begrudges the other, there is no divergence of the extreme judgments of visitors to public gyms. The dedicated powerlifter envies the overweight treadmill pounder for the *lack* of dedication and commitment to a vain recourse. One moment, I am a psychopath enraptured with the tear of muscle fibers, and the next, a *douchebag.*

I believe I'd rather die than live as the baseless animal I am, consumed with *consuming,* growing… *growing* to *die,* oh sweet entropy, my God-

And *you* (metanonfictional alert), foul idler—knowledge seeker, entertainment-indulger, haven't you enough of my *sin,* my perpetual duress of the mind? Ah—my arm aches and my foot throbs—the love—love of *entropy,* my eternal God.

Verbose ramblings of a lunatic?—better than the stringent one-liners of a sage who claims to *know.* You… *you,* I've no name for you, for you are I, and I've become what I've despised. Consider this—the shadow, Jung's theory: What you find intolerable in others is what you find most intolerable in yourself. I have embraced my shadow and my ego condemns me! The incessant pangs of hostile voices are a product of my self-chosen damnation!

Hope… there is hope to be thrust into the military-industrial complex, to be stripped of the ego and to become one with my fellow self-aggrandized title and emblem bearers.

Am I foolish, unfit for service, or should be institutionalized?

A half-gallon of milk, peanut butter, almonds, and whey; I consume while I listen to J.S. Bach and yearn for death. "Pathetic," I think to myself, ~~devoid~~ reprieved of external outlets to project my ego onto, i.e., family and friends.

Boredom is the reality. Bored at work (life), disgruntled and disillusioned with the premise of this game. No—life *is* pleasant, I concur. Life bores me *to* death. What can we do, learn about all the sweet nothings of this reality and progress for the sake of competition with others for the benefit of mating and exponential population growth with improved infrastructure and medicine? Submit ourselves to entertainment and indulge in the flesh of others—*please*—yes, I know, I pummel this concept *to* death and no matter my efforts to relinquish this nihilistic, cynical, misanthropic self-imposed mental cage, I enjoy *it*.

11:49 PM

The man who asked me to guess between two numbers and quizzes me on random occasions with various questions presented me with his two fingers split apart to form a "V."

I said, "Should I reciprocate?"

The man said, "Do you know what this is?"

I knew the gesture from affiliations with past girlfriends and said, "The Vulcan symbol": A *Star Trek* reference.

The man gazed at me with amorous eyes and said, "Who's your favorite comedian?"

I rounded back to my dish sink, and over feverous scrubs of a cheese-stained pot, said, "Carl Sagan."

He stood and gazed at me with wonder, uncertain of my sincerity.

The gregarious woman infatuated with me, Pelagia, asked me, "How are you today, Baethan?" after she spoke small jibes directed at me and signaled curious gestures to which I chose to ignore.

I said, "I'm afflicted with neurosis and psychosis which renders me prone to feeling indifferent and apathetic. How are you?"

Pelagia thought for a moment and said, "Same."

"What was that?"

"Same."

I gazed at her, hunched over a translucent cambro container, and said, "If you felt the same way you wouldn't have initiated a conversation with me."

Pelagia stared at me, a "deer in the headlights" moment, and began to walk away. She called out over her shoulder, "I'm a good actor!"

"Actress?"

"Yes—yes… I'm really a boy. No, I'm really not." She exited into the adjoining bar.

Pelagia returned minutes later and asked me if I enjoy "pets."

I said, "Yes."

"Do you have any pets?"

"No."

"Well, you aren't as heartless as I thought you were if you like pets."

I said nothing and scrubbed harder.

Again, ten minutes later, Pelagia called out from across the kitchen, *"Baethan is the kitchen's Patrick Swayze!"* to which many laughed; I shook my head and continued to ignore her. Pelagia proceeded to initiate conversations with asinine inquiries and invited me to join her and the kitchen crew for discount Thursday martinis at a local bar after my shift.

I said, "No."

Alton and Tyler chuckled while they cooked.

Pelagia said, "Yeah, I knew you were going to say that but I thought I'd ask anyway."

After the kitchen crew departed, the Vulcan symbol man (Howard) approached me while I sprayed a rack of silverware and said, "I heard you're the Patrick Swayze of the kitchen. Is this true?"

"This is not true and I heard too."

"Can it be true?"

I looked at Howard's sly face and said, "Yes, if you wish *it* so."

Howard beamed, snapped his head away from me in one swift jerk, and exited into the bar room.

The gym is an aberrant social affair, a strange product of our advancements. I visit every other day and each instance I do I'm disgusted with how each of us subjects ourselves to artificial stimulation. What are the *true* merits of technological progress when suffering persists in different forms; we suffer for longer in smaller increments.

I find the enormous "jacked" individuals to be incredible and often desire to obtain a physique of similar caliber to inhabit a body fit for my mien. However, I'm inclined to recall a quote of yesteryear's journal by a dead man:

"Envy always lasts longer than the happiness of those we envy."

- Heraclitus (c. 500 A.D.)

January 11th, 2019

11:08 AM

I experienced the most pleasant dream last night since the age of six.[17]

The dream: Early dawn, I stood at my cardboard podium and heard a rustle outside. One of my ex-girlfriends—a hippie I met at a convention who lived with me in my father's home for a year—erected barbed wire fencing in the backyard with two other men. I tackled her, pushed her aside, gripped the barbed wire with my bare left hand, and screamed, "What the hell is this?"

Lacy said, "That's barbed wire, *man!*"

"I know what *it* is—but what the hell are you *doing?*"

"We thought this place was abandoned, and I remembered living here; an ideal place to start a commune."

At once, I lifted her up by the hand, apologized for tackling her, and admired her refined beauty… Long locks of black hair, rectangular glasses on a rounded face, her intelligence refined with the elegance and poise granted to a woman beset by age. We fell in love again—by dream logic, and advanced nine years in the future—by dream logic, to which my character within the dream was oblivious to.

In this dream future I held the title of the most notorious man in the neighborhood, nay—the entire *town,* for the house had been converted into a shelter for the homeless and destitute, replete with livestock, plow trucks, dump trucks, cranes, expansive gardens, and mounds of upturned manure. Over fifty men and women dressed in ragtag clothes bumbled about their business with peasant duty redolent of a medieval town center: baking, cooking, cleaning, hauling, cavorting, tending, idling, smoking, and most of all, toiling. Yes, *my* men and women toiled, subservient to me, while I—dressed in my usual all-black dress clothes—paraded around the commune as co-leader alongside a woman I *trusted.* My neighbors, who had upgraded their homes to the latest technological standards, sneered

---

[17] I found a one-hundred-dollar bill inside a toy store and purchased a large LEGO castle set replete with skeletal warriors and a drawbridge.

at me from within their fine-glossed windows and I *sneered* back from the street—a jovial glee in my expression.

My commune was an unwanted blight on the land and my notoriety had spread to far regions of the state and beyond. The cacophonous noise output of incessant activity disturbed all within a hundred-yard radius—and lo—no leader would be great if *not* hated by his subjects—and indeed I was!

"Your work inspires me," I said to a man who slaved over a grungy kitchen sink with a mound of dishes encrusted with day-old foodstuffs. The man stared at me with a glazed glower—knowing my *work* is to *write*, to *read*, to *enjoy* the labor of others and profit from the suffering of an amalgamate.

"I wish to thank you all for your hard work," I said to a group of men and women converging around a cucumber garden, backs bent, tools in-hand. My accolades were received with silence and I kissed my clever woman in front of the disgruntled residents and… awoke!

Yes… A splendid dream.

The reality: I've consumed, showered, exerted my body, and prepared for a 4PM - 1AM shift as a dishwasher at the "hippest" bar in the city. After my shift, a visit to the gym. I value my intrinsic worth through words and physical strength: a sad little man among other sad little people with sad little hopes and aspirations of confidence while we flounder and paddle against the entropic surf of our minds.

1:43 PM

All art is a sham and a scheme. My ~~debt collector~~ publisher cares about money and is indifferent to the content of my work. I have composed and sent a message in response to the incessant emails and voicemails I receive on account of due payments:

Hello (customer service agent),

I desire to report my disgruntled state and annoyance with whoever directs the marketing representatives and check-in coordinators to bombard customers with phone calls and e-mails with the tonality and intention redolent of a debt collector.

Yes!—this is a *service* and I am addressed as one who "owes." I've answered the concerns of my "remaining balance and fees" twice already; this information must've been lost in translation and/or neglected on behalf of my money not being immediately received and accounted for. The incessant requests for payments are anything but courteous reminders; they are dull distractions and vexations. This verbose complaint I write to you now is the manifestation of combined requests for my money—a tedious distraction to *your* work, which you must read on behalf of your job. Draw the comparison: my self-assigned job is to write, and I've chosen this company to publish my work; the company accepts my manuscripts despite the inane banality of the content due to my money. Writing is at the forefront of my mind every day—my mission, vocation, life meaning—and I enact the will to do so with integral conduct, i.e., your company will receive the money due for progression on my manuscript when I am ready to pay; when I am ready to pay—I will pay!

My projected date for continued payments (as I have already clarified with a representative on the phone) will continue in March, though I cannot be certain due to chaos, and I don't need or want a plethora—of any, "courteous reminders." I've also been informed by a phone representative that I will not be charged late fees (another ridiculous policy redolent of a debt collector rather than a paid-for service). I wonder: Should I bend a knee and pledge an oath of guaranteed payment and capture the act on film for the director who commands his subordinates to solicit customers for money; the absurdity of the practice is equivalent (and exemplified) to the content and length of my (this) vitriolic diatribe on behalf of my genuine disdain for needless bother.

I enjoy this publisher: the name is fitting to the content of my work; I don't intend to withdraw from publishing with the company now or in the future. If I could get along without being prodded by an avaricious corporate tendril every few days, I'd appreciate the service rendered to me "that" much more.

Thank you, (customer service agent), for your time and attention with this disturbance.

- Baethan

January 12th, 2019

2:50 AM

I arrive at the dish pit to an unexpected workload leftover by the absent morning dishwasher. No prior warning. I perform my duties with cold indifference to all around me and strive to be as apathetic and detached as possible; I know the energy I transmit and feel the effects return to me.

I've developed a limp; my right foot is hindered. Still, I walk to the gym and back home—a fool… I hailed a taxi for the first time in my life, wracked by the bitter cold and tender pain in my foot. I return tomorrow for another round and will have clocked over eighty hours of labor this week. I loathe myself and deem the attitude acceptable. Consumption of whey, an avocado, and a jar of peanut butter are my sole sources of dopamine. There is no love. There is no attempt for a social life; in fact, I invest a great deal of effort to subvert a social life for myself and reject all interest. My ego is already validated and I have no desire to validate the ego of others.

People are attracted to me for the "wrong" reasons; there is no "right." I desire to condemn all who attempt to consort with me as "wayward and desperate fools"—alas!—how would I provide for myself if I am estranged from society with no skills of wilderness survival amidst the deadened season of a North American winter? For the sake of my psyche, I deal, as all others do, with *one another*—our sick, twisted, machinations of nothingness and readable creature behavior. I am void of pretense; therefore I garner attention worthy of the magnitude of a train wreck. *"Just what is he?"* wondered my fellow men and women…

I am you.

11:36 AM

I have no desire except the unknown. All food is a burden to my gut. All human interactions are a reminder of the ego and the many ephemeral forms one may manifest.

At the gym, I entered and found an old man in his sixties with long salt and pepper hair and a beard down to his chest, the entire face framed with pampered fur. We greeted each other; I said, "Do you ever wonder why we strive for progress?" and ended up seated with this loon far more

86

mad than myself, who ranted and raved on how he yearns for the past; he lambasted technology and the "damnable kids" of this generation.

"Where's the progress in that?" he summarized after each allusion. *Back in the day...*

E.g., When the mail carrier arrived at 1PM instead of 5PM, when the horse race was judged by eye rather than nanosecond, when people knew how to "build things with their hands," instead of on a screen—*on* and *on*, he rambled in a disjointed fashion similar to myself, only this man *is* a mental savage, a hoary old fool who yearns for the past and complained of feeling "obsolete."

I attempted to provide a reference of an example of one who was born before *his* (the old man's) time, e.g., a woman who may have complained of the invention of the video camera and television—she frequented horse races; after the invention of the video camera, a large proportion of the attendants now stay at home to watch the televised program; the woman finds herself to be one of the few amid rows of empty bleachers.

The old man ignored me and continued—oh—"*Where's* the progress in that"—Bah!—I struggled to suppress my forlorn grimace and refrained from the effort. I glowered at this old man while he gesticulated wide circles of his glorious era of the 1960s. He claimed *I* failed to understand; I agreed, and said, "Well, I'm going to begin my deadlifts," and shook his hand.

He garbed himself in a dirty brown jumpsuit and carried a plastic bag. His breath smelled of alcohol. There is much more I wish to record of this old man: his ignorance of a grand scheme, my allusions of entropy, the inconceivable leaps of "progress" due to the theory and development of "quantum," and the inevitable cycle and rapture of temporal schisms. These notions were overlooked on account of: "Mail is now delivered at 5PM instead of 1PM."

I said, "Well, consider if the automobile had never been invented, you would receive your mail once a week instead of each day due to the exponential population growth. Remove technology from the equation and there would be no population growth; the paradox is-"

"That doesn't matter," spouted the old man.

You're right!—old man! I'm off to wash dishes for twelve hours! Fasting due to lack of time and to promote an overnight recovery of my sprained limbs! Limp across town to a sink where I will proceed to limp back and forth across a kitchen! "Where's the progress in *that?*"

January 13th, 2019

12:39 AM

Yes, to hobble across town after a twelve-hour shift among a dish basin is proper to how I enjoy suffering. Ice crystals thaw from my eyebrows on entering my derelict "home."

Palgia believes that she is "God" and that we are all "God,"—masters of our own realities, a suggestion discoursed in brief throughout our conversations due to her many initiatives to interact with me today; I wonder for her sake: "Why?"

I deny love yet disclosed to Pelagia my secret behavior: I *act* the part of heartless socio/psychopath to estrange myself from others; however, I impeded myself from elaborating *why*...

This document.

If I were to perceive my life from a globe and witness the actions of my character in a time-lapse, to be able to scrutinize the miniature "me" trudge through reality, and study his emotional spectrum, I would be perplexed by this curious being, this fleck of nothing, this mote of selfish selflessness.

1:02 PM

I have declined management's request for me to work on my two days off and reap the benefits of a respite. Despite being a new employee, I've been assigned to train another new employee, a girl, on my return; therefore, my leg and arm must be in satisfactory condition.

The dish basin is a U-shaped domain. When standing at the primary sprayer station faced towards a wall, the dishwashing machine is to your immediate diagonal, forward-right. A complete cycle to wash, rinse, and dry, is a minute and fifteen-second process; once complete, two handles on either side of the chamber are gripped to lift the machine doors and remove the loaded pallet onto the "clean" basin to your right. All dishware must be sprayed and scrubbed prior to the dish machine cycle due to the limitations of the machinery.

Dirtied dishware: pots, pans, cups, cast iron, blenders, plates, silverware, trays, ladles, spatulas, tongs, ramekins, oblong bowls, and cambros of varied shapes and sizes are loaded onto the counter to your left by the kitchen and service staff.

To the rear of the U-shaped basin are three tiny square basins allotted for soapy, clean, and sanitized water, respectively.

Your duty is the optimization of systematic cleansing and intelligent prioritization of what is required to be restocked for the kitchen to maintain efficiency.

You'll hear the words, "Hot," "Thank you," "Sharp," and "Behind," more than any other combined words of spoken conversations around you throughout your entire shift (fluctuations are dependent on gossip and unfocused labor).

Your hands may bleed and you may be burned. You may become wet and grungy; haste and precision are equivalent to optimization; often, these factors, when practiced, negates the mental processes for conscious preservation of clothes; however, an apron is provided. Rags are utilized to grip handles of superheated cookware, to wipe off remaining food residue, and to dry plates and pans. Provided you remain alert of sharp/hot objects, monitor water temperatures, and heed the verbalized warnings of your peers, damage to the body will be minimal. Arm-length latex gloves will protect you from the aforementioned dangers (I've yet to procure a superior "coat of arms" agreeable to my personal preference) and may be worn at the detriment of tactile sensation and dexterous maneuvers; fumbles and the likelihood of shattered dishware may increase.

The immediate kitchen environment must be observed to evaluate inobtrusive moments when one may restock cleaned dishware to appropriate sectors. A frenzied and hectic staff is a poor time to traverse through the narrow walkways; wait for ideal moments—veritable "calm before the storm" openings. If staff members are engrossed with phones and the walkways are clear, *this* is the ideal time to clear your "clean" basin.

If there is no dishware provided to you, clean your station, e.g., dish machine, basins, walls, sinks, faucets; if your station is clean, traverse the kitchen and waitstaff depository and seek dirtied dishware on your own accord. Your peers will be grateful for any initiative you undertake.

Your performance throughout your shift before the end of service will determine the difficulty of the final wave of dishware thrust into your care. You may become overwhelmed, anxious, and disheartened with the abundance and incessant deliverance of dishware—*if:* You dawdled, chatted, idled, texted, complained, or "enjoyed" a break; there is an equal exchange of stress for the brief five to twenty minutes of relief a break may provide; enjoy a break when you know enjoyment is guaranteed.

Inspect your work. Respect yourself. Throngs of hedonists depend on your service. To anthropomorphize the establishment, you are the metaphorical liver. Dishes come in; dishes go out.

7:05 PM

Alton commented on a man who wears a robed attire complete with a hooded cowl to work: "He needs some place to stow his wand."

I flashed a light-hearted grimace and said, "Oh, c'mon now, man."

A half-hour later, I approached Alton and said, "Hey Alton."

"Yeah?" He acknowledged me with a sidelong glance.

"Your comment earlier about the wand pertaining to the man who wears a robe–"

Alton began to smile and turned away.

I continued, "What you said suggested two things about your character: one trait being that you aren't open to new experiences."

Alton looked at Pelagia who stood nearby and said *to her*—for secondary affirmation, "I'm open." Pelagia focused on her activity at the counter, listened, neglected to reciprocate affirmation, and began to depart down the stairwell to the basement storage area.

I continued to address Alton and said, "The second, is that you make fun of other people as a means to feel better about yourself."

Alton's averted visage conveyed disbelief; he said, "Ouch, that's a low blow."

I raised my hands, outstretched to the sides of my head, smiled, and said, "Well, that was a low blow to the robed man too."

Alton said nothing and I hobbled away. Throughout the remainder of my ten hours alongside him in the kitchen, dishwasher to cook interactions, receiving and delivering pans, our communications remained cordial and pleasant.

I've finished Leo Tolstoy's *"The Death of Ivan Ilyich"* and feel numb. The implausible conjectures of what defines a "good" life when we all suffer the same harrowed end of death, overwrought with solitude despite the similar fate of those around you… a fate suffered by millions before you in multitudes of ways… is a *numb* sensation. To envision the imaginary tale of a "successful" judge lost to the throes of madness due to his doubt is an authentic, refined tale of nonfiction relevant to each of us. This hopeless, meaningless existence is alleviated through brief snippets of hopes and joys which, throughout "time," lose the once magnificent wonder and jovial glee felt by unrecallable degrees in childhood. Earliest memories of ecstatic pleasure and transcendent bliss are inconceivable; the moment has been experienced; shattered fragments of a stain-glass window, the frayed fabric of a patchwork quilt, faded charcoal depictions on a cavern wall, the ebb of the final note of a symphony, and the *bygone words of dead men*, are quintessential symbolic representations of the human mind. There is only now.

January 14th, 2019

2:16 AM

Impossible to sleep, everything I am and have been is a disturbance to the mind.

I feel guilty to reciprocate the feelings of others: falsifications of my true being of abject carelessness and vile inner thoughts. I experience nothing but disdain and revulsion for humanity and yet, I am compelled to care, prompted by the care curiosity of others in regards to my character.

I lay on a dirty carpet for four hours, wrapped in a single blanket, and wish for the world to implode, to crumple inward akin to a paper ball compressed to a singularity, whisked away into a void by a nebulous gust of aether wind.

This sick life of senseless pursuits of gross *engrossment* is enough. Yes—enough. I've had enough and yearn for the bitter satisfaction of the intense anguish preceding death. All the times I've laid on the floor, crippled with terror by the belief of my imminent demise by the hands of a psychopath, is my own self-engrossed fantastical delusions of me killing *myself*—yes, the maddened state of a lunatic perplexed by his own thoughts is manifest in my yearnings and daydreams of death. To throttle my own neck and eviscerate my gut is salvation, bliss rendered to me.

Even now, I stand in the dark by the light of my writing device and feel a slight trepidation, an expectation of sudden physical pain wrought by the hands of a murderer.

The Navy won't save me; I fail to save myself. On the contrary, the

Navy will exacerbate my dissatisfaction and entrap me within the realm of the ultimate manifold of delusions. My injured foot may prevent me from my single hope, and if denied, I *will* thrust myself into damnation and seek out cultish regions of the world to enslave myself to.

Damn me and everyone I've ever known with their inflated sense of righteousness, their condemnations, their *justice*. What bothers me most of all is my recent comment to Alton on his perceived character. What overcame me in that moment of my utterance and egoic projection in this world is an intense vexation against my integrity:—how may a repressed misanthrope condemn another for mocking another to make oneself feel better?—is this *not* the essence of humanity, to compare, compete, and strive?—is this *not* the fundamental basis of *confidence*? Does a self-help book written by the Dalai Lama *not* put down those who fail to achieve happiness, does *it not* elicit feelings of inadequacy with the suggested notion that happiness is a status quo to be pursued and attained? Verbose nothingness—all *this* is and ever will be. Reader, I pity you most of any I've ever known. You must know me from somewhere; at some point in our lives we crossed paths and I manipulated you with pretense. You follow along, *interested* in my dread and self-abasement, snug in the warm entanglement of your own fantastical delusional realm in a manner similar to my own—ah!—too meta(non)fictional and verbose for you? Well—this *is* the maniacal lamentation of a man on the edge of a mental cataclysm— awake, when he desires nothing more than permanent sleep!

8:29 PM

Five piglets snorted and huddled together in the corner of a dirtied barn.

A fattened farmer approached from a moonlit archway and leaned on a shovel; he said, "Oh look at my girls, how I love you so."

The piglets snorted.

"*Oh*—my girls... Martha, Betty, Juniper, Starla, and Rosy, how I love each of you *so*... You'll never know. When the moonlight shines down on your pink bodies, I remember all the good times of childhood, back with papa at the kitchen table. Oh, my girlies, how I love and yearn for you each night when I'm up alone in my room—so I come down here to look at y'all and see my little girlies, my little ones, all bright and cheery, sleepy too. You wanna' sleep, my little piggies? I'll watch you sleep now. Stand here all night and watch you sleep, my wee girlies. I think back to old times before y'all were born and I didn't know my way. Now I know my way when I see you, my sacred angels, so beautiful and bright."

The piglets snorted.

January 15th, 2019

8:05 AM

Sweet slumber, your kiss teases;
A lull away from anguish.
Reminiscent of extinguished love,
My heart falters on your pass.
Stay for longer.
Your tender embrace bears
Familiar essence: lost friend,
Newfound acquaintance,
Amiable rival.

"Are you ready?" said a hopeless man to a heartbroken man.

"Ready as I'll ever be; if we don't do this now we never will."

The hopeless man stroked the short barrel of a 9mm handgun, nodded his head, and said, "Do you think *it*'ll hurt?"

"Not if we do *it* right like we researched and planned. Don't even fucking start, *don't* contemplate, *don't* philosophize, *don't*—just do; let's do *it*, right now, no more deliberation, this is *it*, ready?"

"Wait."

"What—Oswald—*what?*"

"I think we should wait until I get a magnum too."

"Why?"

"Well, I have two concerns, one-"

The heartbroken man rested his .45 magnum on his pleated cargo pants, squeezed his nose bridge, crunched both eyelids shut, and said, *"Christ."*

"One being that, I feel like, and think, that we should both use the same gun type for-"

"That doesn't mean anything—what, you want to make a statement or match? Let's do this."

Oswald stammered, swallowed, and said, *"The second* concern I have is that I read a bit about people who shot themselves and lived with rounds the size of a 9mm."

"I can shoot you first and then I'll shoot myself, deal?"

"That would defeat the purpose of this arrangement and you would be a murderer."

The heartbroken man considered Oswald's words for a moment, sighed, and said, "You'll be fine; *it*'s a fucking bullet dude, aim right and aim true. Ready?"

Oswald looked away from the heartbroken man. His crestfallen gaze scanned an unswept apartment floor for answers, for reasons, for excuses, for discernment, for insights, for revelations, for interventions; he fixated on a few burnt crumbs of week-old toast.

The heartbroken man shouted, "Are you *fucking* ready or what?"

"Alright."

"Alright?"

"Yes—alright… I'm ready."

"Good," said the heartbroken man, and he lodged the barrel of the .45 magnum between his teeth, upside down, pressed against the roof of his mouth.

Oswald scrutinized the placement of the magnum, hesitated, slipped the barrel of the 9mm handgun into his mouth in a similar fashion, and settled his lips around cold steel.

The heartbroken man jerked the magnum out of his mouth, turned full-face to Oswald, who stared straight ahead at a dirty white wall, and said, "Don't you *fucking* pussy out on me," and wedged the magnum back into his mouth, three centimeters deeper.

Oswald shifted his eyes to meet the heartbroken man's visage of uncertain conviction; both nodded. The heartbroken man held up his free hand in front of them and raised his index finger, followed by his middle finger… ring finger. Two gunshots resounded, the first louder than the other with a 0.4-second delay between the bangs.

White light: Oswald's eyes opened. He lay on his right shoulder against the floor, convulsed, and gushed streams of blood out from two holes: one in his mouth, the other above his left ear; he thought: *I'm still alive; dear God, this pain is unbearable. I knew this would happen. Fuck you Gerald, you lucky bastard. He got off easy; he isn't moving; yeah—he's dead— head is near-blown off—FUCK—I wonder how I look? Who will find me and how long will it take? I'm such an idiot; I can't take this; I can't take this;*

dear God, please—please—please—please make the pain stop. Make it end. Margaret, George, I'm sorry. Mom—even you dad, I'm sorry, oh my God—just stop thinking—no thought… I can't… I can't… Just stop thinking, can't…stop… I'm going to hell… No, hell isn't real, this pain is—incredible, pain… no—hell isn't real; I'm going to hell, oh my God I'm… stop, can't—thinking… stop…"

Oswald wheezed a final agonal breath and died in a lukewarm pool of blood.

10:15 AM

Dear Diary,

This morning I wrote about the suicide of two men, an instance of which I relished the composition and arrangement of every word. You're a sick little bastard—you diary, you crude, offensive, tasteless amalgamation.

Your paper feels redolent to the exposed flesh of a fifty-six-year-old harlot on the verge of menopause caught half-dressed in a changing room. "Oh my goodness!" you squeal when the curtain is pulled back, yet you blush, unabashed, with a suggestive grin skewed across your countenance.

Your paper thinks akin to a prepubescent schoolboy who has masturbated for the first time in a public library restroom to pornographic images on his cell phone… *Dear* diary, clean yourself and repress the memory.

You're *nasty* and *uncouth;* what have you to say for yourself other than "I," "I," "I,"—what about *me?*

January 16th, 2019

12:47 AM

I scrubbed dirt off of clams and listened to Pelagia announce information which enlightened a facet of my psyche. Tyler asked Pelagia, "How many people have you had sex with?"

Pelagia said, "Well, over thirty women," which exceeds *my* female mates, "and over two-hundred guys."

Tyler said, "Wow."

Alton said nothing and turned away.

I glanced over my shoulder at Pelagia; she reckoned my glance through her own sidelong smirk, and continued: "I'm not a hoe; I just *really* like sex!"

I scrubbed at the clams and mulled over my lot in life, the women I attract and the women I'm attracted to… there is a trend; self-proclaimed, ~~hoes~~ *"Strong Independent Women"* attract me; all have been promiscuous and yearn for sex with many men; a revolt against the ~~patriarchy~~ traditional marriage perpetuated by Christian theology. Praise be the whores, harlots, and hoes of the modern age!—revolt!—revolution!—upheaval!—in the name of polygamy! Monogamy is a sin against nature and humanity. Yes, the temptresses of our time delight me—from afar; I observe the beauty and chaos sown on behalf of males desperate to (re)dominate the once subjugated gender. I rub my hands together and snicker when the strong and independent specimen pursues men to the chagrin of other men; I am often the perceived ~~victim~~ mate, and on my indifference and apathy to the expressed interest, males and females alike are *confused*. Confusion, pity, and often anger! Let the people fornicate and leave me be!

At the end of Pelagia's shift, she approached me and recommended the movie, *The Lobster*, in reference to "all our previous conversations," and suggested I search up the premise due to her inability to elaborate *it* for me; what this means, I haven't the slightest inclination due to my lack of connection to the internet.

At the end of my shift, I donned my merino winter-wear and was hailed by Howard (Pelagia's best friend) and a bartender; he insisted once more on giving me a ride.

Howard said, "Where do you live?—where are you going?"

"I'm alright." I flashed a thumbs up.

"No, *it's* so cold out, let me give you a ride!"

"No, thank you."

"Seriously, where are you going?"

I pulled down my face mask and said, "I'm going to the gym."

Howard and the woman (bartender) eyed me over in wonder—yes, a man who suffers a limp treks a thirty-minute *walk* to the gym after a twelve-hour shift in the *"cold"* weather. Howard said, "What gym?"

"[Name of gym]"

"The one near [Name of grocery store]?"

"Yes."

"I live *right down the street*; let me give you a *fucking* ride!"

"No, thank you Howard, really-"

The woman shouted, "Let him give you a ride; you're crazy!"

I said, "Yes I am," readjusted my face mask over my mouth, nose, ears, and exited the back door. They scrambled to their car and watched me. I'm uncertain if they followed me while I hobbled down the road to my destination.

I called a cabbie for a ride home from the gym. A wispy-bearded man I at first glance thought was a woman awaited me on the driver's seat. I said, "Hello, how's *it* going?"

"Oh you know, another day in paradise."

I hopped into the passenger seat, fussed with my jacket, glanced around, looked the man through his thick circular glasses, and said, "Is this your paradise?"

"I guess so."

"If this is your paradise, what's your hell?"

He shrugged and said, "Ah, this too."

Disappointed, I sat for a moment and thought of something profound to say; I said, "How long have you been a cabbie for?"

"Seventeen years," he said, with a high-pitched, drawn-out voice.

"Do you enjoy the job?"

He nodded—*excessive* movements of the neck, up and down, a veritable human waterbird contraption, and said, "Oh yes, I sure do."

"Seventeen years, I imagine you would."

"Oh yeah, yeah."

"Who's the creepiest person you've ever picked up?"

The man thought for a while, shifted in his seat, and said, "I really don't know... I've never been creeped out by anyone I've picked up."

"In all your seventeen years?"

"Nope, at least not around here."

"Where else have you been a cabbie?"

"Nowhere else, just this area."

I stifled a subtle frown on his behalf and let there be silence for a time. I said, "What is your self-assigned meaning in life?"

The cabbie's instantaneous response of "My children," elicited a smile to my face and I nodded at him: encouragement to continue, and he did: "Three kids, the oldest is twenty. He just got into the marines."

"Ah, nice. I've enlisted into the Navy; I would have gone marines but I have a tattoo on my palm and only the Navy will accept me out of all the service branches."

"Hm."

"You must be proud of your son."

"Oh yes, I'm very proud of him."

"Do you have any military service?"

"No… Second son is seventeen; he's in eleventh grade; he's doing okay I think."

"Does he have any hopes and dreams?"

"He wants to join the army. Youngest is eleven, my daughter. Where am I going now?"

I pointed to our right and said, "The big boxy one with no lights on… right… here."

He flipped on the overhead light of the cab and announced, "Six-sixty-nine."

I handed the cabbie a ten and said, "Keep the change—for your tip."

"Hey thanks man, you have a good night now."

I extended my hand for a shake; the cabbie accepted, looked through me, gave my wrist a weak jostle, and said, "Oh I will, got another five hours of my shift to go."

"Ah—but you enjoy *it,* that's all that matters! Paradise and hell. Take care."

The cabbie turned his head away from me, gazed out his driver-side window, and said, "You too."

10:52 PM

The parents of my lost childhood friend danced alone on the floor of the bar room while I approached for a refill of water. Both acknowledged me in their own moments: the father desired to ignore me; the mother wished to stop the dance and speak; I limped along in silent respect for both, for what their son had become (a chemist), and for what I am now (a dishwasher).

I waited by the road for a cabbie for fifteen minutes and passed a young couple hand-in-hand, both stiff and locked in haste.

The girl said, "The wind!"

The boy said, "Yes, the wind."

The wind blew into their faces and at my back. I may as well have walked and continued to meander back to my residence in the bitter cold due to my twenty-minute wait. Damn this foot and my idiotic running sessions in boots. My physical pains are minor yet my mental pain is a hellish duress of my own conception. My saddened visage greets all and I am deemed unsociable, inconsolable, standoffish, aloof, detached, and indifferent.

I limped towards the cab, met with an enormous woman, said "Hello," entered, and she beckoned me with a surprised smile.

"Hello," said the cabbie.

"When you first saw my face, what emotion did you glean?"

"Hm, tired, cold… and sore." The woman smiled again, and I realized she didn't want to offend me by stating despair, anguish, or despondency, or she hadn't noticed; I'm inclined to believe the latter.

I chuckled and said, "Yes, you're right… I'm sore all over, in my mind most of all."

She nodded.

I said, "How long have you been a cabbie for?"

"Seven years," she said, proud and declarative.

"Do you enjoy *it?*"

"I love *it.*"

We met amiable eyes; I said, "What do you love most of all about *it?*"

"Meeting the people."

"Who's the strangest and most vile person you've ever met in a cab?"

"Oh," she laughed, "That's a hard one." I opened my mouth to speak and she said, "Too many to choose from-"

"I was going to say—too many or too little?"

Her laughter intensified and she said, "I've met many, many drunks and drug dealers."

"Ah. Do you believe there is a true self, or is personality a pretense?"

Taken aback, she said, "Hm, that's difficult to say. I believe we're all different and the world would be boring if we weren't, so *it's* a good thing even if *it* is pretense."

I nodded and closed my eyes. Hot air blew into my face and my breathing slowed. I wished to depart my body; instead, I waited forty-five seconds and said, "What is your self-assigned meaning in life?"

"To take care of my children and grandchildren to the best of my ability."

I nodded again, somber, grim, a contented agreement, and said, "That's all there is."

"Yes, family," she affirmed.

We turned onto my road; I paid my dues, entered my "home," thrashed into the kitchen, slammed my writing device and winter garb onto a padded counter, and cried on behalf of myself, i.e., for the world, for the basis of life, for the utter depravity of reciprocal endeavors, for the desolation of institutions; oh woe—yes, what a sad, tragic, *love* story we engage in. Hormonal outcries; I am deadened and sickened; my act is no longer an act; I have become what I have done—exhibit, dance and whirl with a macabre waltz on this abundant stage of opportunity; I turn to all and squander each moment with a crestfallen gaze, a foolish flaunt, a grizzled countenance.

And you, reader, my tears dry and my mouth quivers with contempt for you.

"You should take *it* easy with mocking your readers, dude," said my father to me, weeks ago, and what would he know of what I know of what others know me to be; he wishes me to become rich and famous so that he may enjoy an imaginative, vicarious ride along the tar-encrusted coattails of a miserable buffoon—his son—wouldn't want to *offend* anyone—now *would I*… Yet if *you* persist with this read, *reader,* you are… nameless, an anomaly, I fail to describe… I fail *to* contempt, to loathe, to hate, to dislike; this requires effort and I am a walking corpse of welt-up ill-humor and hateful judgments.

I "intuit" the voice of my mother: "Baethan has spent too much time with his father and has gone foul; I truly do hate my son." Yes mother, and you have every right; acknowledge what I have become. I implore you, for the love of anything *you* believe, abolish your pity of me, your disappointment, your sympathy, your empathy, and grant me the ~~hate~~ apathy I deserve.

January 18th, 2019

12:56 AM

I arrived at work today, silently responded to the greetings of my coworkers, descended the stairwell to the basement bathroom to urinate, and on the post where I always hang my coat, a copy of my book, *Outbursts of a Privileged White Man; Thoughts of an Egotistical Fool,* stood upright, title outward, with a square "post-*it*" sticker attached which had the words, "Sign me," written across the yellow template. I stood, slack-jawed, shocked, *mortified,* and entered the bathroom. I stared at myself in the dingy mirror and thought, *"I should have never spoken of my writing to Henry,"* yet I *had,* during my damned interview, when Henry—my current supervisor, asked about my hobbies; I offered him a free ebook stub—the fool that I am.

I contemplated my book that loomed on the post on my exit from the bathroom: A monster leaned up against the wall; *it* stared back at me. I ~~walked~~ hobbled past the unaccounted for monstrosity and began my shift.

An hour passed and I scrubbed at a pot. Pelagia, the self-proclaimed "strong independent woman" I've developed suppressed infatuation with due to her promiscuous behavior, approached me from my left, and said, "Are you going to sign my book?"

I turned to face her, smiled, and said, "Ah, *it*'s your book."

"Yes!"

"I was going to sign, 'For a fellow fool,' uncertain of the recipient, though now that I know *it*'s your book, the statement definitely applies."

She blushed at me and I returned to my labor. I may have blushed too.

Later that night, an hour before close, she approached and idled around my station while I sprayed filth off of a mundane object; I said, "What made you decide to buy my book?"

"I was intrigued, I still am," she shrugged. "What made you decide to write a book?"

I opened my mouth with a preconceived witty answer, stopped, and contemplated; after five seconds, I looked up at Pelagia and said, "Pain."

Pelagia nodded.

I shook my head and said, "Who told you about *it?*"

"Ah," she beamed, "I don't want anyone here to end up missing—or dead."

I eyed her, incredulous to the insinuations of my sinister character, and said, "They wouldn't."

She hesitated while I loaded the dish machine and said, "Henry told me the day of your interview. He showed me your book stub and I was intrigued. I ordered a few books and received them in the mail a few days ago, yours was one of them."

I scowled at the mention of Henry and said, "I believe you may have wasted your money, though that is up to your determination."

"I don't waste my money; nope, I never waste my money."

I thought of the Bhagavad-Gita: *There is nothing lost or wasted in this life,* and said, "You would know of that matter better than anyone."

She smiled and I turned away.

I wrote in Pelagia's book:

> *"Pelagia,*
> *"To a fellow fool.*
> *"We are God.*
> *"—[Signature]"*

A cabbie arrived at the gym. I greeted an obese man in his late forties who frowned at me. I presume my aspect—dressed in my usual all-black dress clothes after a hormone-stimulating session, incited him to loathe me.

I said, "Hello sir!"

He glowered at me and said, "You're the one for [Street Name] right?"

"Yes sir. How are you?"

"I'm alright."

"How long have you been a cabbie for?"

"Since August."

"Not too long then."

"Six months."

"Most cab drivers I speak to have been a cabbie for over five years."

He shifted in his seat and said, "We all gotta' start somewhere."

"Who's the strangest person you've ever picked up?"

"You're workin' on *it.*"

"Alright!" I exclaimed, "-What's your self-assigned meaning in life?"

The man flashed me a visage of disdain, threatened a gesture to pull over, and said, "Dude, *it*'s a cab ride okay; you're starting to push my buttons."

"*It*'s only a question."

"Yeah but *it*'s abstract bullshit."

"I understand."

"If you want to talk, talk about the weather or sports or somethin'."

I stared down at my lap and said, "Anything *but* weather and sports."

"I suppose we'll just be quiet then."

I agreed with a head nod and felt tears well up at the corners of my eyes. I felt *sorry* for this man and thought to myself, *"I feel your pain"*: a lie I concocted in an attempt to influence reality and compel us both to a better state of mutual being; I believe I failed.

We endured the remaining four minutes of the ride in silence as the man had wanted. I tipped him more than any cabbie thus far for the anticipated $6.50 fare.

I said, "Have a good night sir," when I had wanted to say, *"I hope your life improves sir,"* though I believed this would've offended him and I thereby restrained myself.

"Yep, good night."

6:02 PM

I requested today and tomorrow off from work due to increased foot pain and visited the doctor's office. The physician recommended an X-Ray; I declined due to no insurance, and have been prescribed treatment of ibuprofen, elevation, and ice.

I've devoted time to a viewing of *The Lobster* with my father at his home on behalf of Pelagia's recommendation. There is no relevance to any previous conversations Pelagia and I have discussed concerning the film's content—the *"reason"* for her recommendation. Pelagia ~~is deluded~~ lied; I believe she suggested the movie to me based on her own interests and agenda, or I fail to understand the relation.

I'm uncertain, despite the movie's genre of "dark comedy," if the premise is meant to be authentic, satirical, or a parody; in all regards, the director/producer failed. I am rendered bored and unimpressed. The forced and blunted dialogue is reminiscent of a David Lynch production—devoid of subtle undertones and supplanted with dry attempts of humor through depictions of mundane social interactions meant to serve as a statement for social relations.

To be single or coupled; to fuck or not to fuck. The ending relieved me (the movie is finished) and captivated me; the allegorical statement the film attempts to convey, in my interpretation, is summarized: Do you ostracize yourself with personal rationality intact, or do you blind yourself to join a society?

January 19th, 2019

1:22 PM

If my life of the past several years had a default theme song while I performed mundane tasks, e.g., maintenance of essential body functions and housekeeping, Mozart's *Piano Concerto No. 4 in G Minor, K. 41: II. Andante,* would be *it,* for the somber intro, the reflective strings, the punctual tonality, the bittersweet pangs of the piano, and the final chords, which suggests more of the same if prolonged.

Bach's *Sonata for Violin Solo No. 1 in G Minor, BWV 1001 - Adagio*, resonated while I arranged myself a seat—to *sit*, uncomfortable, agitated, and vexed, with my foot propped up on a cardboard box mounted on an adjacent chair. Damnable entropy. The flesh *is* indeed weak. I sit and contemplate inevitable death with the emanations of micro radiation of my writing device above my genitalia and intestinal tract, and pass my idled days with the edit of my previous year and the read of new books shipped to me: Charles Bukowski's *Post Office* and *Women,* and Robert Greene's *The 48 Laws of Power.* [18]

Snowstorms are due.

January 20th, 2019

12:55 PM

Snowblower Symphony

Sunday morning dawn.
Lay semi-conscious and listen to
Gentle thrums of windswept
Snow against an adjacent window.
A muffler sputters. A shovel scrapes
Against pavement.
Breathe into your sheet and listen-
One after another:
A whir of choked engines.

6:29 PM

I've finished a read of Bukowski's *Post Office* and am delighted. *Women* is the next read in my queue.

The realization of the implicit fallout of sharing my publication with

---

[18] A middle-aged woman, married, with children, who works alongside Pelagia in the kitchen, asked me one week ago if I had read *The 48 Laws of Power.* I lied and said, "Yes," under the pretense of having read much of Machiavelli and Sun Tzu; I presumed I knew *enough* to answer with my rendition of truth.

those I work with has rendered me powerless against those who take an interest in me. My shameless accounts and honesty, despite my pen name, are veritable chinks in my "armor"—for those who care... Pelagia, the woman who bought a copy of my work for me to sign. My supervisor, Henry, who I gifted an ebook to for his wife to "judge," has exposed me; no longer am I a sociopathic creep... No, now I *truly* am a fool... Though there are upsides: the innate long-term marketing reaped from those who also fail to refrain from speaking *of* me increases potential sales. The detriment to my esteem is only *now*.

On the fifth law of *The 48 Laws of Power:* I recognize the absurdity of all who play for power, and how I, and the woman who reintroduced the tome to my attention who works alongside me in the kitchen—*reads* this *manipulative* text of deception based on claims to teach!—a "national bestseller," for indeed, Greene compiled great works from the most notorious people throughout history and resold the work for his own profit—which *I have bought*... Indeed, the absurdity: Kitchen wenches and dishwashers play a game of power among their peers. I imagine the woman—my kitchen comrade—utilizes what she "learns" in the art of dissimulation and lies to her husband and children, what a joy.

Robert Greene advocates a "defense from power," as a reason for a read, a reason I ascribe to; however, how may one defend against concepts which are essential elements of the human condition without severing your relations, for to enter a relationship is to be entrenched in a power struggle. I maintain my power of powerlessness, enmeshed within the lowest ranks of society, albeit, not by choice, or *perhaps* so... Regardless, enlistment with the U.S. Navy is my primary motive to subvert my mind with inconsequential "thrusts" for power—to defend against the vulgar exertions and extortions of my soon-to-be "superiors."

To speak of my writing is planned ruin; there must be no more.

Power... I scowl and lambast the power-seeker, the social climbers, the self-proclaimed *somethings*. The endorsement of lies and deceptions is a counter-paradigm to the basis of every philosophical doctrine composed for the betterment of society ever conceived, yet, there can be no working order without lies and deceptions, i.e., chaos.

Ah, yes, I recline in a chair, wounded foot up, a stupefied grin splayed over my sheepish countenance; with a full belly, I reiterate: There is no truth.

How I practice the fifth "law" to near-perfection: *"Always say less than necessary,"* in my affairs, and return to the solitary domain of my mind and this template to expulse endless discourses for all the poor, *poor* souls who whittle away the hours with *my* ego instead of their own!—is a riot!

Ha!… Ha!… Ha!…

January 21st, 2019

11:40 AM

After many prolonged mornings laid on the floor of the dilapidated shambles of the house of my late childhood in what once was the old weight room, I've verified that all projections and perceptions of the "self" in a sustained manner are a psychosis/neurosis equivalent to one who forgoes self-identification in favor of a malleable, "fluid" personality. Yes, life is a state of psychosis and neurosis; I reflect on my past…

My younger "self," between the ages of thirteen to nineteen, paid no heed to the opinions of others whatsoever. I believed, in my immense ignorance, thrust among my peers in public schooling, that I was the only one with any "sense," in the literal and abstract meaning. Before I adopted an image of all-black dress clothes for the sake of simple professionalism regardless of the occasion, I wore all-black t-shirts and pants with (too many) chains, loops, and pockets. My long and cared for blonde hair strewn down past my shoulders. I wore black eyeliner on occasion, inspired by Stanley Kubrick's depiction of the character Alex from Anthony Burgess' *A Clockwork Orange* and was often accused of being a homosexual by repressed homosexuals. I would've been bullied if I wasn't feared; I spoke little, and when I did, my remarks cut deep into the ego of my would-be contender, often with an audience; humiliation ensued, and I was immune to retributive defamation. My schoolboy reputation of being "that attractive brooding guy who hates people" enshrouded me as an effortless product of my natural disposition.

Young girls placed themselves in my path and I brought a new one home (on the bus) bi-montly; however, to each of the hedon's discomfort and confusion, I refrained from physical contact. Instead, I ushered each girl to my room—painted black, with overhanging black tapestries, and seated them onto my black bed—and played eerie ambient music from surround sound computer speakers. My companions would sit with me and I'd ask questions, e.g., "Why do you pursue sex with strange boys?"; "What do you think the meaning of life is?"; "What do you believe happens when we die?" The young girls, often horrified, dissuaded, and disgusted, would arrange to leave *much* earlier than arranged, often out the front door within ten minutes to walk home while they phoned a friend or parent(s) to "save" them from the clutches of a warped weirdo and an uncustomary walk. With time, as gossip spread throughout the locker-lined annals of my local public school, the decent girls with stable families began to avoid me and the girls who were prescribed medications from broken families began to pursue me.

Thus, Eliza, a "girlfriend" of four years, deposited her phone number on my porch during our final year of high school. We arranged to meet at the local boneyard, whereupon I charged into her amongst the shadows of overhung tree branches, embraced a supple body, kissed tender lips, gripped a once familiar hand, and led her by my side into the darkness of that warm night; she giggled all the way, her slender arm tugged along by my eager gait. We stumbled over upturned stones and exposed roots along beaten dirt paths, her firm grasp around the back of my neck.

January 23rd, 2019

1:03 AM

Another cab ride home after a night stationed at the dish pit, a gym session, and a trip to the market. My foot has managed a near-full recovery though I expect I'll need to wait another week before I resume cardiovascular training.

"How are you doin' tonight man?" said a large, bald, amiable man to me when I opened the cab door.

"I'm doing well! How about yourself?"

"Oh… You know how *it* goes… Winter cold and freezing rain and everything outside is slippery and frozen."

"Yes, walks outside have proven to be treacherous."

"You walk out in this?"

"Yes."

"Where do you go?"

"I average three miles a day to and from-"

"*Jesus* man, what're you crazy?"

We smiled at each other; I said, "I think so."

He said, "Yeah, this weather, I mean, I think we're gonna' be goin' on cold and snow up until March, according to the reports and the way things are."

"Don't you find human interactions curious in the way conversations often default to the weather?"

The man laughed and said, "Yeah, yeah, well I'm a taxi driver so, ya' know, I gotta' be talkin' about somethin', usually the weather, or politics, current events or something local, ya' know..."

"What's the strangest question anyone has ever asked you—in a cab?"

"Oh man... I don't know, hm, well, hm, ya' know, now that I think on *it*, probably guys asking where the local whore house is."

"Really, that's the *strangest* question?"

"Yeah I pick up a lot of drunks and drug dealers and ya' know, I mean, they say a lot of stuff without thinking first and I often get asked about whores and... yeah-"

"Alright, how about this one then: Do you think the personality is a pretense and that we're all the same?"

"Do I think the personali... Hm, now, ya' know, hm, I don't quite understand the question-"

"Do you think that we're all the same, baseline, and that we utilize the personality to ease our interactions with other individuals depending on the content and situation?"

"Hm, well," the cab driver deliberated; his warm demeanor uplifted my mood. "I think *it*'s a matter of beliefs and perspectives; I don't really know." He looked at me.

I rubbed at my nose and said, "I don't know either."

We connected eyes and chuckled.

I followed up with, "What is your self-assigned meaning in life?"

"Oh, geez, *what is my self-assigned meaning in life,* well, *that* has changed often lately and all throughout my life. I'd say, lately I'm focused on health and trying to get healthier, and treating other people the way I want to be treated."

"Do you find health hard to attain while you work as a cabbie?"

"Oh yeah, definitely, food choice I mean—ya' know, fast food places..." A soda from a popular drive-thru franchise sat in the cup-holder between our seats. "... Sitting down ya' know, and unable to move for long periods."

"I've known the feeling lately. I've dealt with a limp and have been chair-bound for the better part of the past four days, hence the ride from you. I've been made to feel grateful again for all the faculties of my body and youth."

The man lurched up in his seat and said, "Oh, yeah, I've had gout, a form of arthritis in my leg before and was stuck in a hospital bed for eight days and had to walk around with a cane. I spent a lot of time reflecting and am thankful for what I have…"

He missed my turn twice due to our chat; I assured him his apologies were unnecessary, tipped him two dollars, shook his hand, and departed the vehicle.

9:42 PM

A limp no longer; a trudge "home" through freezing rain with no umbrella over sheets of rigid ice and rivers of slush. A bridge encrusted with bent striations of snow. The snow began to melt during the afternoon and froze again with the onset of night. A desolate quasi city: an industrial wasteland of reflected streetlights and lowlife escapades; I work at the oculus of this dreary semi-suburban hub and clean the plates and glassware of drunken patrons.

What life these people live… Neglected dreams and hopeful longings for a warm body to sleep against. Envious and jealous hordes congregate— crowds of conquest seekers and oath breakers. Harlots and charlatans unite under a single roof in the pseudo "high class" domain of a no-name downtown sector of indolence. The city is a quaint district of subverted vices: few speak of the corruption, yet the consummate nature of life permeates all facets of the walkways and littered side streets. A paralyzed man throttles a wheeled chair down a sidewalk at 10mph. Hooded men and wary women veer in and out of tenements and dilapidated houses to and from corner-side convenience stores for cigarettes, milk, a six-pack of beer, and lottery tickets. From within the illusory safety of cars and trucks, hunched-over residents scan the street sides for those who they may compare themselves to. *"Glad I'm not that guy,"* thinks a man down on his luck about another man with a tattered pair of jeans slumped on the outside of his stoop, phone in-hand. *"Look at that hoe,"* thinks a mother of three children while she passes the bars of downtown and spies in a crowd a woman far more attractive than herself; two of the three children scream on the back seat in demand of pizza for dinner. *"People are so stupid,"* thinks a man in a suit as he passes a church-hosted soup kitchen event for the homeless. *"I feel sorry for that woman,"* thinks a retired spinster on the sight of a pregnant nineteen-year-old girl with a stroller in one hand and a four-year-old boy by her side gripped in her other hand. *"Learn how to drive,"* thinks every driver in regards to the unsatisfactory performance of another driver. *"Huh,"* thinks a man when he drives by and reckons the mutilated corpse of a burn victim on the side of the road surrounded by police tape and a congregation of grieving kin; the man cranes his neck on passing, turns his entire torso towards the scene, and continues to stare after he comes to a halt at a stop sign. After thirty-one seconds, a car pulls up behind him, and with prolonged hesitation, the man turns right, on his route towards a one-bedroom apartment, where, on entry, he will greet his preoccupied girlfriend with indifference, sit on his sofa, switch on the power of his television, and think a little more of the burn victim before his thoughts alternate between perfunctory sex and reheated Chinese food.

After Tyler prepared me a calamari pizza with chicken wings, I presented him with the small pamphlet of *The Death of Ivan Ilyich* and said, "I'd like to give you this as a token of my gratitude for the excellent food you cook for me each day."

Tyler gripped the book with both hands and stared at the front and back cover with a quizzical, amused expression. "What's *this?"* he said.

"A story I think you'll enjoy."

"You don't need to pay me back for any of the food I cook for you."

"Well, consider this recompense for existence."

A day prior, Tyler disclosed to me how he believes he is a loser and that he has "given up." He inquired of my future work in the Navy and reaffirmed his reasons why he refuses to join the service despite the misgivings he has with himself for abstaining from the *effort* to join. He believes the military and all the benefits granted "Makes life too easy," to which I refuted that money is a means to an end, and he may invest his money to whichever extrinsic cause outside of his own means of survival at his own discretion. "I get depressed easily," he followed up, and continued, "I also enjoy smoking marijuana too much to give *it* up." Tyler claims to have scored a ninety-eight out of one-hundred on the military qualification aptitude test which would grant him any job he desires; he is a superb chef, an ex-power lifter, and at the age of twenty-five, is one of the most "gentle giants" I've ever encountered. Granted, he may *lie* about his history, and for his sake, with the consideration of his current perspective and depression, I hope he is.

Who am *I* to judge other than *you?*

January 24th, 2019

8:39 PM

My manager canceled my shift today on account of poor business.

I read to fill the void, and when I become restless, I engage in a few sets of calisthenics. I eat, edit, read, eat, read, edit, perform calisthenics, pace, think, prostrate, eat, write, edit, eat, read, eat, and write—write this *now* and think further: *"How much happier would I be if I were to participate in the social game, to attend bars and endure the banter of strangers, to shill out my unnecessary funds on a plethora of pleasures... A smidgen happier?"* I cease to think and continue to read, to eat, to mobilize my body, to break my flesh and mind, to read... eat...

"I took my bottle and went to my bedroom. I undressed down to my shorts and went to bed. Nothing was ever in tune. People just blindly grabbed at whatever there was: communism, health foods, zen, surfing, baller, hypnotism, group encounters, orgies, biking, herbs, Catholicism, weight-lifting, travel, withdrawal, vegetarianism, India, painting, writing, sculpting, composing, conducting, backpacking, yoga, copulating, gambling, drinking, hanging around, frozen yogurt, Beethoven, Bach, Buddha, Christ, TM, H, carrot juice, suicide, handmade suits, jet travel, New York City, and then *it* all evaporated and fell apart. People had to find things to do while waiting to die. I guess *it* was nice to have a choice."

– Charles Bukowski's Women

A few days before I terminated my relationship with Jasmine for the final and third time, I sat in my reading chair and she sat on the arm of the chair to my left. We had just finished an impromptu ceremony of immolating a ring her ex-boyfriend gave her and a ring Eliza had given me, side by side, under a heap of sage in a small earthen bowl. Jasmine's mother called at twenty-minute intervals throughout Jasmine's two-hour visit to ensure her daughter's attempts at intercourse would be interrupted; I understood, though Jasmine didn't. As the ashes of sage cooled, Jasmine mounted herself onto my lap, began to grind against my genitals, and unfastened the top three buttons of my shirt while we kissed. Her mother was due to arrive in ten minutes. I stopped Jasmine and shifted her off my lap, back onto the arm of my chair. We held each other for four minutes, lost in the unspoken feelings of each other. Her mother arrived.

"Do you want the ring?" I asked.

"No, throw *it* away," she urged, and kissed me after a slight hesitation.

The rings sat in the clay bowl covered in ash for a month, undisturbed. A few weeks after our severance, I inspected both, trashed the ring one of Jasmine's ex-lovers had given her, and proceeded to wear the ring Eliza had given me for nine more months.

I read the faded Latin inscription on the inner of the ring one last time: *"Amor Ad Infinitum"* which— Eliza had told me—when translated to English, meant, "I love you forever," [19] and discarded the black titanium circle into a plastic garbage bag tucked inside a kitchen cabinet on the third floor of my old attic apartment. I brought the trash outside later that evening and thought of the ring inside, nestled to the bottom of the bag or shifted into an empty carton of eggs, and dropped the translucent heap into a waste receptacle to be picked up and transported to the dump by my landlords the next morning.

January 25th, 2019

12:00 AM

Reader, who shares in my misery, I address you now before I lay down on a floor for sleep: you wish to engage in my discontent? There is no power to draw from the words of a fool. My slavishness renders you a beast of burden. I implore you to avert your eyes to a pleasant scene, e.g., a mirror, and to stare at yourself a long while. Do you fancy yourself handsome or beautiful? Yes, what a pleasant sight for you; even the self-proclaimed ugly and deformed will rejoice on the aspect of their conduit for being.

---

[19] The correct english to latin translation is, "Love to infinity."

January 26h, 2019

1:43 AM

Howard, the odd mid-thirties man who is the best friend of Pelagia (the self-proclaimed "non-hoe"), enjoys peculiar inquiries and prolonged stares from around corners and from behind door windows. Howard waltzed up to my station at the dish pit and said, "So I'm in the bathroom and these two guys start talking and I'm between them and I'm like—*Jesus*, are you kidding me?'"

I smirked at Howard and said, "You don't like that?"

"Uh, no, I can't pee when people are talking—or looking at me," Howard continued to stare at me from behind thick-rimmed circular black glasses. "Also—I can't brush my teeth when people are looking at me." He snapped his head away, turned full-body, and pushed through the kitchen door to the adjacent bar.

There are an abundance of mundane snippets of randomness to record on account of Howard and I choose the few which please me; I begin to think that Pelagia shared my book and informed Howard of my activities (journalism) and now he goes out of his way to interact with me for the chance of anonymous obscurity; he has succeeded.

Howard glared at me and said, "Do you shave?"

I loaded a tray with plates and said, "Yes."

"Do you need to shave?"

"I don't need to do anything."

Howard huffed, forced a chuckle, and sped away.

Occasionally I catch Howard while he peeks through the bar door windows at me; he averts his eyes, feigns embarrassment, looks back at me with a loathsome, upturned lip, and vanishes around a corner.

Two days ago I performed neck rolls with my eyes closed when service slowed. I opened my eyes and Howard stood to my left; he stared at me. I looked at him. He scampered away.

An obese man of morbid proportions picked me up in a cab from the gym. I'm noticing a trend for cab drivers and obesity. I knew on immediate entry into the vehicle that the man is pleasant and amiable. He said, "How are you tonight?"

"I'm well sir! How about yourself?"

He talked and rambled: a cab driver for twenty years; the strangest people he ever picked up were "two lunatics who claimed to be abducted by aliens." By the end of our ride, he commented on how he has been told by family members that he should write a book. The cabbie said, "I'd name it '*Upstate Babylon.*'"

"Yes, that's a brilliant name, for how people talk, and talk, and *talk*," I motioned my hand in a circle.

"Maybe one day."

"If you're capable and willing, people will read anything."

"Hey, *it* was a pleasure to meet you, truly."

"I agree."

He offered his hand for a shake; I accepted and tipped.

January 27th, 2019

12:54 AM

Dishwasher's Lament

No extent of chaos will impede me this night; I'm ready, primed to work.
Apron on, hot water fills each sink—pots and pans, first of the shift,
Slung from my right—ah!—no time to chat, please refrain;
Stifle your tongue for I've no interest—a pile of plates heaped to my left;
Silverware assorted, tongs, ladles… Yes, I've got this now, I know I do;
A tray of glassware, a stack of bowls—ah—
blackened macaroni rims a pan, *well now*-
Burnt cheese encrusts two pots—regardless—
what, the garbage?—a moment-
A party of thirty?—thanks for the heads up;
now I *know* I'm truly fucked.
Greasy water lines each basin—hold on now, you want *what?*
A favor—sure, right away, though nobody else will keep the cups at bay-
Stacks of pans—a pile of pots—heap them all into soap!-
Let them soak while I scrub the remnants on
this tray—more plates already?-
What's today?—I've lost my senses—the weekend *and* a party…
A second wind—oh joyous me; this deluge of dishware is nothing-
Keep them coming!—*yes*—may the rabble eat and drink!

Hunched over rows of uncouth plates, sprayer
in hand, imagine yourself...
Anywhere but *here*—stalwart and laborious,
suppress each crestfallen notion;
Don't lose your head, align your thoughts—*what?*—another party?
I resign myself to an abundance of filth—*ah*—
scrub harder, enact with haste!-
Piles loom despite bolstered efforts; keep the
pace, not a moment to waver...
I hear guests from beyond the threshold: outbursts, laughter, histrionics.
Music blares and people dance, lost in their moment, and I with my own-
Alone with my mind and mounds of grot,
I fail to discern between either;
What I've done with my life in regard to now: an inconsequential reverie.
Bleary eyes, soaked pants, burned, cut, and scaled hands.
Mopped floor, apron hung, breathe deep and reckon all you've become:
Hate yourself—let the feeling pass; back tomorrow for more fun.

4:55 PM

On the Indecency of Being Human:
    Games: Every word, every action, is a web of social games. To ostracize
yourself from these games is a farce and a surefire path to insanity, for the
validation of your ego is a game unto *it*self. To validate the ego, one requires
another ego to contend, spar, and compete with; comparisons are judged
by outcomes, thereby mates are distributed.
    Self-interest: Your naked body is a template for pretense and deception.
Dress and assume an appearance suitable for your ambitions. Every word
you speak is a lie. To identify with character traits assigned by you or others
is unbecoming.
    One may speak, "I'm honest,"; "I'm generous,"; "I'm caring," and while,
at the moment, these conditions may apply, the conditions also apply in
moments for serial killers and ruthless military generals; the externals for
which you are honest, generous, and caring for are the division your ego
relishes in. Is the married, stay-at-home mother of two children more
innocent than a dissolute baby rapist?—your ego determines, for if *you* are
the baby rapist, there is no wrong, and if *you* are the stay-at-home mother,
there is no wrong.

This is indecent: when one is exposed to be a fraud, a sham, a liar, a scoundrel, a pretender.

Do I project *my* ego onto others egos as though we are one?—*yes;* am I wrong?

"Yes," replied a calm critic, slanted in their conceptualized knowledge of right and wrong; the holder of an identity of someone who "knows" is a great burden and must be shed through the application of self-delusions. *This* is indecent.

You are not the same personality manifest through the pretense of your learned behavior prior to the reading of this sentence. One day you will die: this, too, is indecent.

"Into the same river you could not step twice, for other and still other waters are flowing. The unlike is joined together, and from differences results the most beautiful harmony, and all things take place by strife. That which separates unites with *it*self. *It* is a harmony of oppositions, as in the case of the bow and of the lyre."

- Heraclitus (c. 500 A.D.)

9:58 PM

I've nothing to care for and nothing to aspire for; I bide my time and wait for newfound slavery with the U.S. Navy. This dull process compounds my anticipation for a "ship date." Once the date is determined, the process will persist in being dull, even once I arrive—this I know, and despite my knowledge that the wait for *something* never ends, I nurture an ember of hope. My free time is spent engrossed with words of others and my own, fettered to my chosen vocation, entwined with my self-designated destiny. The escapism of music, namely, J.S. Bach's cantatas, offers me enough distraction to rejoice in the fractional moment of "now" while I recline for short intervals on a chair and close my eyes…

"What do you wish to be?" said a psychoanalyst to an arbiter.
"A good husband to my wife and a good man for the people."
The psychoanalyst laughed.

10:53 PM

I stare at a mirror and speak to myself, unimpressed:

"My life is an apish gallivant back and forth between sites of labor whereupon I feed my body with the profits reaped; look at what you are— know that you reckon a mirror-"

I proceeded to alter my facial expression in accordance with the broad spectrum of emotions a human may feel, e.g., despair, sadness, joy, annoyance, surprise, despondency, jealousy, wrath, resentment, happiness... I altered my pitch, tonality, and speed of spoken word while I studied my visage from all angles.

"Come to me now, death; I yearn for an intruder, an external force, anything but my own hand; I implore chaos to encroach..." and I stood there...

January 28th, 2019

10:14 AM

A malnourished peasant awoke from a five-hour sleep, wrapped in a tangled mess of frayed sheets; he gazed around a dilapidated shanty, stretched his limbs, and idled. His steady and slow breaths rasped. His reddened nose, encrusted with dried mucus, flared open with every forced inhalation. He shifted onto his left shoulder and squinted at five men lying on bunk beds. The peasant rubbed at his eyes with a closed fist and shifted onto his back, splayed on a dirt-ridden pile of sheets. He turned again, back onto his left shoulder, and closed his eyes for fourteen seconds. Again, he shifted on his back and raised his torso up, hunched forward, head slumped; he looked at himself; first his blackened feet, his haired legs, his overhung belly, and he held his hands inches in front of his face. He remained this way for several minutes, and rose up from the bedding.

On emergence from the shanty, the peasant acknowledged the sun aligned with a stark horizon beneath a thick veil of formless dark gray clouds. He returned his gaze to muddied, upturned dirt beneath him.

"Mornin' Siegfried," said a short, fat, joyful man who stood near a moss-coated stone wall lined with uniform shovels.

"By God's feet this mud."

"Yea'."

"Every mornin' this mud… by *God's* feet…"

"Yea'."

Siegfried ambled toward the fat man and stared at him. On approach, after a sixteen-foot slog through a turfy loam, Siegfried stood within arms reach and glowered down at the shiny red cheeks of a plump face.

"Take *it* then," said the fat man.

Siegfried's inhalations hastened and he wiped at the encrustment smeared around the edge of his nose; he thought for a moment—a fleeting mark of consternation accented his brow. The fat man raised his brow in mimicry, folded his arms, and stiffened his posture. Siegfried grabbed at the shovel nearest to the fat man and instead knocked into the handle with the tips of his fingers; he stumbled forward to catch the grip, fumbled, and watched the shaft fall flat, contouring into the mud.

The fat man said, *"Hm."*

Siegfried advanced two steps, bent low, gripped the shovel with both hands, and raised himself up by the fat man's side; they looked at each other and Siegfried said, "What?"

"Droppin' yer shovel already."

"Yea'?"

"Don't be droppin' yer' shovel before you even begin yer' work now."

Siegfried stood motionless; his grip around the shovel tightened.

The fat man performed a single neck roll, gazed straight ahead at the shanty, and said, "Well get yer' arse to work then."

Siegfried broke his stare and trod away, through the mud, up a slight hill, to an eight-foot deep ditch spanned miles through a series of inclines, declines, and into the overgrowth of a dense forest. He descended into the ditch and stood at a four-foot deep segment and slammed his shovel into the watery earth. He repeated this action, alone, for twenty minutes, and began to pant. Sweat soaked through his loins and his calloused hands began to bleed from worn crevices along his fingers and the lower of his thumbs.

Two men joined the ditch, and another, then three more, and soon the mire hummed with the activity of two dozen shovel-touting men outfitted with identical garb and similar morose countenances.

After three hours of labor, a man closest to Siegfried, six feet away, said, "Siegfried."

"Yea'?"

"How do you do *it?*"

"How do I do what?"

"How do you get by? I mean, I want to kill myself, Siegfried… Every day, I mean *it;* I can't go on like this for these bastards any longer…"

"Yea'."

"So, I mean, tell me your secret, how do you do *it?*—you got this, this certain zest about you, this unshakeable will, how do you do *it?*"

Siegfried slung a pile of mud over his shoulder and said, "Yea'."

"You aren't going to tell me?"

"I think of Genevieve."

"Genevieve?"

"Yea'."

"The server girl?"

"Yea'."

The man dug into the mud, chuckled, and said, "You bloody fool, that whore?"

"Yea'."

"Why, she's a real strumpet that one… *That's* what gets you by? You ever bed her?"

"No."

"So you sling mud for these lousy rats all day and think of bedding the server whore—that's how you do *it?*"

"Yea'."

"Fopdoodle."

"Yea'."

"That's not…" the man stopped mid-sentence and forced a disgruntled sigh. Minutes elapsed: one, three, ten, thirty, forty-five.

Siegfried said, "How do *you* do *it?*"

The man whirled around, mortified, and faced Seigfried; he leaned on his shovel, shook his head, and said, "I don't know—I *don't know.*"

"Yea'."

"*Yea'* nothin'—I asked you because I figured you knew somethin' I didn't, with how you work and all."

Siegfried slung three heaps of mud embedded with fist-sized stones over his shoulder; the man watched him, and when he reckoned that Siegfried had nothing to say, he continued:

"I suppose the food, even though *it's* fit for dogs, though there really isn't much else, is there?—besides the food, and when we get back to sleep, I mean…" The man straightened his back. His bleary eyes sparkled with fresh tears he fought to suppress.

Seigfried, without looking up from his labor, said, "Don't cry."

"I'm not."

Eighteen minutes elapsed and a bell resounded from a quarter-mile away.

Siegfried threw down his shovel and joined with the twenty-three other men who had already thrown down their shovels and trotted towards a large wooden structure; he began his own trot, last of them all.

On arrival at a rectangular log structure, Siegfried entered a low archway, stepped into line, and observed a quasi tavern. He tapped the shoulder of the man in front of him and said, "Where's Genevieve?"

"Who?"

"Genevieve."

"Don't know."

Siegfried waited. He clenched his hands together and craned his neck side to side. On his approach to the counter, an unfamiliar old woman poured him a seventy-two-ounce ladle full of overcooked barley; he said, "Where's Genevieve?"

"Away."

"Away where?"

"Take your food and piss off."

Siegfried held his hands out and accepted the bowl. The old woman departed from the counter, veered into a kitchen, and began to rummage through dirtied dishware. Siegfried stood, bewildered, and he continued to stand for two minutes while the other men sat and ate in silence in their respective chairs. He walked towards a staircase and ascended the steps. A dark hallway rowed with eight rooms, four on both sides, loomed before him. He sauntered, a bowl of barley in-hand, down the hall, and listened to the familiar voice of Genevieve; she moaned from behind a closed door: *"Oh—oh—oh—oh yea'—yea'—yea'—"*

Siegfried stood inches away from the door and continued to listen to Genevieve. Steam from the barley whiffed upwards; he sniffed. A man behind the door grunted.

Siegfried lifted the bowl of barley and titled a portion into his mouth.

"Oh—oh—ohhhhh—oh—Yea'!—Yea'!"

"You like, huh? Yeah?"

"Oh—mmm—oh—mmm!—mm!—mm!"

"Yeah?"

Siegfried turned away, walked down the hall, descended the steps, and joined the other men at the tables in their respective chairs. Most had finished their meals and had begun their forlorn trudge back towards the ditch. The last three, excluding Siegfried, followed soon after. Siegfried sat alone and chewed the final portion of his barley. The old woman ventured out from the kitchen to collect the bowls, scowled at Seigfried, and said, "Piss off then; get out."

"I'm not finished."

"You had your time, get out or I'm callin' fer' Thomas."

"A few more bites."

"No—get outta' here, then."

"A few more bites."

"Thomas! *Thomas!*"

Siegfried spooned two mouthfuls and darted towards the exit. He rejoined the twenty-three men in the ditch, pried his shovel from the mud, and began to dig. Five hours and twenty-one minutes elapsed and the same man who had worked alongside him prior to mealtime said, "Ay, Seigfried."

"Yea'."

"I didn't see Genevieve."

"Yea'."

Thirty-two minutes elapsed and the bell resounded again. The men carried their shovels back to the wall, Siegfried among the center of the crowd; he panned his head towards the sky and scrutinized the dim glow of a setting sun behind a darkened gray veil of clouds.

The fat man awaited the men in the same position, posture, and demeanor; he said, "Good job. Good job," to no one in particular.

Siegfried placed his shovel against the wall; his eyes averted to the fat man's boots. He walked into the shanty, ruffled his bedding, and settled onto the dirt, fully dressed.

1:54 PM

A review by *Foreword Clarion* of my first installment of this abject lifelong series highlights what I've attempted to relay all along to my despicable readers; two key quotations:

"This book, then, is not an edifying treatise inspired by other privileged white male writers. Rather, *it* reflects the vapidity which that same status offers Balor. What remains is a well-paired antecedent to a devoid predicate: a raw subject, whose unfettered musings, active

contradictions, and solipsistic renderings of himself are an incisive glimpse of the current state of American psychosis.

"Balor thinks of calling his book 'What Not to Do with One's Life.' Being trapped in the mind of a Privileged White Man turns out to be the perfect opportunity to take stock of one's own psyche."

- Foreword Clarion

I'm amused, for my choice of a title, "Privileged White Man," has evoked the exact sentiments I anticipated. I'm disheartened, for the second half of the title (Egotistical Fool) is far more pertinent to the ~~human condition~~ subject matter, yet, the obtuse social stigma incited by the sight of "Privileged White Man" raises eyebrows and reaffirms biases. *Yes*—these privileged white men are *crazy!*—we hear *voices*, I tell you! If you're capable of reading these words, you're privileged, regardless of gender or race; are you grateful?—you've no reason to be.

January 29th, 2019

8:20 PM

Work canceled due to constant snowfall.

Soon after my shovel hit the pavement at 7:00 PM, the neighbors of my father's abandoned home opened their garages and fired up their respective snowblowers. Within ten minutes, four snowblowers whirred up and down the street. I swear, these people wait, peer out their windows, wait, pace, watch a few segments of television (the weather channel), sip a bit of coffee/beer, pace, peer out their windows, sit, stand, peek out their windows, and all-the-while they contemplate if *"now"* is the optimal time to clear the snow away from their driveways in a manner reminiscent to how they mow their lawns.

I shovel for the sake of my father; he wishes to perpetuate the illusion to any representative of the bank under which his unpaid mortgage is owed that his abandoned house is still occupied (by him). I am the perfect ploy for his design; being his son, this is a mutually beneficial, albeit temporary game.

January 30th, 2019

10:25 PM

After my shift, I stood in the kitchen and stared at grease drip out from the fryer pipes into two large pots. The assistant manager, Ted, approached from behind me, stopped, and said, "You're still here? What are you doing?"

I hesitated, turned towards him, sighed, and said, "I'm watching grease drip out from the pipes."

Ted smiled—a genuine narrow-eyed smile with creased cheeks; he laughed, turned from me toward the back exit door, and said, "Goodnight Baethan."

"Goodnight Ted."

Tyler and I spoke at great length near the end of our shifts. My new voice recorder arrived by mail too late; the conversation would have been of great merit and interest to record in the exactitude and length deserved.

In summation: Tyler considers "our" intelligence (him and I) to be that of introspection. He considers "will" to be the single difference between humans, which defines what we are. He believes the self is defined by the "will," i.e., our chosen delusions.

We agreed that the delusions we chose and experience aren't "bad," neither are they "good"; the delusions are essential: the crux of our humanity, our egos. Tyler, this unassuming man, tucked away in the corner of a kitchen, engaged with the preparation of fried food and side dishes for drunks and socialites, astounds me. I've never met anyone with a similar will.

"How's *it* going Baethan?" said a nineteen-year-old dishwasher that works at the neighboring establishment.

"Ah... I'm well... contemplating."

Tyler, who stood by, hood up, headset on, said, "Don't contemplate, just live."

"This life," I began, outside in the frigid winter night while Tyler inhaled drags of a cigarette, "I don't understand-" The three of us stood under the glow of back alley city lights and shivered.

"You're not supposed to," he remarked with an empathetic smile.

I stood and icy winds battered my face. I looked to my left, to my right, down, around, and *had known* I'm not supposed to understand.

"The first sign of the beginning of understanding is the wish to die."

- Franz Kafka

My fasting, cold showers, and severance of all friendships has been an act of self-flagellation and nothing more despite my pre-contrived reasonings, yet, I persist, despite my (self-)knowledge, due to perpetual discomfort being the single ailment to my "psychosis," condensed into the framework of painful self-consciousness paired with the belief that there is no "self." Everyone is the same beneath the pretense of *everything* derived from culture: upbringing, personal knowledge, clothes, mannerisms, demeanor, and speech—we *all suffer the same*. Solipsism is irrelevant; my intuitions of others are most often correct and hardly ever not due to my focus on the social condition—the *human* condition, with myself as the blank template on which I reflect and reverse-engineer the body language and demeanor of all others *with an understanding of my own behavior.* Animals… *you're* not excluded, despicable reader.

"You think too much," is what I often hear whenever I decry the pretenses and delusions seated at the root of the ego, as if the judger who ascribes themself as someone who thinks less than I do "knows" what the "correct" amplitude of thought is.

Tyler is a veritable psychiatrist/psychoanalyst and he deemed me to be *humble.* I informed him of my recurrent bouts of self-loathing, and how these states are externalized by my ego and perceived by me as hatred directed at me from everyone who knows me. "Some would say, schizophrenia," I quipped; we chuckled. I stacked clean dishware into matching assortments akin to a child organizing toys by variable size, shape, and color, while I said, "I refuse to believe that jargon. I'm egotistical for the sake of my writing, engrossed in my act; therefore, I'm self-obsessed."

"That's not *bad* though, you're like just about every other person in our age range."

I sprayed dirty plates and desired to scream—a vehement outcry of despair. I didn't.

January 31st, 2019

12:47 PM

Seated in an arcane lecture hall, sixty-two intelligent masses of tentacled flesh the size of mature oak trees listened to the discourse of a tentacled mass of flesh of equal size garbed in a resplendent celestial mantle: A Professor of Universal History. Spanned in a wide half-circle arc around the professor's ethereal desk stood four-hundred and three beach ball-sized translucent globes mounted on pointed podiums.

The professor writhed and spoke a telepathic discourse into the mind's of the pupils with a dialect that sounded reminiscent to the English language (for the sake of relative translation): "So what we have here is a quandary—for example, consider subject thirty-six: the universe of Hop-Gish; there is, within this elementary confine, a habitat which hosts peculiar creatures that believe a variegated spectrum of paradigms as to how and why they exist." The professor levitated towards the thirty-sixth globe in the arrangement and waved two hooked tentacles over the zenith. A spinning orb colored with variegated hues of green, brown, white, and blue, centered within the globe. "Before I continue, does anyone have any questions?"

A distended mass of amorphous flesh near the back row of the assembly interjected a transmission of thought akin to: "These globes represent dimensions and realities crafted by the Gyokuhn, this I understand; however, what is to prevent the possibility of the Gyokuhn from also being an indefinite suspension within a globe crafted by creatures of another reality or dimension unbeknownst to our kind?"

The professor thought of a conjecture: "Nothing."

The lecture hall buzzed with wayward thoughts reminiscent of: "That's odd."

The professor overpowered the deluge of unrestrained theories, postulations, hypotheses, and propositions electrified throughout the domain with a nullifying thought comparable to: "Yes, *it* is odd."

4:06 PM

I'm amazed by how I wake at 9:00 AM and lay on the floor upon my sheet for two hours, engaged with the idle process of thought. To remove myself from the floor is tremendous mental labor and I often procrastinate with shifts back and forth onto either of my sides; I sigh, sigh again, breathe in slow rhythms, and wish to lose myself in a void best encapsulated in sleep—to return to the realm of non-dreamers and be still.

"Life is what you make of *it*," I heard spoken to me the other day by a weary bartender who resents her job and who expresses her disdain for people.

By 11:00 AM I stiffen my body, turn, balance my weight onto a knee, and rise; this moment is the worst of each day, even worse than the lapses of daydreams I succumb to before the evening ritual where I hesitate to prepare for sleep and yearn with every essence of my being to do so. The shower is labor; I start hot, clean myself, and shift the water to a full blast of cold; this endeavor is a far cry from a macho pursuit, rather, a reminder to "feel."

After, I stand naked in front of a mirror and see an average man in every respect, neither impressed or disappointed: there is *just* flesh.

To dress is a process which lasts half-an-hour to an hour dependant on how distracted I become with the preparation of food, impromptu note-taking, internal planning, and periods of contemplation where I stand, disengaged from any process whatever, in favor of a narrow-eyed stare at walls, flooring, fixtures, and miscellaneous items.

First the briefs… the undershirt, a sweater/overshirt, socks, and if I am to attend a session of dishwashing, a button-down shirt with "shirt stays" attached to both the dress shirt and overshirt. The pants are last, secured with a belt… readied for a social excursion. I return to the mirror and look over my body, again neither impressed or disappointed, but perplexed by the curious behavior I exhibit and my metrosexual manner of style, for I desire to impress none, yet I present myself in a way which, if *it* were to become sentient and speak, would say, "Look, look, I have undergone an effort to prepare myself for *you* to scrutinize me!" Neither a fop or dandy, others often remark of my militaristic bearing and severe demeanor.

By noon, I revise a few pieces of writing and prepare for a new entry devised from the morning's idle bitterness; this act grants me solidarity, unity, solace, and equanimity—for the moment, and I break away to shovel yesterday's snowfall. Now, I have several passages of pertinent text to record in regards to what being human is: a conversation conveyed through messages between myself and Tyler; he offered me his phone number and a *hug;* I accepted both, for his benefit, though in retrospect, I no doubt derived "more." The following messages, sent by me, and Tyler's responses, are invaluable.

I initiated with a quote:

"Now, there is nothing of which a man is prouder than of his intellectual ability, for *it* is this that gives him his commanding place in the animal world. *It* is an exceedingly rash thing to let anyone see that you are decidedly superior to him in this respect, and to let other people see *it* too… Hence, while rank and riches may always reckon upon deferential treatment in society, that is something which intellectual ability can never expect: To be ignored is the greatest favor shown to *it*; and if people notice *it* at all, *it* is because they regard *it* as a piece of impertinence, or else as something to which *it*s possessor has no legitimate right, and upon which he dares to pride himself, and in retaliation and revenge for his conduct, people secretly try to humiliate him in some other way; and if they wait to do this; *it* is only for a fitting opportunity. A man may be as humble as possible in his demeanor, and yet hardly ever get people to overlook his crime in standing intellectually above them. In the Garden of Roses, Sadi makes his remark: 'You should know that foolish people are a hundredfold more averse to meeting the wise than the wise are indisposed for the company of the foolish.' On the other hand, *it* is a real recommendation to be stupid. For just as warmth is agreeable to the body, so *it* does a mind good to feel superiority; and a man will seek company likely to give him this feeling, as instinctively as he will approach the fireplace or walk in the sun if he wants to get warm. But this means that he will be disliked on account of superiority; and if a man is to be liked, he must really be inferior in point of intellect."

- Arthur Schopenhauer

Tyler responded: "This is how I get by and find myself being amiable to almost all persons of any age, religion, culture, sexuality, etc.: I mask myself to blend in (lower my intelligence to match theirs, I love to call *it* 'matching vibes'). I've let go of some of my intellect, willingly. I was sick of choosing above my fellow man. I didn't like how I could throw away people and replace them. And for that ego, I relinquished my ego and pride as best I could. Started doing more drugs and started showing love and appreciation and understanding. I've lost much but have found much more. Hence why I chose to follow this route. I still feel like I'm hiding my intelligence and not using *it* in fear of being alone… and even worse, I fear I'll lose appreciation for life and for the simpler things. I'm scared of the mass money and of the responsibilities I'll have to inherit if I allow my intelligence to be known and used… I want freedom. And so I stay at home and cook. I'd rather be happy, humble, and unknown. I have essentially given up on my ideals of success and replaced them with ideals of genuine, personal peace. My question to you is, do you think I'm a waste? Should I do more?"

I responded: "To answer your question, I'll quote—again—a Hindu scripture this time, *The Bhagavad Gita*: 'There is nothing lost or wasted in this life.' To go beyond that, I'm appreciative of your self-disclosure; I never expect similar returns when I reveal my shadow the way I did for you—by way of crestfallen lamentation. Success and progress for the sake of humanity is a moot endeavor. Entropy is the true progress, and for what does humanity propel themselves toward if not that? I write, work body and mind, consume, defecate, and abstain from all relationships (albeit this one is agreeable thus far); I don't consider myself a waste on this account and I don't believe you should either if you are truly pursuing what makes you happy. I assume you are uncertain what makes you happy, thereby you question yourself and ask for my opinion—perhaps as satire… or perhaps you are genuine in your expression of pain as I have been. I don't know the answer though there are many people either of us could ask who would claim to know what's best for us both and humanity as a whole. My writing is my only solace, an engrossed expulsion of filth. Intelligence, to me, is a sham, just as everything else is— ideas, proliferated by charlatans. There is no truth. Cook and consume at will and die alone with your backpack beneath a pleasant tree." [20]

The following morning I received Tyler's follow-up: "Tranquility consumes me as I read your response. I do not know what makes me happy for I am forever doomed to feel this sickness they call 'chronic depression,' but I know *it* to be melancholy. Happiness does come and *it* never lasts long enough for me to take a breath. I feel as if for other people, happiness comes much more easily and lasts longer, however my cynical afterthoughts meshed with my propelled self-testing gives me no chance to accept happiness. More likely than not, this is a system I have accepted to enter long ago. A system of limited and controlled happiness… For the simpler fact that I loathe finding myself comfortable in life. Oddly enough,

---

[20] Tyler had stated earlier at work in response to my inquiry, "What would be your ideal way to die in any imagining you can think of?": "A nomadic death, alone, beneath a tree."

I express my melancholy with pride while my happiness is seldom shared, where as much reluctance fills the tone. I am convoluted and to many people, I am a perplexed individual. But that's okay with me man, life is what I make *it*. 'Your' [21] goal to be a millionaire means nothing to me for I want to live a life without anger, anguish, jealousy, hate, pettiness, malice, [and] expectations. I chose to live a life of intangible goals long ago and in that respect, I am richer than most. I know I cannot prove my worth and I really don't care. The ones close to me get a glimpse of me first-hand and know what I'm capable of... And respect me even more for being who I want to be, not what I should be.

"Am I happy? Perhaps I am and don't know *it*. But at the cost of my negative feelings, positive feelings will be amiss. I know when I should be happy even though I don't feel *it*. And for someone with melancholy, that's the best I can get as of now. I do not think I'm a waste, not yet. My pursuits of mental and emotional growth have always been my priority. The goals I have set for myself have all been met. My gut still tells me that I should do more in the hopes of my parent's acceptance or to meet the agenda my peers have set for themselves, but I do not want to follow this path. Guilt, shame, inadequacy should not drive me in life. A life of anxiety is something I will gladly pass up.

"I laugh when I'm in physical pain or deep emotional anguish. And I cry deeply, snot and all, when happiness consumes me. I am not normal. I pay no mind to my reasonable trauma or obstacles. I actually find fun in the chaos. I find *it* to be challenging and refreshing. I have seen many tragedies in my life and have become extremely hardened. But show me a toddler who cries because they are alone in the dark and I will cry with them. For I remember that exact pain when I was a child. I am a being of empathy and perhaps that's the reason for my pursuits of personal solidarity. For I know, I have the innate ability to inspire others, that my vibes supersede me and if I am not careful, my negative feelings will be projected. And so, I am the way I am. You now know most of my psyche when *it* comes to my day to day."

I responded: "Your psyche is a reflection of my own! I believe you describe the mind of all, including those who refrain from and never will take the pains of introspection to consider what you've expounded. A single tear fell from my right eye while I read your response, on account of the brief glimmer of what I feel is 'happiness' fleeting through me, an empathic

---

[21] "Your," meaning, "Anyone's"

response. Chaos promotes change while order is stagnant, thus we strive to become... something 'greater' for some, while you and I are aware of the trappings of riches and fame, we subdue ourselves and temper impulses to deceive and manipulate in favor of personal virtues. By comparison to our 'power' and sex-obsessed peers and the remnants of expectations we still cling to, i.e., hope, we may be considered losers, wretches, low-lives, or incompetent—idiotic—foolish—stupid!—all these opinions are harmless, yet the ego demands validation. I too met my goals, and now I am disillusioned. I validate my own ego and don't desire to validate others; I ostracize myself to spare the feeling of others and internalize my apathy. I abstain from entertainment and also seek hardships/challenges, though lately, all paths appear to be of a bland and desolate color: Melancholic. There, we have shared facets of our neurosis/psychosis.

"Would you agree that there's nothing you hate more than being pitied?"

Tyler responded: "I hate pity along with general ideas of sympathy towards myself and others. Empathy is what I prefer."

I let *it* be, and our ~~conversation~~ relationship ended.

FEBRUARY

February 2nd, 2019

1:51 AM

A recorded dialogue between myself and a haggard cab driver after a midnight grocery store and gym visit:

I said, "Hello sir."
"Hey bud, where you goin'?"
"[Street name]. How long have you been a cab driver?"
"Oh, twelve or thirteen years on and off."
"You must enjoy the work then."
"The hours are long and stuff sometimes but ya' know the drivin' part of *it*—meet different people, never in one place, always in a different area most of the time. Not like bein' stuck in a cubicle—stuck in a factory where there are no windows to look out or anything' ya know."
"That's true, in fact, the last job I had was at a factory, and my biggest gripe was that there were no windows at all."
"Oh yea'!"
I paused, waited for the driver to speak further, and continued, "Even the job I work at now, there are no windows."
"Where do you work now?"
"Right now I work at [Bar name]."
"Oh okay… where do you work?—in the kitchen or-"
"Yeah. Yeah. And there are no windows there."
"Is the kitchen in the basement there, or is that another restaurant?"
"Uh—that must be another restaurant." A moment of silence elapsed; I said, "Who is the strangest person you've ever picked up in a cab ride?"
The driver laughed, scratched his head, and said, "There's a lot of em'. Probably the scariest one I've picked up ya' know was where was… I picked up this one black guy; this was about six—seven years ago, picked him up right up at [Street name], and I get him in the cab; he's goin' to [City name]; I get em' to give me the money upfront because anything over twenty bucks they like us to get our money upfront ya' know. He pays me. I get down one exit. The dispatcher asks me where I am. We're testin' the new radio to see how far the range is on *it*. Now I drive the same car pretty much every day, so you know what your radio looks like in a car and everything like that. But the radio I was driving in this car in this particular time had

133

a little bit of white paint up at the top of *it* for some reason. I don't know why, but, I was lookin' at the radio and I'm just like—'oh yeah I'm just goin' past [Street name] headed south.' The dispatcher said, 'Oh yeah your radio sounds really good! Sounds good!' So I get down one more exit… and I got two state trooper cars comin' off the off-ramp to box me in the front; two more speed up behind me and back me in from the back… and ya' know how they do those felony traffic stops on T.V.?"

I lied and said, "Yeah."

"They yell 'Driver put your car in park! Driver throw your keys out the window!' And they did that stuff when they pulled me out of the car, and when they pulled the guy out of the back seat they weren't so nice when they pulled him out."

I chuckled.

The driver continued, "So—he had pistol-whipped his girlfriend, walked over to the gas station to have the clerk at the gas station call a cab… and… he still had a 9mm, loaded, tucked down in his front waistband." We met eyes and I raised my eyebrows to acknowledge the fear the cabbie must've felt in that moment. "And he sat behind me the whole time." The driver gazed at with an expectancy of shock outlined in his uncertain grin. "So, I was like…" A long pause; I said nothing; the driver continued, "But I picked up some—I picked up one, one time too, but I didn't get him far, I got him like a block away from the hospital; the guy had escaped from a behavioral health unit at the hospital. Feel like I always get the weird ones."

"The insane asylum?—or the-"

"Jut-ju-just the weird calls sometimes, ya' know…"

"Hm. Well you can notch me down as one of the weird guys that you pick up."

"Why are you weird?" The driver giggled and leaned his elbow against the cab door.

I stared straight forward, hands braced on my thighs, and said, "Yes. What is your self-assigned meaning in life?"

"… I had one time where I pulled up to a house, and I beeped the horn, and nobody came out, so I sat there for a few minutes; I called the number they gave me—no answer. So, I like, I pull up a little bit, and I'm a little ways from the house, and for some reason I looked down the side of the house, and just as I did, one of those sheet ropes come outta' the second-story window." I chuckled again. "And I'm like—okay? And I was gonna pull away but I was like—I ju—I just gotta watch, and see if whoever is comin' outta' this window is gonna fall out of the window or somethin'.

I didn't know if *it* was a guy or a girl comin' out, or if *it* was a kid tryin' ta sneak out—middle of the night, ya' know. So, I'm lookin' and the next thing I know, I see—after I see the sheet rope come down I see this guy hurry up and climb down and he's runnin' towards my cab with—he has his boxers on and he's got his clothes in his hand." I laughed. "And he comes to the cab and yells, *'Hurry up get outta here—get outta here!'* What *it* was, was, he was messin' 'round with this married woman, and her husband came home early. He was hidin' in the closet upstairs while she was down tryin' to distract the husband so he could find a way to sneak out."

"Turn here. That is an excellent story. So the man was sitting in only his boxers in your cab?"

"Yeah well I mean I stopped a block away and he had put his clothes on and his pants on and stuff… *it* was just really weird, ya' know, *it*'s like…"

We pulled up to my "home"; I said, "I need to call your company to pay by card, I should have informed you sooner, but I had a preference to ask you questions instead."

The driver laughed.

1:44 PM

Yesterday, in the kitchen of the bar, Pelagia informed me she experienced a recent miscarriage and still hasn't dealt with the "psychic trauma."

February 3rd, 2019

1:27 AM

Pelagia insisted on cooking me a meal; on my decline, she persisted with offers of various items. I walked away. Tyler also offered to cook me a meal; I declined; he shrugged. Fifteen minutes later I procured for myself a bowl of rice, broccoli, and two small chunks of red meat; I ate the meal, estranged from my coworkers, while they chatted in a circle at the far end of the kitchen. Pelagia abstained from initiating conversation with me for the remainder of the night. Tyler behaved with no deviation; we bantered in brief and spoke our good-natured farewells to each other by the night's end.

Lo, the nature of man and woman.

A recorded conversation with a decrepit cab driver after tonight's gym visit:

The driver said, "Hello."

"Hello sir. How are you?"

"Good. Where to?"

"[Street name]." I buckled my seatbelt and sat while he recorded documentation on his clipboard. "How long have you been a cab driver for?"

"Oh just 2002."

"Geez, that's seventeen years?"

"Yeah seventeen—eighteen years."

"You must enjoy the work then."

"Well... yeah, *it*'s... *it*'s the easiest job I've ever had."

"Who is the strangest person you've ever picked up?"

"Oh God." The cabbie thought for a moment. "Ya' know... When people get drunk they're out of their head. And they don't know... where they are or where they're goin', or some gay people—ya' know."

"Have you ever had any gay people hit on you?"

"Yeah—oh yeah."

"What do you enjoy the most about the job?"

"Uh, I can do *it*. See, uh, see my canes?" The driver pointed between the seats at two modest wooden canes. "I can't go without them. I have progressive muscular atrophy. But I can do this. Ya' know, I like *it* because I can do *it*. *It*'s easy. Meet people, talk to people. Make some money."

"Lately I've experienced difficulties with my foot, being young—so *it* makes me think about when I'm your age in the future too and what I may start to lose in my own mobility. How old do you think I am?" The cabbie switched on the overhead light and grinned at me.

"Mmm... Sixty-six."

"I'm gonna be sixty-six in March."

"Ah!—so I was close."

"Real close."

"What is the hardest part about dealing with the lack of mobility in your legs?"

"Well... you get used to *it*, doing things that you once could do—you can't, ya' know you can't... jump and run; you can't run (he repeated)... No huntin' now... No motorcycle now... Can't ride a bicycle... Can't *run* (again)." The driver laughed and a long pause ensued. "You're limited to the things—when you have something in your power that's great; you're still living."

"Do you believe that we are all the same when you take away the pretenses and the clothing that we wear… no matter what our genetics are, our parenting, or our heritage?"

"We're all the same?"

"Yeah, and-"

"Well our minds are different."

"What unifies us is suffering."

"I think everybody's different. The way they think, the way they act."

"You don't think *it*'s pretense?"

"I sorta' don't understand your question."

"I'm—I'm not too sure that I understand what I'm saying either. I don't know—I think there's a baseline human understanding… that, no matter, as I said, what your origins or your heritage, or your upbringing, we all… experience this reality in the same way, and the main unifying characteristic of that, is how we suffer. Yes—our minds may be different, how we think, but that's a product of our experiences."

"Now—did you go to college?"

"No. I read a lot of philosophy… and psychology and sociology; I'm trying to understand the human condition. I think that we all speak to validate our egos, and that's the whole reason why we maintain relationships with other people: *it*'s a reciprocal act of ego validation."

"You'd be a good professor."

I chucked at the driver's sincerity and said, "I'm not trying to preach to anybody."

"Now—you don't let me go by your place."

"Alright, *it*'s up on the right here, near the end of the street. I ask you these questions because I like to seek alternate opinions on these ideas."

"Oh yeah—everybody's different. Stop here?"

"Yes, here."

"Here?"

"Yes." The driver didn't stop. "Stop here," I affirmed.

"Right here?"

"Yes, right here."

9:26 PM

We're sane as children, blank templates spawned into this familiar reality. Life molds, shapes, and ebbs us into patterns of behavior, i.e., insanity, in various formats, i.e., culture.

The African woman born on the fringes of the Bronx in New York believes she is different from a Japanese man born in the nexus of Tokyo. The first layer of pretense is the distinction of race, gender, and kin. Physical/mental aptitude, deformities, and abnormalities endowed through genetics is the second layer, though these characteristics are often the most esteemable manifestations of identity an individual regards as a unique bestowment or right (especially intelligence in *its* many forms). The third layer is affectation, clothing, and speech: tools for manipulation and deception. The fourth layer is a culminated social judgment of recognized accomplishments, achievements, derelictions, and honors wrought by an enactment of the will.

Void all pretenses: empathy and suffering remain.

February 5th, 2019

7:11 AM

I dream of distant planets, bygone worlds, arts and passions lost, and faces I once called friends. Memories ache.

11:13 PM

By day I dream of death in the most uncanny of circumstances. Every car which passes me by on the side of the road, I yearn for *it* to hit me head-on, yet I "know"—this is wholly undesired, in truth, for the pain elicited and the trauma sustained to the body would be anguish and agony. To slip and fall on the ice behind a snowbank and crack one's head—dead phone battery… temperature dropping, paralyzed, one can't scream, speak, whisper—*only* breathe… in, and out…

On my trip to a school auction this morning to assist my kitchen supervisor/chef, Henry, with the loading and unloading of outdated electronics, we discussed many aspects of human duality and experiences. I suggested and agreed to ghostwrite a novel detailing his life experiences through the transcription of his spoken word, verbatim, in real-time. My voice recorder will be utilized to ensure accuracy and refinement. I've dug my own grave; shovel dirt in my mouth and place dainty pebbles on my closed eyes.

I loathe myself and suffer the onset of sickness; a dreary cough and scratch at the back of my throat warn of imminent disfunction.

I walked down the street for two miles with a full pack, two grocery bags, and closed my eyes while chill winds blew over semi-frozen puddles; I felt the warmth sapped from the downturned contours of my frown and dared a glance at my rosy cheeks and dour eyes in a storefront reflection. Bars, restaurants, barbers: all closed for the night. I walked alone on splintered ice: a shambler, a dead man among dead men holed up in their homes. The flicker of television sets glowed from third-story windows.

I retire to a floor now, with this gaping hole in my heart equivalent to every human account of woe, every tale ever spun, every fabricated lie, every gospel. Sleep.

February 6th, 2019

11:05 PM

Ghostwriting is easy; I prefer the task as opposed to *this* dreadful labor; to record, transcribe, and embellish the thoughts and memories of another with your own artistic flourish is a wholesome endeavor. We all have a story to tell.

Henry, is a sixty-one-year-old man. A foot smaller than myself in height, his girth is formidable, though his acclaimed strength has diminished over the years due to an arm injury and the onset of accelerated entropy. His eyes—brown and blue (complete heterochromia), pierce out from a grizzled visage set beneath a pair of thin eyebrows. His short grayed hair, often styled with minimal effort, begins to thin. His presence commands authority, though when he speaks, his uplifted voice connotes one who would rather be engrossed in whimsical conversations. He's stout and hardy, with a diversified history of culinary, crime, martial arts, and travel. I'm fond of him, for he rules the kitchen with an iron will; his stalwart position, fixated on the task at hand, scrutinizes the "big" picture and the dynamics of a functional staff.

A recorded conversation two days ago with Henry, unbeknownst to him (at the time of recording), in a cargo van, on our way to pick up items he bid on and won from a school auction warehouse:

Henry drove us down the highway and said, "Great view of the skyline here."

I said, "The Adirondacks are a beautiful place. I'm weary of *it*."

"Why?"

"Same scenery over and over again, all day and… same people, same town—people like to say 'small world,' but, *it*'s really just a small region."

"Yeah."

I paused for a while, pained with my habitual deliberations and blunted affectation; lack of daily social interaction and forced abstention from speech while in social settings dampens grace and charisma. "I yearn to see the world and people of different cultures before I die."

Henry acknowledged me with a nod and said, "Have you traveled at all before?"

"I traveled down to Florida—I lived down there for-"

"Where in Florida?"

"I went to Orlando, and I stayed down there for about a month, and then my girlfriend at the time, she uh… she tried to sleep with my roommate, who was the artist, and I was the—I was the story and character writer, and the brother was the programmer of this idea that we moved in together for, so… I had to choose between a career with them, or my girlfriend at the time, and—like a fool, I chose her. So we moved back to New York… things didn't change, we ended up splitting—again, but uh… had a few more roommates that didn't work out; more jobs, that didn't quite work out either, then I ended up moving back in with my father… That's when I decided that I need to pursue my writing." I reflected on my past, stared out the windshield, and summarized my sentiments with, "Funny how things turned out the way they did."

"So, I just want to understand this better, and I'll explain why I'm asking you these questions after, so… is *it*… Do you feel *compelled* to write? Do you feel like: 'Oh my God if I don't get this down on paper I'm just going to go crazy?'"

I smiled: a broad, dumb grin, and lowered my stare out the windshield to my lap. "Uh-"

"Now—now let me start over with this, because, I have a multitude of life issues, and I've had to reinvent myself at least three or four times, ya' know, about getting over being a troubled youth, that whole process and experience and trying to make *it* in the world, find my own person, the right relation, ya' know—failed marriage, travels in Europe, Russia, Ukraine—the stories I have from there are crazy! And every time I tell any of these stories people always tell me 'Oh my God you gotta write *it* down—you gotta write *it* down'—and I'm *trying* to—and *it*'s probably the most difficult thing I've ever tried to do; I love *telling* the story; I hate *writing it* down!"

I met eyes with Henry, flashed him an enthusiastic grin, and said, "You can tell me the story and I'll write *it* down."

Henry immediately said, "Alright. Deal. *It*'s a deal."

I sat, flabbergasted, unexpecting of my seriocomic suggestion of something I had already intended for my own merit to be *accepted*, for Henry had been unaware of my voice recording of this particular conversation—a story in *it*self.

Henry continued, "Every time I try to sit down and think and write this story down, I write a few sentences and just give up, ya' know?"

"Perhaps you could... (I stuttered)...you could-"

"Record *it*?"

"-*record* yourself speaking."

"I *tried* that! I tell you-"

Henry answered a phone call; I waited in silence. He resumed with renewed excitement expressed in his demeanor on the immediate end of the call and said, "So—I lived—uh, one of the jobs I had—I rode two ferries to work every day, and the ferry ride was lovely, so already back then I thought, 'I know, I have all this time on my hands,' so I bought a new recorder, and I thought, 'I'm going to record all these stories I have,' and at the time-"

Henry swore and answered his phone again; he quipped a directive, ended the call, and resumed: "Uh, so, I bought a new recorder, and I would stick *it* on my dashboard, because I was staying in a car basically, a ferry car, and I would just tell all these stories—but, they had this software called *Dragon Speak,* and you could train *it*—*it* was kind of in *it*s infancy, but you could train *it* to recognize your voice, and *it*-"

"*It* would transcribe *it*."

"But *it* wasn't very good at the time and things didn't work out very well—and then—and then!—I'm just way more animated telling the stories to a person than I am talking into a machine. So, uh, yeah if I had somebody I could tell the stories to, even if they recorded them, or we record them while I tell the story, ya' know what I mean?—and we could transcribe *it*—well not transcribe *it* but turn *it* into a-"

"First-person story format."

"Yeah!—because, when I think about *it*, each one of these stories I remember exactly, in a very engaging autobiographical-fiction, and I even thought of a title; so my father used to call me [Pet name], I was the [Pet name] of the family. So I thought a great title for the book was: [Book title]. And, you know, make the culinary the core, but the side stories are about getting out of jail, getting into jail, going to do this and that or whatever, but the culinary is always going to be the subject theme right? Alongside short stories, or maybe recipes, and ya' know, but I thought [Book title] was a unique book title.

"*It* is."

"And the subtitle."

"Yeah the subtitle is a nice touch. What do you have in mind for the cover art?"

"I haven't even gotten that far—I have *no* idea. But I think the story would do well, ya' know depending on—I'm looking at this as—my wife doesn't know half of what I've done in my life, ya' know? I was on a contracted train, doing an American and Ukrainian joint venture for an upscale hotel and restaurant, and my wife at the time was selling advertisement—so she's part of the stories too, and I don't *get* America; I don't-"

"I don't like *it* either."

"My wife is younger than me-"

"I have no reference for comparison though so…"

"-Yeah. So people ask me since she's so much younger than me 'Well how did you guys meet?' And I'll try to be funny and say, 'Well I was twenty-one and she was three; I met her on the schoolyard and we've been dating ever since.'"

I neglected to display any sign of humor and continued to listen.

Henry continued, "Because a lot of people like—okay I'm sixty-one, she's forty-whatever, *it* doesn't seem like much at all, but when you say I'm twenty-one and she was three, that sounds like a lot, ya' know what I mean?"

"Yes."

"So… um, but uh, my experiences and stories are incredible, but that's what makes them so unbelievable because they're true! And uh… and just the things I've gotten into and out of in my life. So, my thought was, *it* would be a real interesting… I don't know anything about my dad, except, from the time I can remember when he was around. I know he wasn't born in the states; I know he grew up in this country after the war, but I don't know anything about him—I really don't! I wanted to know what made him tick, what made him the way he was, and, I want my daughter to have some kind of reference to me, for how *crazy* her dad was! Ya' know, so I think this could be an interesting read, maybe *it*'ll be something she picks up when she's thirty and has kids and decides to read, even if *it* isn't published, even if *it*'s something archival, *it*'s worth *it* to me; however I do think *it* has some marketability. There's a certain element of the craziness of the book-"

"If you're serious about this, we could arrange something, and... I could be your ghostwriter."

"I just, I don't want to—I don't—I don't know how to—what—what's that service *worth?*"

"I'm uncertain."

"So find out. Let's try to find out."

"Alright."

"Because *it* has to be something that's worth your time, ya' know? I know *it*'s worth my time because I definitely want to get this going, but *it*'s gotta' be worth *your* time; otherwise, what's the point? So I would see what *it*'s worth as far as your time goes, and then uh, ya' know we can work *it* out, the best time for both of us, a couple hours a week or whatever, that type of thing."

Our conversation veered into how the end of his current role as supervisor and head chef of the bar kitchen will transpire by the closure of the next three weeks; he offered for me to work for him full-time or part-time, my choice, at his new domain of work where he has been hired as head chef.

I said, "*It*'s funny how no matter where you are in the hierarchy, we're all just cogs."

"Oh yeah."

"Even the people phasing you out, they're all just cogs too."

"Yep. That's why I like doing my own thing, being in charge of-"

"Self-sufficient."

"Yep."

February 7th, 2019

11:47 AM

What more is there than bundles of fleshy fibers entwined in striations of sinew bound around calcified marrow and fat deposits which ebb in and out of the bloodstream? Ah—you enjoy pulling up onto bars and pushing off of a floor—do you?—eh?—you *buffoon,* you ninny; look at yourself, at what you do, and for what reasons? Are you mad and desperate—no—no—the flesh is weak, and the mind… feeble. Well, continue to push up and off of your damn floor and pull up onto bars!—swing yourself around and gallivant to your death, you imbecile, you creature of nauseous habits.

When I write, agitation wanes, the spirit is subdued, and I once again align with the placement of mortals.

6:45 PM

At a meeting with the chief of my Navy recruiters, I've settled for the rating (job) of CS (Culinary Specialist [Cook]) on account of the duties and granted qualifications. My current ship date for May 5th will be forwarded to a sooner date once I reenlist for active duty instead of the reserves. I've been asked to volunteer for a Special Ops qualification test and have agreed.

Should I be happy?—oh, the happiness, I wonder, what *it* is, to be assured of my liberation from the need to worry about finances ever again, that I will be able to afford a luxurious home, cars, and wife if I desire, with the men at the recruiter station as proof of their claims.

Is this happiness, when these same men suffer the same; I reckon their inhibitions, their pain, and the doubt each feels, gleaned from the contours of their faces while they speak.

The chief said, in a one-on-one discourse with me, "You gotta be a leader for these kids Baethan, especially when you're at boot camp; you know what the real world is like; you've been in and out of shit jobs, shit relationships, scrubbing toilets, cleaning dishes, factory work; you're how old?"

"I'm twenty-seven."

"Yeah man, I was twenty-three when I got in the Navy, flat broke, no money for anything, living paycheck to paycheck doing factory work and jumping between jobs. By the time I got out of boot camp I had six grand in my bank account. A year later I bought a $30,000 car; still had money in the bank, and a few years after that, since I had no bills, I saved and bought a home for a hundred grand out in [City name]. Life is good now, no worries, and these kids straight out of high school—they think life is all rainbows and sweet cakes—they've no fuckin' clue man. You gotta set an example for these kids—you'll be that guy laughing while everybody else is bitching about how much the shit they're in sucks, because you *know,* man."

Am I predisposed for any vocation, role, or preset?—no, no design that satisfies me, for I have no desire. I am nothing but my will.

"Ill—ill—mentally ill!-" shouts a paragon of human virtue; the mask sloughs off and reveals a husk, a hollowed vessel, a *thing* devoid of life.

A conversation with Henry on the ride to his home after we loaded his van with the items from the school auction:

I said, "Do you believe there is a true self, or that *it*'s all pretense? By pretense I mean how we act, the clothing that we wear, the culmination of our experiences in life, our genetics, and our parents; *it*'s a process that-"

"Well I think *it* absolutely is an outcome of life experience. Um, the choices you make whether they're bad or good, the things you have, ya' know, I think that, um… I've uh… The majority of my life I've started out working basic jobs for just about nothing; however, as an adult, I don't think I've attained that 'Renaissance man' I always wanted to be. I think what ended up happening was, I ended up becoming more of an observer than a participant. I think I screwed my chances up a long time ago, so what I'm trying to do is make the best of things that I can to create a positive, nurturing environment for my child, so she can grow up with a healthy start. So I figured, if that's the best I can do with the rest of my life, that's enough. That's kind of where I am."

"What do you mean by you were aspiring to be a 'Renaissance man?'"

"Well… I thought years ago that the people who seem to be one step ahead of life, who seem to know the right things to do and the right people to meet, the right things to say, the right places to be at, the right business to be involved in—just the people who seem to have *it* together so easily; all seem to have come—that I've met—all seem to have come, from the background of… controlled chaos. And, so, I'm trying to—I don't think necessarily consciously, but subconsciously, I'm trying to get a little of my own controlled chaos, putting myself in all kinds of situations where you would think having survived them, would have given me those abilities somehow. Things like that!—I mean—I don't know. I'm a high school dropout. Uh, I spent a lot of years when I was younger—because I was just a crazy kid—and… uh, I had a fabulous upbringing, lovely parents, ya' know but I totally went a different direction; I totally went a rebellious direction… and, out of all of that nonsense, I've been able to make a decent living, marry a wonderful woman and have a happy family, and uh… and uh… so I'm thinking you know in some ways, I've done good, but in other ways, um, I feel like I could have… um, ya' know, I would accept jobs overseas in a country I've never been before, just because *it* sounded cool, and I figured *it* out, ya' know, how to live, how to get to work, how to dress up, so, I've done that often. I mean I went to [Country] back in the early 90's when *it* was still ya' know, [Government], and I worked in the [Country], and in the [Country], and all these different places to work, and—just became *it* sounded like a cool thing to do; I once spent a year in an intentional community down in the forests of [State]. I spent two years salmon fishing in [Country], and a lot of these experiences were not that pleasant, but, I learned many things and went through poverty—I mean I'm basically fearless. That's why I started a career in business."

I said, "You could say that those people who seem to have *it* all together on the surface—they were your models because they were almost the quintessential aspect of controlled chaos; however, *it*'s funny you say 'controlled chaos' right after you mention that (those people) because I was just going to comment and say '*it*'s those people that have *it* all together on the surface that have *it* least together out of all of us.'"

"Yes that's very true."

"That's exactly what I mean about pretense—is that people identify with certain characteristics or achievements or failures that they've experienced throughout life, and *it* manifests as personality."

"Yeah."

"But underneath all that, what unifies us, is suffering, because we all suffer the same way; *it*'s a universal human condition."

"Yeah."

"So when you peel back the layers, *it* doesn't matter."

"Yeah I mean ya' know, let's take Jamison for example—the owner of the restaurant; so, when I first met him, I was really kind of in awe of his success—I mean he's done *so* well for himself, and, ya' know, he's much younger than I am, and uh, but then I found out the way he treats his wife and kids?—and I'm like 'I don't envy this guy at all,' ya' know; he doesn't spend time with them, he's too busy with everything else, too busy with the business, doesn't give them the time of day, ya' know. I think he's lost sight of what's really important in life. So, I went from envying him—now I pity him, uh…"

"Pity is the worst feeling you could connote to somebody. To pity somebody… nobody likes being pitied."

"Oh you mean to be the recipient?"

"Yeah, yeah…"

"Oh I see."

"Most people don't know they're pitied. I think I'm pitied often."

Henry gazed at me, shocked. "No! Why would you think that?"

"The way that I act purposely whenever I'm in a social scenario. I tend to…withdraw entirely-"

"Yeah."

"-because I think that nothing good can come from speaking. Even in this situation like now, nothing good can come from *it*; however, here we are, and I speak because I have an unsettled mind."

"Uh-huh."

"Let's say for instance when I'm washing dishes and everyone is bantering and having a good laugh, I like to keep away, and I often take on a countenance that looks sad-"

"Uh-huh."

"-or dismayed and serious."

"Uh-huh."

"I think I'm pitied on that account."

Henry quipped, "I don't think so."

"No?"

"No—I don't think so. I think uh… I think you're not at the right age range to be pitied. I think sometimes what happens is that, sometimes I think people pity Margaret (the old dishwasher) because of her age and what she has to do to get by and sometimes *it*'s physically hard for her, and she's often exhausted. People pity Margaret because she reminds them of their own grandmother or whatever; I think they see you as eclectic, ya' know, and I don't think-"

"As what, you said?"

"Eclectic. You kind of have a peculiar personality, and I think that's pretty much the extent."

"I've never heard that word before."

"Eclectic?"

"Yeah."

"I don't know the exact definition of 'eclectic'; how I mean *it*, is… Let me think of a different word… Uh…"

"I've been called 'eccentric.'"

"*It*'s similar (The words aren't similar). I think eccentric connotes (denotes) a lifestyle you've had for a long time; ya' know, like the old guy who lives in the house and traps his fireplace because he believes people are going to come down his chimney to steal his electricity—*that*'s eclectic."

I laughed.

Henry continued, "I mean—that's *eccentric*... eclectic, I think is different. Eclectic is um... okay, ya' know the guy who wears the robes to work?"

"Yes."

"So, he knows... he *has* to know that his choice of dress and mannerisms, style—*it's* got to be a little bit questionable to some people. He's too intelligent *not* to know."

"I empathize; I've also worn robes in public, paired with a cowl."

"When most people see him, they think of a harmless, kind of a weirdo."

"Harmless weirdo?"

"Yeah—he's a weirdo but he's harmless. And uh, but when you take the time to talk to him—he's brilliant; he has an amazing mind, *it's* no wonder he worked ten years at a bookstore. But he's definitely quirky, he has his own mannerisms about things—*okay,* I have *it,* I can explain 'eccentric.' Eccentric is a person who makes personal life choices which can be contrary to the norm but doesn't hurt himself and is comfortable with *it*... That's eccentric."

"I'd say I'm fairly eccentric. I spend all my time in a house that's completely empty, that's been abandoned. I've sustained a wayward lifestyle for the past two years from the time I went to a commune before I came back to this area. All I own is a device to do my writing-"

"Uh-huh."

"-and a backpack with all my essential clothing. That's *it*. So I spend my time standing around, and all I do is read and write; on that account of me relaying this information, I've been called eccentric."

"Did you find *it* interesting that Pelagia went out of her way to buy your book?"

"Yes. I also found *it* unsettling and I informed Pelagia that I believe she wasted her money. She told me she never wastes her money. I told her that she would be the best judge of that. That's about *it*."

"I think she did *it* more to kind of get a reaction out of you."

"Yeah, she posted a little sticky note on *it* downstairs in the basement with 'Sign Me,' scrawled on *it*. When I first walked in I was flabbergasted. I didn't expect that at all."

Henry chuckled and said, "I think the most interesting thing was that your *lack* of reaction made *it* all the more interesting—because everybody expected you to react differently."

We discussed the restaurant's menu of the establishment where we work for the remainder of the three-minute drive before arriving at the warehouse.

February 9th, 2019

12:40 AM

Today I learned how to butcher duck.

"Oh woe and pity—the hypocrisy!" laments a naive reader, "When will my eyes glaze over with *genuine* entertainment?... Oh, pity to this fool."

Margaret has quit her job. I have taken up the mantle of full-time dishwashing for two. From noon to midnight, Monday to Saturday, I mull around the kitchen and perform the duties of a wench. Afterward, despite my pathogen-induced sickness, I sauntered to the gym amid thirty-mile-per-hour winds blown headlong against my indifferent countenance and performed the typical compound lift routine and ran akin to a hamster on a wheel... and now, I dedicate time in the wee "burning the midnight oil" hours to transcribe two dialogues recorded within the past two hours while oatmeal cooks on my portable element. A conversation with a young man at the gym:

I approached while the 5'5 ball-cap and wife beater-garbed man stared down at his phone, earbuds in; he saw me in the full-length wall mirror, removed one earbud, and snapped his head up. I said, "Do you think *it*'s absurd, as human beings in the modern age, that we come here and do this shit?"

The man stared at me, circumspect, and said, "Why?"

"As a means to counter entropy, for our physiology, for everything that we've read on the internet and in books that tell us how great weight-lifting is for you, while back in primeval days, we were supposedly out hunting mammoths and doing things with our bodies that actually mattered that sustained our strength naturally—and now here we are," I raised my arms and looked around me... "doing this *shit*."

The man beamed and said, "Right?"

"Don't you think *it*'s absurd?"

"All of society is pretty absurd—yes."

"Alright, I agree."

149

"I agree."

We both smiled from ear to ear.

I said, "Well, that was on my mind-"

The man laughed and compelled me to laugh; he said, "I think you're right; I think the way society is today is pretty absurd."

I turned to resume my futile activity and said, "Alright."

"That's what keeps us sane, right?"

"Yes."

He *laughed*—oh yes, he laughed aloud, with a jovial glee!—and said, "You gotta do what you gotta do." I nodded, returned to my station, and resumed dumbbell flies.

I admitted to a cabbie of my sudden use of a cab service for transportation ever since a foot injury, and how now, despite my foot being healed, I persist in using a cab service due to excuses, e.g., bad weather, feeling ill, overburdened with groceries—all conditions I would endure in my recent past on account of ~~discipline integrity~~ foolishness. Cab drivers are my clergymen.

A key point I remember of my confession near the end of our route:

I said, "Do you ever find yourself so overwhelmed with being human that you fall to your knees?"

"Yeah, I get overwhelmed often."

A peppermint candy rattled in the empty drink-holder next to a fountain drink purchased from a local gas station.

I paid my fare and said, "I'm glad to know you're overwhelmed often; I am too. Take care."

"Yeah."

February 10th, 2019

1:55 AM

I greeted a short, stout, ballcap-adorned, facially-pierced woman, who avoided eye contact with me throughout the entirety of our interaction and laughed with the nervousness of a self-conscious schoolgirl:

I said, "How long have you been a cab driver for?"

"Um—two and a half years."

"Do you enjoy the work?"

"No," she giggled. "I used to when I first started but, *it*'s kinda played *it*self out now."

"Have you gotten sick of the people or-"

"Um, some of them; the pays not very good either so… but *it* pays the bills—barely but *it* does." She smiled.

"What is your dream job?"

"Um I'd like to be famous for my music," she giggled and blushed. "That's my dream job."

"What music do you create?"

"Um—I sing R&B music."

I misunderstood and said, "The… The United States army music?"

"R&B, not army."

"Oh—oh *R&B-*"

"Yeah."

"Ah. I was going to say I didn't know that the army employed singers." The woman laughed.

I continued, "But they do—now that I think about *it*."

"That's funny."

"Do you ever do any gigs around here?—like bars or clubs or anything?"

"Um—[Town name] usually."

"Do they pay you?"

"No," she laughed again.

"Oh, so just volunteer work?"

"Pretty much. I do *it* because I love *it,* and I'd like to get paid for *it* someday…"

"I understand; I'm a writer, and-"

The woman grinned and interjected, "Same thing."

"-I had my first book published—yeah pretty much—and I'm not expecting anything from *it*. I intend to publish each year until I die."

"Because ya' like *it,* right?"

"Yes, and, if I didn't do *it* I believe I'd off myself."

"Yeah."

"There is literally nothing else to this world, other than sex and consumption, and *it* sickens me, so I need to find a creative outlet, therefore writing."

"Yeah."

"*It*'s the only thing that I know how to do… efficiently, [22] at least."

---

[22] Consistently*

"Yeah."

Weary of my self-exposition and eager to reap droll content, I said, "Who is the strangest person that you've ever picked up in a cab?"

The woman answered with intermittent bursts of giggles, "Oh Jesus there's too many for me to answer that—there are a lot of strange ones. I honestly couldn't even tell ya'."

"Oh I'm sure you could."

"There's just—just a *lot* of strange people I've picked up in my cab—my cab days."

"Maybe I'll work on that count"; I let there be silence for a few seconds and we both began to snicker.

"I don't know," she reminisced, "I couldn't even tell ya' who is the strangest of them all."

"Well just, the strangest of the bunch. Anyone that comes to your mind, I'm interested."

"Um... I had a guy, 'OD' (overdose) in my car. Um, I've had another guy, um, huffed aerosol cans in the backseat, and, um, he literally peed his pants, and, and like no-" Our combined laughter overpowered the quiet car radio. "-So many strange happenings..."

We pulled into an alleyway parking lot. I said, "Where are we going?"

"Oh someone else called who's also going to [Town name] so I'm picking them up."

"Okay, cool."

An obese and disheveled bearded man in his late thirties entered the backseat.

The driver said, "Sup Larry?"

Larry said, "Hey."

"Going home?"

"Yep." A paper bag crinkled behind me and I smelled the unmistakable stench of fried food.

I turned to the driver and said, "What is your self-assigned meaning in life?"

The woman chuckled and said, "I have no idea."

I turned towards the backseat and said to Larry, "How about you sir?"

"What?"

"What is your self-assigned meaning in life?"

"Huh?"

"Your self-assigned meaning in life."

He expelled an involuntary burp and said, "An upside-down cross."

I laughed.

"Yeah," he reiterated, "An upside-down cross."

"Do you mean that in the religious context, or do you mean that as symbolism for what your life is?"

"I could care less."

"Alright, I'll take that as the symbolism then... I wish I could care less."

The driver giggled and said, "Amen to that."

We rode in silence to Larry's destination; he paid and departed. I also paid in equal respect.

9:06 PM

Once upon a time, an idiotic linguist crossed the outskirts of a jungle threshold into a small village of a tribe of barbarian cannibals. A plume of discolored smoke rose upward from a massive fire adorned with the fresh carcass of a young boy impaled through the mouth and out the anus by a thick tree branch.

"Hm," thought the linguist, *"The flesh of that lad blisters and bubbles in a peculiar manner,"* and he strode forward, towards the village nexus where four dozen tribesmen danced, engrossed in a ritualistic fervor around the blackened corpse of the boy; chants resounded: guttural ululations and prolonged bellowing.

"Greetings! Hello!" announced the linguist in the supposed native language of the mob. Three four-foot spears lobbed through the short distance between the linguist and the convergence. Two of the spears skittered across a stretch of dirt to the linguist's right and one spear impaled the flank of his left thigh. The linguist screamed a pained cry and collapsed to his knees; amidst the throes of agony, he held up both hands to ward off an onslaught of serrated stone knives and crude clubs.

February 11th, 2019

1:50 AM

Accompanied by the dead master's compositions of the baroque and renaissance period emitted from the low-quality speakers of my writing device, I march through the deadened town of my youth for three miles with a 38 lb load of groceries strapped around my back after a training session at the gym. I forsake cabbies; the service is a method for dupes and invalids. Open jacket and hatless, I incline my determined visage to a veil of toxified clouds… ah, to be alive is a marvel; I smell the sweat of my armpits; I hear the steady rhythm of my breath, and I reckon a fraction of the burden of man at the frontal seat of my thoughts—a throne of the damned. Feed the body.

2:53 AM

"You can't fix stupid," is a common adage stupid people quote from a popular comedian of this era whenever aforementioned people witness a stupid act and desire to elicit a cheap laugh.

Is "stupid" a condition to be fixed? The stupidest people I know are also the happiest. While the smart man laments his ill-contrived plans and unsatisfactory fortune, the stupid man shits himself and grins.

7:18 PM

Reader, I address you again—yes, my new routine—you'd believe me to spin fantastical tales estranged from my reality, would you? "Fantasies I could concoct of my character and life would be far more enticing"—I retort to the thought I have implanted into your mind, whether you agree or disagree with the initial implantation.

Despise me for my truth, my boring, mundane reality parallel to your own. Chisel away the wondrous and mystical lives of your favorite persons and you will reckon a mirror.

Oh—you hoped to be entertained in reading this, did you—*after all I've written*, how could I be so—*so* heartless and dismissive?—*so* impudent and unimaginative? What a bitter little man I must be!

I've neared the end of *The 48 Laws of Power*, a well-organized and formatted summation of the treachery and deception employed by past leaders and charlatans, and have added to my own repertoire of "understanding" what is known as the fundamental human condition.

You silly and naive reader, with your fanciful ponderings and pitiful boredom. How you may one day sift through the words presented before you and dare to chuckle on behalf of the foolishness, or to absorb an entire span of text in one gross sitting and reflect on naught but a few passages which tickled your narrow passage of reflective potentialities.

Long for a fantasy, do you?—to escape from the humdrum mundaneness of your self-prescribed reality? Are you depressed? Feeling low? Discomforted by my sudden and inexplicable irreverent outburst against your support? Good. Despise me, for I have truth as my useless albeit bold ally.

My boredom is now yours, while I stand and squander my time with the consumption of foodstuffs, engage in regimented sets of calisthenics, read of corruption, write *this,* and *wait* for my departure to America's Navy boot camp where I will be molded into an impeccable slave fit for a role I have diminished desire to perform: a Culinary Specialist (CS). [23] I have memorized the "Sailor's Creed" and now allocate mental space for the "11 General Orders of the Sentry."

"I heard you're joining the Navy! That's impressive!" said the social relations manager of the bar where I work while I sprayed hot water over a pan of poultry grease.

I raised an eyebrow, shook my head, and said, "I find your position more impressive."

"My position isn't nearly as important."

"Drunks and harlots gotta eat too."

We laughed. *Oh…* reader, *we* laughed… at the expense of the patrons, ourselves, society, this whole damned world.

"If you want to tell lies that will be believed, don't tell the truth that won't."

– Emperor Tokugawa

---

[23] I've accepted the rating of CS due to the CBD oil discrepancy and the lack of other ratings available to me *due* to the aforementioned discrepancy despite my qualifications and initial declaration to my recruiters of "I'll accept any rating except one involving a kitchen."

February 12th, 2019

4:42 PM

I admit *it:* I'm a fraud and a sham. With my second revision of last year's journal installment for clarity, before I submit the manuscript to my publisher, I'm abhorred and appalled with myself that I have fallen back into the domain of my father's now-abandoned home.

Why is there shame on this account?—with my mother forsook, why do I desire to extricate myself from my father and subject him to a similar fate? I regard all others as piecemeal scraps of human nothingness. I sit alone with my hands folded in my lap, blinds closed, and stare at a shadowed wall. My ideals of adventure, hardship, the pursuit of compassion and a cause worthy of my esteem, are now mere flecks of the written word, to which, on my reckoning, I am disheartened, for I am not alone in hypocrisy and delusional proclamations.

To say you are something, or that you will be "this," or "that," is a vulgar demonstration against death. To become anything more than what you are is at the expense of resources and the wellbeing of other entities. Many strive to transcend what human is, to be Godlike, and to what detriment? Many would conceal the extent of the toil and labor required to achieve a commendable feat, to amplify the awe they inspire… to be validated… fame and fortune, a namesake remembered *beyond* death.

This is no excuse. This is no pardon. The truth is *always* ugly. I've no cause to be excused *or* pardoned.

I think to my past, years before, to my early youth, before I had any conception of what life is beyond what laid before my eyes…

9:57 PM

Alas, there is no honor unpunished. A glory is equivalent to an indictment.

A silk-laden bed overhung with purple-streaked yellow tassels.

A voluptuous naked woman sprawled the length of her body out before a handsome young man seated at the keys of a grand piano. She moaned and pressed her enormous breasts against the ruffled sheets. *"Do* play that one again—the one you played for me when we first met."

"You liked *it*, did you?"

"Oh, yes, very much."

"I do recall now… let me think, ah—yes, number one, in F major… andante," the pianist began to play the first few notes.

"Oh yes—this one!—this one is magnificent! Who's the original?"

"My dear," he began, his key-presses slow, calculated, with space between each note for words of his own, "I wish to say… this was mine… nonetheless… the credit goes… to Chopin."

The woman arched her back and tucked her thighs against her belly, bosom poised at the zenith of her frame. The pianist peered over the contours of the piano and stared at her figure.

"Oh," she cooed, and twisted her waist and abdomen into the folds of the bedding. "This is so beautiful…"

"I'm pleased you're pleased."

"Play another for me, a different piece, when you're finished?"

"Anything for madam."

"Don't call me that."

The pianist missed a key and said, "Alright, miss!"

The woman lost her air of playful grace and said, "Nor that."

"What shall I call you then, if not your name?"

"You ruin the music with your talking."

The pianist played the remainder of the composition with quiet strokes while the woman posed and stole glances at a rectangular floor-to-ceiling mirror embedded in the wall behind him; she continued to contort her limbs within the confines of the loose bedding and arranged herself to be exposed at the flank and shoulders while her lower body remained concealed by a furled red blanket.

The pianist finalized the last few chords with a pronounced force, an expertise unreckoned by the woman. "This is how you make me feel, oh, nameless one," he muttered, and flipped through several pages of his composition book, stopped at a Joseph Haydn sonata marked by many angular scribbles and annotations, and began-

"*Oh*—you play *beautifully!* So very beautifully…"

February 14th, 2019

1:11 AM

This life—to put into words the anathematic sentiments I withhold for my fellow man, woman, and our designs in this bizarre world—is impossible; no sculpture, painting, music, or string of words could summarize the abandonment of care. *So,* I employ myself for twelve hours in a kitchen, apply myself for two-and-a-half hours at a gym, return home to feed, sleep, and repeat the process, day by night. I disdain all entertainment on account of no time for *it,* and no interest if I *did* possess the time for *it.*

This is no laughing matter, yet I laugh, for the abject futility-

"oh—oh—*oh*—no!—*no!* Anything but a nihilistic diatribe! Please!—I beg of you!"

Ah, damn you and your meta(non)fictional self-expository interruption!

"Your life is beginning to bore me; in fact, *it* has for quite some time now. You've gone lax on your fiction and poems and I am averse to the character you are becoming. I think you should write something new and witty, or perhaps profound. I desire entertainment, and I find your self-inflicted pain and sorrows to be humorous and to my utmost delight. If you would supply more content redolent of your allegorical heartbreak and mental duress on behalf of humanity, I'd be pleased and content, *but* only if you condense your outbursts into a brief summary with proper formatting and syntax. To sit and read through a lengthy paragraph is wearisome."

And so, I gritted my teeth and finalized my imagined encapsulation in a brief paragraph for my average reader. Now go, begone, close the book or negate the screen, oh… *oh,* wait, I have something for you:

~~Never mind. Maybe later.~~

"You're a genius," said the dupe to the charlatan.

"Thank you, my friend, I owe my talent to God."

"God is a good man."

"I think you're a heathen."

The dupe fingered his right nostril and said, "I think I'm in heaven."

"Oh-" The charlatan's eyelids fluttered. "-you flatter me."

Now, what was *that* about?—something irrelevant and preposterous with no grounds for any merit? Do I waste my time ~~and yours~~? I'm publishing this. I stir my oats and laugh.

11:13 PM

Another stretch of labor from the onset of waking. With no time for adequate food preparation, I seize the opportunity to fast, return home, and resume where I stood the night prior.

This—*this* is the meaning of my life, to stand with my thought depository. I refrain from all conversational initiations and eye contact with my coworkers. When spoken to, I answer with dull affectation, in short responses, at a volume loud enough for only the interaction initiator to hear.

Happy Valentine's Day. I had intended to write a love poem today, though the hour draws to a close, and I'd rather sit and stare at a wall.

11:48 PM

Love to Love

Look at me, I exist; notice my gestures and ways I flick my wrist.
Notice me, please; I'd like to know more about you
So that we may stay up all night engaged in coy banter
With topics ranging from shared cultural phenoms,
Entertainment pursuits, hopes for the future, and manners in which
We'd copulate, for I love to love, *it*'s all I know;
I wish you'd join me, but don't stay long.

February 15th, 2019

11:40 AM

Yes, I have become this document. I speak and seek conversation with the sole intention to record the social implications for reflective study about what I once believed and believe now.

Every paradigm and mode has been shattered: a relinquishment. There is only silence; this too, will alter throughout my experiences. Perhaps one day I'll desire to settle and start a family, whereupon my selected mate will read through my history and true thoughts contained in this series of text, and think, *"Oh..."*

"Blessed is the man who, having nothing to say, abstains from giving us wordy evidence of the fact."

– George Elliot

February 16th, 2019

2:11 AM

I swear—another ten hours of labor, a combined hour-and-a-half of walking my routes, and a subpar visit to the gym, dissuaded by thoughts of my own death—I've no time!—hark—*hark!*—this is no cry for help, no lead for sympathy, self, you cannot begin to fathom why you exist—*think*…

A driver almost (mock) struck me today on my walk home, I believed with intent to startle or frighten me, however, I stopped, reminiscent of a deer in headlights, and gazed headlong at the oncoming vehicle, and—by the God(s) almighty, I hoped chaos would overtake my supreme order.

These damn people at the public gym; my initial amiability towards my fellow man and woman is mistaken as interest in communication and relationships. On my midnight visits, there is always a woman named Mia who utilizes the elliptical machine while she giggles at a television program positioned a foot in front of her face. She maintains a slow, steady pace for up to two hours, and proceeds to stretch her back afterward for twenty minutes. The other recurrent visitor is the old "Where's the progress?" man named John; he performs one set of low weight flyes on the cable machines for fifteen reps and proceeds to walk on the treadmill for forty minutes.

Both of these people consider this their "exercise."

I walked down my home road the other day on my route to the bar and met with a little old woman who lives at the end of the way, donned in her beanie, sunglasses, parka, mittens, with a leash held taut with a toy dog at the end of *it*—little bastard yipped and growled at me—the woman muttered to the dog: "Yes, *yes,* I know." What did she know about me that the dog also knew? "He needs his exercise too," said the woman. She smiled at me: a witch and her hound.

I'm amazed some people consider walking a mile or two to be "exercise." Walking five to ten miles a day is my passive life, between my routes, pacing, treadmill runs, and mode of labor.

"Be careful out there! Keep warm! Stay safe on the ice! Don't talk to strangers!" Mia said to me on my departure from the gym.

I grinned and said, "I already did."

John, by her side, said, "We *are* pretty strange people," and the door shut between myself and them. I was gone, out of earshot, and I spoke aloud to the wind—"Oh, you silly people have no idea how strange I am," nor I—them! I'd read a journal written by both of them, or perhaps I wouldn't, depending on subject matter and talent. I imagine Mia would write day-by-day of the children she babysits and of her "productive" gym sessions. John would write on how this world is lost to the new age and on how the "old simple ways" are lost.

There never *is* "living simply." If you live a simple life, you're a simple*ton*, with simple problems of great complexity (due to the nature of how people perceive their own problems)—which I suppose is what I am, considering oats boil on my cooking element; I'll consume, sleep, wake, and return to a bar to perform the same mundane labor I've performed three consecutive days prior to earn my room, sustenance, and pay to have this tripe published and marketed—for the *glamor*, the *honor*, the *privilege*, the *esteem*—oh, yes, watch me fade into oblivion.

Three wind-induced tears escaped my eyes, blew back towards my ears, and crystallized against my cheeks.

February 17th, 2019

2:51 AM

Near the end of my shift, Pelagia approached me at the dish pit: typical behavior I expect from her throughout the day despite my forced standoffishness and withdrawal. She persists, and I indulge in her banter, albeit my input is brief, juxtaposed with her lengthy and wordy expositions of topics ranging from dreams, ideas, thoughts, food offerings, suggestions, and inquiries of my character and/or life.

In this particular instance, she spoke her farewell to me; I turned to her to address her and spoke my farewell… and, to my unexpected pleasure, she enclosed me in a hug, to which I reciprocated with equal affection. We pulled away after a three-second embrace and gazed into each other's eyes…

Now, I consider everything I am of a man, and everything I know of her being a woman; at that moment, I shared in a mutual exchange of love—for I acknowledged her with empathy expressed in my visage when we separated, and in her regard of me—yet, I know *it*'s a sham.

There is no titillation on my behalf... how long *it*'s been since I have been, I can't recall. Years... years ago...

The temptations of a self-proclaimed (non)hoe who enjoys gratuitous sex?—and for her, to be interested in a man who strives to ignore her, we are similar in our wretchedness; therefore, the attraction is paramount. Or, I'm another notch to add to the belt of egoism and validation, a vacuous trophy for the debauched.

Pelagia will no longer be employed alongside me within the next ten days; she has been hired to co-manage a nearby restaurant with a theme of healthy foods. With this in mind, after our hug, and the consideration of our combined previous interactions, I've ordered her a quality bust of Hippocrates and a plaque inscribed with his words, "Let food be thy medicine, and medicine be thy food" as a gift for her.

3:56 PM

Law 41 of *The 48 Laws of Power* is: "Avoid Stepping into a Great Man's Shoes"; the theme is to slay your father, i.e., You are your own father.

Yes, I am surrounded by my father's aged symbols—the familiar architecture of my youth while I live in his abandoned home. My father's shadow encompasses me; he urges and wills for my "well-being" out of a desire to validate his provisional capability by accusing me of stupidity if I am to forgo his providence and advice.

Out of necessity—to escape psychological duress, I relinquished all inherited possessions, joined an intentional community, practiced asceticism, and dedicated my life to the recording of useless thoughts; this mode of being is complete estrangement from my father's hedonistic background and postal working career; *however,* I am again entrenched, and have reverted to a quasi-dependency, though in actuality, I would be better off once again in my own apartment for the psychological benefit opposed to the monetary gains I acquire from residency in a dilapidated house. I have mommy *and* daddy "issues"; parental figures are a scourge to be shed. There is only my writing while I anticipate news of my forthcoming father: The United States Navy.

By the grace of being alive, there is nothing to satisfy me: no divination, vocation, pursuit, accomplishment, philosophy, treatise, creed, pledge, oath, method, paradigm, theory, discipline, or love. The absence of commitment and care fosters hope for anything *but* the expected. I am committed to *this:*

A little man hobbled along an ancient dirt path and stumbled over a brick of gold.

"My God," he spoke aloud upon his recovery and inspection of the impediment to his gait, "I'm rich; I'm filthy *rich.*"

"Nay," resounded an ominous voice from the adjacent shadows of overgrown brush. "You wish to keep the thing for yourself?"

The man gripped onto the brick, fearful and eager to flee with his find, though the material held firm to the path. "Who are you? Is this yours? You can have *it!*"

"Man," began the somber, discordant ululations, "If you could see what I see of you now, a reflection of humanity presented to me through the aspect of your avaricious figure knelt over a brick-"

"Who are you!" screamed the man, and he pulled harder at the gold; his battered shoes dug into dirt and sweat formed along his brow. He grunted, panted, and on several failures, swerved his head in all directions, for the voice which beset his ears now resonated from within.

"Upon sight of you, I pity."

The man exerted one final attempt with an exasperated puff of expulsed air, clambered to his feet, and scampered down the same route whence he came with concurrent glances to the brick of gold and back to the path before him.

February 19th, 2019

1:18 AM

"According to the Elizabethan statesman and writer Sir Francis Bacon the wisest policy of the powerful is to create a kind of pity for themselves, as if their responsibilities were a burden and a sacrifice. How can one envy a man who has taken a heavy load for the public

interest? Disguise your power as a kind of self-sacrifice rather than a source of happiness and you make *it* seem less enviable."

– Robert Greene's The 48 Laws of Power

I visited my father for dinner; he clasped a hand onto my right shoulder from behind while I engrossed myself with editing and said, "I want to let you know I'm very proud of you and of the man you are." My father has expressed his remorse and disapproval of being cast in "such a foul light" in the first year of this pointless journalism endeavor; his concern amuses me, for the sheer immensity of the nothingness ascribed to my own work by me is the paramount feature—and he *cares*.

A concubine traveled a vast expanse on horseback to the home of a notorious hermit known for his peculiar art. Her multicolored garb fluttered in the wind and revealed supple features of her body to the dissatisfaction of the hermit when he opened his triple-latched door at the sound of her eager knocks. The concubine stepped one foot into the doorway, held a weighty tome up by her head, and said, "Did you start writing these excerpts with the intention of publishing them?"

The hermit eyed the concubine, her coy grin, brazen short-cut hair, defiant stance, and hopeful eyes; he sighed and said, "No, and yes; the idea attracted and repulsed me throughout writing, even on completion I hesitated, though now I'm committed for life."

"I'm not reading your book with the intention of obtaining wisdom. I feel that this experience, along with every other one, is a process of realization for my ever-evolving quest to seek more information about myself. There are no selfless acts, *right?* I started reading your book this morning with no idea that *it* would contain bits that 'hit home' at the right time." The concubine paused and scrutinized the hermit; he gazed at her with indifference expressed in every contour of his face. She continued, "I own and have read parts of the *Bhagavad-Gita* too. 'There is nothing lost or wasted in this life'; that reminds me of the second law of thermodynamics or entropy. Energy is neither created nor destroyed, *it* is only transferred."

The hermit opened his mouth to speak, refrained, and attempted to shift the door shut, though the concubine's body blockaded the doorway, and the allure of her presence evoked a dull empathetic response from deep within him; '*There she is, and here I am,*' he thought, and said, "The self is an intangible product of pretense. Many would disagree due to the ego.

164

I presume you identify with solipsism if you desire to undergo rigorous introspection; I advise you against this due to experience, for my own mode of being is a self-engrossed delve into the 'self,' and by extension the human condition; I'm a sad and disappointed man, as a result. Your comparison of entropy and the aforementioned quote is astute. I place all my faith and hope with entropy."

The concubine postured herself a few inches deeper into the doorway, cleared her throat, shifted her hips, and said, "When I say 'I' or 'myself,' I'm not referring to my 'self' as most folks do. I'm referring to my whole self: past, present, future, intangible, higher, mortal, ethereal, physical... Without that acknowledgment then *how* and *why* do we proceed through life and not lose ourselves to the constructs of a shamelessly 'evolving' world? I've transcended the ego through meditation and have seen my silver cord. After that, a lot of change began in my life."

The hermit glared at the concubine and said, "What is your silver cord?"

"*It* links the physical body to the higher self. Last year I was going through a rough patch, and at the time I was avidly practicing hot yoga. One day after an intense Balkan Method Hot Vinyasa class I went into Shavasana to meditate... I heard nothing, saw nothing, felt nothing. I was nothingness. I experienced a sensation equal to a bolt of lightning strike from the base of my sternum and expand outward into the abyss; I saw an opalescent cord-chain grow from me, what looked to be a double helix. I later told a *very* dear friend of mine what had happened and he explained what *it* was."

The hermit continued to glare, unblinking, and said, "A man once told me that he saw the walls of his bedroom illuminated with the golden light of God and was changed ever since."

"Well," the concubine's eyes narrowed and she looked the hermit up and down with a wearied countenance; an impression overtook her, that she had, at that moment, met with a new, unfamiliar, and uninspired man, "I believe in myself. I am my own God. That experience expanded my sense of self."

"If you transcended your ego, why do you defend *it*?"

"*It*'s part of me," the concubine snapped.

The hermit shifted his eyes over the concubine's shoulder and observed the sun halved by an ocean horizon.

The concubine veered out of the doorway and waited for the hermit to initiate with an action or spoken word. Four seconds elapsed, and with jovial venom expressed in her tonality, she said, "What is ego transcendence without an ego?"

The hermit feigned a yawn and said, "To transcend the ego would be to elevate yourself above the ego—to strip *it* from your humanity; *it* would no longer be a part of you."

Without another word spoken, the concubine turned, mounted, and urged the horse into a full gallop. The hermit's book, once clutched with reverence by her hand, laid in the dirt a meter away from his feet.

February 20th, 2019

1:15 AM

I yearn for days, a little over a year ago, when I suffered the apex of self-induced insanity. Two, two-hour strength training sessions a day while fasting at the bodyweight of 135 lbs at the height of 6'1. Grocery store labor. The wretched inner ego spoke lambastes while I prostrated alone in a small square room—windows layered with opaque plastic, and I shed tears onto a carpeted floor. My writing achieved a certain 'oomph' while I sustained a madness of self-perceived maligning. Albeit I'm *still* afflicted with 'intuitions' and projected ego-speak if I am to refrain from the flow of thought—such as now; however, I no longer care, for I ~~understand~~ comprehend myself, and accept the conditions of my humanity.

Parental issues have abated, alongside feelings of inadequacy and worthlessness, due to the holistic experience of the *unique* perspective I project among the *sameness* of my fellow man and woman; this belief I have, that 'we are all the same,' is the root of my personal duress.

Socrates, Buddha, and Jesus as *characters* never existed—the men *may* have, though the paragons of philosophy, spirituality, and virtue, respectively, as the general populace knows of them due to symbols read on internet venues or in books, is moot. How do I 'know' this? These men were *just* men, human beings who suffered, lied, and died, the same as anyone else. They are names, glamorized as glorious symbols for the ideologies each represents. Is Jesus not an idol for the Christian god?— what *blasphemy*, son or not.

The books and lectures fail to record the gray areas: shortcomings, failures, hypocrisy, mundaneness, vices, grievances, of every individual deemed "great."

All achievements and advancements are at the detriment to the greater good of man.

"Ah—no," said an opinion, "Fire is the quintessential example of advancement that allowed humanity to persist and evolve."

What of *it*, I wonder, if we were to still be fireless hominids, deprived of the Promethean boon, lost in the darkness with nothing but insufficient rations of raw meat, berries, roots, and vegetation. Imagine the beauty and the spectacular brevity of life, the incalculable terrors, the insurmountable odds… oh yes, we're *much* better off with civilization, where we grow old, occupy ourselves with fanciful nothings, and seek stimulation with all the achievements and advancements we've attained, yet none of us would know what *it* **is** to *be* ~~alive~~.

What of *it?*—after a metanonfictional exposition of my character development, I validate that I'm ~~sane~~ a functional member of society, designated for the military.

Now I lay me down to sleep, I pray for Death to come and reap.

2:51 AM

While I washed dishes this evening, I failed to imagine the suffering of one burned to near-death over a pyre and afterward thrown into a cold, lightless dungeon cell filled with stiff hay.

February 20th, 2019

6:02 PM

I sit within a street-side bar at a table in the middle of the most active part of the city and gaze out the window towards the rows of shops, eateries, and bars—my domain of labor being one of these venues. A bartender has asked to serve me water; I've accepted; he called me "friend" on deliverance. Upbeat acoustic bluegrass music plays. I'm the single patron. 10 lbs of steel-cut oats, 5 lbs of almonds, and a bottle of apple cider vinegar are in my backpack to my immediate right. A new box of condoms and a bottle of silicone-based lube is in the top compartment of my pack.

I wait at the bar in the expectancy of an effeminate married man who has solicited me for sex at the establishment where I work and arranged for this meeting. He desires to perform fellatio on me and for me to "top" him; I accepted to meet him after little persuasion out of curiosity and boredom. He is late.

8:18 PM

I endured an hour at the bar, seated at a table closest to the window, and noted the steady influx of socialites and drinkers. When I stood from my position, estranged from the convergence, my aspect drew stares of intrigue from many women and glances of unease from a few men. I stay away from these damnable cesspools of hopeful fornicators for a reason—yet there *I* was—hopeful expectant of homosexual fornication.

I proceeded to edit last year's writing and corresponded via text message with my would-be partner while he waited for his wife to leave his home; he said, "You have a great body by the way."

"Thank you. Fine flattery."

"Are you bi?"

"I think so. I'm mostly bored and disillusioned."

"I hear ya. Been with many men?"

"No, one other for strictly sexual means, older than myself. I didn't enjoy *it*. Yourself?"

"One a long time ago… What did you not enjoy?"

"The male form, and we didn't connect well."

"How old are you?"

"Twenty-seven, you?"

"Thirty-six. You're pretty cool my friend. My wife is on the phone with friends now."

I waited ten minutes, messaged, "I'm going to head out. I tend to avoid bars," donned my pack, thanked the bartender for the water, and departed. On my arrival at the abandoned house of my father, our conversation resumed; he messaged, "Damn… I wanted you so badly tonight. Can you host?"

"I can host, though the conditions aren't comfortable."

"Why so?"

"I live an austere life with minimal furnishments and sleep on the floor."

"Sounds rough. Oh God I wanted to make you happy tonight."

"You may be unable to make me happy. The decision is yours; if you're too circumspect of meeting a stranger to be ass-fucked in an unfamiliar house, I understand."

"I'm glad you do. I'm free Monday, let's do then?"

"Alright."

"Excellent! Send me pictures of your delicious body! Please."

I didn't.

Why I subject myself to circumstances I am uninclined for is a matter of whimsical fancy and ego validation. Some men desire me to penetrate them, some women do; the men are more impudent than the women and I've yet to experience what factors render intimacy with a man to be unpleasant in the ways I have with women. I predict more of the same. Flesh is consistent.

February 22nd, 2019

1:32 AM

Howard, the peculiar bartender who peers through windows and acts bizarre to elicit reactions, has gifted me Ayn Rand's *The Fountainhead* and *Atlas Shrugged;* I am indebted to him.

I've finished *The 48 Laws of Power* and am compelled to reflect on the top five laws—per the text—I practice in my writing in order of magnitude, "1" being the most prominent:

1. Recreate yourself.
2. Assume Formlessness.
3. Make your accomplishments seem effortless.
4. Enter action with boldness
5. Plan all the way to the end.

Despite my "power" practiced through thoughts committed to action, I forsake all my power by committing myself to the U.S. Navy. The longer I must wait to ship out and begin boot camp, the more I am concerned and confound myself with the immense possibility *other* than the path I'm currently on; a four-year commitment is a long time to "serve your country" in a field I have no interest in (food service). I may postpone my ship date or enter undesignated for a Yeoman slot—absurdity and foolishness abound; I enlist for the potential travel, medical/dental benefits, and a slanted perspective of the human condition I may experience and record for the sheer engrossment of being alive.

At the end of *The 48 Laws of Power*, there is a preview to the proceeding book by Robert Greene: *Mastery*, which began with a quote by Goethe. Enthralled, I read onward and digested several passages I stopped and reread on multiple instances:

"**This inclination (towards a particular subject) is a reflection of a person's uniqueness. This uniqueness is not something merely poetic or philosophical—it is a <u>scientific fact that genetically, every one of us is unique</u>; our unique genetic makeup has never happened before and will never be repeated.**"

- Robert Greene's Mastery

Yes, this statement is agreeable; however, three pages prior, Greene had recapped the progression of the human species and our shared physiology due to evolution—the basis of humanity; in the realm of mastery, the above-quoted applies.

"**If we don't try too much in life, if we limit our circle of action, we can give ourselves the illusion of control. The less we attempt, the less chances of failure. If we can make *it* look like we are not really responsible for our fate, for what happens to us in life, then our apparent powerlessness is more palatable. <u>For this reason we become attracted to certain narratives: *it* is genetics that determines much of what we do; we are just products of our times; the individual is just a myth; human behavior can be reduced to statistical trends.</u>**

"**Many take this change a step further, giving their passivity a positive veneer. <u>They romanticize the self-destructive artist who loses control of him- or herself.</u> Anything that smacks of discipline seems fussy or passé: what matters is the feeling behind the artwork, and any hint of craftsmanship or work violates this principle.**"

- Robert Greene's Mastery

I agree and disagree with several points from these brief passages pulled out of the context of *Mastery* and shifted into my own egotistical realm of self-reflection.

If Greene disparages people who believe genetics determines much of what we do, why does he assert the "scientific fact" that genetics is what makes every one of us unique? We *are* unique in what we do—hence mastery... this is a conundrum.

I remain to be the self-destructive artist in the sense that I am primed and readied to forgo all friendships for the sake of continued practice, i.e., *Mastery;* my spiral into the unknown realm of chaotic indifference is no passivity or positive veneer (as I've made clear on my occasions prior; I've even considered the original title of this series to be *What Not to Do With One's Life*), this—*this* is an act of work; this is by no means effortless—*easy*—yes, and I persist despite my health and other obligations/priorities. Self-destruction *is* romantic.

The individual *is* a myth of our own designs. Human behavior *can* be reduced to statistics and has been for centuries—this is "scientific fact."

"We are just a product of our times," yes, this statement is foolish; on the contrary, *time* is a product of humanity, and culture is determined by a conglomerate of individuals with power wielded by each through the application of mastery.

Greene has developed a "mastery" of the consolidation of ancient history and wisdom rewritten in succinct format and proliferated as quasi self-help books; therefore, he is granted power through the acquirement of money, and what he invests in with that money—I don't care; therefore Greene is powerless to *me*. Albeit, I enjoy his writing style and the synopsis of world events accentuated by relevant margin quotations from famous and notorious dead historical figures.

I agree: In the realm of "mastery" we are unique, though the underlying fundamental condition is suffering, experienced by all. I must discover if Greene's propositions of what constitutes an individual's "uniqueness" extends beyond what I have already read in the preview and have thereby purchased *Mastery* (successful marketing); if not, my ~~mastery~~ belief of this condition has been postulated.

February 23rd, 2019

12:21 AM

An attractive young woman, a little younger than myself, exercised her thighs on a cable machine. I had never seen her before and we studied each other through the walls of mirrors. At the end of a dumbbell press set, I walked over to her, and thought of saying, *"I don't get out much; would you be interested and available for sex?"*

I said, "Excuse me." She (pretended that she) hadn't seen or heard me and gazed at my feet through the corner of her eye while she adjusted a weight pin. A loud beat played from her earphones that I could hear over the even louder club music piped into the establishment through an overhead stereo system. "Excuse me," I repeated.

"I'm sorry!" She stood, hunched, mouth agape, and pulled both earphones out from her ears. Mock surprise overcame her, or perhaps authentic, I can never be certain—nevertheless—a pleasant face ogled me expectantly.

I said, "What do you think of the conditions of society that we're in now, opposed to, say, the primeval times, and the fact that we're here right now doing this shit?"

"Doing what?"

"What do you think of the fact that, right here—right now, we're working to improve our physiology, opposed to what would come naturally if we were to live in the primeval times?"

"You mean like evolution? Like how we evolved?"

"Yeah—I mean to ask—do you think *it*'s absurd that we have establishments like this?"

"No."

"No..."

"No," she affirmed.

"Alright."

She laughed. I looked away, grinned, strutted back to the bench, and resumed my dumbbell sets.

"Certain writers, of whom I am one, do not live, think or write on the range of the moment. Novels, in the proper sense of the word, are not written to vanish in a month or a year. That most of them do, today,

that they are written and published as if they were magazines, to fade as rapidly, is one of the sorriest aspects of today's literature, and one of the clearest indictments of *it*s dominant esthetic philosophy: concrete-bound journalistic Naturalism which has now reached *it*s dead end in the inarticulate sounds of panic.

Longevity—predominantly, though not exclusively—is the prerogative of a literary school which is virtually non-existent today: Romanticism. This is not the place for dissertation on the nature of Romantic fiction, so let me state—for the record and for the benefit of those college students who have never been allowed to discover *it*—only that Romanticism is the *conceptual* school of art. *It* deals, not with the random trivia of the day, but with the timeless, fundamental, universal problems and *values* of human existence. *It* does not record or photograph; *it* creates and projects. *It* is concerned—in the words of Aristotle—not with things as they are, but with things as they might and ought to be."

- Ayn Rand's Introduction to The Fountainhead

I write this ~~novel~~ metanonfictional magazine with the intent of *it* fading on the moment of conception. My thoughts are bygone relics of what no longer is: an account documented on behalf of my ego, and later thrust into oblivion.

I'll leave the verdict to you, reader, for I will not return to *this*, and these thoughts may only exist with a reader to comprehend them:—if my writing is not both romantic *and* naturalistic.

February 24th, 2019

1:59 AM

Pelagia thanked me for the Hippocrates bust and accompanying plaque; she hugged me at the end of her shift, one more sensual than the previous. I chuckled.

My physical strength increases and my focus improves with every task I engage.

I deadlift at midnight, alone with my reflection.

On my solitary walk home from the gym after a Saturday night shift cleaning up after drunkards, whores, and the despicable, invisible snow began to fall and coated my hair with a powdery dew. Civic trucks spewed salt onto the main roads. Pizza delivery vehicles and taxis hastened past at regular intervals.

This account of mundane superfluity is reinforced with my *feeling*, which lasted from my departure from work, to my session at the gym, to the walk through the city, homebound, and *now*—where I stand and consume a can of sardines and prepare the nightly pot of oats: I reflect on my feeling of *hate*… Yes, not quite as monstrous as indifference, though a step above; I've improved; my hatred proves I *care*.

I care to hate the envious and resentful. I care to hate the unhappy who wish and strive to reduce others to their level of unhappiness. I'm surrounded by the hateful *and* loving in the kitchen, from the cooks, to the waitstaff, to management, the bartenders—and there I am, at the heart of the activity, the one person every staff member interacts with on account of their consumption and deliverance of waste and unwanted orts.

At the *Peaceorama* I attempted to subvert my ego with a lack thereof: a hubristic effort. Thereafter I attempted to divert my ego to a wholesome pursuit upon the realization that human life is impossible without the ego, and failed, due to the ego being "unique" in *it*s expression (i.e., *mastery*).

My hate is based in fear, for what my ego would become if I nourished and cherished my long-repressed *malevolent* indifference, to endeavor on the sublime route of corruption and deception, e.g., criminality, ambition, villainy; I could be all of this and more on a whim if I desired… this is the scary nature of the human condition—for we all could, no matter your touted benevolence, "good" deeds, magnanimity, virtues, and precepts; there is an error, miscalculation, misjudgment, disillusionment, and most important—chaos.

Hatred is tamer, discreet, and legal.

"The man-worshippers, in my sense of the term, are those who see man's highest potential and strive to actualize *it*. The man haters are those who regard man as a helpless, depraved, contemptible creature— and struggle to never let him discover otherwise. <u>It is important to remember here that the only direct introspective knowledge of man anyone possesses is of himself.</u>"

- Ayn Rand's Introduction to The Fountainhead

Perhaps my belief of all people being united through suffering is my faint hope to externalize my own repressed ~~psychopathy~~ humanity; I ~~refuse to~~ am fearful to acknowledge this possibility. All people lie, to themselves most of all.

3:08 PM

I wake at two o'clock in the afternoon to a setting sun and pensive emptiness.

February 25h, 2019

4:27 PM

A blackened field, charred to the dirt that once flourished with ripened corn, expanded beyond a red-lined horizon. Corpses of men littered smoldered divots. Morning air is tainted by the onset of rot.

A young boy approached a corroded iron fence: a three-mile wide barrier between a countryside road and the carnage; he gazed upward and reached for a decayed head crowned with mottled gray hair impaled on one of the innumerable fence spikes. The boy's bottom lip quivered. His youthful hand withdrew before contact, braced the bar below the spike, and recoiled to his chest, palm upward, fingers outspread. The boy looked at his bloodstained hand.

7:09 PM

I arranged to meet with the effeminate married man, again, downtown, at the same location. Entertainment seekers of varied social class and manner hurried by to converge at an event hosted at the city civic center.

My height, malnourished, with blackened curled hair made up into a haphazard style, the angular-faced man veered out from the dim light of a shopfront enclosure and hailed me, "Baethan?"

I stopped: an abrupt termination of my stride. "Yes."

"I'm Jimmy," he outstretched a gloved hand to me and beamed.

"Oh. Hello Jimmy. I didn't expect you here—at this location," I gestured both hands up to the title of a jeweler's shop above our heads displayed in bold white print against a black backdrop.

"Yeah—shielding from the wind."

We shook hands and continued to walk in the direction I had intended for, towards his home. Jimmy fumbled with his hands and eyed me up and down; he said, "I gotta tell ya' man, I'm nervous as hell," and forced a pained laugh.

I met his gaze while we walked and said, "I understand, you-"

"I mean I'm doing this to my wife and—I really wanna' do *it,* don't get me wrong."

I halted my walk once again; he followed my lead and we turned to face each other. Jimmy continued, "I mean I *really* wanna' do *it,* and you had to walk all the way here."

"Don't worry about me walking. I understand you want to be faithful to your wife-"

"Yeah."

"-and perhaps we shouldn't proceed with this arrangement if you're feeling..."

"No I really want to," his eyes lit up; he waved his hands down both sides of me, inches away from contact, "and I think—as I've already told you—that you've got a *great* body!"

I resented his statement, smiled, and said, "Thank you, but-"

"I'm just—I mean I'm doin' this to my wife and..."

I nodded and said, "Alright."

"I tell ya' what, let's do Wednesday night at five."

I stared at him for a moment with a warped projection of sympathetic disbelief and said, "I work all day this week-"

"Really?—Damn!"

"From two until ten, often later. *It*'s either now or next week."

"I guess next week then... shit!" He scratched the back of his head, said, "Hey I'm sorry brother," and reached out to shake my hand again. I reciprocated with a half-hearted jostle.

"*It*'s alright." I turned to go.

He opened his mouth to speak, closed his mouth, grimaced, and from thereon, he no longer existed, for I had retraced my steps to the central roundabout, deliberated my next course of action, and proceeded to a corner-side store for twenty-four eggs and a gallon of milk.

I have no intention of meeting with Jimmy next week, or ever again.

There is something peculiar—certain depravity, about a middle-aged married man who meets with a stranger with the intent of performing oral sex *on* the stranger, receiving anal sex *from* the stranger, and referring to the *stranger* as "brother."

This morning I contacted my recruiter and informed him of my decision to enter basic training as an undesignated rating [24] due to my disinclination of being a culinary specialist. My recruiter acknowledged my request; therefore, my contract renewal *should* be expedited with a ship date designated for March at the latest.

My "plan" is to "strike" for an "MC" (Mass Communications) rating while I undergo the life of mundane drudgery and servility (I'm accustomed, and imagine this won't change in the military); a side-career in journalism would improve the skills necessary for my personal vocation of ego distillment.

"Many of the greatest masters in history have confessed to experiencing some kind of force or <u>voice</u> or sense of destiny that has guided them forward. For Napoleon Bonaparte *it* was his 'star' that he always felt in ascendance when he made the right move. For Socrates, *it* was <u>his daemon, a voice that he heard</u>, perhaps from the gods, <u>which inevitably spoke to him in the negative—telling him what to avoid</u>. For Goethe, he also called *it* a daemon—a kind of spirit that dwelled within him and compelled him to fulfill his destiny. In modern times, Albert Einstein talked of a kind of <u>inner voice that shaped the direction of his speculations</u>. All of these are variations on what Leonardo da Vinci experienced with his own sense of fate."

"—Finally he (Buckminster Fuller) decided upon suicide as the best option, he would drown himself in the lake. He had a good insurance policy, and his wife's family would take better care of her than he had been able to. As he walked toward the water, he mentally prepared himself for death.

"Suddenly something stopped him in his tracks—what he would describe later as <u>a voice, coming from nearby or perhaps from within him</u>. *It* said, 'From now on you need never await temporal attestation to

---

[24] Undesignated sailors must "strike" for an available rating while they are serving onboard a ship to begin a career; meanwhile, undesignated sailors are the equivalent to a full-time custodian/dishwasher/sentry and are thus treated as invalids by peers and officers.

your thought. <u>You think the truth.</u> You do not have the right to eliminate yourself. You do not belong to you. You belong to Universe. Your significance will remain forever obscure to you, but you may assume that you are fulfilling your role if you <u>apply yourself to converting your experiences to the highest advantage of others</u>.' Never having heard voices before, Fuller imagined *it* as something real. Stunned by these words, he turned away from the water and went home."

- Robert Greene's Mastery

The ego manifests in a myriad of ways.

Hm, these are *classic* cases of mental illness—*no doubt!* These unfortunate individuals should've been institutionalized! Four out of five "experts" agree!

The greatest egos are afflicted/blessed with "unique" manifestations of delusional perceptions that fit a "rational explanation" in alignment with their time, i.e., culture and self-knowledge of how one relates to society. One may only conceive inner self-talk to be "God" if they are taught by an external source what "God" is. Daemons, spirits, your next-door neighbor's seance sessions, the government broadcasting commands into your brain, the wraith of your dead aunt, there is no difference in what you *believe* your ego to be; all must be *learned* to project.

For me, ~~telepathy, clairvoyance,~~ "schizophrenia," and thin walls/ceilings were my "rational explanations" on account of words I read on a screen—printed in books, and the spoken words of other human beings: no longer; I bow to myself, for my cross-referencing of lies and focused introspection has enlightened me of the truth of all *sanities*.

"I'm cured! Praise god!"

- Alex, in A Clockwork Orange (1971)

February 27th, 2019

1:40 AM

An uncanny circumstance is when one packs two cartons of cottage cheese into the bottom of one's backpack and thinks, *"This isn't a good idea;*

nonetheless, I'll proceed anyway on account of my evaluation of the situation," and on the trek to a destination, one slips on a patch of ice, falls onto one's lower back, breaks a carton of cottage cheese due to the impact, and thereby fills the bottom of one's backpack with coagulated curds. I'm thankful, for I am "one" in the circumstance, and this is part of God's divine plan; His holy design has shown me the light.

...the reading that I see. I cannot say it was manifest to the multitude, but to those few to whom it was already a token of her fallen morning, lost, but as it seemed to obtain there... then the import, after they all the examples of unchangeableness with respect to the end came... and so... in their countenance, and thus, as of God's being set... His light designs shown me the light.

MARCH

March 2nd, 2019

1:01 AM

A human mortal with the body of an immortal Goddess sauntered into a restaurant; she addressed a group of nine men seated at the bar: "Which one of you will be the one to sleep with me this night?"

All the men turned their heads on the sound of the angelic voice and beheld the incalculable grace and impossible features of the woman standing several feet in front of the archway of the door, framed by rows of blurry car lights visible from outside the establishment's immense wall-windows. Seven of the men responded with a gesture or a brief verbal agreement to be the one to sleep with the woman. Two of the men averted their eyes and looked down into their respective glasses of alcohol.

The woman sauntered on red stiletto high heels towards the two uninterested men who sat side-by-side, stood between and behind both, and said, "You two." The men glanced over their shoulders and winced at the perfect beauty while the seven other men watched in awe. She continued with a voice of subdued thunder, "Why will either of you not sleep with me?"

"You're too beautiful," said one.

"I have a wife," said the other.

The woman seized the man who claimed her to be too beautiful by the arm, wrenched him off his stool, and escorted him out of the bar. Flabbergasted and terrorized, the man submitted and allowed himself to be hauled off to the back seat of a limo with a driver obscured by an opaque glass barrier. "Drive," commanded the woman, and the driver did. She turned to the frail, middle-aged man beside her and caressed his balding head. Her supple lips pressed against his chapped lips, once, for three protracted seconds, and she pulled away, content with the manner his hand trembled on her own.

March 3rd, 2019

12:25 AM

"I want you to try to enjoy this as much as I will," said the woman reminiscent of a Goddess; she mounted the balding man upon a mattress of purple silks aligned with overhung red tassels on each side. Flickering lights projected from rows of wall candles penetrated the sheets and illuminated the enclosure with a tinted orange glow.

"Oh," groaned the man. "Try?"

"Yes, you don't deserve this do you?" The woman rocked her pelvis with the man's five-and-a-half-inch penis wedged within her vaginal canal. "Oh, yes, but you love me, all of me, don't you?"

"I-"

"Don't answer."

The man obeyed and watched, stupefied and struck with an implacable horror while the woman serviced herself.

I'm afflicted with a deep sadness; I reject all love. Crystalline reflections on a thin layer of snow on the sidewalks of Main Street during a midnight walk home distracted my mind from the horrid reality of my self-deprivation. I yearn to be manipulated; the sensation validates me, yet I abhor those who attempt… A quandary: to hate those who love.

Pelagia is the new head chef, a temporary position for the next three weeks. I said, "How do you intend to apply 'The Laws of Power' with the acquisition of your new position?"

She went on to lambast the old chef, Henry, who had left to never return; I enjoined her with the banter—indulged in her judgments, and expressed my disappointment with his conduct in regards to my ghostwriting (lack of finances to pay me), and for the passive-aggressive remarks he made against myself and other members of the staff. However, this poisonous banter ceased when I spoke a distilled venom; I said, in no particular order, "You gossip"; "You are volatile about others behind their back"; "You don't know yourself."

Pelagia veered in and out of the kitchen while I finished my labors, both of us hurt by my words. She spoke her "goodbye" from across the room and we locked eyes for a brief moment before she spun towards the door and pushed herself out into the night.

Pelagia messaged me two hours later and expressed how her desire to invite me to "tea and conversation" at her home had been nullified on account of being repulsed, embarrassed (she slipped on grease), and insulted. She believes I am "Intensely prideful, yet impulsively ignorant."

4:31 PM

The woman reminiscent of a goddess returned to the bar and beheld a young man of Olympian standards seated between thirteen other men, two empty stools to his left, one empty stool to his right; his powerful aura of overt masculinity, intimidating physique, and flawless visage tempered the other men to silence. The goddess and the Olympian reckoned each other; his sky-blue eyes pierced into her own radiant green. He slammed an empty glass onto the counter, stood, and strode towards the goddess. Both continued to acknowledge the other with infallible gazes, and while he shortened the distance between them, the goddess said *through* him, "Which one of you will be the one to sleep with me tonight?"

"I am the one." The Olympian's immense chest pressed up against the goddesses' well-proportioned breasts.

"Yes," she said.

All thirteen men at the bar conceded; seven men glanced up, and on observation of the two resplendent examples of humanity, reburied their countenances into their respective drinks. Three men rustled on their stools and moved their lips to speak, though they did not. Three men recognized the voice from the night before and chose to remain entrenched with their current pain and woe.

"We're a match made in heaven," said the Olympian; he mounted the goddess atop a bed of purple sheets overhung with red tassels; his pronounced abdominals slid over her supple belly as he entered her and lowered his face inches above her own.

The goddess glared through him and squeezed her breasts together with her biceps.

The Olympian stared at his orange reflection captured in her corneas and proceeded to enter and leave her with powerful, rhythmic thrusts.

March 6th, 2019

1:16 AM

Well, I've done *it* again: I've "fallen in love." I felt *it* encroach; the sinister tendrils of interest have magnified to infatuation and engulfed me with the long-lost, albeit well-acquainted feeling that we name "love"—yes, I say *it*.

Pelagia, the damned harpy, has bewitched me with simple laws of human nature: she has garnered my attention nonstop since I began my labor at the bar and has behaved in a way suitable to my esteem; we are broken and retained in similar modes of self; therefore, we identify with and ingratiate each other with our egos.

After a night of suppressed emotions and restrained eye contact, when Pelagia and I were alone, she said, "I'm sorry for lashing out at you."—concerning her comment of me being, "Intensely prideful, yet impulsively ignorant."

I stared at Pelagia; she looked down and moved to walk away; I said, "You don't need to be." She waited for me to expound; I didn't; however, I followed up with, "I accept," and turned back to my labors.

Minutes later, I walked over towards Pelagia's station to procure any dishware in need of cleaning. I looked at her and saw the pain, sadness, and remorse etched on her face. She looked at me, and her eyes welled up with newfound tears. We gazed at each other; I advanced three steps and embraced her in a hug. She wept, *a little*, and whether the tears were forced or authentic, I, the bearer of another's inner anguish, gripped her tighter, for the duress is shared among us both on account of her pain—dissimulated or genuine—being my own; and my own, her's. We disengaged and said nothing. She has a peculiar manner of pulling her beanie down over her face and back up over her forehead—adorable; I don't understand the idiosyncrasy and never intend to ask; to know would negate the enchantment. I nodded in understanding and she stood, embarrassed and forlorn.

On my return to the dish pit, I began to curse and hate myself with renewed vigor, for I felt the sincere care for another fester to the forefront of my conscious thoughts.

She deposited a few pans by my sink; I ceased my labor and said, "When I said you don't need to be sorry, I meant that you shouldn't be."

"Why?"

"Because I agree with you." We smiled and chuckled together. "However," I continued, "I don't understand how one can be *impulsively* ignorant."

"That… was a poor choice of words," she admitted.

"You contradict yourself. A hypocrite."

"Yes-" she provided me examples of my recent hypocrisy in relation to our verbal skirmishes.

I beamed with an unwarranted satisfaction and said, *"It's* amusing to me that you deem me a hypocrite, for that's the name of the book I'm currently working on." We laughed, and I expounded through my laughter, " 'Outbursts of a Contented Hypocrite; Thoughts of an Enlisted Slave.'"

The conversation became convoluted and multilayered henceforth for the remainder of the night. We spoke our goodbyes and while I mopped the floor I knew that I must visit her for "tea and conversation," despite my past proclamations of self-assigned social ostracism and sought-after notoriety among any tribe I associate with—there is always *one* foul temptress—a wanton succubus—a deceptive courtesan; I am drawn to these manifestations of self *due* to my aforementioned proclamations and conduct: no strings attached. Sir Galahad—there is no such legend, for legends exist only in mind.

At the gym, after training, while I donned my boots for departure, the woman who receives great pleasure from a conversation with me, Mia, began to speak: polite and easy-going, I endured her flattery and compliments on my strength progress and discipline... I inspire her, apparently, more than any other she's seen at the gym, due to my "tenacity and desire to improve for a cause (The Navy) rather than trying to impress girls when you take your shirt off-" a bold assumption to make on my behalf; I stymied discussion of *me* with an inquiry:

"Do you believe there is a true, authentic self?"

"Yes."

The conversation evolved from identity being a constant state of becoming, to her belief in reincarnation, to inner voices; I asked what manner of inner voice she hears and she disclosed to me that her inner voice directs her to engage in friendly discussions whenever possible and to help people whenever she can-

"To validate your ego?" I interjected.

"Yes, I only ever experience a friendly inner voice; I never judge people because I don't like to be judged. I feel good and *it* gives me purpose whenever I help someone."

"Do you experience a first-person or third-person inner voice?"

Her countenance shifted to a quizzical pondering and she said, "Never first-person, always a guiding, helpful voice that suggests I do something or one that brings a particular person to my attention."

"So, for instance, if you saw a young girl crying on a bench, would your inner voice chastise you if you were to ignore her?"

"Hm, no, *it* would say something like, 'There's a girl crying over there, what are you going to do?' and if I were to walk on past the voices would stop. I feel good about myself whenever I follow my inner voices' lead and what *it* suggests. What about you? Do you have an inner voice?"

I closed my eyes for a single second, inhaled, and said, "Yes… My inner voice is… malevolent, hateful, and disparaging. I'm compelled to pursue self-flagellation and abstention from relationships whenever possible while also behaving with dignity, grace, and integrity for the sake of society. I must always be working and must abstain from entertainment; if I fail, I am ridiculed and tormented by a man and a woman: two manifestations my ego assumes."

"Oh… *Oh* sweetie, why?"

I laughed… Damn *it* all, I *laughed,* shrugged, and endured more of Mia's ~~flattery~~ ego; if I knew, I'd know myself, and would have nothing to become; I'd be awestruck with the brevity and depth of my self-acclaimed wisdom and succumb to atrophy-before-entropy.

I returned home and checked my phone. Pelagia sent me a recording of a song she wrote, recorded, and played on an open windowsill twelve years ago: a two minute, low-quality recording of her singing and strumming a guitar; the harpy has the voice of a siren.

"I'm reading your book right now in bed," she messaged.

We arranged to meet at her home for "tea and conversation" on the 10th of this month.

I'm primed to enter the manslayer's den.

2:37 PM

Within the year 1979, in the city of London, there lived a boy named James who acquired a giant pair of jeans. He inspected his newfound possession in a department store changing room mirror and beamed. The contours of the oversized navy-blue denim billowed out from his small frame. He spun in place and peered over his shoulder at the bottoms hung in a loose rumple on a tiled floor; the top expanded fourteen inches outward in diameter around his waist.

James hopped in place, giggled, and ran his small fingers through a mop of youthful blonde hair on top of his head. He inserted a large black belt through the jean's waistband and pulled the strap taut to the final notch. Between each loop, mounds of crumpled fabric jutted out. He bent over and rolled 3/4th's of the pant legs up—just above his heels, and barged out of the dressing room, delighted with himself for all to see.

"*My,*" said the cashier; she raised a purple fingernail of her right pointer finger to her lips, unsure whether to smile or frown.

"Yes!-" James squealed, "Yes! Yes! *Yes!* Yes!"

The cashier's eyes narrowed and she braced both hands against the edge of the counter, thumbs underneath, eight fingers topside. "Right." Her visage settled on a grimace and she snaked an arm forward to accept the money James tossed down: bills folded into tiny, perfect squares. The cashier fumbled, cursed under her breath, and on the verge of an outburst, the implausible assembly of bills unfurled. "Thank you," she muttered.

"Yes! *Yes!*" James bounced in placed and locked gazes with the cashier; she stared, horrified by his bulbous and strained green eyes, and imagined the jeans were a misshapen weight preventing him from lurching upwards through the ceiling and beyond. James lumbered between the department store racks towards the exit, his gait reminiscent of a crippled old man burdened with a full diaper.

James emerged into a bright, rare, cloudless and sunny day of London and screamed; his fanatical ululations garnered the attention of thirty-eight passerby. Men sneered, boys jeered, and women turned away, though one little girl approached: a familiar schoolmate of small stature, with ear-length curled red hair, and a face full of freckles around a close-set pair of beady brown eyes; she said, "James!—your *jeans*… they're *enormous!*"

"I love my jeans—I really do—Margaret!—Don't you love them too?"

"I-" began Margaret; her nose wrinkled, and she stopped, observant of the way in which James bobbed upwards and down akin to a wound-up mechanical toy, the way he swayed in expectancy of her answer, and his stupefied grin which prompted her to reciprocate a malformed smile of her own. "Yes, your jeans are lovely."

"Well you *can't have them!*" he yelled, inches from her face; she retreated two steps, flustered, eyes closed, brows raised, head sideways, steadied herself, and opened her eyes with intent to chastise and critique, though James had bumbled several meters down a cobbled street toward his uncle's home.

The reinforced wooden door to the street-side home flung open and James' uncle looked up from the desk of his study. "James…" he began.

"I *love* my *jeans!*" James hollered; he assumed various leg-dominated poses, accentuating the disparity of dimensions between himself and the denim.

"James, those jeans are much too large for you; you look ridiculous; take them off at once."

"No! I love them, Gregor!"

"Did you just purchase those?"

"Yes."

"Do you have the receipt?"

James extended his arms straight over his head, trancelike, and lowered them—palms flattened over his chest, down to the jeans, whereupon he aligned both hands to steady against his rotating hips. "No!"

Gregor leaned his elbows onto a pile of paperwork, clenched his nose bridge between the thumb and middle finger of his left hand, pushed his rounded spectacles up closer to his eyes, and said, "James…"

"I love my jeans!"

"… Alright James."

March 7th, 2019

2:33 PM

Ayn Rand was a crusader who wanted to save man from himself.

Two fools sat on the edge of a flat boulder embedded into the sands of a vast beach, hand-in-hand.

The woman sighed, smiled, and said, "Are you entirely cynical or do you find beauty and joy in the abnormalities of life?"

The man stared at the edge of a night sky framed against the ocean's edge: a harsh blackened murk against a tapestry of stars; he closed his eyes, thought for a moment, cocked his head, averted his gaze to the bottom furls of the woman's plain white evening gown and said, "Life to me is an anomaly. There is beauty in the most mundane… That's a multifaceted philosophical question, and to answer *it,* no, I'm not entirely cynical. There is beauty in suffering."

"I understand. There being beauty in suffering is the reason why I find part of our interactions to be beautiful."

The grips of both their hands enfolded around the other tightened.

190

The man said, "I understand."

"I don't necessarily like that I'm becoming more comfortable with you in this manner. However, I am open and upfront… I thoroughly enjoy hugging you."

"To disclose that you're open and upfront is a pretense. Regardless, every hug I've shared with you has conveyed an array of intense, convoluted feelings that I've enjoyed all the same."

The woman's grip relaxed; she adjusted her posture and said, "*It*'s not a pretense."

"I believe *it* is," the man spoke with a tonality devoid of emotion, "in a similar manner of when one declares, 'I'm honest.'"

"I agree—but not in most situations for me."

They sat for a long while in silence and listened to a muffled wind blow over the expansive grasses of plain lands to their rear and the still seawater to their front. Both leered at the nothingness, internal and external; their breathing synchronized, and each waited for the other to speak. Their bodies numbed and the interlocked web of their hands dampened with cold sweat. The woman said, "Sometimes I feel like you're trying to strangle me with my words. *It* won't work."

"The feeling is self-imposed."

"I know," said the woman; her eyes glazed, unblinking, and she stiffened from foot to head.

The man exhaled: an exasperated, subdued acknowledgment of the rift between them despite the proximity of their bodies and the entanglement of their fingers; he said, "*It*'s in our nature to be hypocrites."

"I'm exhausted right now." The woman slid a few inches away from the man though their hands remained entwined, suspended between them over the smooth rock. "I would love to continue a conversation that challenges me beyond what I thought was-"

"I acknowledge that my cold, impersonal, and awkward demeanor is a pretense of indifference, and that I know you seek a lover opposed to a chess player, though isn't *it* stimulating nonetheless?—perhaps for me at least; there's a flair of comedy about our relationship and I enjoy you immensely."

The woman whispered, "You've awakened me."

"A little distilled emotion did the trick, a dash of charisma?" the man winked and tugged at her hand.

"Silly—human *me*."

"Yes, I had thought that you liked me better when I was cold and heartless."

"That's not true."

"Understood."

"I just like you as you until I don't. Goodnight." The woman shifted her legs, moved to stand, and the man renewed his hold on her; his thumb pressed light against the top of her palm and he said, "Yes, I understand enough to cancel our meeting three days from now and to refrain from communication except in a professional manner."

The woman turned to him, looked down at his stern visage, and said, "I'd prefer otherwise. We maintain our remotely professional relationship during work hours together and we follow through with our plans."

The man's face twisted and revealed a perplexity unknown to himself; he said, "I want nothing from you. What do you want from me?"

"If I were to say nothing, you'd think I was lying. If I were to say sex and physical comfort, you'd think you were right. If I said simply to be as we are, you'd be skeptical."

"You're right."

The woman's face softened; she said, "I know. The truth is, I have no idea—though you're lying when you say you want nothing from me. Maybe 'want' is the wrong word…"

The man stood and leveled his gaze with her own; eyebrows raised and shoulders back; he said, "I admire your truth. I'd prefer everything you said except the 'nothing,' for the benefits of my physiology and the experience, though my rational facet urges me to refrain. I have no idea either." He winced, shrugged, and continued, "And there, you have my admittance of feelings and motives, unabashed. Well done."

"Checkmate. I feel the same."

"Did you get what you want?"

"Not yet. Did you?"

"I'll meet you in three days. Goodnight."

"Goodnight."

They both stood and focused on each other's eyes; diminutive grins accented their somber expressions, and they sat together, fingers still interlaced, and persisted in this manner for sixteen minutes. Neither spoke or moved, though both breathed deep cyclic rhythms. The cold sweat between their palms dried and they separated with the acknowledgment of each other's suppressed sadness.

March 9th, 2019

2:03 AM

Pelagia is headed to my home via an "Uber" vehicle; she is drunk. I hate myself, not on her account, but because I hate to love.

No, I sat with this woman in the downstairs restaurant office through the earlier midnight hours and we exchanged sentiments. We are both unhappy; therefore, we are attracted to each other. We agreed that hate and love are synonymous.

March 10th, 2019

4:00 AM

I'm drunk on two glasses of red wine and a shot of tequila. I'm ~~in love~~ infatuated with Pelagia, my supervisor. Last night we engaged in intercourse on four instances over five hours; interspersed between these sessions, we conversed on life and enjoyed the idle carnal pleasure of each other's supine bodies.

After my shift, at midnight, I entered the adjacent bar and waited behind Pelagia, her boyfriend—Ryan, and a half-dozen other patrons. I stared at the back of the bartender, Howard—Pelagia's best friend and the man who has gifted me *The Fountainhead* and *Atlas Shrugged*. Ted, the social relations manager, offered me a drink, "on the house," for he encountered me first; I accepted: my first glass of red wine in years.

Ryan heard my order of the wine, acknowledged me, stood, and walked out the bar door; I noticed only his short stature and thinned hair. Pelagia urged me to sit in Ryan's empty seat; I sat; she pulled my stool close to hers, and I imbibed on subsequent two free glasses of red wine and dined on olives and sweet pickles. Pelagia's hands rubbed my legs, shoulders, and back. I walked her home to the apartment she shares with Ryan and arranged to meet her at 2:00 PM today at her home while Ryan—who she claims ignores her requests for sex and steals money from her—is away.

March 11th, 2019

2:34 AM

I love to love and hate to hate; hypocrisy, yet, there is no differentiation between the reversal: love to hate and hate to love; how can one discern between two extremes of the same spectrum?

My relationship with Pelagia deepens; joy and despair compound in equal measure due to this progression. Yes, there is much to lose and nothing to gain, for I desire only to enact my best character for her in my final two months before shipping out indefinitely with no intention to ever return. This matter is what I feared, though the relationship adds a dimension to my life, one that I cherish for the temporality and fickleness.

Pelagia is the most intelligent woman I have ever been intimate *and* carnal with. I desire to manipulate her out of fear of being manipulated, ~~though I refrain,~~ and the admission of feelings and thoughts I relay to her are unfiltered and foolhardy. I've concluded, despite my desire *to* be manipulated by another—for manipulation is not implicit of "evil" or negatively—I'm fearful of vulnerability. I torture myself with love. My ego shifts with years bygone.

12:15 PM

"Your false self is the accumulation of all the voices you have internalized from other people—parents and friends who want you to conform to their idea of what you should be like and what you should do, as well as societal pressures to adhere to certain values that can easily seduce you. *It* also includes the voice of your own ego, which constantly tries to protect you from unflattering truths."

- Robert Greene's Mastery

Greene would be an excellent ally to undermine the American Psychiatric Association; however, I believe the intent of his discourse is estranged from my own, for this is the final paragraph of the selected literature—affirmative empowerment:

"Your *true self* does not speak in words or banal phrases. *It*s voice comes from deep within you, from the substrata of your psyche, from something embedded physically within you. *It* emanates from your uniqueness, and *it* communicates through sensations and powerful desires that seem to transcend you. You cannot ultimately understand why you are drawn to certain activities or forms of knowledge. This cannot really be verbalized or explained. *It* is simply a fact of nature. In following this voice you realize your own potential, and satisfy your deepest longings to create and express your uniqueness. *It* exists for a purpose, and *it* is your Life's Task to bring *it* to fruition."

- Robert Greene's Mastery

Here, Greene's proposals begin to unravel due to the artificial mysticism of his claim; "something embedded physically within you," is reminiscent of a phrase one would hear uttered within the flaps of a soothsayer's tent at a carnival. The proceeding claim of the reader's uniqueness further aggrandize his words; the reader *wants* to believe in their own uniqueness and competence, and Greene is aware of this. He claims to "know" of phenomena beyond our understanding... *how*, if we *don't understand?*

"-powerful desires that **seem** to transcend you"; "This cannot **really** be verbalized or explained. *It* is **simply** a fact of nature." What pomp! What circumstance! What constitutes a person's uniqueness cannot be explained, yet *it* is a (scientific) fact of nature? I'll leave this puzzle to ~~the American Psychiatric Association~~ my *unique* reader, for I'm finished with my musing of what the ego is—there is, by the ennobled words of a recognized author (Greene), *nothing* to understand after all: Better to refrain from thinking on what you cannot understand—by fact—and instead read and compile the words of others into one large tome and regurgitate the concepts of others in a succinct, "educational," self-help doctrine.

A sad and disappointed man.

7:22 PM

I've terminated my romantic relationship with Pelagia. I love her, for her wickedness, for her cruelty, for her humanity. I wish I could be with her forever so that we may deceive each other with benevolence and enjoy the sanguine comfort of the mutual understanding elicited by the aforementioned deception. I hate her for her boundless love and selfish energy; she is beautiful.

March 13th, 2019

1:31 AM

Pelagia reinvigorated our romance after I resolved to refrain, and failed against her will; I reciprocated, eager to do so. My curiosity for her abounds and I am enraptured; we are a study for each other, a psychoanalytic delve into the social aspects of human deception. We embody dissimulation and manipulation. We "read" each other's ~~minds~~ gestures, body language, and calculate behaviors to identify genuine thoughts and feelings, and disclose this information to each other. I believe we are both ~~empathetic~~ ~~"psychopathic"~~ pathetic and desire to fill each other's symbiotic voids elicited from an embedded self-hatred.

Pelagia desires to please and be cared for, to overcome her deprived childhood of debauchery and dissipation; I desire the same (not to say my childhood is of similar experiences)... *We say*—to each other, that we desire these designs; in actuality, we desire to be annihilated; we desire to proximate ourselves near an outspoken mind akin to our own to reveal the faults of our characters—to be destroyed, broken, obliterated; we desire to suffer-

For the sake of *joy*—to be *reborn,* to understand the inner mechanisms of each other's psychology so that we may better understand our own.

I'm drained of energy after interactions with Pelagia, to my morose delight; oh, she is lovely, and has yet to disclose any negative remarks of my character to me other than, "You are intensely prideful and willfully ignorant." What more is there to say? I yearn to be burned to ashes and arise anew; this woman is capable and has yet to apply herself. I'm a romantic stoic, what more may *I* say?

9:57 PM

I've commented on a young waitress' intelligence and clarified this was not a compliment: instead, a challenge—for a conversation after her shift. She believes there is a true, authentic self. I intuit that she believes I am obsessed with the intellect. *No*, there is only an obsession with "why" and "how."

March 14th, 2019

12:21 AM

While the last table of guests of a slow Wednesday night calmed and finished their meals, a dishwasher and a waitress engaged in rhetoric inside a server's station:

The dishwasher said, "Alright—so on the idea of 'true authentic self'… Do you believe that there is one? Now, would you like me to present my theory to you first, or would you like to present your theory as to why you believe-"

The waitress smiled, swayed, and said, "I want to listen to your theory first."

"Alright."

"I'm just curious so—to hear you explain more."

"Alright. So let's say that, we're born—we are… all the same; human babies: we are pure ego. We are manipulative."

"Yeah."

"Would you agree that babies are manipulative because they are pure ego and only care for themselves?"

"In that sense I guess, yeah."

"Alright."

The waitress suppressed a chuckle.

"So we'll go from there then. As life progresses we accumulate experiences through our parenting, our culture, our environment, then, that's when our personality begins to manifest-"

"-Definitely."

"-and personality is just a pretense, and *it*'s how we get by—for instance, what I'm wearing now, is just a projection of what I want people to perceive about me, and as you see I wear the same exact clothing each day—a dress shirt, and *it*'s a respectable presentation, so people are immediately inclined to have a snap judgment about my character. Everything about me—my demeanor, my posturing, my facial expressions, my gestures, *it*'s all learned behavior that's a product of our accumulative experiences."

"Like our environment."

"…Yeah. So the self isn't authentic because, *it*'s just… a giant pretense."

"Well in the beginning, but once you get older like now especially like say when you get your own house, you really do become, what people like to say in their 20's, they're finding their self because you really are finding who you truly are because you don't have all these outside factors kinda controlling who you are cuz' *it*'s true! Especially the way you grew up, that way, *it* puts you on the path for the type of person you are; I definitely agree with that. But then *it*'s after when you still have these environments around you… or just, you, *utilize it?* Cuz' like, even like, I'm in school now, and like we're talking about—and *it* makes a ton of sense too sometimes—you just bind by that, and then when you do realize—I guess what you do after that *it* kinda makes you the person who you—like to really be authentic—there are people who aren't authentic I would say, those are people that just—the people who won't settle in life who keep like, I don't know—and they don't have one path." The waitress grinned.

The dishwasher said, "So you're looking at *it* from a finding yourself *into* adulthood perspective?"

"I guess in a way yeah."

"See, I'm seeing *it* from a general, humanity perspective."

"Mhm, I see that."

"As I said from when you're born, you're just an egotistical baby that wants food, attention, and comfort. And then, the moment afterward as soon as you're exposed to whatever environment you're in, you are immediately *shaped*. And then your character starts to develop from that. So-"

"-There are millions of little pretenses then. But…"

"And—being pretentious doesn't necessarily have to be bad, and neither does manipulation, and babies are masters at manipulating because guilt and shame haven't been taught yet."

"Mhm."

"*It*'s the only way to survive—even right now the interaction that we're having is manipulation, because we are impacting each other's perspectives."

"We are."

"And I'm impacting your own thought processes right now simply through speech, and that is just pure manipulation."

"You're right."

"You have affected my own as well. So *it*'s just mutual manipulation."

The waitress giggled and said, "You just love sayin' that word don't ya?"

The dishwasher smiled and said, "Yes, *it*'s common."

"*It* is common."

The dishwasher stared down at the floor and muttered, "In everything." He closed his eyes, inhaled through his nose, opened his eyes, gazed up, and said, "Alright. So have I convinced you?"

"Yeah. I uh, yeah, the way you were looking at *it* yeah, I see what you mean, but… I mean, the question that you're asking, yes, but *it* makes *it* sound like, we're also robots, and we all have no choice, I mean to a certain extent—like you said, we *are*, but I think to an extent. And then after that *it*'s like really—eh, *it*'s like adulthood and some people realize what they want to do when they're ten years old."

"On the contrary *it*'s not so much robots, but more… automatons, and we're all wired to learn behaviors in a certain way—so yeah, in a way *it* could be considered robotics, but we are *animals*."

"Yeah, we are animals."

"We're no different than say… well not that we aren't different, but we have the same chemical makeup of every animal on this planet-"

"-Yeah we're closest to mushrooms."

The dishwasher raised his eyebrows and inquired, "Our ancestry is closest to mushrooms?"

"Yeah on our ancestry tree we're closest to mushrooms. Look-*it*-up."

"I thought *it* was uh, sponges."

"Sponges are also on the family tree—I see what you mean. Yup!—that would be closer yeah…"

The dishwasher nodded and said, "Alright, I'll leave you to *it*." He extended his hand. The waitress reciprocated with a giggle, a limp wrist, and said, "Thank you, I appreciate *it* too," and giggled again. "Keep your mind thinking—that's good."

"Yes," said the dishwasher, and he turned to depart. "Have a good night."

"You too."

12:30 PM

Pelagia, the manslayer harpy, has entangled me in an emotional drama. She lives with a forty-two-year old-man, Ryan; he is a chef, guitar player, and per Pelagia's opinion: a brilliant man in the field of oddities, trivia, and the mundane, i.e., per my opinion, a pedant of the innocuous. She is dissatisfied with her relationship with Ryan due to his refusal to engage in sexual intercourse with her. I've met Ryan, once, at their apartment, a few hours after Pelagia and I engaged in sexual intercourse on their shared bed (on which they sleep wrapped in separate blankets). I've never been subjected to a more hateful, disdainful, and distrustful stare in all my life; the contours of his lips quivered into an unstable smile when I indulged him on the subject of his favorite literature. Pelagia observed us interact with the intensity of a deprived astronomer peering through the Hubble telescope.

Pelagia desires to rid herself of Ryan, though she is dependent on his validation and the sentimental superficially of his words. Occasionally, Ryan agrees to a sexual whim and the cycle of begging and self-hatred repeats. The anguish of their shared complacency is a comfort to both. I've attempted to upset the balance once, on my own accord, with a plan to speak to Ryan myself and inquire of the extent of his "cares." Ryan isn't on the lease of their apartment and Pelagia's opinion of their relationship is a matter of flux and calamity.

I am an emotional release for Pelagia; at work, she is my manager and supervises me; we've developed a superb empathy for one another, and I'm almost certain of our shared "psychopathy," for we understand *too* well, to the point of embarrassment, where even thoughts may be discerned and interpreted without a word spoken. In this manner, we desire each other, yet hate the reality of our attraction. Our union annihilates all pretense, and we have nothing left to show but the selfless, conscious, construct of flesh that we are.

Our shared empathy is of a null understanding of what love is.

Pelagia discloses and elaborates a plethora of her secrets, psychological upsets, and self-conscious focus to me—though I believe she does this to all she meets, as a personal test conducted for potential mates, to verify whom among the vast pool will accept her for what she portrays herself to be. She desires to please men—many men, as often as she can, without injuring those who she fraternizes with (dissimulation/deceit) so that her ego may be satisfied. Her strategies are blatant and graceless, which bestows her with an endearing charm, one of innocence and naivety, though she achieves this with a ruthless and cunning social intelligence. Once healthy and fit, she has now gained an unhealthy amount of weight and struggles with her loss of sexual power over men. Her beauty and elegance which once intimidated men unworthy of her esteem when combined with her social savviness, has been supplanted with an awkward uncertainty—though still beautiful, there is a vibe of doubt about her, to which men capitalize on, and when rejected by her—no matter how slight, these men will begin to treat her with contempt and malice opposed to admiration and respect... all due to a negative self-image prompted by the physical form.

Pelagia's desire for children is a tragedy; she yearns for a baby to raise on her own accord with the belief of her innate paternal abilities, yet she is unable to reproduce without a guarantee of the child's death. Impregnated with Ryan's sperm, she has suffered the loss of a recent abortion and has "yet to deal with the psychic trauma."

For myself, Pelagia is a catalyst for insight, thus, while she lamented in the basement of the bar we work at and expected my console (instead I informed our manager—who is also her close friend—of our "developing feelings for one another" and prompted him to console her instead), I proposed that I will pay her a full month's rent of nine-hundred dollars and draft a contract which will permit her power over my residency until my ship date as a method to end her duress with Ryan.

Oh *yes*, what sickness ails me—what foolishness—I hope, for the sake of my spirit, that she accepts the contract I've devised; I also hope, for the sake of my soul, that she rejects:

Temporary Residence Terms

This agreement is in relation to the apartment lease owner, Pelagia [Last Name], and the temporary resident, Baethan Balor.

On ___ / ___ / ___, the temporary resident will obtain rights to reside in the apartment of the lease owner. By 05/01/18, the temporary resident must relinquish rights to reside in the apartment of the lease owner.

The lease owner may, at any time, at their own discretion, chose to evict the temporary resident from the apartment under the name of the lease owner; subject to this circumstance, the temporary resident is ineligible for financial recompense of any sum of the $900.00 paid by the temporary resident to the lease owner and this contract is rendered void.

On ___ / ___ / ___, until 05/01/18, the lease
owner and temporary resident are to be the only
residents occupying the apartment under the name
of the lease owner.

The lease owner and the temporary resident
understand that if the **temporary resident** fails to
comply, this document may serve as justification
for legal prosecution.

Pelagia [Last Name], Lease Owner:_____

Baethan Balor, Temporary Resident:_____

I've wept in this woman's arms on behalf of the defilement of trust;
I've exposed my intent; we've manipulated each other to the point of
contempt, broken our wills, disenchanted and demystified every aspect of
the potentials of "love" in less than a week: I'm ready for marriage.

March 16th, 2019

2:04 AM

A night at the adjacent bar of my workstation alongside Pelagia, the
bartender Howard, and a few others—I am distraught and riveted to
exclaim that I am enraptured by Pelagia—with a will to be; I desire to be
executed with hateful love before my leave to east Illinois at the border of
the Great Lakes.

I'm enthralled by a malevolent witch: her spell cast over me—by
my own desire to be charmed! Yes, she engages in intercourse with her
boyfriend, no doubt, yet I proclaim my adoration for her—her faults and
all the humanity that she is! I drink red wine and feel her hand rub against
my leg while her boyfriend stands nearby and knows… I embrace her in the
basement while her hands rub against my erection, and she returns home
to her boyfriend's erection wedged between her thighs—I presume!—for
what else? Ah! What equanimous beauty is this!—life engagement of the
game, the one true game! My oats cook on a stovetop and I wonder, what is
it that I'm *really* after, my prerogative, my directive, my nexus… Ah—*this:*

this recording of every semblance of memory, for every mundane detail—
my life, for any to behold and cast judgment in reference to themselves.
Alas!—I am embittered with the cause of my own design.

March 17th, 2019

3:18 AM

Two more glasses of red wine seated alone at the bar; a few women and
one man spoke to me. One woman spoke inches from my face and brushed
her shoulder against my own: slim, fit, in her forties, a blonde with long
hair and somber blue eyes.

Earlier I had admitted to Pelagia that I think to myself that she is
a ho often, and in fact, have twice in the day; she had inquired of this
matter and I replied with truth, for the thoughts we speak are projected to
others and acknowledged. In fairness, I confessed that I am a "douchebag,"
for this is my status rendered to me by fellow judges of humanity—for I
fraternize with a woman judged as a "ho" by a majority of my peers. Thus,
my character (apathetic, industrious), in conjunction with this woman, is
judged in accordance with our interactions: She is my manager; and I, her
dishwasher and emotional support. After my blatant affirmation of her
suspicion of being thought of as a "ho," she summoned me into her office
with a request to "use me" for a particular matter. I entered her office and
she cried onto my shoulder. I held her for a while and gripped her tight,
though my thoughts raced with insults and proclamations of love.

Thoughts being our reality, she sensed my altered disposition the
longer we embraced each other; slight increments of disapproval with her
conduct and form incited me to lax the grip of my hands and to rub my
fingers in mechanical circles across her back while I thought of the growing
pile of dirtied dishware at my station upstairs. "Don't think less of me for
this," she wept.

"How could I think less of you?" I thought, and said nothing, insecure
with the manifestation of my own maliciousness; Pelagia sensed this too,
and pulled out of my arms. I intuited that she desired to push me away,
disgusted, yet she backed away with a slow retreat, gentle and unaffected.

Pelagia continued to lament her conditions: many varied factors—the
least of her concerns being the disclosure of my thoughts to her. Even after
the mutual denouncement of our character, she continued to engage me

for interactions throughout the remainder of my shift and we arranged to meet again tomorrow (today) in order that she is not alone on the date that marks the memorial of her grandmother's death.

This woman... I will not pity her, for I know she *chooses* to fragment herself for the sake of the approval of others—the most sought-after validation being emotionally unavailable men; she chooses this in a manner akin to how I choose to be hated, to be vilified and scorned, to avoid relationships. I often fail, and am instead admired and pursued—to my egos delight—by those I wish I *could* pity. Pelagia and I are the perfect match.

March 20th, 2019

12:58 AM

Pelagia and I met at a coffee shop before work and engaged in a forty-five-minute conversation on the topic of the essence of our relationship. The conversation was recorded by my recording device, though the dialogue between us is diluted and muffled by the varied voices of other patrons. In summary:

I conveyed to Pelagia my expectations of our relationship and the finality of what our relationship will be once I depart for basic training.

Pelagia and I pity each other as much as we adore and abhor each other. Hatred hasn't been experienced by either of us due to a lack of experience of love for one another.

When Pelagia speaks to me, she imagines I am "nonhuman," in the sense of my character being devoid of the fundamentals of social etiquette; she imagines my body to be "dissolved in pixels" and is left with only my mind to interact with.

Pelagia pities me for reasons she is unable to explain; she cites my peculiar "pretense" although we have discussed the pretense of humanity being a projection of culminated experiences manifested through an ideal chosen "self." Still, she pities me—for reasons *she* cannot explain—yet I know... she pities me for her understanding of life in accordance with her experiences and perceives my own life to be an example of one who lacks in experiences and is therefore pitiable. I pity Pelagia for her adoration of someone (me) she pities, for what she desires to fulfill in herself is the satiation of her desire for me *to* desire her; we adore each other for we are fit for each other's voids.

Society would perceive us and remark: "Lo, over ther' yonder goes a ho and a douchebag."

At work I must assert masculine energy to dissuade Pelagia despite her being my direct supervisor and strive to subvert her yearnings for validation; I hoped she would choose another man for this outlet and leave me with my inner peace, though she claims her work and cooking suffers if she feels unloved—therefore *she* is unable to work with "love"… yes… pigeon-holed into a quasi advisor role, I am abhorred for my asserted dominance by coworkers, all-the-while vulnerable to subtle attempts to emasculate me due to my subordinate position in the workforce.

This fickle game of push and tug is the cause of my chosen desire to uplift the designs of my life, though the energy is inverted: the woman pursues me, and I, the pursued, react! Masculine and feminine energies are polarized—in the *workforce,* though out of this setting, there is a role reversal, and my… how we do indeed adore and abhor each other…

We've arranged to meet each other again for coffee this morning, to expound on the sweet nothings of our nonexistent future.

I drank wine alongside Pelagia and her boyfriend Ryan at the bar. Ryan and I discussed the author Hemingway. I recommended to him, written on a napkin, Hemingway's short story, *The Short Happy Life of Francis Macomber.*

11:34 AM

I sit in a coffee bar now and squander my time waiting for Pelagia— yes, the social element of life has drained me of all personal thought; she supplanted my mode. I will never forget what she is: a harpy.

11:33 PM

I interjected at the bar into the relationship of Pelagia and Ryan; drunk on four glasses of wine, I asked Ryan:

"Do you love Pelagia?"

Ryan said, "Yes."

"Then fuck her."

And so there was a mutual agreement; I hope they live in contentment and happiness, for I am an outsider in all affairs. There is nothing else to us. I am nothing in a void of shit. There is an emptiness in me while I type this at a bar. I love Pelagia, in the adulterous manner, yet I admire her for her extensions of love. I wish to let her go; there is nothing else.

My self-assigned purpose is to write. The bartenders I've spoken to have no idea of their purpose in life. There is emptiness in all lives. Consumption, defecation, procreation—and now, in this particular context consumption is the singular constant: I sit in a bar…

Our lives are an ephemeral joke. I can't help but to laugh at the absurdity of my emprise. Of what I am, I have no idea. There is a mote of care, and I wish to help others to find themselves. I love, for the sake of hate.

When I cry, I may as well laugh, for there is no difference in the expression.

The judgments of others are fleeting motes of *garbage*.

March 21st, 2019

1:34 AM

A slit in my finger and a belly full of alcohol is null to the pain I feel for my love of Pelagia; we admitted this condition, intoxicated beneath a full moon, where we cried, and laughed into each other's arms. We kissed, and held each other, for a time I wish had been forever *and* unmemorable, yet I condemn myself with the memory by this act—I stand now, drunk, in my home, and engage in sets of pushups, consume a can of sardines, a cup of cottage cheese, and two bananas.

Ryan had sat at the other end of Pelagia while I engaged the bartender—who happens to share the same name as me—with the inquiries of, "Do you believe we are all fools?" and, "What is your self-assigned meaning in life?"

The bartender believes he has no meaning in life and that nobody is a fool—the conundrum of this belief system is equalizing, reminiscent of death; I desire to be equalized, even now, while alcohol courses through my veins and I desire nothing more than to be in the embrace of Pelagia's arms, my own arms around her, hands clasped against her contours, fingers through her hair, lips pressed against one another's, all-the-while—*locked*, in the *moment*, by a gaze into each other's eyes, heedless of other individuals, society, culture, civilization… there is *only* us.

A Chinese fortune cookie shared with me by Pelagia reads, "If you judge someone, you have no time to love them."

Is love not a judgment?

10:38 AM

Sober.

I laid on the floor, hungover, analyzed the previous night, and have reached a newfound comprehension of the relationship between Pelagia and myself.

The "mother" issues resurface.

Pelagia has "father" issues.

I exert feminine energy in my social relationships; I react, for I don't seek validation from others. I exert masculine energy through my work; I assert, for work is how I validate myself.

In our interplay, Pelagia and I pity each other; this is the basis of our "love," our understanding; we wish to consume one another, to break down, destroy, to annihilate; I believe this is *true* love.

I ignore her, and the more I do, the more she asserts herself, for she wishes to pity me as she would a child, yet I treat her as I would a girl in need of protection. When Pelagia is rejected the emotional validation of men, she reverts to an infantile state and becomes overly self-conscious of the judgments of others due to a dependence on approbation.

This is all-too-familiar...

We are self-conscious of each other, and we both believe we are capable of understanding the true intent of one another due to the fixation of our thoughts. The communication is multifaceted, for instance:

I began to think of ending the relationship with Pelagia as our shift progressed. I stood at the dish pit and reckoned the energy of our coworkers around us, *their* perspectives, and synthesized the combined thought pool into a directive that I perceived to be most beneficial for my current scenario; this behavior is what I imagine a "psychopath" to "feel"—*not* genuine care, but care which is in alignment with an ambition for the *self*, i.e., survival. To observe and glean the complete "picture" of interrelated events and to understand the ethics of a culture and how minor events will ripple outward and affect *your* reality.

When you delude yourself, you delude others. Am I mad to believe that Pelagia is a genius?

We enjoy the way we inflict suffering on each other, for the promise of joy hangs akin to a slackened apple from the Garden of Eden; our mutual directive is *knowledge*, self-knowledge, from each other. Neither of us *cares*—only for ourselves… yet we are ambitious in our work, and we have adopted each other as *projects*. Something to shape, an element to understand, a mystery to solve, and this is *only* because we understand one another; she claims to agree with everything she reads about me in my book; is this *"evil"* manipulation, or is she truthful? If she is truthful, I know what she is; she is myself. ~~: a "psychopath."~~

12:24 PM

Obscurantism:
Noun
1.   Opposition to the increase and spread of knowledge.

This word, with origins of conception based in the nineteenth century, summon to mind torch-bearing fanatics converged at a library of antiquity. Alexander the Great would've touted this word as his dogma.

A modern torch-bearing fanatic is a veritable sedentary social networking hacker.

March 24th, 2019

2:40 AM

Drunk again., ~~this is the final time.~~

I've met with Pelagia, also intoxicated, and terminated our relationship, again, for everything that never was or ever will be, for our unrequited "love," for what we "knew" of what love is:

A douchebag and a hoe?—many would perceive; I will never forget her face, her delightful visage. I care for nothing of the men or women she's been with or who she's with now. What is felt is human, a reckoning of *love*, the intangible essence of being… I don't understand *it*. There is no "psychopathy"; there is no "sociopathy"; there is only deviance from empathy, compassion, and equanimity. Psychology is a crock of nothing; I am appalled… I miss Pelagia already.

I stand, drunk with tears in my ears in the abstract comfort of my father's abandoned home and cry—for the sacrilege of humanity: ourselves,

Pelagia and I—mere motes who have no desire, no care, no reason, yet we "love," for what *we* understand.

There is forbearance in our wills. We are sanctioned by our lies.

I sat with an older woman and chatted with her at the bar while I consumed wine and a mixed drink; the woman placed her hands on my legs and arms, leaned in close, and stared into my eyes. Pelagia sat at the opposite end of the bar with her boyfriend, Ryan.

Yes, *it*'s selfish to cry; I've stopped, and stand affronted by my state of being, with full acknowledgment of everything that could be, the temporality of existence, and the loss of what I never had. A trace of solace manifests in my heart, for the merit of change, growth, and becoming.

I reiterate: There is no "psychopathy," no "sociopathy," there is only human, in the full spectrum of hate and love. The "psychopath" may hate himself and therefore be misanthropic, though a "psychopath" must love to hate. Is the manifestation of a "psychopathic" character the "truest" conception of a realized self? Acknowledgment and practice of virtues proper to a culture for the sake of survival: manipulation and adaptability… Yes, a "psychopath" is counter-culture—counter-*society*.

3:36 PM

Sober.

A "psychopath" possesses innate understanding, a mastered empathetic capability, yet the world and other humans are perceived as resources— as they *should* be, when life *is* a game of consumption. A "psychopath" expresses love through the mastery of their "self"; what contribution this provides to society is a byproduct.

A "psychopath" is vilified jargon; society is deluded by the term on account of media; one thinks of serial killers, perfect physiques, murder… demonized, and *always* misunderstood. The term *it*self is a delusion, a label created by the APA. Swallow your damn antipsychotics and be still!

6:55 PM

I respect my fellow man, yet there is something hideous and grotesque in my own reflection; a thing unnamed, dissatisfied, malcontent… when people see what they want to see when your aspect is reckoned, there is a diffusion of true authenticity of character. The *self* you know *yourself* to be is only real to you while others paint over the colors of your tapestry with their own designs.

I shook the hand of the dissipated man whose "girlfriend" I mounted on several occasions, sat with him for a drink, discussed philosophy, and bantered on the merits of the writings of Hemingway; Ryan may believe I sleep with "his" woman, a woman he fails to live up to the expectations of—in accordance to her perspective of him; yet what I see, is a hallowed husk of a man, overwrought by drug use, who follows Pelagia akin to a lost puppy dog. I see only a slave—in everyone, to our self-appointed meanings, our feeble whims and fleeting opinions.

Pelagia lied to Ryan and convinced him that she does not sleep with me. Pelagia lies to me and I choose to believe her. I lie to both of them without speaking, in my countenance, my gestures, my actions—all are pretenses for the sake of the betterment of my goals, my survival; I believe Pelagia behaves this way… Ryan, too, and all involved in this small circle of interpersonal relationships, and those related to every multifaceted circle of connections branching outward—all involved, *yes*—humanity: we are all the same, though the vast majority would deign to believe of the supreme uniqueness of their individuality, in the delusions of their personality. Some are impervious to the suggestion: a self-inflicted ignorance… though who is a fool to judge?

Yesterday morning, on my way out the front door of my father's abandoned home, I glanced at and held my gaze on my copy of Aristotle's *Nicomachean Ethics* positioned on an outdoor table within an enclosed porch. I thought of all I had betrayed of my previous *self:* my prevalent states of intoxication, my lust for a devious—wanton woman, my desire for self-destruction… the hedonism—all those I've condemned before. I have succumbed, in the brief time employed at the bar, engrossed by the culture. No longer an outlier in observance, I've enmeshed with the crowds of bar-goers and stood, glass of wine in-hand, at the centerfold of throngs of those no different than I: Lost—every one of us, throughout the resonant blaring of music, the sweat, the cacophony of speech, the touch of a hand against a shoulder, the rub of fingers down one's arm; there is an emptiness full of the potentials of what will never be.

When I hear "Hello," I think, *"Why?"* and proceed to lie if I am inclined to speak.

I've thought more about the actions and reactions of the interplay between Pelagia and myself: I began to copulate with her the day she assumed the role of my direct supervisor; I ceased all communication with her on the night of her final day of employment. Her closest workplace friends, Alton and Howard, have terminated their employment in the kitchen/bar, respectively, to join her at a new health food restaurant which opens a street away, with her as their direct supervisor. I predict the social affairs conducted within the new establishment will undermine the ethics of a respectable business. What merit is a respectable business?

I begin employment with a fresh slate, with a strange reputation entailed to me, one I am indifferent to; my choice to sever relations with Pelagia has solidified the general perspective of a douchebag and ho [25]— in my mind, and no doubt her own—for this moment; her newfound hatred (what I desired from the onset of our relationship) may tempt her to defame me and draw attention to her self-perceived victimization. Pelagia's relentless pursuit of me and my submission to her whims for the sake of my own agenda (experience, writing material, self-insight) is successful. Pelagia's reputation is critical for her success with her upcoming responsibility and she made a point to conduct our affair in seclusion. Anything she, or I, say of our terminated relationship to others, will shine a light on the deficiencies of our characters—a matter I am impervious to; my dishwashing role is estranged from the opinions of my peers and my station on the east coast of Illinois beckons me in a month and a week.

Henceforth, I resume my daily routine of writing and reading in the afternoon before work and attending the gym at night after my shift. The bar is anathema to me. I have repelled the manslayer—foul harpy and temptress, and have emerged from the fray unscathed, with my confidence intact... I loved and hated; our relationship represents a tumultuous maelstrom of inconsistent energies: lies, dissimulation, manipulation; unfortunate circumstances prevented what could have been an extraordinary lifelong correspondence and partnership.

---

[25] A relationship founded on lust is a strong predictor in the manifestation of character traits becoming of a douchebag and a hoe. I am a notch on Pelagia's belt, and she is a pseudonym in my book; I believe this may have been one of her motives, to which I am happy to provide her the means to sustain her love/hate, or adoration/abhorrence, or bitter contempt. I hope she is indifferent, or at best, content.

March 25th, 2019

2:08 AM

"I often think that he's the only one of us who's achieved immortality. I don't mean in the sense of fame and I don't mean that he won't die someday. But he's living *it*. I think he's what the conception really means. You know how people long to be eternal. But they die with every day that passes. When you meet them, they're not what you met last. In any given hour, they kill some part of themselves. They change, they deny, they contradict—and they call *it* growth. At the end there's nothing left, nothing unreversed or unbetrayed; as if there had never been an entity, only a succession of adjectives fading in and out on an unformed mass. How do they expect a permanence which they have never held for a single moment? But Howard—one can imagine him existing forever."

- Ayn Rand's The Fountainhead

March 27th, 2019

9:13 AM

Pelagia arrived at the bar's kitchen last night while I closed alone despite her no longer being employed at the establishment. She observed me around the doorway; when I looked up, she walked off down the hall. I had expected behavior of this manner, yet *so* soon, and *so* flagrant? Minutes later, while I swept, she returned; we reinitiated communication.

Pelagia stood, expectant, and nodded.

I nodded; we both smiled, and I approached with the feeling equivalent to the anticipated, dreadful excitement of the first drop of a wooden roller coaster.

We arranged to meet for dinner at a local sushi restaurant.

I now attempt to treat Pelagia as I would a woman I desire to pursue; I predict she will be repelled by me. Pelagia doesn't seek *my* attention; she seeks general validation. I will exercise tact with my interest.

A mongoloid wallowed at the edge of a lake of mud. "Oh, I enjoy this mud," he blubbered, and displaced his arms in vertical swings back and forth. "I'm filthy," he commented to a passing wind; his eyes slanted, nose crinkled, and brow furrowed.

I gifted Robert Greene's *The 48 Laws of Power* to one of the two owners of the establishment, Walther, where I am employed, and asked him, "What is your definition of love?"

A few hours later, Walther approached me while I worked and said, "Love is an oasis, always wet. Love is a well, never dry. You fill your cup, and *it* sustains you 'til the next thirty moment. And, in the rarest of loves, you are their oasis too."

I said, "Your perspective of love is romantic. Are you a father, or husband?"

"No, I am neither."

"I ask because I imagine you would be great at either role."

"Ah, well, maybe. I think my perspective of love is rather practical."

I failed to understand over the kitchen noise and said, "Is rather what?"

"Practical."

"How so?"

"You need water to live, correct?"

"So you compare love to a feeling that is required for the physiology of your body?"

"I don't know; if we knew, we wouldn't be talking about *it*."

"Ah, we know the weather, and that happens to be the most discussed topic of all."

Walther chuckled and began to walk at a slow pace; he said, "You obviously haven't been keeping up with the meteorologists." A brief pause ensued. "I think my perspective of love is allegorical with suitable visual imagery."

We halted and faced each other; I said, "*It*'s more metaphorical, there isn't any-"

"What do you do when you're thirsty and you're at a well?"

"Drink the water."

"And if the well is empty, you're unsatisfied."

"And if there was water in the well, *it* could be poisoned."

On my statement, he turned from me and continued to gaze over his shoulder, bearing the aspect of a man who had more important matters to attend to than a discussion on the philosophy of love with a dishwasher.

To love is to surrender yourself to an entity you hate, be *it*
a person, object, idea, or yourself, to embrace the polarity
of unification, to worship your self-destruction.

11:55 PM

Three glasses of red wine. Emptiness of the mind; self, remember
this moment, drunk—do *not* edit a single drunken word; remember how
Pelagia made you feel.

Pelagia sat alongside her boyfriend at a bar, after you shared a pleasant
dinner and drink, alone with her, at a restaurant across the street. You sat
with her and received her woe, her dread, her sorrow, and what do you
have of *it* but your own miserable dejection, alone in the night with a can
of sardines, a banana, and a jar of peanut butter? You paid for her and her
boyfriend's tab, you fool!—yet, you desired all of *it; all* of what you are
is *now*. You drunken bastard, don't you understand your wayward path,
your notions of romance? She doesn't want *help!* No! You sorry pleb; focus
on your task; what's wrong with you? Haven't you everything you desire?
What is a confiding glance, a promising eye, a feminine hand across the
shoulder, or a knee pressed against your own? Even a warm body to hold
onto—you have nothing, and what of *it,* you idiot—you lament to a screen;
you pound a keyboard for the sake of yourself. You blithering cretin,
why—why, imbecile!

She makes you feel human.

March 29th, 2019

12:11 AM

I finished my workout at the gym after a night out with Pelagia and
our workmate, Beatrice.

Both discussed their unhappy home lives and their outlets—male
companions (myself included, in Pelagia's case), while I drank a discount
martini.

The conversation ebbed on and I listened to the accounts of these two
women and their infidelity, ate a large chicken salad Pelagia bought for me
(against my desire to pay), and stared at rows of alcoholic beverages against
a mirrored wall. People bantered around me. Pelagia rubbed against me,

cast sidelong glances in my direction, stroked my legs, set her hands on my shoulder, and I *looked* at her.

Yes, I looked at her, this is all; I saw a void, an empty canvas, a reflection of the emptiness—a permeation of the spirit. I listened more—to the female bartender and my two companions; I heard nothing, a vile strain of nothings, from all angles. I sat with my beverage and finished the plate of food with a few fried chips set aside... I looked at Pelagia and she looked at me. I felt as though I loved her, uncertain of what love is, though the feeling was there, present, palpable; I yearned to kiss her and refrained. Instead, I withdrew, abandoned all pretense, assumed a cold, callous demeanor, and questioned why she invited me out despite me telling her earlier that day that I look forward to seeing her again. Pelagia answered, flabbergasted, confounded, at a loss: she expressed accurate observations of sensory input we had shared.

"Forget about me, Pelagia." I turned away and raised my near-finished martini to my mouth.

"You'd like that wouldn't you?"

"Yes, I would."

I watched her veer out of my peripheral vision, her eyes bleary; I didn't watch her go.

I haven't cried; I haven't lamented, I haven't "felt"; I don't intend to; there is nothing. I have no reason. I haven't tried to understand; I don't care—is this human, to desire to *not* care? I want, yearn, and desire, for indifference, for apathy, for an enemy within humanity.

I asked the entire kitchen staff and a few waitresses what their definition of "love" is. Most didn't want to begin to think of *it;* others expressed their lack of capacity *to* think... one young girl with thick-rimmed glasses giggled at me, blushed, and said, "I don't know, um, warmth and pleasure." I think she's right, and what of *it?*

I'm too selfish to love. I desire to hate, to convert this hatred to love for the sake of the self—to experience suffering for the sake of joy: an ephemeral transition between the equanimous sentiments of love and hate elicited through oxytocin and serotonin—to "become," until death; I am food. I "know" the way. I apologize for nothing.

Pelagia appeared at the end of my shift while I swept—again, a wraith, a she-devil, hellbent on the crystallization of her aspect within my mind's activity. She entered the kitchen doorway, spoke my name thrice, and whistled for my attention akin to how one would summon a dog. I bent my knees and peered at her, twelve feet away, between the silver counters of the serving station; we locked eyes. I gazed at her with a visage which suggested, "Really?" She returned my gaze with the look of a contented stoic and sidestepped out of the kitchen—our eyes still locked until our line of sight was broken by her maneuver. Witch.

Pelagia aspires to read of herself under the pseudonym I assign to her with meanings connotated to my interpretation of her character; thus, she attempts to be in my reality; she is a stranglehold on my creativity—I choose this, for she is a distraction from the mundane disciplines I enact with each bygone day.

An imbecile hunched over a dish basin and swirled coagulated water with his bare hands. An amalgamate of food clogged the entry to a drainpipe. The imbecile pushed on the amalgamate and continued to agitate the water. He sniffed, thought, *"Not bad,"* and listened to the suction of air through the slotted entry points. He watched the last of the yellowed water trickle downward and he prodded an opaque mound of white cheese adhered to the side of the basin with his right pointer finger.

"Yo Baethan," said a voice from the imbecile's rear; he whirled around and scanned the kitchen for the face correspondent with the sound: "Ima' make some fish bro, you want some, son?"

The dishwasher's lips loosened and he called out over the idle banter of waiters and waitresses, the sizzle of broccoli in a pan, the superheated air of an oven ventilated on opening, the dull thwack of a knife pressed against a cutting board, the monotonous tune of a radio song, and the discussion of next week's customer party agenda between an astute manager and disinterested employee. "Yes, thank you."

"Aight."

March 31st, 2019

3:29 AM

I am enraptured by nothingness. I chat with Pelagia, Beatrice, a bartender and a bouncer; all believe me to exert a "dominating energy," though all confide that I'm a "bit insane."

An aged beauty of a woman approached after Pelagia and Beatrice departed and left me alone. The woman called me by name due to the bartender's disclosure. Her husband sat and watched her embrace me; her nose grazed my own and she said, "I see you with your girlfriends tonight; I hope they don't mind."

I said, "I have no girlfriends; they all use me for validation, in a manner similar to the way you and I are validating each other now."

"Oh stop that nonsense." She pulled me closer and interlaced her fingers around my back.

"We all need someone to validate us, such as the way you and I embrace."

The woman slackened her hold of me, leaned back, and gazed into my eyes while I held the contours of her supple back in my palms. Her husband continued to watch us from the opposite end of the bar; I met his apathetic countenance for a moment and nuzzled my chin against the woman's shoulder.

"If you say so, Baethan (we had introduced ourselves to each other a few nights prior). This is a really long hug."

"I'll let you go then," I said, and let go of her.

She grazed my shoulders and arms with splayed palms and pierced into my soul with *want*. I turned away and raised a glass of red wine to my agape mouth.

APRIL

April 1st, 2019

2:15 AM

A month from today, I relinquish every belonging I own except a new moleskin journal and a set of clothing in preparation for the U.S. Navy boot camp: this is no April fool's joke.

My weariness of this realm of the world has climaxed manifold, at several points throughout my youth and young adulthood—to the present, whereas now, I await my final excursion.

I expect to meet many women—they've overtaken my mind with recent happenings… Pelagia, most notable, prominent, dominant, *singular;* one woman is always enough at any given point. I enjoy being entrenched in a mire of romantic machinations, more so if the experience is a detriment to my health and discipline: the greater a ~~challenge~~ hatred to overcome for the sake of this feeling we call "love."

Beyond women (though what else is there for a man, within the confines of a holistic, realistic, perspective of being?) I hope and aspire to be broken, to learn a plethora of skills, to develop disciplines, to achieve, to excel; I expect to be disappointed. The U.S. government glamorizes the military to civilians by the sentiments of proposed "honor" and "courage" in the name of the industrial war machine. In actuality, I expect to become the ultimate cog, enlisted for luxurious enslavement.

10:20 PM

On September 16th of last year, I vowed to myself to venture on foot, away from the town I reside in, to relinquish all relations and material items—indefinitely, on April 1st, 2018.

I haven't been derailed due to chaos; instead, I am constrained by order.

There is no "socio," "psycho," or "neurosis"; *yes,* devout followers of neuroscience and sociology—the brain *is* chemistry—a product of experiences, yet what is an institution, an organization, an entity, to determine the "right" and "wrong," the "sane" and "insane"; the proponents of what constitutes a healthy mind are in alignment with a productive workforce and therefore a safe, efficient society, governed by a doctrine of ethics and virtues by a hierarchy of *fools;* to overturn this fundamental notion, to acknowledge the merits of an individual's life, no matter how estranged and contorted one's perception of reality may be, is art. There is harmony in the designs of a serial killer, a pedophile, a terrorist, a rapist, a tyrant (Genghis Khan meets the criteria of all aforementioned titles)—a sublime element of the individual enmeshed *with* the whole: Essential, inescapable, we see ourselves in these characters for each represents a facet of humanity; without actions committed by the cruel, villainous, barbaric, maniacal, hateful, murderous, vengeful, and treasonous, humanity would be rendered *inhuman*. We *are* culture, from the first hallucinogenic orgy around a cavern fire, to the first "artificial" intelligence to emulate empathy, there have been untold atrocities committed for the sake of untold benevolence. When you dismiss the lies and shame, you reckon an animal intelligent enough to adapt, socialize, and cooperate for the sake of *it*self as the primary motive. The limitless beauty of perception has inspired the most extraordinary acts of cruelty and mercy in equal proportion; there is no other way.

My personal duress of the mind has abated with the onset of self-understanding; the "self" being what we "know" as empathy and the intuitions we apply: there is *no* "self"; there is *human,* from the malformed circus freak afflicted with a brain tumor that renders him devoid of empathy, to newborn twins conjoined at the head—there is understanding—the topic is banal, a wearisome back-and-forth, akin to philosophy and what constitutes the *way* and *being*… The answer is ~~destruction~~ ego, a perpetual cycle. This humanity: I gaze at my naked body and my hands which create these words by utilizing a device created by the actions of others, to be published, proliferated, and distributed; *my* perception, no doubt to be condemned as ignorant, baseless, tripe, is part of the *whole*. An anarchist, a revolutionist, an egotist or individualist—or a *fool?*—these are *words,* and what power they impart is merely a *thought*.

I'm aghast by the dependency of others—their need for validation by those who tout their credibility to diagnose… to diagnose another human being at a loss with themselves: a being unable, or unaware of their own *ableness* to *think*… To think… that's all there ever is; all else is nothing.

Happy Fool's day!

April 3rd, 2019

1:08 AM

I visit the "tavern" next door after my shift, an establishment owned by the same two individuals who own the adjacent establishment where I work, for two glasses of red wine. Within, I took my drink to an empty six-person table situated at a corner and enjoyed the first few sips. A spider crawled along the edge of the table; I watched *it* move in the reflection of a wide wall-window. I finished half of my drink and moved to the last seat in the bar. To my left, a man recognized me and outstretched his hand past his companion who sat next to me.

"Do you remember me?" he said.

I looked at him. "No."

"You're the guy who stopped into the coat store on the corner street a few weeks ago," he began to laugh; a large smile overtook his face the moment he had started to speak, "You stopped in and made my entire *year.*"

"Oh? Yes, I remember now—you."

The man encouraged his friend to listen and continued, his gaze shifting between the two of us. "You came in and asked me a question I'll never forget; you said 'Hello. Do you have a coat in stock that will make me look less like a douchebag?'"

"Yes, and you couldn't help me; I don't think a change of coat would help me anyway." I raised my drink to him, expressionless despite their exacerbated laughter, and thereafter, the three of us engaged in philosophical discourse of consciousness, reality, and their self-assigned meanings of life. The man holds a degree in philosophy and deems the boon useless; he works in a retail store and spends his free time on mountain hikes while partaking in alcohol, marijuana, and mushrooms. His friend—a self-accredited nihilist, wakes every morning and thinks, *"Oh why—here we go again with the same old shit."* I've been recommended a book by Max Stirner, *The Ego On Its Own.*

Pelagia desired to meet with me and I informed her of my location.

"I push you away because I don't like being the other man," I said to her; this being a half-truth, for there are a multitude of reasons why I strive to avoid her, yet I embrace her within my limited sphere of what I know as "love."

Pelagia said, "I know… I know…" and looked away.

I love this girl; she destroys me.

I said to her, "What is your definition of love?"

"I knew this was coming."

"How—are you reading my mind again?"

"No, everyone you work with tells me that you've asked them this same question."

"... *Everyone* I... Why the hell would they *tell* you..." I gazed downward with a resolute desire to disbelieve her, yet accepted the reality of the social norms, of how people talk, how they relay, how they observe—I being one, a single drop in a torrential deluge, only I tell *myself*—to remind me of what no longer exists at a point in the future.

Pelagia proceeded without heed of my disdain; in essence, she said: "I don't think love deserves a definition."

I shared my definition of love with Pelagia; she exemplified our relationship with a Venn diagram example: love and hate being two circles; the overlap being "us."

What would that overlap be? Contentment? Indifference? Equanimity? Peace? I didn't ask her.

What is the emotion between love and hate?

What is the point between empathy and pity?... Sympathy.

Between love and hate, there is no understanding.

Pelagia pitied me for my "lack of experiences" and praised me for "going out to the bar all on my own." She is incapable of hate or love in regards to me. This is bizarre. I enjoy *it*. She requested that I work in the new eatery she manages whenever I can from now until I depart. I will attend her dish room tomorrow.

We hugged outside the bar at midnight and refrained from "more" due to potential observers—at her chosen discretion. I hastened "home" on empty roads and cursed aloud with her name at the tip of my tongue.

2:02 PM

My father visited me in his abandoned home out of a strong desire to see me. I stood in my briefs and cooked breakfast; he arrived when I had just begun to eat. His first comment: "Pumped up!" in regards to my physique. I stood, indifferent, and chewed.

He relayed to me the activities of his neighbors and commented on how I don't stop by for eggs in the morning anymore.

I said, "I don't stop by anymore."

"I know—why not?"

"I don't want to."

"Why?"

"You're a bad influence on me."

"Oh sure, Baethan. I'm the guy who raised you and loved you all your life and I'm the one responsible for all your bad behavior? Really?"

"You said that, not me, so if you want to get yourself worked up about *it,* go ahead. I don't know why you're taking *it* personally."

"You just told me that I'm a bad influence on you—I'm your *father;* how could I not take that personally?"

"Yes, you're my father. I'm a grown man, that's why you're a bad influence on me. Me even being in this house is a bad influence on me. I know you don't believe in energy, but I do, and your energy is disdainful and loathing of humanity… contempt."

"I do believe in energy."

"Why would you tell me you don't if you do?"

"There are many things I should have never said to you. So I'm the reason why you hate people too? You've always hated people."

"I hate people out of a desire to love. You contempt people; there is a difference."

"Yeah, whatever Baethan." He trailed off to the basement to seek a lost pair of sunglasses, returned after a failed search, and began to speak of his obsession with quantum and the existential crisis he experiences despite his advanced aging with the relation of how nothing can exist if quantum is to be proven "true."

I compared the short, brutal lives of ancient barbaric tribes in the South American provinces to modern man—modern man, overcome with time… time to *think.* I shared the sentiments of the man I talked to at the bar last night with my father:

As a civilization advances and comfort is attained, members of the civilization begin to speculate and contemplate; philosophers proliferate, and the overall malcontent and unhappiness of the people begin to increase.

The conversation veered into the matter of how I will be severing communication with my father and everyone I know once I ship out to the U.S. Navy.

My father said, "Why would you cut me out of your life?"

"That's how I choose to be."

My father paced through the empty kitchen and lambasted me for my past "mental health conditions," my current state of mind, and informed me there is something "wrong" with me. He requested a hug immediately after; I embraced him as I would a totem pole.

"Get off the steroids, buddy," he said on his way out the front door, "they're fucking with your head."

I stared at the clothes I had folded on a chair, *surprised* by his baseless accusation, which clarified to me his complete lack of understanding of my perceptions of our relationship. I maintained a calm demeanor throughout the entirety of the interaction.

"I don't take steroids," I uttered in a manner of abject simplicity, to imply the statement I spoke shouldn't have been necessary.

"Yeah, sure," said my father, his back to me; he went out the front door, deliberated on the enclosed porch, and departed in his truck.

The man I spoke to at the bar last night shared one brilliant thought that confirmed my biases (therefore brilliant):

"Philosophy determines brain chemistry." With the exclusion of trauma and genetics, experiences culminate as philosophy, whether at the forefront of your thoughts or repressed—oh, damn *it* all, I can only ever know myself; best to placate my obsession with the self and accept my ego for what *it* is: boundless.

April 4th, 2019

7:54 PM

I attempted to meet with Pelagia to discuss the exact parameters and expectations of our "relationship." She said, "If you intend to scold me, tell me what you don't like about what I do, make me feel like a bad person, or to tell me you no longer want to communicate, save your breath… Tell me now and I'll abide. I've had enough stress and disdain."

I said, "Out of that list of presumptions, I've only attempted to cease communication with you on many occasions. I had intended to discuss our exact feelings to determine whether we should progress or relieve each other of our 'relationship.' I understand that this has already been answered. I will no longer communicate with you; I'm pleased you abide. Goodbye Pelagia."

I met with my recruiters for my final preliminary fitness testing before basic training; to run the circuit and work the body with men and women for the sake of a common goal—all younger than myself—felt phenomenal. I'm impressed by my own abilities and stamina in relation to my peers, though the pride I feel with my physical training throughout the past few years is leveled with the concept of entropy, always at the forefront of my thoughts. My worldview is framed with a hazy gray outline of degradation around a diminished blue ember of "becoming" at the centerfold. Yes—the extent of my physical progress has spearheaded to this point—in less than a month, when I will be tested, broken, and molded… Bah, what glamor, what pomp; basic training will be too easy and lax. If not for my hand tattoo, I'd be a marine. Even to be enrolled in a special operations program, what glory is there in any arbitrary test of the body—to exert and consume ad nauseam? Oh, but *it*'s enjoyable, to exert, to consume, to *be* human—for the glory of your *country*.

No—I am routed to learn the culinary profession and attain the required documentation and skills to one day open an establishment of my own if I ever desire… *if.*

An editor slid a six-hundred and eighty-four-page manuscript typed in size elven Times New Roman font, with two triangled fingers, across a polished oak table. A writer at the opposite end of the table peered up from the space between his legs, cleared his throat, and said, "What did-"

"Your long-winded expositions are a bore and you'd be better off without all the philosophical dribble, especially if you want to establish an audience. Everyone has a philosophy of their own; there's no interest in that sort of thing. That's what self-help books are for, and let me tell you, I see enough of those pass through here. To write that you hate your readers is… well, *you* know, folly. If you strive to be hated and vilified, this simply won't sell; you create a predestined flop—*knowingly,* and yet… You truly do waste your time; I almost can't believe *it,* and, to be frank—from what I've read, I sympathize as to why you hate yourself, though I could never understand *it.* You must hate me then, too, to be subjected to my opinion— to have to endure the sight of me? Being that I am the one with power over you in this situation, I imagine you *must* be hateful… Well, no matter, this manuscript needs too much work for me to even begin a synopsis of how to improve *it.*" The editor removed her rectangular glasses and revealed the brilliant gloss of her eyes against the soft incandescent overhead lightning cast off by twelve arms of an electrical bronze chandelier. "I'm appalled—I'll tell you. Your 'stories,' or rather, colorful paragraphs, are merely unfinished concepts, as if you had an idea, attempted to formulate a coherent wordage, and puttered out once the slightest hint of genuine effort was demanded. Why did you choose to spend your time writing this? You really are everything you say that you are, and I'm a bit sickened to have you sitting before me... Well?"

The writer stood from the chair he sat in, leaned over the table, reclaimed his manuscript, straightened, stood steady for one second, bowed—a slight incline of his head, said "Thank you for your time," turned, walked seven steps to a heavy-set mahogany door, gripped a cold-steel knob, twisted, stepped through the doorway, turned, and smiled through the vertical slit between door and wall.

The editor watched the writer go and listened to the muffled thud of the mahogany door against a wooden frame. She grimaced, leaned back in her chair, turned her head, and stared out the horizontal spacing of plastic blinds strewn over the fourth story window of her office at rows of tenements, factories, and shops of a twilit city coated in dust.

April 6th, 2019

2:21 AM

I sat at the bar adjacent to the dish basin where I labored and drank wine after my shift. I bantered with the bartender, Pat, and an ambitious young girl; she shone a light into my life.

The bar emptied and I sat alone with the bartender; Pelagia and Howard arrived, to my surprise, and sat at the two seats adjacent to me. An uncomfortable dialogue elapsed, with me at the centerfold of the bittersweet nothings and trivial inconsequentials.

Pelagia's boyfriend Ryan arrived; I said to him: "Ryan, do not pity me. Hate me." He looked away, laughed... and laughed, his eyes dead. Pelagia overtook his attention and I leaned back in my seat.

Howard and I discussed the nature of our condition; he empathized with my suffering at the moment and implored me to refrain from concern over someone (Pelagia) who does not know themselves and desires only validation; I cried a single tear, a reaction to Howard's empathy, my face a slate of stone; what I felt was an icy acknowledgment of what never was: love... though I loved Pelagia, in a moment—a few days, perhaps, a moment on the floor of my father's abandoned home with our hands clasped together, naked, side by side, the warmth of our bodies comprising the accumulated knowledge of all that mattered to either of us. A joke: to stare into each other's eyes, smile, kiss, and comment offhandedly on the temporality of all things, as if we were immune to the nature of our jest, and that the moment would last forever. I'm disgusted and mystified—to "know" how insignificant these sentiments will mean to me at a future time, to the immense gravity the thoughts impose on my mental state *now*.

I stood in the rain a half-hour past midnight and watched Pelagia walk alongside Ryan, homeward bound, together, as they should be; I felt the subtle pangs of renewal.

I knew all along, in our entire engagement, from start to finish: Pelagia had been the predator, and I, the prey, *willing* to be reaped. The reversal of masculine and feminine energy served as the catalyst for my current state. Pelagia desires the impossible from a man: A condensed masculinity, an unemotional hunk of meat, though if she found *it,* she would enact every method within her power to emasculate this hypothetical man. She still pursues me—to observe me... a haunt... a wraith. I must abstain from alcohol and local bar attendance, for my sake and her own.

April 7th, 2019

2:18 AM

A night at the bar with two glasses of red wine. I interviewed the bartender, Pat, and compiled notes while he spoke. My inquiry: "Pat, I intend to write a poem titled *Bartender's Lament;* I desire for you to relay to me a sequence of your worst possible day at work."

Pat relayed his grievances, annoyances, and perturbations.

I've never once pursued a woman; always, the woman has initiated first, and I reciprocated. Every woman I've ever been "romantic" with has been masculine, a misandrist, a feminist, affected with low self-esteem, or bored. Women have attempted to emasculate me in every relationship I've ever been in (except one—who suffered the lowest self-esteem of my relations); some succeeded and experienced grotesque empowerment of their spirit at the detriment of my own. To be pursued as a man, I've never experienced a desire to pursue. To only know the feminine facet of a relationship, I've yet to express a masculine role, to be the initiator, the force of action, the "conqueror." Though I've mounted many women, perhaps I delude myself, from what *is;* from an internal perspective, I've always been the reactor in another's act.

I walked along the bridge between towns on my way to my dish pit station and met a man for the first and last time by the name of Dyer. He urged me to guess how his name is spelled. After nine attempts, I succeeded. I said, "What's your definition of love?"

"To protect your family, to always be there for them… What is *your* definition of love?"

"To surrender yourself to what you hate, be *it* an entity or idea, to embrace the polarity of unification, to worship your self-destruction."

"Sounds toxic."

"Yes—yes *it* is."

"I don't know about that. Are you on your way to a college?"

"No, I'm on my way to a dish pit."

"Oh. You work in a restaurant then."

"Yes."

"I work in a restaurant too, also as a dishwasher."

We stopped at a crossroads and I said, "Do you destroy your ego for the sake of your children?"

"Oh yes, my family destroys me every day."

We shook hands.

Children are templates, loved for compliance. If your child burns your house down to a few girders and foundation, you may hate them. Some practice unconditional love: an art form. If the child is receptive to discipline and correction after the transgression, you may love them. You may love your child the moment of birth, prenatal, mid-conception, or as an idea, for a child demands love: another ego to depend on for survival; the parent's ego is destroyed and renewed if they choose to love the child—a perpetual cycle. If the child is hated, the parent's love of their own ego is the reason; surrender is the reversal.

On occasion, a child may be sold into slavery, or butchered and eaten; in these circumstances, the ego pertaining to "love" and "hate" is irrelevant. Consumption prevails. Entropy is God.

2:52 PM

The fifty-year-old woman with sensual features attempted to be intimate with me last night while I stood at the bar; her husband sat by and observed with a docile grin plastered over his face. "You're an interesting person; you intrigue me," she said, akin to what many others have shared on behalf of their perceptions of my character. "You're tentative; don't be tentative, that's bad," she continued between her points of physical contact.

I, a miserable fool, estranged and friendless by choice, vying to be hated, indifferent to the outcome, am *curious* to an observer—I reckon, in a way similar to the way one perceives me through eye, one is also interested enough to read; thus I hate you, reader, for your senseless intrigue, for your egotistical reasons to indulge in the selected sufferings of my existence. You may have paid a paltry sum of money for this product; I may receive a negligible percentage of that monetary value if I am still alive by the time of your purchase, and if I do, I'll clarify now, that the contribution compels me to ebb my hatred into a softer emotion, perhaps loathing, or disdain, though if I didn't hate, there would be no potential for love. Thank you.

April 8th, 2019

12:41 AM

I met an African American man with a short grey beard and cropped hair, at least fifty-five-years-old, by the name of Gary, at the gym. His demeanor, pleasant and humbled, compelled me to call out after a deadlift set, "Excuse me!"

Gary removed his earphones and nodded at me.

"Why do you lift weights?" I asked.

He approached, slow, calculated, and stood erect a few feet before me, at the height of 5'9, with a lean physique similar to mine. The moment he spoke I reckoned a man who had been through the hell of his mind and back. I regret not having premeditated a recording session, for the dialogue verbatim would have been a phenomenal memory to record in the exactitude of the moment. Throughout our discussion, we touched on one nodestone of insight: Gary claims there is a critical difference between "drive" and "ego": The ego is capable of serving the collective of humanity as much "evil" as "good." Drive, however, as a standalone

231

principle—according to Gary—is the product of a self-loving *and* humble character.

I said, "How may one's drive without the backing of an ego serve humanity in a directed manner? In essence, you would become 'one' with the 'collective consciousness,' a veritable cog, removed from individuality."

The conversation veered to many alternate routes: modes of living, thoughts being the true nature of our realities, and there being no difference whether we think or speak a thought. I listened, for most of our interaction; Gary often stopped at intervals, chuckled—embarrassed, sidestepped, and asked a self-conscious, "What?"

I said, "I'm reflecting and contemplating what you're speaking to me."

"*It*'s rare to meet someone who truly listens, who is genuinely open and willing to educate themselves."

I nodded, and he continued; we persisted in this way for half-an-hour, while I stood in the center of a hexagonal deadlift bar, and Gary, beside a pair of dumbbells he had abandoned on my summoning of his attention.

"I'm sure we'll see each other again," said Gary, "Let our conversation be a memory, in the past, for what *it* is."

I said, "I'll be ready for you next time." We nodded, smiled at each other, and resumed our energy exertion side by side, groan to groan; mutual respect for the breakage of muscle fibers, akin to two brothers in the trenches of our minds; we checked our forms in the mirror before us, wiped the sweat from our brows, and went our separate ways.

2:45 PM

Bartender's Lament

"You look miserable; must you be so sad?"
I said "I'm neither," and turned away from the woman to polish a glass.
"I'm a bartender too, you know, try to have a bit
more class. To look like that, well-"
"What can I get for you ma'am?"
"Nothing at all, I'm here to relax."
"I see. So you're a bartender, for how long and where?"
"Twenty-three years, towns 'round the country,
my dear—would you mind?"

"What?" I addressed her with a twinge of a
grin while two old men stumbled in.
"You're too austere; look at a mirror before each
shift and say: 'I love what I do.'"
"How can I serve you folks tonight?" I said to the two.
Both stammered and slurred; one said, "Food?"
"I'm sorry sir, the kitchen is closed, if you'd like a dri-"
"God *damn* you," he blurted, and went hand-
in-hand with his friend out the door.
"See now," the woman smirked, "you come off like a jerk."
"*Sure*. Any recommendations on how to improve my work?"
"*Oh* yes—many, now, to begin: you look like a dweeb;
"Your posture is poor, tuck in your shirt, the hair needs a trim,
"Your smile is contemptuous, your demeanor—disdainful-
"Ah, boy, even the way you *move* is grim;
brighten up, enthuse, be playful!
"Open with a joke—go on then; don't *ever* frown."
"A critic walked into a bar, sat down, and opened her mouth."
"Lousy, pish-posh, you understand? To attack *me* is crude;
"Learn to be a gentleman; you're uncouth, bland, a *real* bore;
"You make polishing glasses a chore; there's no fun, no rhythm,
"You haven't got an act. You're too stern with no tact."
I laughed. "My transgressions are many and my merits are few—"
"Don't forget I've many years in this profession over you;
"I'm unimpressed, to say the least. Give me a beer: demonstrate.
"Yes, a lack of flair, grace, and zest; from your
simple pour I can tell the rest."
"Inform me ma'am, I know you're the best—please, put me to the test."
Her smile faded, displaced by a glower; she
muttered, "Sarcasm just lost you a tip."
"You *really* think I give a shit?"
"An irredeemable, base, intemperate fool. No wonder you're hated."
She stood from the stool and left me to ponder,
Alone with my reflections at an empty counter:
What manner of man I am.

1:41 AM

I waltzed into the gym, intoxicated on two glasses of red wine, and strutted up to the man I engaged in a dialogue with the day prior: Gary. Voice recorder on:

I yelled across the open expanse of the room, "I've had two glasses of wine!—just to let you know."

Gary uplifted his head from a cable row machine, burst with laughter, and said, "How old are you?"

"I'm twenty-seven."

"You look a lot younger than that."

"I'm told that often. I want to know what you think is the difference between drive and ego."

"What's the difference between drive and ego?"

"Because, I'm thinking, of altruism-"

Gary stepped closer and we stood, man to man; he began: "Okay. Drive... drive is that one thing that is naturally pure; you can always think about your actions on that drive. Now ego, that's a whole different thing because you don't care about anybody else but yourself; there's no true purpose behind *it* but your own self-worth. Now when you have that drive, that 'oomph,' that push, *it's* like *it's* pushing you. Now ego, you can tell someone has a big ego out of the gate: they're not humble; they're not settled; they're the type of person that wants all the attention and has to have *it* all the time, and they don't take anybody else into consideration.

"Now, that drive is a whole different thing because *it's* like 'oh my mom is in the hospital and she's sick, and all the bills gotta be paid and I gotta make sure the bills gotta be paid.' Now the ego states: 'I don't give a fuck if you're in my way; I'm just gonna' mow you over and don't care who I take with me.' You understand what I mean?"

"I do. I recall you making the comparison of Hitler, and his ego; however what he did for his country and his people, they all believed they were in the 'right,' so to speak."

Gary cringed and said, "Ego."

"Yes, and ego is what drove him to create acts of altruism for his country."

"Yeah but how many millions of people got killed because of *it?*"

"This is-"

"Now—that drive will push you to the point where, 'Okay, we have a max amount of people, we got all these cities in ruin, how we gonna' build *it?* We gotta find the solution; how we gonna' build *it?* Where we gonna' find a place to build these things. *Drive,* creates positive change. Ego will create a massive hurricane that will bring nothing more than destruction."

"How can you have drive without the ego?"

"You have to have a mixture of the two, but you can't just run purely on ego."

"That's where humility, tolerance, and temperance come into play."

"Right, knowing your position and knowing your place and to have enough respect to say: 'I love myself, and I'm not gonna' walk down this road. I love myself, and I'm with this girl but I'm not gonna' sleep with her cousin.' I love myself enough to say: 'Okay, I need money but I'm not gonna' rob this bank."

I nodded and said, "Would you mind listening to my definition of love?"

"Sure."

"I'm interested in your opinion. To love is to surrender yourself to what you hate, be *it* an entity or idea, to embrace the polarity of unification, to worship your self-destruction."

"*Well,* love is a broad thing, and love has many interpretations depending on the individual; your definition of love could be totally different than mine, which is simply, perfectly fine; that's how the world works."

"I believe I asked you what your definition of love is before."

"Yes."

"What did you say? I forgot."

"Me too," Gary turned his head aside and laughed, heartfelt and embarrassed.

"I don't think you had an answer the first time-"

"-But you gotta' understand one thing and one thing only; like I said, *it*'s the one thing that makes us human, *it*'s the willingness to say, 'Okay, I'm gonna' stay here and do this even though I know *it*'s bad for me, and I'm gonna stay here because I'm comfortable.' Or, think of the bigger picture, and strive to be better than what I used to be; why wallow in pain when I can push myself to success and happiness? And even in that, there's pain, before you get to that level where you find success, because we all gotta go through what we gotta go through in order to reach the next level. Now you can stay in that hole, in that pain, in that misery, or you push through that pain, and that hole, and that misery, and have a good life. There are people that would rather sit home and do nothing, and they get what they get; then you get the ones that go out there—and they hustle; now maybe there's someone in-between: they just exist, the nine-to-five person who settles and says, 'Alright this is all I'm gonna' get, and I'm not gonna' get better than this.' So you got the individual; which one do you choose to be? Do you choose to be the person who sits home and does nothing with their life and *fails,* for the plain and simple fact of *not trying.* Or you can be that person that says, 'I'm not gonna' go any further,' or you become that person that has that high drive, high motivation and says, 'I'm not gonna' take what life has to offer—there's more. I want the 'more.' I want to become the five percent, or the one percent that does what he likes, so you get to pick and choose how you navigate, and *it* becomes your life.

"*It*'s just the same thing as money, and I find *it* kind of funny because people say they have no money yet all they do is sit at home and drink all day, or they'll sit at home and watch sports—or, ya' know, or, they'll use drugs, and they have nothing, and they'll complain they have nothing. And then you have the ones who have a shit-ton of money whose fuckin' miserable as all hell. Miserable!—all hell! You got all these rich people out there that throw themselves off, and they have everything their heart could desire—anything in the world! But they're still fuckin' miserable, and then there are the ones that are right there, in that sweet spot, that say, 'I don't need a whole lot of money, but I know I don't wanna' live like that, and I'm happy, right here.' So *it*'s tryin' to find that balance of, 'Okay, how much money do I need, and how much am I willing to live on? What are my standards of living that I will not budge from? *It*'s like I was talkin' to an old friend today, he works at [Warehouse]. I work at [Warehouse], but I clean three places; I also detail cars; I also glass windows, and everybody thinks that I'm crazy. I don't have a lot of money, but I live the life that I wanna' live. If I want to go out to eat—I go out to eat. If I want a new pair of shoes—I got a new pair of shoes. I mean I have a shit-ton of money in savings, but I'm able to navigate and survive how I want. So *it*'s like trying to find that equal balance of how you want to live, how you gonna' justify your means of your life. Do you want to be like a huge amount of the population that blames everybody else for where they're at? Or do you want to be between the five and the one percent of success that say, 'Okay, I can make something of my life,' and how far am I willing to go? How far am I willing to push? How far can I take this? So when *it* comes to life *it*'s all about the individual interpretation, but you have to pick and choose; *it* goes back to that statement I said before: 'Either you do or you don't; you will or you won't.' Like I said before, *it* applies to everything."

"Do you believe that there is truth?"

"There's always a truth."

"Do you think *it*'s our basic sensory perceptions?"

"The truth is under all the bullshit and all the garbage that is fed to everyone. You can tell yourself a lie, every day—all day, same lie, all day, every day, every week, every month, and every year; your mind, over time, will look at *it* as being true, while somebody else will look at *it* as being wrong. This goes back to the whole Hitler thing; in his mind he felt that what he was doing was the right thing to do, and the rest of society said, 'No—no, that's *fucked* up, you just can't be killin' masses of people and takin' all their shit like you own *shit*.' That's what I mean; *it*'s the same thing when you have a crooked politician whose like, 'Okay, your bill won't go through unless you give me x amount of money.' So like the average drug dealer, 'You're on my block, you're on my street, you're on my corner, and if you deal here I'm just gonna' have to kill you.' Now, look at any form of truth, in writing... *it*'s all dependent on the individual. The same person that sits there and says, '*It*'s okay for me to get high; *it*'s okay for me to drink; *it*'s okay for me to cheat; *it*'s okay for me to abuse my spouse and abuse my kid'; they think that *it*'s right and the rest of society views *it* as wrong. So *it* all depends on the individual."

"The last time I talked to you, you seemed to be an adherent of the collective." Again, Gary unleashed a vibrant guffaw; his eyes sparkled. I rushed to speak, for he opened his mouth to cut me off every three words I spoke: "But there can be no collective without the individual, and the ego feeds into altruism, and that's the only true form of altruism, is if you bolster the ego-"

"Well I'm not saying there is no ego; you can't be all drive or all ego; that's the thing; there's gotta be some other element in that, in *it*'s purest form."

I said, "And if your purest form is the ego-" Gary laughed again—a theme whenever I spoke, "-whatever you give out from that, that happens to benefit society, that is altruism in *it*'s purest form."

"Yes!—but nine times out ten, the majority of the individual—with their ego—does *what* with *it*? What do they do with *it*? How many people's lives get ruined and destroyed behind *it*?"

I opened my mouth to speak, and before a syllable spilled off my tongue—Gary *laughed!* I said, "That's a fundamental of life—consumption; the holy trinity: consumption, defecation, procreation-"

"But you gotta' understand as a whole. A lot of times, *it's*—I've heard this before, and I couldn't understand *it* until I reevaluated *it*, and I heard *it* again, and again, and again, in *so* many different ways: Other human beings will always do what is in our best interest; when we don't do what is in our best interest you could hurt a lot of people, you could hurt yourself, for what level of push? What level of drive, leads to the point of going over the edge? So there has to be a certain balance—so yes, there's ego in there, but how much? How much narcissism is in that? How much of not caring, not evaluating, stepping on people, kicking people down, is in that? I understand what they say with war, and life: casualties will happen, but how much destruction is enough, and how much destruction is too much? Where do you find the balance in that?—where do you find the truth in that? That's the overall question. *It's* like somebody who owned a grocery store and somebody was sittin' behind the counter, and somebody got kids at home, and instead of workin' a living wage to feed their family, they're out robbin' that grocery store. How much is too much? How far is too far? How little is too little? As individuals and as people, we can't find that balance.

"Look on the news, look on the media—oh *it's* a black and white thing: bullshit. There's this thing and that thing: bullshit. What's actually there, that you don't want us as humans, to really see. You have sports, you have music, you have television, you have movies: all that stuff is a piece of a blind. What is *it* that you're not really showin' us? Are we really slaves? What is there?"

"I think that we're all slaves to ourselves, at the least, and that we're all slaves to something, even those at the figurehead. Power is enslavement to whoever you rule."

"Well… in all honesty if you go back in the day and look at the richest man in Babylon, and if you break *it* down section by section, is that you're enslaved to the person you owe money to. And then you have *it* so where you go through time and move forward you have so many populations and so many races that are captured and put into slavery against their own will, and then you come into modern day, where you have your actors, your movie stars, and your great big businessmen. Another form of the slave: people that can't pull themselves out of in front of their television, and now they sit home all day and watch the television; that's another form of slavery, the person who cannot bring themself past the fact that they don't need to drink, to watch movies, take drugs, beat on people—*it's* all a form of slavery; you're in bondage to something in some form or other."

"On that level I think we're all slaves to each other."

Gary laughed: an amiable, agreeable expulsion. "You don't listen to anything when you come in here?"

"No. I would but, I like to be in…"

"The moment?"

"Yeah. Hearing whatever self talk or-"

"What is your nationality?"

"American, I was born in this city—the hospital."

"I understand you were born *here*, but what is your ethnic background?"

"I took a DNA analysis once: Welsh, and Great Britain."

"So you're British?"

"Also Welsh, but yes, Great Britain too, with some mixes of other origins, though that's the predominant."

"Cuz' my fiancé, she's German, and something else."

"I'm often thought to be German; I've been called an Aryan… whatever, many times."

Gary muttered, "Ignorance." He shifted on his feet, eased, and said, "Now why are you going to the Navy if you don't mind me askin'?"

"Writing, and the experience. I want to observe the human condition."

Gary chuckled. "You could rent a movie."

"What do you mean?"

"There's plenty of Navy movies out there… You want to be on the *frontline*."

"Ah, I'm going in—well, I was disqualified from most of my opportunities because I admitted that I used CBD oil, and they classified that as marijuana, and I was going to be on a submarine-"

"*Why* would you admit *that?*"

"I know, *it* was foolish of me, truly foolish, so now I'm going in as a culinary specialist, and I'll at least acquire the documentation to open my own restaurant if I ever want to by the time my education is finished. While I'm in I will aspire to become an officer."

"Culinary officer?"

"No, a naval officer. I'll attempt that route once I'm in, so that I may experience what that 'power' is, as much as I don't want *it*."

"… You can experience that right at *home!*—with a cat or a dog!" We laughed together; Gary continued, "Get off the couch! Don't pee there! Don't eat that!"

"*It*'s not the same as lording over your fellow man."

We laughed the hardest we both had throughout the entirety of our conversation.

Gary said, "In that case become a supervisor! 'Hey, hey, I told you, first time; not now, get back to work; who told you to put that pallet there? Move that over there; move that over here…'"

I extended my hand and said, "Thank you for taking the time." We shook hands, stolid and resolute. "I appreciate *it*."

"No problem."

"Gary, I'll let you get back to *it* man."

"Hey, don't be so hard on yourself."

"Oh… That's what ego is all about."

"Not necessarily. Got a girlfriend?"

"I did for a bit, somewhat, well… many in the past, bygone."

"I've been divorced twice; *it* gets better." Gary smiled and reinserted his headphones while I sauntered to a water fountain.

At the end of my session, I approached Mia, the woman who often utilizes a treadmill from eleven until midnight. She commented on my progress, my hair, my physique, and her happiness for my happiness. After a brief exchange of formalities, I said, "Mia, this may be crude or distasteful to you, but I don't care: Would you like to be 'fuck buddies' until I deploy?"

Mia readily accepted. There was no pursuit. We groped each other and kissed, just the two of us in the otherwise empty facility, in the perspective of all nine of the rounded ceiling cameras, and arranged for me to arrive at her home on the 11th.

I checked my phone and had one missed call after two days of nothing: Pelagia. Coincidence or energy? She left me a voicemail and proclaimed to miss me. I called her and left her a voicemail stating that the best course of action for us would be to meet for sensual passion.

Pelagia called my phone at two in the morning while I prepared my oats and transcribed the previous dialogue between Gary and me; she informed me that she knew I visited the bar, what I drank, and what I've spoken to people; she has "spies": bartenders, and my peers who relay my actions to her—she claims. Pelagia lamented that our paths haven't crossed "coincidentally" since she agreed to abide by my request for her to never speak to me again.

Yet, *I* return her call and speak to her again—for what end-

Illustrations in the *Bhagavad Gita* manifest in my mind, of a man and woman locked in tumultuous copulation; the great fall begetting wrath.

April 11th, 2019

10:46 AM

Copulation with Mia before I met with Pelagia at the bar. Ryan wavered around Pelagia at her seat.

I stayed with Pelagia until the bar closed and we endured each other's disdainful companionship. I asked her to accompany me to a hotel room. She deliberated an answer for fifty seconds. I sipped my wine. She rejected me on account of her cat's tenth birthday and her exhaustion.

"You've already slain me Pelagia; what more do you want?"

"I love you for the human you are," she said, and held the back of my hand.

"I don't have friends."

"You have friends whether you want them or not."

I sipped my wine again. We were never friends. We were two generals locked in battle and we have emerged from the ruins of a conflict with our "selves" intact and altered.

Ryan ordered a drink from my right. I said, "Hey Ryan." He looked at me. "Do you pity me?"

Ryan's face warped with befuddlement; he said, "No, not at all; you have your whole life ahead of you, and you haven't fucked *it* up like I have my life." His expression twisted to a huge beaming smile and he unleashed a faint sound reminiscent of a giggle.

I said, "Should I pity you-"

"No."

"-or have sympathy for you?"

"No—no, I don't even have sympathy for myself."

I observed Ryan: Frazzled hair, apathetic grimace, respectful clothing, trimmed facial hair... and his eyes. I said, "When I look into your eyes I see a void."

Ryan nodded, thought for a moment, and said, "Hey, at least *it's* in three-fourths time."

"Three-fourths time?"

Pelagia had been listening and chuckling at our "conversation"; seated to my left, she interjected, "Yeah, three-fourths time, like in a song."

"Oh," I said, "So when *it*'s slowed. So, a void in slow motion?"

Ryan said, "Yeah," and drifted away.

Pelagia proceeded to share her sentiments of weariness: her eighty-four-hour work week, and the proclaimed nonexistence of romance between herself and Ryan. These sentiments were interrupted and stymied depending on who entered or departed the vicinity. Pelagia commented on how she enjoys looking at my face and misses our conversations. While I listened, my mind convulsed on the contingency [26] of our relationship. We gazed into each other's eyes; I said, "You and I could sit here, stare at each other, not speak another word for the remainder of the night, and look like a couple of weirdos to everyone around us, though we would understand each other more than if we were to speak."

I leaned close to her; we continued to stare, our countenances shifting with subtle twinges of emotion; my mind raced with thoughts: *"I've loved you Pelagia; this can't go on, for the betterment of ourselves and those affiliated. I think you're a sexy, intelligent woman, and would have you on the floor right now if not for civility. We must end it. We must end it. Leave me with my wine and forget me."*

Pelagia closed her eyes. I waited for her to look at me again and said, "I *should* be recording this conversation so that you could one day read all the bullshit you've spoken tonight."

Pelagia said, "Fuck you," twice, throughout her verbose defense: all valid claims of humanity; I didn't disagree with her qualms or hope to discredit her opinions; I only knew what was between *us:* a tired travesty.

"You're too intelligent," she said, to my extreme dissatisfaction.

"Too intelligent for *what?*"

"For life."

"You aren't going to emotionally manipulate me. After I first acknowledged that I'm aware that you'd like a lover and not a chess player, you've spoken the word, 'check,' to me twice in conversations since then, and I had no longer been playing chess."

We drank; she turned to a few others to her left and bantered. Her

---

[26] I choose to spend time with Pelagia at social venues and she chooses to share a bed (regardless of the sexual activity) with Ryan each night. I depart for the Navy with no intent of return for a minimum of four years. Pelagia refused my contract and chose to live with Ryan, a man she claims to distrust and have no feelings for.

hands returned to my body first, then her words returned to my auditory perception: sweet nothings.

My eyes welled with unrelinquished tears; my upper lip twinged from suppressed animosity and sadness; we gazed at each other for a time again. I looked at her and drank. She stood, in expectancy of a hug, a touch, a kind word, a farewell...

I turned my head towards her, said, "Fuck you too," twice, consecutively (she had not heard me on my first utterance), drank the remainder of my water, stood, donned my pack, thanked the bartender, avoided the sight of Pelagia's aspect, and pushed out the front door.

That I may expunge Pelagia from my mind and immortalize her with the solemnity of a funeral rite, a brief animal study:

Pelagia, at the height of 5'5-5'7, a (guessed) weight of 175 lb - 185 lb, carries herself with the haughtiness of an esteemed empress and the probing curiosity of a schoolgirl. Irish ethnicity. Gemini zodiac. There is a slight stiffness in her gait due to being hit by a car several years ago. She is voluptuous, on the verge of unhealthy, though she retains an elegance of the body that is often betrayed through her actions. Her weight is a matter of great self-doubt/consciousness, more so due to her being fit and active throughout most of her young life.

Pelagia's visage is often sly and rueful, weary from the toils of restaurant labor. Her plaintive eyes penetrate. Her full lips accentuate a soft, feminine voice. Her body is tattooed. A subtle assertiveness is prominent in her manner: the force of her tenuous social interactions. "Unladylike," in the classical sense, she is a veritable brute in how she conducts her relationships. Her hair is a short, wild, black, mangled array; she decided to shave bald when our previous kitchen supervisor, Henry, commented on the length of her hair being, in summary: "Unprofessional and uncouth," a month or two before I was hired. Her modest clothing is often form-fitting and she is unabashed in her expression, body and mind.

Pelagia is covetous, thus I knew she would be my greatest and unwanted workplace adversary. She is practiced in the art of duplicity, emasculation, and culinary arts. The manner which her eyes fixate on others, observe, and scan the immediate environment is akin to a tigress on the prowl, though the beast is confused, and desires to establish a professional, respectable reputation within the community while also accruing males within the same community to "feed" on; she is at odds with herself. Pelagia thrives on the respect and admiration from those she vies to devour most of all:

men most prone to reject her; the challenge is a stimulation; the conquest is a status symbol: validation. No matter how self-deprecating she must become, once the male submits, he is emasculated.

Pelagia's social spirit is vigorous and ambitious; her introspective nature is hateful and distrustful. A superb chef; she believes food to be the best expression of love. Despite her grievous, debauched, and wanton past, she pursues a dream of inventing a new, novel way to cook, to own a restaurant, to become a famous chef, to enjoy a roadster life—motorcycle style, and to retire to a farmhouse replete with gardens; I hope she succeeds. Her sense of humor shines. Her authentic smiles are wholesome. Her laughter is jubilant—a harpies' throes, a siren's enchantment, a slayer of men; I loved her.

3:41 PM

Ayn Rand's theory of objectivism rejects skepticism. I consider myself an absurdist, a utilitarian, a romantic, and many labels of philosophical paradigms, though *most of all,* a skeptic. I'm skeptical of *being* a skeptic. The material world, per objectivism, is the only fount of reason to be trusted, the singular source of knowledge—and anyone skeptical of this, well, don't bother!

Oh yes, I'm skeptical—skeptical of the capabilities of human reason, skeptical of the reality our reason permits/constrains us to perceive, and skeptical *of* the reasons behind every meaning any man or woman has ever given me for their existence—my own included, and *it*'s "truly" absurd.

"Mathematics," shouted a pragmatist, his chin raised and arms crossed.

"A theory," snorted a skeptic in response, his grin contemptible, and his legs spread beyond shoulder width.

"For what reason do you choose to be ignorant?"

An absurdist entered the small eight-by-eight foot room illuminated by two string-operated incandescent bulbs; he clenched an accordion and pushed the ends of the instrument together to create one, singular, doleful dissonance. "Mathematics!"

The pragmatist winced and said, "Your argument is invalid; you don't choose to be ignorant for the sake of mathematics."

"But you see," the absurdist began, his visage overtaken with a stern glare fit for an Egyptian monument, his hands clasped tight on both compressed ends of the accordion, "Your theory of mathematics renders you ignorant." He decompressed the accordion and compressed at a rapid, unrhythmic pace. The absurdist dropped the accordion and raised his hands between the two string-operated bulbs: two straight vertical arms over his head; he clapped; three-and-a-half inches of space measured between the full arc of his hands between each intermittent connection of his palms.

The pragmatist departed the room, journeyed into the busy streets of Manhattan, retucked a disheveled section of his dress shirt, walked several feet until he could no longer hear the resonance of the accordion—which had begun to sound off again—through the ill-constructed apartment walls of the building he had exited, and hailed a taxi.

"Hello sir," said the taxi driver.

"I don't know where I am, but I need to get to Maple Ave."

"Alright," said the driver, and he turned halfway to meet face-to-face with the pragmatist who had slid onto a back seat cushion, "but first, I want you to know that the words I'm speaking to you now are a brief account that serves no function other than to validate me with your attention. Today I washed between my toes in the shower for the first time in two weeks and I was disgusted by the accumulated dirt that rinsed down the drainpipe. Afterward, when I toweled off, I felt much cleaner than usual, though I looked in the mirror and thought of my ex-wife and was compelled to cry. Well, I began to weep, and after about two minutes of weeping, I decided I needed to freshen up before I went to work, so I got back into the shower and ran a bit of hot water over my face and then switched to cold. I stepped out, looked at myself, and felt like a new man."

The pragmatist waited a moment; he said, "Okay."

The driver nodded, turned to face the road, situated himself, coughed once, scratched his nose, and merged with a line of vehicles behind a red light.

April 12th, 2019

1:35 PM

Money is of no consequence for me at this point. I have secured my desires from now until deployment; thus, I have informed my employer that "-if the powers at be would rather me removed earlier, I will not object."

Henceforth, until April 27th, I will think of only malevolence, disdain, and contempt, unabashed and unrestrained, while I engage in my labor. I will meet my fellow man's contemptuous upturned nose with my own, a deluge of negativity emanating from every pore of my body—for management, most of all. I've lost respect due to my deplorable relationship with Pelagia, and I'm certain she maligns me amongst her wide social circle of *very important people*. There is no recourse; let the damned be damned; I ~~need~~ desire more time to edit my "work" and to read John Locke before deployment. There will *always* be time to serve and obey.

April 13th, 2019

1:49 AM

Midway through my shift, hunched over a dish basin, I scrubbed a dozen pots. My new supervisor, Ned, approached me from my left and said, "Hey Baethan, many people would consider this mundane and low-level work, but I appreciate what you do."

"What?"

"Washing dishes, and everything else… You seemed upset when you came into today."

"I was attempting to project contempt and disdain, and have failed."

We smiled, his of a brotherly manner, mine of a satirical play. Ned put his hand on my shoulder and walked away.

Yes, thoughts are indeed objects. My malevolent mental activity directed at my peers *always* elicits an immediate impact whether I am engaged or disengaged with them in conversation; I believe that the thoughts of others are a synchronization. Energy is empathy and vice-versa.

I am unable to feign ill-will; for a time, authentic disdain and contempt is feasible—often, though to sustain a pretense… this is impossible, for all, even "psychopaths," for they experience empathy most of all. Strange, to think of being eviscerated with a sharpened stick amidst the shadows of a cold winter night, your killer may cry on your behalf, and they may as well be laughing. Thus, is virtue a pretense? Is personality a pretense? If all learned behavior is a pretense—experiences culminated into personality, what is the authentic self if not pure ego?

Oh, brothers and sisters, we are lost. Among each other, we meander and grapple.

After a strength training session I ran home from the gym, intoxicated on two glasses of red wine. A man stumbled along the sidewalk at an intersection; he blubbered, wept, coughed, and shouted, "Sir! *Sir!*"

I stopped. "Yes?"

"A phone, please… a phone."

"Certainly."

I walked towards the grievous man. A foot-and-a-half shorter than myself, perhaps a bit older or the same age, he hobbled and tugged at a ripped *Breaking Benjamin* shirt and choked. Tears streamed down his face. We met and I handed the man my phone; he dialed '911' and summoned a police officer. While he spoke, I powered on my voice recorder. We reinitiated the conversation and waited for the officer together. Chopin's *No. 1 in F Minor, Andante,* played from the speakers of my writing device within my pack:

I said, "What happened if you don't mind my asking?"

"There's a lot of shit goin' on brother," he veered away from me, paced, and held his head with both hands. Tears poured from his eyes. "I did nothing dude—I-" he choked, paused, and exhaled.

I said, "Hey," and put my arm around his shoulder; I pulled him against me for a half-hug. He collapsed for a moment in my grip—a *moment;* I towered over him. His head nestled into my chest. He became rigid, pulled away, and shouted: a barbaric plea.

I said, "Is somebody injured?"

"Nobody's injured, motherfuckers—I'm about to throw up. I tell ya' right now motherfuckers think they're playing games buddy—they'll go to prison, I mean right now." A long pause; I waited. The man wiped his eyes and blurted, "I did nothing! I did nothing, this motherfucker—he's playing games with me bro like fuck you bro I'm not gonna' sit here and take that. Bro, I've been sittin' here doin' dishes for you for the past fuckin'— three weeks, but yet nobody wants to fuckin' do the dishes, but yet you want to come downstairs and come here, and complain and complain and *complain*—and *bitch,* and put your fuckin' hands on me and kick me outta' the fuckin' house. But yet you got all these mother fuckers doin' drugs in the house, okay. I'm about to put mother fuckers in fuckin' jail, for fuckin' life, that's what I'm gonna' do. Mother fuckers want to play fuckin' games with me—okay, I'm gonna' ruin your life, you ain't never gettin' your kids back, bet you'll like that… Never did I ever fuckin' plan this, fuckin' sick of fuckin'…"

A police officer pulled up in a van, rolled down his windows, and addressed the man: "What's goin' on bud?"

The man wept and placed his elbows on the open driver-side window of the police car. I stood behind the man and observed.

The officer said, "You okay? What are you crying for?"

"Because dude—there's a lot goin' on now that's why."

"Do you need to go to the hospital?"

"No I don't need to go to no goddamn hospital. No!—I'm pissed off because I'm sittin' here on [house address], but yet this fuckin' big ole' argument, *blows out;* I don't know fuckin' why, but, yet, I get fuckin' hands put on me, and all this crazy shit. I got fuckin' scratches and fuckin'—and fuckin' all this crazy shit on me."

"Who'd you get in a fight with?"

"This fuckin' dumb ass mother fucker."

"Here, let me pull in here." The officer drove into a nearby parking lot.

The man began to walk away and I stood motionless; he turned, a few meters away from me, and said, "Thank you so much; I appreciate everything."

I said, "You're welcome," and began to run.

April 14th, 2019

3:57 PM

I clocked out at the end of my shift and entered the adjacent bar. Two women around the same age as me, a blonde and brunette, sat and chattered at the far end of the room. On my entry, the bartender Pat, who I've established a friendly rapport with based in philosophical debate, said to the two: "This is Baethan; he's a writer."

"Oh! We're *both* creatives," said the blonde.

"Yes, we like art," said the brunette.

"Very creative."

"We're into expression."

They continued this way for five seconds, and on their scrutinization of my apathetic glower, I said, "I don't know why Pat felt *it* necessary to inform you of my writing; is the act supposed to impress you?"

The blonde's narrow cheeks rounded into a smile and she said, "What do you write about?"

I cringed at Pat, turned to the two women, thought *'Tripe,'* and instead, said, "The human condition: poems—theories—philosophy—short stories—autobiography." The women nodded their heads. *"It's* a bunch of bullshit, like all writ-"

Both laughed. I turned to Pat, asked for a drink, and proceeded to ignore them. Both stood and left for the dance floor; each eyed me on passing; I raised an eyebrow. Pat rounded the bar, planted kisses on their cheeks, and embraced both in a hug. While Pat poured me a glass of wine, I said, "Pat, please don't do that to me again."

"Sorry man-"

"I mean, I get *it;* you attempt to assist a fellow man with copulation, however-"

"No, well, I don't know-"

"It's all very heartfelt-"

"Yeah well what can I say, geez man," he slid the wine to me.

The manager entered and the three of us discussed the merits of the new chef (Ned)—the manager's personal friend. I heard, repeatedly, from the manager's mouth, "He's a good man. Yep, he's a *good* man," as though this were meritable. In my dealings, I've concluded that Ned is a pragmatic sycophant; sounds like a "good" man to me.

After the incessant praise for another man, I waited for the conclusion of the conversation and said, "When I first met Ned, we sat together at the bar, right here, and he flattered me to all hell."

The manager said, "Here?"

"Yes, right here," I pointed to two stools between us. "I had told Ned that he flatters me and urged him to stop, though he persisted."

Pat cleaned the bar and said, "Well who doesn't like to be flattered?"

"I don't; flattery is self-serving; the flatterer desires something from you, even if just validation."

"See, Baethan," Pat sighed, "I don't know what *it* is about you, but… you just, you put this negative spin on everything, like what's wrong with other people validating each other; is that bad? Is *it* really so bad that people find pleasure in making each other feel good?"

"Well, this is entering the realm of ethics, and I'll close on flattery by saying that not even a dog likes to be coddled and praised to excess, so what makes you think a man would?"

"Alright, fair." Pat continued to clean and reckoned me with sidelong glances. He said, "Now about your negativity: You come off to me as… ah, arrogant—*well,* not arrogant, but like you think you're better than people; you're disdainful, or behave as if you know better."

One of the two restaurant owners, Walther, entered the room, and the four of us stood together in the dark. A sports channel broadcasted from a wall-mounted television garnered the attention of the manager and Walther while Pat and I spoke of my character.

I said, "Haughty."

"What? Hottie?"

"No, *haughty.*"

"What does 'haughty' mean…" Pat looked at the others; both returned his gaze with a vacant stare.

Surprised and disconcerted, I said, "Haughty: *it*'s midway between prideful and arrogant."

Pat conceded that I'm "haughty." I discussed with the men whether each would prefer to be pitied or hated. The social relations manager preferred to be hated. Walther failed to answer the question, and instead confessed he had always fantasized about being terminally ill and having his condition known to the public.

"That's a weird fantasy," I said.

Walther pointed a finger at me, widened his eyes, and said, "Don't *you* tell me what's weird about *me!*"

I laughed, and I may as well have cried, for this man—a man who fantasizes of being terminally ill for the sake of pity—a man who wrote a high school thesis on the matter of how 'altruism doesn't exist'—a man who had recently conducted a charity event at the bar for a friend who is a terminally ill cancer patient… Did Walther, by extension, fulfill his fantasy by hosting this event through a vicarious second-handed premise?

We discussed fate and determinism, to no avail. I asked, "Do you believe virtue is a pretense?" and followed up with, "I believe we are all 'sociopathic-' " Thereupon, before I could expound on my lack of belief in any diagnosable "pathy," I lost all credibility. Walther exited the room, disgusted by my claims and questions.

I stayed with Pat for a while and we delved into discussing the American Psychiatric Association (APA). Pat had understood what I meant, and we both agreed that "sociopathy" is the wrong word, though we were unable to think of a substitution. Perhaps "base," "bestial," "intemperate." Virtue is a credential we don as a mantle—our "character," our "pretense," as a survival mechanism, to fit into a societal role. The "family man," stripped of his virtue, would continue to be a "family man" for the sake of his propagated ego (seed) and would maintain relations with each member of his family for the sake of himself; he would relate to each member per the time he considers required to maintain each individual relation. Embellish the man with established cultural virtues, and you have yourself a "good" man. Is the "sociopathic" family man "evil" if he achieves the same end through alternate methods of behavior?

Society is fickle business; I'd take the brief position as chieftain of a tribe of barbarian cannibals until my first social blunder renders me flayed alive and skewered over a bonfire, any day.

The term "sociopath," coined circa 1929-(30), is a modern terminology to describe "mental illness" or unwanted social behavior. Contemporary jurists ascribe what "normalcy" is for the sake of law and order. Is this *truly* "good"? Is there no "evil" in dictation?

"Principles of action indeed there are, lodged in men's appetites, but these are so far from being innate moral principles, that if they were left to their full swing, they would carry men to the overturning of all morality. Moral laws are set as a curb and restraint to these exorbitant desires, which they cannot be but by rewards and punishments that will over-balance the satisfaction any one shall propose to himself in the breach of the law."

— John Locke's *Essay Concerning Human Understanding*

I stood akin to a sentry and observed the creatures of the bar until 1:00 AM. The holy trinity [27] lay sprawled before me; I partook, and approached a young, attractive, raven-haired girl with deep somber eyes who had validated me with many furtive glances throughout the night whenever she disengaged from her boyfriend. I said, "Hello."

"Hello," she stated as a query.

"Do you have a boyfriend?"

She smiled; a coy blush flashed onto her visage. "Yeah." She pointed to a jovial man engaged in a half-dance with two male friends.

I said, "Alright," gazed at her one final time, and departed.

---

[27] Consumption, defecation, and procreation.

April 15th, 2019

4:10 PM

A craven beast thumbed through a mound of human bones from deep within the recesses of a blackened cave. "Ah," *it* spoke aloud with a voice reminiscent of a moribund field bird, "I suffer no other recourse." The beast clambered up from an abysmal grotto onto multileveled planes of rock enshrouded by darkness, perceptible only to *it*—the contours and passageways of intricate chambers: a second-hand instinct, for the whole of the beast's life, *it* has known only the reclusive providence of what *it* calls "home" through vision adapted to perpetual night.

The sleek body, mottled with coarse black and gray fur, hunched forward with a grace bearing semblance of a poised recurve, primed and ready to pounce with two distended arms coiled with sinewy muscles. A dozen foot-long bony fingers radiated outward from calloused six-inch diameter palms. An angular face composed of sharp cheekbones, two opalescent beady eyes, and a high forehead with skin spanned taut down to an enormous beaked maw stared out from an oblong vertical entry point of the secluded cavern. The dim light of a nearby city shone through the varied spaces between tree trunks far below. The beast crept up to a ledge and stared over the edge of the mountain's pinnacle; *it* opened *it*s beak, clacked two ends of the calcified bone together twice, and descended, engaged in a silent sprint. The beast's hasty strides encroached on the countryside; surrounded by prey, *it* selected a roadside cottage. A blue car had pulled into the driveway; the beast saw a woman through the rear window seated in the driver seat. A young boy sat in the passenger seat.

The driver's side door of the car opened: "Just wait your turn next time and *it* won't be so bad."

"But Daniel *always* gets to go first," whined the boy, and the passenger door swung open.

"I don't care *who* gets to go first; the point is—is that you need to learn to be patient. You can't always get what you want and when you act like *that* you make us both look bad." The woman rounded the vehicle with an armful of square cardboard boxes. "C'mon, let's go inside for dinner and get you ready for a bath. I just want to let you know how disappoi… James? *James?*"

The boy listened to his mother's voice fade and the incessant pound of two padded feet. A relentless gust of cold wind blew between two of the six powerful digits clasped around the boy's head and buffeted his terrified eyes. The boy opened his mouth to scream and tasted rot. Blood trickled down his scalp from four incisions inflicted by serrated fingernails. His body a ragdoll, suspended by the neck, dragged along dirt, stone, and the tips of pointed rock wedged out from the earth; his feeble hands grasped and clawed at the colossal appendage wrapped around his face while his lower back and legs shredded and tore up the side of the mountain. Darkness overtook his senses and the grip of the appendage tightened; he began to suffocate, and attempted to scream, to cry, to beg. A whetted maw eviscerated the boy's abdomen; he hung limp, hoisted into the airy blackness of an abyss, and convulsed to the sound of his intestines spill as the appendage jerked upward and snapped his neck.

April 17th, 2019

1:58 AM

Treks back and forth across town on foot with a tactical pack braced against my back, from the bar where I'm employed until the 27th of this month, to the grocery store, to the adjacent gym, to Mia's nearby home for frequent wine and copulation, to back "home," where I feed, sleep, read Aristotle and John Locke in preparation for basic training, engage in simple calisthenics, edit last year's documentation, and write—*this;* my life, in essence, is refined to the elements of pleasure and exertion of body and mind. There is no love nor hate; therefore I experience a state of equanimity, at one with the dish pit, a glass of wine, a conversation at the bar with a stranger, and with a weight hauled up from the floor— relinquished, ad nauseam… the cycle of each day is equivalent to an entire life: marginalized and fleeting.

11:13 AM

At the bar, I discussed with Pat and a stranger a myriad of topics for an hour and twenty minutes. A touchstone of this conversational array: towards the end of my time with the two, the stranger had exhausted himself of exposition and scrutinized his phone screen.

I said to the stranger, "Do you believe that virtue is a pretense?"

"Well that depends on what you mean by pretense; how would you define pretense in relation to virtue?"

"An embellishment of the ego."

"An embellishment of the *ego*... how?"

"There would be no 'human' without the ego, and the ego, first and foremost, is concerned only with the best means to achieve survival. Civilizations produce a culture determined by an amalgamate of individuals that desire to cooperate for survival. These individuals determine ethics based on the immediate environment and the best methods of production in alignment with the environment suitable for survival. We shape each other's egos with behavioral expectations, in other words, virtue."

"Right, alright, I can see that."

"With the idea of virtue being a pretense, do you believe that we are all 'sociopathic?'"

The stranger tapped his phone with both thumbs, drank the remainder of his scotch, looked up, locked eyes with me, said "Yes," shook my hand, stood, shook Pat's hand, wished us both well, and departed.

All people lie.

April 18th, 2019

3:02 AM

My, how I've fallen from my self-designated precepts; at the bar again, I met with many self-proclaimed acquaintances and friends—all enemies to me, one of them being Ryan, Pelagia's ~~starry-eyed~~ diminished boyfriend. After listening to a brief summary of his overdue library rental fees, I recommended for the third and final time, *The Short Happy Life of Francis Macomber,* by Hemingway.

Ryan sipped his beer and nodded.

I continued, "The characters remind me of the situation between you, myself, and Pelagia."

Ryan frowned and gazed downward at the floor to my right. "Oh."

"Yes, and, I'd like to tell you now, that whatever was between Pelagia and myself is now over, and there is no recourse from this matter; I thought you should know." Ryan eyed me with a circumspect gaze and bobbed his head ~~akin to how a bobblehead doll would bounce after being hurled by a jovial toddler down a long, narrow, abandoned highway road.~~

I extended my hand for a shake; we shook: a grim jostle, and veered away from each other at a natural inclination to disengage from the unsavory conversation.

A beautiful young black-haired woman arrived shortly after I received my wine from the bartender and had chatted with a few fellow workmates.

"Oh howdy-dowdy-doo?"

"Oh yes, that's nice, how about you?"

"Oh her-da-der-da-day."

I asked three men if they believed virtue is a pretense and if the terminology "sociopath" applies to the human race; two agreed, one—the bartender (who happens to share the same name as myself), is combative, and disagrees with everything I speak as a modus operandi; I appreciate this behavior.

Pelagia arrived and sat with Ryan a few seats away from me at the bar while the black-haired woman went outdoors for a cigarette; she had compelled me, by her beauty alone, to wait for her to return.

The black-haired woman, Sara, offered to buy me a shot to share with her; I refused, though we proceeded to talk of the "self," our definitions of "love," her meaning of life, my upcoming deployment to basic training, how she once hit a bird while driving in a car (she laughed and cried simultaneously—there can be no other way), and a small Japanese hieroglyphic tattooed at the nape of her neck: "Strange."

Pelagia offered me a beer she had no interest in finishing herself; I accepted, with a tentative touch and tender gaze… at Pelagia; we met eyes—Sara and her roommate between us—and shared a mutual expression of what may have been the final vestiges of "love," bygone or in the moment; there was a summation of acknowledgment—of the destruction we had sown on one another. Pelagia pulled her beanie over her face, an idiosyncrasy I adore, her eyes wet, face sullen, and I looked away, to gaze at the alcohol-lined wall and compose myself before I turned to face Sara, and said, "May I have your number?"

Pelagia swung her head in our direction—the moment Sara proceeded to nod. I reached into my jacket pocket, procured my phone, and Sara insisted on entering the digits herself. "What for?" She inquired.

"I'd like to take you to a hotel room."

"For what?"

"For temporary intimacy before my deployment, in a neutral setting."

"Why a hotel?"

"I live in an abandoned home-"

"That's beautiful. Hotels are too sterile, though."

"And I sleep on the floor, *it*'s rather embarrassing."

"*That's* beautiful."

I leaned back in my chair, wine in-hand, and scrutinized Sara; my face twisted into an amused grin of satisfied wonderment. Strange indeed. "Yes, I reckon an abandoned home, and sleeping on the floor with me, a total stranger, in the aforementioned home, would be a particular expression of art."

Sara said, "We could go to my place—though-"

"Not tonight."

"Not—yeah, not tonight. I did just meet you after all, and-"

"-You may change your mind in the morning when you're sober."

Sara shook her head. "No."

And so wry expressions were cast, subtle footwork enacted, hand gestures conducted, and amiable touches received. Hands were shaken, bittersweet sentiments shared, and a determination to amplify my suffering by means of the throes of passion, pursued.

5:29 PM

"And Anaxagoras would seem to have supposed that the happy person was neither rich nor powerful, since he said he would not be surprised if the happy person appeared as an absurd sort of person to the many. For the many judge by externals, since these are all they perceive. Hence the beliefs of the wise would seem to accord with our arguments."

- Aristotle's Nicomachean Ethics

April 20th, 2019

1:30 AM

Invited out to the bar where I work by Howard, I expected to meet with *only* Howard for a cerebral discussion; instead, I was met with the trio of Howard, Pelagia, and Beatrice: the unholy three who have found themselves drawn to me, and I to them, for they exude debauchery, and I have been eager to become incontinent... though no longer, due to the incident I have saved on my recording device:

256

Drunk on six glasses of red wine, I sat, disinterested with everything and everyone; Pelagia left me alone at the booth. I closed my eyes and an amiable enemy approached and sat across from me: Cyrus, a young, ambitious, intelligent musician. His countenance: bright and cheery, a juxtaposition to my dreary and forlorn frown; he said, "I had an interesting night."

"How so?"

"A lot of very intimate conversations."

"What have you developed?" I said, with a slight hint of apathy.

"What have I developed? Uhhh... An understanding of my "self," an understanding of other people, optimism for the future. Ummm. Lusting for a better version of myself so I can face the future in a more dignified way. Lots of things."

"Lusting?"

"I love *it*. I can't wait!"

"You're passionate."

"Yes. Yes."

"So you're not content with what you are right now," I stated with flat affect.

"Who is?"

"Some would say the Buddha, some would say sages, but do you believe that–"

"The Buddha's dead."

"Exactly. Sages, are they not equal to a fool?"

"Which sages?"

"Sages: the ones who sit on mountains and endure chilling winds; the ones who proclaim to know that they know nothing. Are they not fools, just like you?"

Cyrus smiled and said "Everyone's a fool man."

"Exactly."

While we spoke, those around us quietened, until our discussion was the foreground to the soft bar music. The bartender, who listened intently to our conversation, began to ululate: "Whoa whoa whoa whoa! Except for this guy *here!*" He pointed to himself.

I leaned on an elbow, cocked my head, locked eyes with the bartender, pointed at him, and shouted, "No—you are the *biggest* fool to proclaim that you are *not!*" The bar vocals silenced; rock music ebbed from the ceiling speakers.

"Hey brother–" slurred the bartender in response.

I said, "Yes."

"I think you're the biggest fool for proclaiming that I'm a fool, and by proclaiming yourself that—I think you're the biggest fool here!"

"Gee wiz—I hope so!"

"'Gee wiz?' You just completely proved that you're a fool by saying 'gee wiz!'"

"I am."

"Shit."

"And I have-" I truncated myself due to laughter, heartfelt and sincere. Pelagia stifled a giggle at the bar. Cyrus sat across from me and grinned from ear to ear like a fool.

I said, "I am the biggest fool in this room."

The bartender said, "Oh is that what you know? [Indiscernible]. You won't."

"I won't what?"

Cyrus interjected: "Cage match!"

The bartender shook his head. "You don't want a cage match."

I chuckled akin to a childish madman and said, "I would gouge your eyes out with my thumbs. I would tear into your throat with my teeth and drink your blood in a cage match. That's how much of a fool I am."

Pelagia laughed; the bartender and two patrons muttered of my "craziness."

Cyrus spoke to me, seemingly oblivious of the agitated people around us, "Do you believe in God?"

"I believe that we are all God, so yes."

"Do you read a lot of Nietzsche?"

My eyes widened and softened. "Yes."

The bartender shouted to me, "What's your first name?"

Cyrus continued, giddy and thrilled, "I knew you did. I knew you fucking did—read a lot of Nietzsche."

I averted my attention from Cyrus, annoyed that my conversation with him had been stymied with a putative "authority figure"—the bartender; I shouted back, "Why do—why do you care? Why?"

"Why do I care?"

"Yes!"

"Why do *you* care?"

"Because I don't!" I chuckled, "Because I'm a fucking fool, man! A word is a word. We are all the same."

"No, I don't believe that."

"We suffer the same, that's what unifies us."

"Uh, no we don't suffer the same; people are gonna suffer something different."

"What will I suffer as opposed to you?"

"Uh, fury of myself."

Cyrus roared, jubilant and carefree: "Cage match!"

The bartender said, "That wasn't appropriate."

I said, "Do you believe there is a true authentic self?"

"Yeah whatever you're talking about, is like, no, like *it*'s, *it*'s, some fuckin', curiosity—no."

"You say your 'self' as though *it*'s different than mine-"

"Whatever you believe in, you're talking through alcohol."

"Your 'self' is the same as mine, altered through a pretense of virtue—that's what prevents us from actually engaging in a cage match."

The bartender braced both arms on the counter, leaned towards me, and said, "There's no cage, but there will be a mat."

"*It*'s metaphorical man!"

Cyrus shouted: "No! I want a literal cage match!"

Pelagia stood from the bar, approached the booth I sat in, and acknowledged with me a downcast gaze of motherly disappointment; she said, "Can I have my jacket and my bag please?" while Cyrus and the bartender argued over the potentials of a cage match. I abided, and laughed at Pelagia, for her insolent and unfounded belief that her opinion of me vexed me.

The bartender said, "Hey."

I stood and approached the bar. I extended my hand; we began to shake, and he arched his pointer finger in my grip and began to tickle my wrist. I said, "You like to tickle me?"

"Why not?"

"I don't know, that's why I'm asking."

"Would you like to find out more?"

I said, "For what?" The bartender persisted in the tickling of my wrist. I loosened my grip and he held firm. Genuinely astonished, I said, "This is the most curious sensation I've experienced in a month."

The bartender looked at me square in the eyes and said, "Wow—I am *very* sorry for you-"

"To have someone tickling up and down my wrist!"

Pelagia sat with her boyfriend, Ryan, and complained: "I'm fucking tired. Okay, I don't know where my phone is. No, I have my card—I don't know what fucking time *it* is, and I *just* want a *fucking* god damn shot."

"I'm very sorry for you," the bartender reaffirmed, his gaze locked on mine.

I paused, looked at him while his finger grazed my wrist, and said, "Why?"

"Because that's the most curious sensation you've experienced."

"In a long while, yes."

Cyrus stood to my left and said, "We gotta take this dude to the strip club and get him some new experiences!"

I said, "Would that satisfy me?"

"Yes *it* would!" Cyrus beamed.

I said to the bartender, "Are you eager to close?" while Pelagia continued to complain of the lack of service being rendered to her even though the bartender had already "rung a bell" and announced he will no longer be serving. The bar closed at midnight; the time was 12:30 AM.

The bartender ignored Pelagia and said to me, "I am *very* eager to close. I *want* to close."

"But you're not."

"I'm not?" He glared at me.

"Isn't that what you said?"

"No, I'm *very* eager to close."

"You tickle my wrist and then you look at me with hostility-"

"I'll tickle your wrist and I will tickle you with hostility."

I laughed.

Cyrus interjected, "Are we doing shots or not?"

"No we're not doing shots," muttered the bartender.

I reinforced the bartender's verdict: "No, he's (the bartender) fucking closing."

Cyrus said, "Alright, that's cool. I'll just finish my beer."

The bartender continued to glare at me; I said, "A fellow human being staring me in the eyes, staring at me with hostility for the enemy that I am."

"A human being? I'm gonna smack you in the face with this mat."

"Please do. *It*'s like a hammock to me, to have somebody stare at me like I'm the enemy that I am. I want you to pick up that mat, and slam me right in my fucking face, right now."

"If you come around this bar *it*'s not gonna be good for you brother."

I moved an inch and Pelagia shouted: "Stop! Stop!" I did, without her heed, for I only *listened* to the man behind the bar.

The bartender repeated, imploringly, "If you come around this bar *it*'s not gonna be good for you brother! Are you gonna be the one to test *it?*"

Pelagia whined, "Stop *stop*—please *stop!*"

The bartender asked me, "Are you gonna be the one to test *it?*"

Confused, I announced, "This is not hostility—this is brethren!"

"No, *it*'s not brethren."

"Why not?"

Pelagia interrupted by shouting, "I just want to pay my tab, take a shot, and *fucking* leave—like that's all I want to do right now."

The bartender ignored Pelagia; his eyes still fixed on mine, he said, "If you come around this bar bud I'm gonna fuck you."

Cyrus said, "Hey Crayton, I know you love playing chicken, but, do you wanna pour some shots real quick?"

The bartender said, "Nope—not at all," his eyes resolute on my own disillusioned gaze. My eyes began to water, and I realized the futility of the entire situation of the moment, the foolishness of all involved, the temperance of some, the incontinence of others, and the abject absurdity. I said, "How have I offended you... I want to know. How?"

"There's the door brother."

"I don't want to fight you."

"I don't have to fight; this is my bar, get the fuck out."

"I understand." I retracted from the conversation, donned my pack, reapproached the bartender who remained stalwart by the bar, his eyes locked on mine; I extended my hand. AC/DC's *T.N.T* began to play from the speakers above us. With a scrupulous hesitation exemplified in the bartender's hand extension, he accepted; I shook the man's hand as a starving man would the hand of a man who had provided a wholesome meal, and departed without another word spoken.

Damn this journal—this trite, this nonsensical pandering...

I've gifted the remainder of my books and possessions to my closest enemies and have maintained a plethora of quasi acquaintances to sustain me throughout my constant interchange of labor between dishwashing, personal hygiene, editing, writing, strength training, and running four miles "home"—to the abandoned house of my youth—and to and from the gym each night. I consume, reflect, read, ponder, and ruminate. I have achieved the greatest state of fitness I have ever known my body to exhibit; I expect this condition to improve as long as my flesh cooperates. Abstaining from relationships on a personal level for over two years (excluding with my father and Pelagia) has compelled me to speak to every stranger I come into contact with.

Yes, I could mull over all my noble exploits and deeds, of what I've committed to assist my fellow man, to aid, to uplift, to endear and validate, and the same for my sisters, though they are few, for relations with women—in my experiences, always tend to be grounded in sexuality. Creatures of mutual desires, we yearn *to* hope.

I love my role as a dishwasher; I will miss the work, for *it* has become who I am for a greater portion of my young adulthood to the present. I am a seasoned veteran of the craft; every shift is a test of will, integrity, stamina, grace, speed, and efficiency—*though,* the realm is limited, and I have mastered what is essentially a labor fit for an imbecile, or an incompetent… or a fool… Yes, I *will* miss the labor.

I entered the adjacent bar to the kitchen where I'm employed with a glass bottle of water in-hand, prepared to partake in my ritualistic-two glasses of cabernet after my shift in preparation for a session at the gym, and encountered Pelagia; I gazed at the back of her head for a moment and wondered: a thoughtless wonderment, and sat three stools away to her left. A self-proclaimed "weird" couple sat between us; the man unintentionally rubbed my leg with his hand and said, "Sorry I keep rubbing your leg," despite only doing so once.

I said, "That's alright."

The man smirked and peered up at me from behind circular spectacles; his small, pudgy stature hunched against the bar, and he said, *"It*'s weird."

I said, "If you think *it*'s weird to rub your leg against mine then why do you?"

"I don't know." He laughed.

"Perhaps you're weird."

The man smiled at me. I looked away to the glass that Pat filled on my behalf. The bar bustled with activity and I immersed myself with the amalgamate of nameless voices: animals uttering vocal signals of dominance, flatteries connotated with lust, and sweet, *sweet* nothings— silent ululations of unsettled minds immersed with phone screens, their individual energies projected outward and converged at a nexus of self- hatred rooted in doubt rendered palpable by one who closes their eyes and listens-

Pelagia touched my shoulder and said, "I saw you and thought I'd say hi."

I turned my head towards her and said, "I saw you and avoided you."

262

"Oh, well, okay." Pelagia left me be and sat where she had been seated before.

I departed the bar after one glass of wine, utilized my free "shift drink," and didn't tip.

Eleven days until deployment.

11:24 PM

I often wish to sit; sometimes I do for no longer than twenty minutes. I lose myself to the silence of mental duress, the restlessness of thought: A veritable hail of fire and brimstone. To shut this out, and forget: Everything you ever were: Memories of childhood friends, obsessions, passions, full of life and vigor, enraptured with the essence of what you'll become… and to *be* possessed by the imagined image of yourself, only to live, and persist on living, where every substantial point or reckoning beyond the point you *just* lived heralds a new "self," with new expectations, new engrossments: a template.

Is virtue pretentious? Some tell me, "Yes," and exhale a sigh of concession. Others say, "No," and expound on the matter of being human— for instance: Saving a kitten in a tree for the betterment of humanity and the sake of *good*, "How is that a pretense?" one presses the inquiry.

I respond: "To save the kitten is for the sake of your ego and your belief that you contribute to the betterment of humanity. The virtue of being benevolent and magnanimous towards a baser animal is a lesson society has instilled in you, to which, even if there is no witness to your action, your ego will benefit due to your belief."

I'm met with a sidelong head shake and a spoken, "No"; nothing more.

April 21st, 2019

1:45 PM

Every morning is the same, and has been for the last three months: Awaken from the darkened floor of what once was the weight room in my father's abandoned home. In the empty quarters, I languish with my thoughts and listen to birds sing, wind rustle, kids scream and play, cars pass, neighbors banter, and the reverb of lawn equipment.

On this particular seventy-degree Fahrenheit morning, I've opened the front and back doors to allow a subtle draft to pass through. My typical dampened and stifled living quarters (a featureless kitchen) has been illuminated by an afternoon sun; I breathe steady and focus on the breeze against my calves while I record these sentiments.

Before I arise from the floor, after a period of five minutes to two hours, depending on the severity of my existential reflections, I engage in as many sit-ups as possible for two minutes, followed by a set of pushups until my body fails me. I exit the empty chamber, enter the kitchen and partake in a glass of water, followed by a tablespoon of apple cider vinegar mixed with three tablespoons of water, followed by another glass of water. I consume an ounce of sauerkraut from the jar, and during this brief period, I begin to arrange my paradigm for the day: activities ranging between reading, writing, editing, consumption, physical activity, and if I am scheduled at the bar—work. Today, I am not scheduled to work; therefore I have time to record a synopsis of my general day-to-day activities for a somber time in the future when I'm malcontent with "being" and seek to entertain myself with words I no longer identify with.

I consume a can of tuna, sardines, a green tea capsule, and a fish oil capsule. A sweet potato boils utilizing an electric portable stove top element on the kitchen countertop to the left of a cardboard box—my podium— where I stand for most of my time in the building. The sweet potato is a deviation from my normalized consumption, whereas I would partake in sautéed broccoli, pepper, mushroom, spinach, and three eggs, spiced with garlic powder, cumin, and black pepper; the sautéed segment of the meal, when finished, is poured into a bowl over a handful of blueberries, blackberries, raspberries, almonds, and cacao nibs, spiced with Ceylon cinnamon. I mix the conglomerate with a spoon and consume.

Periodical calisthenics. Shower. Sardines and a banana. Read (John Locke's *Second Treatise of Government*). Study the *Eleven General Orders of the Sentry* (U.S. Navy jargon). Steel-cut oats and whey protein. Stretch, pace, amble, prostrate.

Boring. The mundaneness of my reality, observable as the product of my immediate material world, is the single reliable aspect of "truth" I may rely on to record as accurate per my faculty of limited human reason and understanding.

The more I learn, the more I desire to unlearn.

Three days have elapsed since I sat with Sara at the bar; I have received no correspondence with her since. I intend to abstain from any bar and from the consumption of alcohol in preparation for deployment, and to avoid those who desire to care about me.

As a secondary passion, I work to ruin the remnants of my good-standing reputation among my superiors at the bar where I'm employed through vitriolic questioning and manipulative tact.

Yesterday I entered the workplace and found myself among the company of men hostile to my presence due to my cold, callous, flippant, and brazen behavior—a privilege allotted to me due to my position as a dishwasher: the lowest man on the totem pole. I turned to the chef and the two cooks and addressed them with an upbeat acknowledgment: "Must we suppress ourselves for the sake of cooperation, the beasts that we are? Or should we all *whistle* and lose ourselves?" My supervisor whistles throughout the entirety of his shift; this obnoxious habit is an expression of his vacuousness and a blatant disregard for the consideration of other employee's soundness of mind.

One cook: A large African American man with a history of a prison sentence and origins from "The Hood," as he proclaims, responded to me, with utter nonsense—a complete miscomprehension of any matter I spoke of.

Moments later, my supervisor approached from my left: A sycophantic man who once flattered me for my work ethic *and* character… a man who whistles throughout his shift—to escape from the realm of *thought;* he looked at me with a disparaging grimace. I said, "Do you experience regret, having flattered me before as much as you have?"

"What do you mean?"

I said, "Would you think that a dog would enjoy being flattered?"

"Yeah, they love *it*."

"I've known dogs to lash out and bite when they are coddled and pampered."

"Yeah, they do, they get arrogant."

He grinned, amused and intrigued. I turned away, and moments later, while I hunched over a dish basin, pan in-hand and pad of steel wool in the other, I heard, "Woof woof!" from my rear.

I snapped my head over my shoulder and saw my supervisor observing me; he glanced down on my acknowledgment of him, and gazed at me with a softer expression. I addressed him with the severity of one who had been mocked—for there is no other explanation. I relaxed my expression and said, "I don't name myself as 'dog,' although that may be your opinion of me at the moment due to my behavior, *it* was a-" My supervisor had approached my side again with a *pretense* of goodwill expressed in his demeanor; I truncated my sentence on account of this behavior, smiled, and said, "I think I remind you of your son."

His smile faded to a befuddled stare. "No."

Neither of us spoke to anyone for the remainder of our shift, nor did my supervisor whistle.

April 23rd, 2019

2:17 AM

Mia has "fallen in love" with me and asks me often if I'll ever return to visit the city while we lay together in her bed post-coitus, to which I respond, "No: to do so would be a personal failure." I visited my father for two hours after three weeks of forgoing his company and he asked me the same query, to which I similarly answered him.

Lo! The dish pit is my domain, and has been for four months. My final week employed within the bar kitchen begins in the afternoon of this day. To commemorate my inconsequential downfall I've decided to shed my dress shirt in favor of a black Henley shirt, and to shave my head, military recruit style. I've accrued notoriety due to my now bygone relationship with Pelagia, post-shift bar activity, and my "weird" behavior among my peers in the kitchen.

Oh, yes, let's begin-

On the Pretentiousness of Virtue

"How is virtue pretentious? You can't just *pretend* to be virtuous; you can't pretend to be patient—that's absurd; you can't pretend to be wise—that's preposterous; you can't pretend to be courageous—that's ludicrous!"

"Quiet, you pitiful, pious, imbecile," shouted a craven wretch, "and pay heed to the words of an abominable fool, for they have more merit than any scripture or creed you hold as a personal 'truth' near and dear to your heart."

"I will not; your theories and proclamations are despicable and against humanity."

"Very well, yet, there you sit, a damned hypocrite; now, reckon this 'truth': We are beasts, creatures who instill our progeny with ethics and morality conducive to a preconceived society."

"We are men of *God!*"

"Shut up, damn you! Ethics and morality are tools of manipulation, to which 'we' (beasts) wield with excellent efficiency against each other. Suffering unites us; empathy is the channel—a conduit of the shared understanding for what we experience (dependent on culture) to be *virtuous* behavior. One 'practices' virtue for the sake of the ego, i.e., insurance of genetic proliferation, cooperation among a group, and self-preservation. The 'practice' of being virtuous is equivalent to the manner one may practice an art, profession, or *game*—most notable, the actor/actress— veritable quintessential expressions of the *game* of life: both tragic and comical."

Now, to review the essence of each virtue and proceed to analyze, in brief, each correspondent behavior in relation to culture:

Chastity: To "Save oneself" for a mate "worthy" of oneself. To promote yourself as "chaste" is to declare your virtue for the sake of enticement. To proclaim yourself as chaste is to *destroy* your virtue, i.e., what never was.

Temperance: For the sake of yourself, i.e., health, public opinion, you temper your desires and the base hunger of being a creature. Health and public opinion coincide at the potentiality for longevity, increasing the odds of copulation and/or validation.

Charity: Altruism, in the purest expression, is nonexistent. There can be no selflessness without selfishness. A martyr is the greatest egotist.

Wisdom: One may only be wise when cross-referenced by another, or when one shares their acquired knowledge on account of experiences; otherwise when left to one's own devices, learning to *not* ingest a mushroom that incites nausea and fever is a simple act of animalistic self-preservation.

I can't be bothered; a virtue in one province is iniquity in another.

Cannibalism: Yummy.

April 24th, 2019

12:50 AM

I conduct my shift in silence.

There is never a reason to speak except to inform, or to instruct and obey orders; all else is futile.

Walther said behind my back in passing while I scrubbed a pot, "Well look at you, ready to be shuttled into space," in regards to my new aspect: shaved head and simple black shirt. I'm regarded with wonder and confusion, revulsion and admiration. Most notable in my interactions throughout the course of my silent labors is the lack of pity. No... Only I felt pity for my brethren, for those who judged me with greater respect and reverence due to manner of dress, style of hair, and chosen slavery... Yes: I pity my fellow creatures for their simplicity.

My direct supervisor considers himself an aged "stud"; his accumulation of visceral fat causes hint to be self-conscious and he compares himself to his peers—myself, most of all, for my age and enlistment with the U.S. Navy.

Waitresses who once ogled me now turn away, dismayed by my slight alterations: the superficiality of their lust repelled by my active will.

A dress shirt accentuates one's physique; those accustomed to my four-month employment garbed in *only* a dress shirt, with no deviation, now reckon my unembellished body. Every man older and stronger than myself looks upon me with relief and superiority—to compare oneself to another, though these judgments I relish more than any praise, recommendation, or exaltation; I welcome the smug and contented grins and the self-accolades of my overfed brethren.

When silent, the intrinsic pandemonium of other's internal machinations ripples throughout... the *mindscape;* oh, and a lovely reckoning we all share when we observe with our eyes instead of listening to the lies we ululate and garble into each other's deadened ears—for what do we *hear...* sweet *nothings.* Empathy is observation; eliminate the diluted nonsense of the spoken word—veritable symbols etched into the *soundscape,* for what cause, other than to *command:* thus, speech is manipulation. A human body and the visage adorned atop is also a conduit for lies... alas, who can one trust but oneself—one's *thoughts,* the intuitive projection into the realm of a perceiver—for we only "know" each other. Trust yourself, whether you "love" or "hate" (yourself).

One week until deployment.

11:00 PM

I've stood in the basement of the bar after my shift for the past three days and have utilized the company's wireless internet to finalize the editing of last year's manuscript. I stand now, with my writing device propped on top of a stack of boxes. A can of sardines, a banana, and a bottle of water is situated to my left. I engage in calisthenics every five minutes.

My recruiters have informed me that my ship date has been expedited two days sooner than planned: April 29th. Five days until deployment.

April 26th, 2019

12:23 AM

Damnable nothings and idle vexations: My recruiters picked me up for an impromptu meeting forty minutes after I awoke the previous morning to verify my background check. My fingerprints from four months ago were insufficient due to a "glitch" in the system; this "glitch" was known months before and my recruiters had decided to inform me within the last twenty-four hours—three days before my scheduled ship date—and now, due to the waiting time incurred on the processing of my new fingerprint documentation (which may not be validated due to a burn on my index finger), my deployment date has been postponed to May 9th.

On the fifty-minute drive back to my "home," I engaged in a recorded conversation with one of my three recruiters, Adam: A thirty-three-year-old man, with a history of seven years service in the Navy, a father of one child, and married to a stay-at-home mother who spends her days playing World of Warcraft. We stared straight ahead at a highway:

I said, "I don't think friends are worth having."
Adam said, "Depends on the type of friend."
"A competent friend, who can teach you skills, is worth having."
"Having someone who compliments your weaknesses is a good thing."

"Yes, if you're in the same field, and you're working together, but then you would be allies. If you had a friend who complimented your weaknesses but you weren't working together towards a similar goal *it* would just be a reminder of your shortcomings and how to improve yourself."

Adam said, "Some weaknesses you can't improve. From a military standpoint that's why snipers work in twos."

"Spot each other. Keep each other in check-"

"And cover each other's weaknesses."

A prolonged pause elapsed; Adam continued: "At the same time the bonds *those* people form are much different than regular friendship."

"*It*'s a brotherhood. Comrades."

"Today people use the term 'friendship,' *way* too loosely. Today at a high school, you can ask a guy how many friends he has and he'll say, 'Oh I've got two-thousand-nine-hundred friends.' Okay. But you don't. Out of two-thousand something of those people, you'll only spend time with a fraction."

"I recently read a statistic on [domain] that 73% of a person's social media friends, aren't people that would even be in their social circle, if not for social media domains."

"Yeah—makes me think of my wife and her 'friends'... There's my home exit!" We passed an exit ramp on a highway and remained silent for two minutes. Adam said, "So what other topics do you like to study?"

"I'm big into consciousness and the human condition. Sociology, psychology, every now and then theology. Mostly those, and philosophy, though lately I've deviated from philosophy. In my writings, I'm breaking down what *it* is that makes for a 'good' human, and how we validate each other, and our 'sociopathic' elements—even though that terminology was coined in 1930–*it* is essentially an umbrella term for antisocial traits and other traits that are not-"

"Normal."

"Yes—or traits that are desirable by a functioning society."

"Sociopaths seem like the best investigators."

"Yes—and I believe that 'sociopaths'—or a 'sociopath,' is just a baseline human being that hasn't been taught any virtue. They don't care to practice virtues that they know, and they only practice virtues when the behavior benefits them. Hence, you're only courageous when you need to be; we are temperate for the sake of ourselves; we claim to be wise to impress our knowledge onto others or are named wise on account of others perceiving themselves to be deficient. *It*'s all a gross indulgence of our 'self,' and, *it*'s

difficult for me to maintain social relationships because of *it*—because of...
all my thought directed towards this-"

"So is that to say that an introvert is a sociopath? Because they have
antisocial behavior and brain chemistry?"

"To go the 'Myers Brigg' route for the introverted and extroverted...
is, see that's just *it* man—these *labels:* 'sociopath,' 'introvert,' 'extrovert,'
all the other *pathies.* 'Schizophrenia' is so overdiagnosed that anyone
whose hearing voices—which is the natural dictation of our egos—is
'schizophrenic' now. Nobody trusts themselves or their intuition. People
who are 'schizophrenic' are just self-obsessed and project their ego onto
other people—or, aliens or government mind control—they can't *bear* to
handle their thoughts themselves—so they project *it* out, and delusions
or hallucinations may manifest as a result, but they're really just self-
obsessed... *It*'s bullshit.

"But, 'introverts'... I consider myself to be an 'introvert'; I've taken the
Myers Brigg test; I'm mostly introverted: 90%. But, I think that extroverts
are *more* 'sociopathic' because of how they really put themselves out there,
and they want the validation—but there are different *types* of *'sociopathy';*
there's different—see there are all these *labels,* and *jargon*—to name these
conditions that are deemed unacceptable by society, but really, *it*'s just to
put people down and to enforce doubt so the masses may be more easily
sold prescription medication, psychiatry, and psychotherapy—and that's
really all *it* is—*it*'s a big marketing scheme. *It*'s all *bullshit.*

"Thinking of this, has been my primary locus of thought lately, and
I'm eager to get into the Navy—for the culture, and the study of *it,* to
travel abroad and experience all the different peoples and engage with
their cultures and learning of their psyches and how they interact and... I
am, *just*—*it*'s validation—*it*'s one big fuck-fest and everybody's eating and
shitting... the holy trinity: procreation, consumption, defecation: that's
all life is.

"You listening to me spew this out now, is a validation, for me; you'll
respond, and I'll respond—and... *It*'s really *just* nothing: soundwaves,
projected back and forth. I'm disillusioned, on account of all the philosophy
I've read, the study of the mind, and everybody says—we'll not everybody—
but we all *apparently* have imbalanced brain chemistry, people hearing
voices—I mean these processes have been ongoing since the dawn of
man; before we developed speech, we were all hearing voices and intuiting
each other's body language, our gestures—we were *interpreting each other.*
But now, *it*'s deemed 'schizophrenic,' for people are self-obsessed and

afflicted with self-doubt. People don't want to believe or identify with the interpretations they intuit from other people because these 'voices' are really a *reflection* of themselves.

"I don't speak, and I'm often sad, so when people see me, they pity me, and I, in turn, pity *them,* for I pity humanity for what *it* is; therefore, I pity myself because I'm human too, so *it*'s a self-fulfilling cycle of negativity, and I can't seem to dig myself out of this rut due to everything that I have *read.* The curse of knowledge; *it*'s bullshit—*it*'s nothing; *it*'s all taught: shame, the virtues, proper behaviors.

"I'd love to be a chieftain of a tribe of barbarian cannibals; what virtues would they have? *Completely* different. *It*'s dependent on culture, and culture is an amalgamation of individuals."

"Which constitutes a society."

"Exactly." I sighed, surprised with how I had rambled, and how Adam had listened.

"So what's the... how would you want people to behave? Let's say we get everyone to accept that what they're seeing is projections of themselves; let's say everyone became aware of that; does everyone just stop—does the world stop turning? Where do we go from there?"

"I think that the notion of progress should be relinquished entirely; to break *it* down entirely—see I've never been asked this before... You could consider me a total anarchist, where I would love for people to accept the ego for what *it* is, and truly embrace their base humanity. The only way to give back to humanity is to be completely egotistical and engross yourself with what you enjoy the most."

"So to act on our most primal instincts."

"Yes, and, through that there would be anarchy. Savages."

"Yeah, well, not savages because we would still practice ethics. Human sentience is to know the difference between right and wrong."

I shifted in my seat and said, "That's just *it* too—ethics and morality are fickle."

"So what's the purpose of your writing lately?"

"Ah... to contemplate what my personal philosophy and creed are, and I've come to find... *it*'s just, anarchy, really; to realize and acknowledge how everyone is deceiving and using each other, and... to act out of reason... emotion... reason *guided* by emotion; emotion is what makes us human. I think that developing quantum computing and artificial intelligence is the most foolish path that humanity could take."

"Because of the singularity?"

"The singularity—yes… that, to me, is synonymous with doom."

"*It* can be. I mean we can postulate all we want about *it*, until *it* happens—if *it* ever happens, humanity will be altered and shaped by something potentially far greater than *it*self."

I spoke with disdain, "*It* could be the greatest thing that ever happened to mankind."

Adam spoke with a hint of optimism, "*It* could be; *it* could be an emergence between robot and human, that we could rebuild ourselves for any purpose we need at the time. Who knows. We could end up with 'terminators,' where computers and machines take over the earth and systematically wipe everything out. *It* could be a dud—the singularity could happen, the 'AI,' *it* knows what *it* is, becomes self-sentient—self-aware, and clones *it*self of *it*s own awareness; we don't know—we've never done *it*."

We sat for a while in silence; we had entered my city; fifteen minutes remained of our car ride. We had looked at each other at rare moments throughout our dialogue to relay emotional information in relation to our spoken words.

I said, "I read a story called *I Have No Mouth But I Must Scream*, and the premise was a dystopian horror world; *it* was inside the mind of an artificial intelligence that had taken over and wiped out the entire human race, and *it* assimilated, or 'consumed' five human beings that *it* chose to torture for eternity. They trek through barren hellscapes; everything is computerized, digitized, and *it*'s a grueling horror; they're surrounded by creatures and darkness; they're ripped apart and reassembled—they die over and over again in gruesome ways but then, they are reborn, and they join each other-"

"So *it*'s like a retelling of… the Greek titan that has his liver ripped out and eaten every day by the…"

"Ah yes what was his name-"

"The titan, gifted man fire-"

I murmured, "Prometheus."

"Yeah."

"That's also similar to… Sisyphus: the man condemned to roll a boulder up a mountain—*see that's* progress to me: to roll a boulder up a mountain and *it* just falls down again—and he rolls *it* back up. That is, in essence, the entire nature of humanity—of life—*it*'s just a cycle. I mean—the singularity, as we know *it*, and discuss *it*, and theorize, *it* is the end of a cycle; *it* is like recreating the 'matrix' in *it*self. I *mean*—all these ideas converge! People seem to have the same basic ideas that are projected through the media; we all seem to know what we're coming to, but we go that route anyway; *it*'s like we yearn for doom… we yearn for destruction; we love *it*."

"Well *it*'s one-half of us."

"Yes. To love the destruction: *it*'s a catalyst for growth. We want to destroy ourselves and we love every moment we achieve a step closer *to* that. I recently was in a relationship with a woman that I hated the moment I met her, and then—she pursued me, as a male would pursue a female; after three months, I finally caved; *it* was the most beautiful act of destruction—to be with her—that I've ever experienced—because she was so *incredibly toxic,* and I was toxic to her as well, and *it* ended with such grievance… I feel like a whole new person because of *it:* in a way, not a whole new person—altered."

"You take parts of every experience. You aren't the same person one day to the next."

"Even this last moment, this second; there is nothing; *it* doesn't matter; there is no true 'self,' just ego and inclinations. There is no true intelligence; there is mastery."

"Do we take a right or go straight?"

"Straight."

We sat at a red light in silence and listened to the outdoor ambiance of passing cars alongside us on the four-lane road.

I said, "I think that admitting to using CBD oil was probably one of the best mistakes I ever made."

Adam snickered and said, "Why's that?"

"I'm going to culinary school now to learn the same kitchen work that I've been accustomed to for most of my life, and I know that I'll be considered to be low… class, essentially, and I prefer *it* that way… I've always been accustomed to *that*. There are low expectations of intellectual capacity, and I am free to think; I won't be fully immersed in the task."

"You'd be surprised how much power the low-class chef has."

"I don't want power."

We pulled up to my "home" and parked.

"But you'll still be shocked by the amount of power that food has on a ship. Your ability to get *things*… like, this guy I knew, a CS-2, his name was Bell—see this pin?" Adam pointed to his uniform at one of the many spangled badges across his chest "*It*'s enlisted service warfare specialist; he would send me people that he knew couldn't pass the test for portions of the qualifications for this—at least the reactor portions, and, he'd give me a chicken sandwich, and *it*'s not mealtime—and he just gave me a free chicken sandwich and all I had to do was give these three guys ten minutes of my time to help them study. So that, in-turn, made him look better because all the people under him are getting this coveted thing."

"A coveted chicken sandwich?"

"No—no, *this*," he pointed to the pin on his chest. "This carries a lot of weight."

"That's amazing."

"Yeah—this stupid little pin made of fuckin' nickel and tin."

"I thought *it* was amusing earlier, when I was sitting in the Navy office: One of the E6's came over, and he saw me reading the *Eleven General Orders of the Sentry;* he started to grill me on the rankings and insignias: He was attempting to teach me. *It* was right after I had been informed that my ship date was pushed back to May 9th."

"So you didn't give a shit?" Adam chuckled.

"Yeah, so I was—I was looking at him but I was looking through him, and my eyes began to glaze over; I could tell he thought that I had a lot to learn in the realm of... respect, because there he was showing me his insignia, obviously very proud, but to me, he is just a human being, and the only denotion his rank has is related to how much he's paid or how long he's been in the service for; that's really *it;* these people," I scoffed, "they parade around with their medals and medallions and their stripes... and their honors... and *it*'s just *pitiful* to me. I know that I'm going to have a difficult time assimilating with the culture; that's the only thing I'm concerned with: I know myself well enough to know that I'm an anarchist, soon to be among a culture of-"

"Order."

"-pompous elitists and—order—yes. There's a difference between being egotistical and being elitist, and I imagine that the more colors and stripes and beautiful badges one has on one's uniform, then the more hubristic and prideful that they are."

"Depends on the person."

"True."

"Like I give no fucks about any of this—I wear *it* because *it*'s part of the uniform and you have to."

"I'm sure *it* warrants some respect and admiration from your peers, though, any amount of envy yields equal... hatred..."

Adam proceeded to inform me of the meaning of every pin attached to his uniform for two-and-a-half minutes. I thanked him for the conversation and departed from his vehicle.

April 27th, 2019

1:08 AM

I pity everybody and myself, for our humanity.

Intoxicated by two glasses of wine, I asked a few pool players what their self-assigned meaning of life is: "I don't know—nobody can know," and "To build my business," were the two answers I received. Both accused me of being "Dracula," and inquired if the wine I drank is blood.

Beatrice suggested that I record her as a character in my book: We wished each other well while she scrubbed pans. I stood, a tactical pack strapped to my back, hands braced against the dish basin brim; I thanked her for her compassion, understanding, and conversations; we hugged twice.

An African American bartender wished that I learn as much as I can and to grow and prosper in the Navy; he desires to become his own boss in a year.

Walther fumbled with a shank of raw prime rib and said to me: "Ah, a fine, exquisite piece of human rib—prime, as it were, from a sedentary specimen, lined with plentiful fat reserves."

I stared at the plastic-encased shank and said, "No lack of that."

Walther poured me a free glass of wine; I asked him what song he hums to himself throughout the day; he said, "Nothing in particular, just random tunes that come to mind."

I asked a young woman near the pool table what her meaning of life is; she said, "I'm an orthodontist; I cure people's mouth diseases."

"That's more of a vocation or an occupation."

"I don't know what 'vocation' is."

The nearby boyfriend of the woman said, "I'm sorry for you."

The woman sneered at him, turned to me, and said, "What's your name?"

"My name is irrelevant."

She narrowed her eyes and said, "Fuck you."

"I ask you what your meaning of life is and you ask me what my *name* is—now you reckon me with disdain featured on your countenance. What of *it*?"

"I don't like you."

"I'm pleased with your forthcoming opinion of me; an honesty of your caliber is a rare trait. I'm an asshole, this I know for myself, and you have pierced the veil of my nature within two minutes of our initial meeting."

The woman turned her body away from me, followed by her eyes, her head, and she veered away to sit down with her boyfriend. "He *does* look like a vampire," she said to her boyfriend.

"Yeah, he's fucking awesome—and weird as hell," said the boyfriend.

I drank my wine, ignored both, and watched pool balls ricochet into cubbies.

The bar bouncer closed his eyes and nodded his head to the club music; I approached him and said, "Look, what do you make of what you see?"

"A bar."

"And the people—look at them."

"Yeah, people sitting at a bar and standing around, talking."

"Imagine them naked, and think of what their true designs are; think of their haired nipples, gashes, bodily excretions-"

"*Alright,* get the hell away from me man if that's what you're going to talk about," he suppressed a laugh.

"I don't care if you want to hear what I have to say, or if you don't like me—I want you to *think,* damn *it* all, of what I envision of the sliver of human filth you see before us now: look, and view the mingling, the absurdity—the people talk of nothing and yearn to fuck—*to fuck-*"

The bouncer laughed and said, "This isn't the place to be talking like that."

"There is no other place; there is only now with these human specimens, and you—and *I,* how we observe our fellow fleshy sacks and persist with consumption and defecation day-after-day—that's all there is!"

"*It* is what you make of *it.*"

"Of course," I said, and swigged my wine.

Confounded—everything: each conversation is contrived and foolish. Dirtied dish water drains down a pipe. I'm a dead man, soul and spirit. My employment as a dishwasher is terminated.

A rotund mass of flesh lurched within a cavernous recess. Two plump, gray, elongated limbs snaked away from the mass against cold stone and slithered towards prey gifted from a master stood on the precipice above the darkened lair. The prey: a naked middle-aged man, slit down his abdomen and stitched together with a simple strand of cotton thread, lay spread-eagled, afflicted with full-body paralysis, and whimpered on the cavern floor.

One of the two pudgy limbs encroached under the dim light shone from the master's quarters above and approached the prey's left foot; a toothless gap at the end of the limb opened and closed; two adjacent holes reminiscent of blackened eyes sniffed and snorted. The gap snapped open and encircled around three of five toes, relinquished hold, and flopped onto the prey's foot.

The prey screamed a muffled wail, his eyes wide and fearful on sight of the abominable appendage slackened over his calf.

"Now, now," the robed figure of the master called from above; the prey gazed upwards and observed one gloved hand outstretched towards the monstrous serpentine flesh—a gesture of reckoning, "Your body will serve as fuel for something far greater: a vessel for my craft. Your suffering is equatable to my joy."

The second appendage encroached from a shadowed alcove to the prey's rear and plopped onto the prey's face, slid off, and latched onto his right ear; a slight suction incited the prey to wail. The first appendage meandered up onto the prey's thigh, past his genitals, and settled on top of his stitched abdomen.

"*My*—she learns with unprecedented haste!" sang the master.

The prey convulsed despite paralysis; one maw clamped onto the abdominal thread and pulled; the other appendage detached from his ear, slithered onto his forehead, and compressed an open maw over his right eye.

The master lowered his hand to his side, stood stiff against the bright backdrop of an immense concave gothic ceiling, and said, "Your lamentations are harmonic to us!"

The appendage situated at the prey's abdomen broke the seam of thread and wedged into the incision inches above the naval. The prey foamed at the edges of a wracked mouth and revealed two crooked rows of teeth outlined by strained lips; his body quaked and trembled in a helpless fit of futile effort: Three fingers and a thumb flexed against the cavern floor.

April 28th, 2019

2:51 PM

Oh… J.S. Bach's *Mass in B Minor, BWV 232 / Credo - Crucifixus,* is a glorious treat to the ears: a perfect cold shower serenade. To be without the pleasure of music will be the most difficult trial throughout basic training.
"Oh-o-say, can, you, see! By the dawn's ear-ly light!"

April 29th, 2019

1:36 PM

I strode into a grocery store checkout line at 11:56 PM with a hand basket filled with 12 cans of sardines, 12 cans of tuna, two bunches of bananas, a jar of sauerkraut, a jar of peanut butter, 5 sweet potatoes, and said to two service clerks, "Alright, so, would you rather be stabbed in the heart by a long blade, puncturing out through your back, and the blade remains wedged in you so you have a choice to pull *it* out; or, you are shot off-center in your abdominals by a .50 caliber round."

The bagger girl snapped to attention and said, "Do I live?"

"No, you're mortally wounded."

"Stabbed in… no, *wait*—wow, both of those options *suck*."

The man at the register acknowledged me with glazed eyes and said, "Man, why you gotta make me think about this kinda shit; I just want to go home."

I said, "Well, if the thoughts disturb you, feel free to discard them at your own volition."

"I mean…" he continued, "Damn, there are… just, too many variables involved. I mean, I could bleed out—only if I pulled the blade out—and *it*'s wedged in there—man, c'mon, usually your questions are much nicer."

The girl laughed and said, "I like this one, but I still don't know; both of those options suck."

I said, "Yes. Have a good night you two," and departed with my fish-filled pack.

11:24 PM

The hermit opened his seaside cottage door and beheld the concubine mounted on her steed. "I've come back for you," she said.

"I see."

"I stopped by a few days ago to see you and you either weren't home, or you hadn't bothered to heed my knocks. I wanted to say goodbye to you one last time."

"Goodbye."

"No-" The concubine leaped from her horse and grasped the hilt of a saber strapped to her hip. "The extent of our interaction deserves more than an underwhelming finish." She hastened to the cottage doorway and met the hermit's resolute stare with her own dispirited visage.

"The extent of our interaction had already transpired and *was* an underwhelming finish. Remember me or forget me as you will. Goodbye."

The concubine stood, saber hilt in-hand, and scrutinized the hermit; he gazed at her with sorrowful eyes and reckoned her unembellished beauty: garbed in a large, simple, purple gown, her shortened hair unattended; he acknowledged how her unburdened left hand trembled; the way her lips curled into an uncertain grimace—a mouth which desired to grin and instead settled on a displaced expression of defiance. How she waited signaled an overwrought desire to speak despite deliberate suppression.

The hermit said, "I pity you."

"I know this." The concubine's countenance softened; she released the hilt of her saber, mounted her horse, regarded the hermit with an empathetic smile, laughed, and rode, homeward bound to a distant mountain village.

MAY

May 4th, 2019

12:58 PM

"Have you ever watched a fly drown?"

White-foamed waves lapped against the shores of a sun-warmed yellow beach and cast a sparse mist over a middle-aged man and a young woman sprawled on top of two separate beach towels colored solid green and blue, respectively.

"No," said the woman, and she shifted her legs to form a seventy-degree angle.

"The other day a fly buzzed in my bathroom; I heard *it* and went to find *it* with a piece of junk mail." The man sighed, squirted suntan lotion onto the tips of his left middle and index finger, smoothed the two fingers over his forehead, and spread the cream down to both cheeks; he rubbed in circular motions and murmured, *"Oh."*

"And?"

"So I swatted the fly, which had settled on the wall above the toilet, and *it* corkscrewed away from the wall and flew into the toilet bowl."

"You watched *it* drown?"

"Well, I watched *it* swim around for about five minutes. A little bit of *it*s guts popped out due to me swatting *it* but that didn't seem to impede *it*s swimming abilities. I began to spit into the bowl and aimed my saliva at the fly."

The woman removed a thick black pair of sunglasses, set the item to her left in the sand, turned her brown-skinned head towards the man to her right, closed her eyes, and said, "You're sick."

"Two out of the eight globs landed right on top of the fly and caused *it* to panic. Do you think saliva is potent enough to begin the digestion process of exposed fly organs?"

"No."

"So after that I stood, walked away, and forgot about the fly. An hour later I had to shit. When I returned to the toilet I saw the fly still swimming like *it* had been when I left. They're tenacious little buggers... I pissed and shit in the toilet and watched the fly ride the waves-"

"You *really* are sick. My *God.*"

"Ah, well—so, the fly seemed unaffected from swimming in piss-water, and my shit had sunk to the bottom of the toilet, and I wanted to flush, but I didn't want to flush the fly down without learning something first."

The woman titled her face towards the overhead sun and frowned. "What did you learn?"

"I wasn't sure if a fly could drown—I mean, I know they *need* to breathe, but I was curious how long they could survive under piss-water." The man laughed, finalized the application of cream beneath his eyes, and lay, legs flat, both arms at his sides, eyes closed. "I wiped my ass and laid the sheets over the fly; *it* crawled out from underneath and resurfaced in a snap."

"This is disgusting."

"Hold on—so, I squatted down for closer observation because I wanted to see the death throes of a fly-"

"Jeremy—*are you* fucking serious right now?"

"Hold on... Well, I reached into the bowl and plopped half of the wad of toilet paper over the fly and sandwiched *it* between the-"

"Oh my *fucking* God—you *reached* into your own shitty piss-water?" The woman sat upright and glared at the man to her right; he smirked, opened his eyes, sat upright, hunched over, adjusted his swim shorts, and placed his left hand onto the woman's back; she said, "No!" and stood.

"At least let me finish."

"Alright just make *it* fucking quick. I really can't believe you."

"I washed my hands after, what's the big deal? *So anyway,* the fly managed to escape from the toilet paper and resurfaced. Now *it* was attempting to climb the side of the bowl with a newfound zeal; I blew *it* back down into the water, tore two foot-long lengths of paper off the roll, and laid both strips over the water. The fly was now submerged with no way to escape and I shifted onto my knees with my head a few inches above the bowl to watch. At first *it* seemed confident and moved slowly; a few times *it* paused and rubbed *it*s two front legs together like flies do—only *underwater,* upside-down... that confused me, but anyway—after about forty-five seconds *it* began to speed around the perimeter of the bowl and desperately nudged *it*s head against the paper. *It* did two full laps before *it* suddenly stopped, twitched about four or five times, then *it* was still... I removed the paper and poked *it* a few times to make sure *it* was dead, and *it* was—no movement, so I flushed and washed my hands."

The woman had turned towards the ocean. Long amber hair billowed off her back due to the encroachment of hot northbound gusts. She stood, statuesque, and waited. The man said nothing. She said, "Why did you tell me that?"

"Just something interesting. Did you like *it?*"

"No… no I didn't. I actually lost respect for you and I'm seriously creeped out."

"Oh c'mon, *it*'s just something guys do." The man shambled to his feet, moved to touch the woman's neck, and she began to walk away towards a Jeep parked a half-mile away at the zenith of a grassy hill. The man followed several paces behind her.

May 5th, 2019

1:30 AM

On one of my last nights employed at the bar, one of the owners, Walther, informed me that the "Ball Game," a fantastical bloodsport practiced by the ancient Olmec civilization, is a myth.

… What is the point of history—*anything*—if all stories are myths and inaccurate retells of the past? "Those who fail to learn history are condemned to repeat *it*"—and is *that not* the cyclic nature of humanity regardless of whether or not adolescents cram for a social studies test?

I romanticize the *idea* of the "Ball Game": To imagine the dirt-laden inner cloister of a resplendent temple, the cheers, the applause, the jeers—the lean, athletic, powerful bodies of men astride one another in the pursuit of death, for glory; all "win" at the end, granted an honorable end.

No… the Roman colosseum is equivalent to a modern football stadium. The Holocaust: a glory. Japanese samurai: a fraud. Would *it* make any difference?—*no*—for we would bloat ourselves on relics of the past and gloat of our ostentatious accumulation of trivial knowledge in regards to the acts and words of men and women *long dead:*

"By the Gods, I hate every fiber of your being; when I look at you, I see a worm."

"You've spoken your last."

The two Norse swordsmen charged headlong over an expanse of stark-white snow, met iron with iron, and burst into a cloud of multicolored confetti.

A single word fails to express the state of "apathetic" or "phlegmatic." The words themselves elicit the sentiment, expressed through the definitions assigned to each: more words, conjoined with other words to express aforementioned words… instead, I proffer a conception of apathy:

A man returned home after a run, winded and red-faced; he entered his front door, stepped six paces forward, and stopped. He looked around his home, at the furniture, at his orange and yellow running shoes, at the grass-green walls, at the refrigerator in an adjacent kitchen, at a pile of magazines on a coffee table, at a ceiling fan, at photos of his girlfriend and brother propped up against an elegant oriental statue depicting an old woman seated on a stone bench.

The man cleared his throat and returned his gaze to his shoes; his eyes followed up the contours of his bare calves, to his navy-blue shorts, to the slight overhang of his stomach; he held his arms out before him and observed the smoothness of his skin, the swathes of hair rowed along each arm, to his hands, fingernails, cuticles, to a minor nick on his thumbnail. He walked towards a reclined chair covered in a faded brown flowery tapestry and sat, head skewed to the side, left leg outstretched, the other leg bent at a right-angle; he shifted, and crossed his left leg over his right leg and stared at the wall at the opposite end of the room. He focused on his slow, steady breaths, straightened his head, leaned back against the seat, removed his left leg from atop his right leg, and braced both feet on the floor. He sighed, closed his eyes, leaned forward, and felt for the strings of his shoelaces; he untied his shoes with his eyes closed and allowed his head to droop between his knees. He smoothed his hands over his shoes and fingered the spaces between the laces. He removed the shoes, set both to the left of the chair, raised his head, leaned back, and sat—head slack against the back of the chair, and stared at the wall at the opposite end of the room.

A man I've known since the age of thirteen, a long-lost "best friend" named Lars, pulled up alongside me in a run-down car, stepped out, greeted me with a hug after over five years of no correspondence, and introduced me to his girlfriend. We arranged to meet… to "catch-up."

We talked at a diner and spoke of "sociopathy" and virtue on account of my questions. The conversation proved to be vapid.

I met Lars and his girlfriend at their apartment later that night. Unremarkable words were spoken. I consumed two glasses of red wine and two slices of a terrible five-dollar pizza. My estranged friend drunk himself into a stupor and smoked bowl after bowl of marijuana; his twenty-two-year-old "runaway country girl" partook in the same activities. We retired to Lars' bedroom, where he and his girlfriend lay together on his floor mattress in a room filled with trinkets and items I recognized from our teenage years. Junk and garbage littered the room, arranged in neat piles between knick-knacks and an assortment of video game peripherals, mosh-pit memorabilia, empty cans of *Red Bull,* a giant jar of rotten pickles (a feat to achieve), and *Mike's Hard Lemonade* bottles arranged at various heights atop counters and shelves surrounding a large flat-screen television. I sat in Lars' computer chair, powered on my voice recorder, and talked of bitter nothings until midnight:

I said, "You're making me think back to all the times when I had spirit and zest."

Lars gazed at me, stretched out on his side atop the mattress—his back to his girlfriend who sat behind him, and his head propped up on a pillow, facing me. "Spirit and zest… when was *that?*"

I began to chuckle and broke into unrestrained laughter.

Lars continued, "Dude I've always remembered you as… at first glance gloomy, but at a second glance just really, intuitive, and intelligent, like…"

"I hate being called intelligent, more than anything."

"Well *it'*s a burden and a gift, I guess. You feel the burden inside, where I feel like *it'*s a gift because I do a lot of *stupid shit,* but then like, I do something and *it'*s like, *'Yeah,* that's *correct':* self-gratification—that's when I feel, the most intellectual, whenever I pull something out of my ass and *it* fixes the fucking problem whatever *it* is at-hand. I'm not incredibly intelligent but-"

I said, "You're intelligent, you're just not that smart."

"I suppose that could be taken either way—I mean I'm open to-"

"Well your intelligence is your capacity to learn, and smart is… the capacity to make beneficial decisions with the knowledge you've learned; *it'*s 'wise' in a sense."

"So I'm a quick learner but I'm not wise."

"Yes."

"I suppose I *do* forget things, but I feel like I have become *quite* smart, I just don't care about certain things, so… your decisions, I may not find them justifiable to give my attention to, but, that does not mean that I don't comprehend or don't have the capacity to do *other*-"

"That's the 'intelligence'—is that you *know* what path you're taking, and that's when you condemn yourself or you feel good—*so* good in fact that when you do choose to make the right choice for yourself… for instance: the easy gratification of video games; *it*'s not a wise choice, but *it* is the most satisfying for you."

"Yeah…" Lars stretched out on the bed. *"It* is quite satisfying… and like, not to be completely away from my own life, just like, sometimes in the intermission of doing so, being *able* to, and making the choice *of* being something *else* for a short amount of time, or as long as you continue to do so, you know what I mean, *it* could be anything: etc. etc.? Like that, *it*'s nice to have the fuckin' *option*. Do I have to play then? No. There's been plenty of times when I've been like, 'You know what I think I'll play'—and then I just, don't. So, instead I watch this short horror film, or this documentary, or maybe I'll make something in *MS Paint*—make little pixel characters; just delete them when you're done and everything like that but… somethin' to do, something to *create;* I'd rather be a different person for a little bit, because you're always going to come back to who you actually are; *it*'s not like you could *hide* that; you could hide that from other people but you can't hide *it* from yourself which is, exactly who and what I'm talking about."

"I devoted all of my time to writing and I was with only myself constantly, so, I behave the way that I would around others in a similar manner that I would behave alone, and, I have no friends because of *it*." I laughed. "And *it*'s harrowing, because I prefer *it* that way; I put people off; I've become more of an asshole than I ever have been in my entire life, because I strive to be devoid of pretension, yet people perceive me *as* pretentious, *because* of how I behave… *it*'s convoluted…"

Lars quipped, "Almost not worth thinkin' about bud."

"No. But I do… I think too much… But what else is there…"

"You can only be as right as you think you are. Because if somebody else were to tell you that you are 'something' and you believe them, then you *are* at that level, but if somebody tells you that you are 'something' and you believe you're more than that, then you are, at the bare minimum, that 'something' that you imagined… Likewise, if you feel like that's not true, and you feel like you're not worth the praise you're receiving, then you are *only* as much as you allow yourself to be, which is how much you believe you *deserve*."

"We evaluate ourselves based on the community that we're amongst; *it*'s a reflection."

"But also where you come from: everything that you've experienced up until this 'very' decision. *It*'s not just where you are, or who you're a part of, *it*'s everything put together to make this eternally concurrent spearhead of existence, *for you;* you've never been exactly what you are before nor will you ever be again."

I held my head with both hands and muttered, "Always changing."

"Exactly."

"From the last moment to the next, there is no 'self.'"

Lars affirmed, "Well *it*'s all 'self.'"

"The ego-"

"Because to have a *'self,'* one would simply have to exist; I can't get into how you can tell whether you fucking exist or not because that's a whole different scheme, but, if you exist then you have a 'self,' whether you refer to *it* as 'self' or whether someone refers to *you* as, their, 'self,' pointing at you… So for you to say there is no 'self,' is irrelevant, because 'something' exists, so there is at least one 'self' in existence…"

"The universal or interconnected consciousness, that's why I asked you earlier if you believe there is a 'true, authentic self,' because you're right—there *is* a self, and *it* permeates all of us: the personality is pretense; the virtues are facets of a personality that allow us to thrive…" A long pause ensued between the three of us; Lar's girlfriend laid beside him and stroked his arm. A small fan blew on us from the corner of the crowded room. I continued, "Every morning when I wake up, I wish to die. That hasn't changed, but I persist, because life is an expression; *it*'s work, so you persist, to work your body and your mind, 'til you die, and you make the most of *it*… reap the enjoyment, to thrive. Enjoyment—to thrive, happiness derived from the practice of virtue… *Work* should be enjoyable."

"But *it*'s not for all. Some people don't like the feeling of hard physical labor. Some people don't like the feeling of non-physical labor; take a construction worker and put him in a cashier position—he's not gonna feel comfortable, *it*'s not what he's used to—*it*'s not what he *likes*… *it*'s not what he knows… Then take a writer, put him in as a personal trainer for a mixed martial art, he's probably not gonna be in the same mindset; he's used to sitting at a fucking desk, not rippin' fucking deltoid presses and backward spin claps."

"When I was at the attic apartment in [Town name] for six months, after I returned from the intentional community, I took Hop Gar classes for about a week, and I ended up sitting with the proprietor discussing architecture and his mathematical achievements instead. Once I exhausted conversational opportunities with him, I just stopped attending... I think now is a good time to leave you two to thrive."

"We thrive when we want to."

"Yes." I stood, leaned down, and shook both of their hands.

Lar's girlfriend spoke to me for the first instance since Lars and I began speaking: "Well thanks for coming over—hanging out."

"Thanks for having me. Take care you two. I'll see myself out."

Lars said, "Alright man, we'll have to get together again before you leave, so we uh—can say our sayonaras and such."

"Agreed."

"But *it*'s good to see you; thanks for hanging out. I hope you had fun and shit, you know."

"I did."

"*It*'s always nice to talk, bullshit around..."

I nodded, acknowledged them both with a genuine smile, averted my eyes, and departed with no intent to return.

May 7th, 2019

12:27 AM

I departed my father's abandoned home to visit his home. Always entangled in my father's affairs—by *choice*, has afflicted me with doubt; he is the last person I am to sever relations with: the one person who has cared for me my entire life (excluding my mother) and knows me better than everyone, except my*self*, despite his authoritative proclamations of otherwise.

My father insisted on preparing me a meal of my choice before deployment. I accepted despite feeling apathetic about the arrangement and said, "Consider yourself the executioner granting the last rite."

"Feel like you're being led to the chopping block? You will be intrigued that *it* (the military) is hardly a chopping block."

"No, I desire to be considered dead by everyone I've ever known."

"Say goodbye to your privacy and solitude."

"That's no issue, only a preference."

"Giving up your people here for a whole new set of people."

"Yes."

"Life goes on."

Homemade sushi: I ate one out of the eight full-length rolls and lost my appetite upon my utterance of, "Thank you for this; I know how much you enjoy my jovial, upbeat company."

"I always do… even if you are a pretentious douchebag kid."

I stared at the rolls on my plate, the wasabi, the hot chili sauce, my adjacent hand, and said, "This is why I dislike accepting offers of any kind from people, especially food; the receiver is rendered vulnerable to chastisement and must endure the now-revealed authentic sentiments that are otherwise withheld until an opportune moment."

"Oh get real will you. You were my favorite kid up until recently, until you started talking about how you are going to 'slay your father' and all that fucking bullshit; I get no respect from you, but whatever, I'm used to *it:* used and abused, walked all over all my *fucking* life."

I remained silent for several minutes and stared through the open screen door while my father puttered back and forth through the small kitchen space; he wrapped each individual sushi roll with aluminum foil, stowed ingredients in the fridge, cleaned counters, and placed dirtied dishware into a sink. I said, "Why the fuck am I even here? All my life I've never asked you for anything."

"You're right Baethan, you have never asked me for anything—ever, I've always just provided for you, and you never asked to be born either. I think everyone your age is just a kid; quit taking everything so seriously; the drill instructor is going to love tearing into you."

"I know you think I'm ungrateful and pathetic."

"Yeah and I know you think I'm a scumbag old man who does nothing but sits on his ass all day smoking dope and watching T.V.—who gives a fuck. I'm your fucking father; I get *no* fucking respect from you; if I behaved like you with my father… Now you're telling me that you're going to cut all communication with me when you leave? Why—I think I deserve an explanation." My father's furrowed and bloodshot eyes scanned the environment for a temporary occupation; he settled on pouring himself an ice-filled glass of lemonade.

"I thought you didn't care about what I think."

"I *don't* give a fuck about what you think."

"Then you shouldn't be bothered if I cut communication with you."

"No, I won't be bothered—what do you think, that I need attention from you?"

"Validation, and alright."

"I don't need *any* fucking validation from you; I validate myself, and if you want to stop communicating with me then *fuck you;* I don't give a shit."

My father's eyes hadn't connected with mine throughout the dialogue; I sat for five or six minutes, stiff, and gazed back and forth between my plate, at the eight uneaten sushi rolls, the fridge, the screen door, the kitchen table, and my right hand, outstretched against the side of the plate. A single grain of brown rice adhered to my thumb.

My father said, *"It's* really nice outside tonight," and moved to sit out on the edge of the stone porch.

I sat and contemplated my position… the circumstances of my life, my conception in the womb of my estranged mother, to my youth: every three-egg with toast breakfast my father prepared for me as a pre-teen boy, every lunch, dinner, intimate conversation, vacation, words of praise, the providence he's provided me each instance I've failed and utilize even *now,* the Christmas mornings, orchestra concerts, amusement parks, movie sessions, words of advice, every authentic hug… and my self-hatred for accepting all of *it.*

I stood, went to the bathroom, urinated, washed my hands, wrapped and stowed the remainder of my uneaten sushi rolls, cleared the table, gripped my writing device and departed out the door; I descended the steps adjacent to my father and said, "Thanks."

My father said, "Leaving?" and we met eyes. "Why are you pissed at me?"

I stood six feet away and said nothing.

"You're going to need thicker skin, boy, if you want to stay in the military; you're gonna learn to swear too." I stared at my father, allowed the hate to glean in my eyes, and gestured my right hand for him to continue. "Have fun," he said; I broke my gaze with him, turned, and walked away without a word spoken, to the boneyard, where I practiced another mile-and-a-half run, edited last year's manuscript atop a tombstone for an hour, trekked back to my father's abandoned home, and packed the remainder of my foodstuffs and clothing into my pack in preparation for a trip across town tomorrow to cancel my gym membership, donate all my clothing except for what I'll be garbed in, and stay overnight at a hotel.

I received a message on my phone from my father after packing: "I don't care what you think about me. However, I *do* care about you. I love you, Baethan." I didn't respond; I don't intend to see or communicate with my father again and will depart his abandoned home in the early morning to ensure this outcome.

My mother and father are the victims in the context of me; I am a nexus of hate, wrought upon the world by their love. If I had faith, I would pray for them. If I had money, I would provide for them. If I had retained the capacity to accept love, I would love them.

May 8th, 2019

8:28 PM

I stayed overnight at a motel, woke, visited the gym for my final session, submitted my complete manuscript of year two of this documentation, and waited for my recruiter, Adam, to pick me up. On the trip I spoke of my subdued glee and eagerness to depart for a new way of life. My backpack filled with hygienic items and the clothing I wear is the extent of my belongings—my "net worth."

Five days ago, while cooking the last batch of my steel-cut oats, I moved my arm over the pot's ventilation and sustained a second-degree burn, three inches in diameter, on the underside of my forearm. I thought nothing of the wound, applied ice, and continued with my routine. On the car ride to the station, I mentioned the injury to Adam and showed him the fluid-engorged blister: "We'll need to show the Chief and see what he says." I concurred and thought nothing of *it*—pleased with my absolute liberty of the nothingness I retained, my void of relationships, and the intrinsic wealth of my extrinsic poverty.

On arrival at the station, the Chief snapped a photo of my blister, entered his office, engaged in a phone call, exited his office, and informed me that I am unqualified to ship to boot camp until the burn has healed. My ship date has been postponed (for a third instance) to May 22nd.

May 9th, 2019

6:34 AM

On the news of my deployment postponement, I donned my pack, visited the local town market where my recruiters are stationed to stock up on food (9 cans of sardines and 12 bananas), stopped at the local bookstore, bought a copy of Aldous Huxley's *Brave New World,* walked four miles southwest to the center of the city, and found a small sanctuary for the homeless sustained by the donations of local restaurants, churches, and operated by a small agency of paid employees.

I approached a large congregation of homeless men and women converged around (and within) a small wooden gazebo. A dozen sets of eyes turned to me and I waved; a few waved in response, and many began to inquire of who, and *what* I am.

"Are you a cop?" said a young man around my age.

"No, I'm a denizen of the world in need of temporary housing."

An older man stepped down from the gazebo and pointed to a young, attractive African American woman who veered around the corner of the house and walked towards the group. "You'll want to speak with her," said an older man dressed in ragged blue jeans and a stained grey t-shirt.

The woman approached me; a warm smile overtook her countenance and she said, "Hello, I'm Tina, how can I help you?"

"I'm in need of temporary housing."

"Alright, follow me," she gestured towards a large two-story house. We entered through the front door, sat at a modest receptionist desk, and after a lengthy discourse of my "situation," Tina offered me a tent, a sleeping bag, free access to the overabundance of food (most is discarded due to excess donations), and apologized to me on behalf of the rooms being occupied in the house we sat in, and the adjacent house which serves as an extension to the establishment.

Last night I trekked to the local train station, erected my tent on flat terrain in the surrounding woods, and read until sunset: this will be my mode of living until the 22nd and I am grateful for the opportunity in humility.

I've met and spoken with a plethora of people—dozens, most notable, a man named Joey, a former personal trainer who has taken a great interest in me due to my pursuit of physical fitness and enlistment in the U.S. Navy.

The burn on my forearm *will* heal—damn *it* all.

6:07 PM

I woke from the tent and felt empowered, enthralled with my position in life; a somber hope unfettered. A walk back to the shelter for breakfast, a four-mile walk to the local gym near my recruiter's station, and a four-mile walk back for the house dinner. An opportunity for work this morning eluded me. I've enough funds for two weeks' worth of food. The blister popped and drained down my forearm while I read this afternoon.

I stare at nothing, and those around me in this home eye me with curious wonder. After two hours of conversation with the downtrodden, ambivalent, and *content*, I departed for the position I've secured near the train station with an eagerness equivalent to the vigor I once demonstrated for deployment to boot camp.

8:46 PM

Before I departed from the shelter for the train station, I spoke with a man named Tim while five other residents sat around us. Tim is a fifty-four-year-old man who thanked me for my (yet to transpire) service to "my country." On my first day at the shelter, while I stood and read in the gazebo, many residents converged around me due to the popularity of the spot—Tim being one of them; he had spoken a vehement and belligerent diatribe against a few women who manage the laundry room. By this impression, I confirmed, due to *image* and *observation*, that Tim is a base man—as many have confirmed with me due to first impressions; an elaboration on my error:

I informed Tim and two other older ladies who praised me that I entered "the service" for selfish reasons and "to serve my country" is at the bottom end of the metaphorical totem pole on my hierarchy of priorities.

Tim said, "Why do you join?"

"To write of the experience, the travel, and the benefits."

Tim disclosed (I had given my voice recorder to the manager of the previous gym I attended) that he had served in the Marine Corps for twenty years and proceeded to share his stories on account of my inquiries. Tim killed three people as a sniper: An enemy sniper five-hundred yards away after his (Tim's) partner had been shot (Tim watched the man's head decimate and spill brain matter); a young boy no older than age eight strapped with explosives beneath his t-shirt (Tim missed the shot with his rifle, leaped into a .50 cal turret, and "sliced the boy in half"); a man who drove a van filled with explosives (the suicide bomber's vehicle exploded after being assaulted by Tim's incendiary rounds).

Tim experiences flashbacks and awakens in the middle of the night "screaming at the top of my (his) lungs," though the nightmares have frequented him less in recent years. The emotion he felt while he killed another human, and upon reflection afterward, is "blank."

"Nothing personal. I was just doing my job," Tim said.

I shared the stories Tim relayed to my recruiters; all three laughed and condemned Tim as a fraud and a liar.

May 10th, 2019

4:41 PM

I've been granted the privilege to sleep in the conference room by command of the shelter director: a kind and magnanimous woman. On the conveyance of my scenario and circumstances to all who ask, I am regarded with approbation.

7:48 PM

Seated alone at the end of a long rectangular conference table with a belly full of pork, sweet potato, and a large mixed vegetable salad, I experience a sensation equivalent to what a megalomaniac CEO or manager would feel upon the acquisition of a new shareholder.

May 11th, 2019

8:43 AM

An objectively hideous and obese woman with a tuft of short frazzled hair named Jessica has approached me for conversation and began to speak of her incredible multifaceted delusions; she droned on about her past lives as Countess Bathory, Mary Shelly, and the experiences of her past deaths. She spoke of her encounters with ghosts, interactions with spirits, the occult, and her undeath. She claims to be a witch, a "famous voodoo expert," a tap dancer, and an opera singer. She speaks to her "twin soul" and is haunted by "alien faces in the dark."

Diagnosed with "Schizophrenia," "Autism," and "Split personality," Jessica confided in me her extensive experiences and ailments. After a lengthy exposition, I attempted to "help" her with an account of my own experiences… to convince Jessica of her self-obsession proved to be moot, for she admits to being self-obsessed and *content*. Her demons are her own, and she validates her ego with the craft and donation of knitted hats. She has relinquished all responsibility and depends on the providence of social security and halfway houses such as the one I occupy now, though this house is a testament to her permanent state of transition for the remainder of her life.

After I shared my sentiments of rational processes concerning how she projects her thoughts to external entities to preserve her ego, I said, "Well, I need to head out to the gym, though I'd like to close out with the statement, *'Sometimes* our intuitions are accurate.'"

Jessica nodded her head and looked away.

Oh, the (in)humanity.

4:38 PM

Ten mile walks each day to and from the gym and back to the shelter through the center of a city center rife with human activity has rendered my face tanned and browned, for the first time in years. Even dozens of miles away from my previous residency, I am honked at by those in vehicles who pass me by along the highway pedestrian lanes. My assumptions and presumptions of what this could mean are irrelevant, for I find, as I've aged the past few years, that even though virtue is a matter of pretentious ass-grabbing, *it* is essential for cooperation and therefore civilization.

My experience, welcomed into the halfway house's microcosmic culture, is an excellent segway before basic training.

My father believes I am already in basic, and there are those who I've informed I will deploy for the Navy on May 1st/May 9th, who may eventually pass me on the highway, and think, in essence: *"That's fucking Baethan, I can't believe that asshole lied about joining the military; what a pitiful loser,"* and I'm improved on this account. My mote of flesh struts down the concrete byways, Main Street, and atop gravel-strewn park walkways, poised and proud.

May 12th, 2019

7:03 AM

Yesterday evening an altercation transpired between Tim and an African American man named Roy due to a literal imbecile named Chris (who "showed me the ropes" of the establishment when I first arrived on account of the negligence of the employed staff) begging for cigarettes. After the heated verbal dispute between Tim and Roy naming each other "child rapist," "drug-dealer," "asshole," "douchebag," "pussy-bitch," and "fucker," Chris hobbled towards me, eyed me with shame expressed in his countenance, and said, "This place is fucking crazy man."

"All this over a cigarette?"

"Yeah nobody will give me a cigarette," Chris muttered, and I observed his large, overhung stomach, the pockets and divots indenting his face that signaled the numerous acne scars accumulated throughout childhood, the permanent grimace stretched over his visage, his slumped posture… at the ripe age of thirty-one, this man carried himself in the manner a fifty-year-old cripple released from a hospital after the recovery of a spinal injury would hobble.

I said, "I'll buy you cigarettes, let's go."

"Really? You would—you don't gotta do that, you would?"

"Yes, you were kind enough to assume the role of my guide when I first arrived here; I'll repay your kindness with kindness." I leaned off the wooden railing that I had balanced my body on and began to walk towards the nearest convenience store. Chris shuffled behind; his worn running shoes scraped loose gravel deposited throughout the driveway. Side-by-side, we approached the center of the city. Inside the convenience store, Chris treated the employees with impersonal regard and demanded cigarettes, a large iced coffee, and a large candy bar. Afterward, he trotted outside and allowed me to handle the transaction. I departed the store and found him, idle, with his broken phone in-hand.

"I broke my phone screen the other day and I've been waiting for a call from the housing woman for five months. She finally got back to me today and then I broke my phone."

"Do you know her number?"

"No I was gonna… write *it* down but I forgot to."

I handed Chris the product I bought; he thanked me, and we proceeded back towards the shelter.

"What is your self-assigned meaning in life?" I asked.

"My what?"

"Your self-*assigned* meaning in *life.*"

"My meaning for... life..." he contemplated for three seconds. "My meaning in life is fool evil."

"*To* fool evil? What do you mean?"

"I do many evil things so that I can get respect and get along with other evil people but I'm not really evil so I need to fool *it.*"

"If you commit evil acts, even if just to impress other men, the outcome is still evil."

"No because I only do evil things for evil guys and I'm not really evil so I'm fooling evil."

I walked the remainder of the distance to the shelter in silence while Chris commented aloud about his developing intimate relationship with another young homeless girl.

8:22 PM

I've lapsed into a state of melancholy once more; while I stand and read outside, on the porch, or behind the halfway house, I intuit the unwanted thoughts of those around me who decree my desire for attention; I retreat, sullen and dejected, to the conference room after a meal of canned tuna and a banana.

I've no desire to speak to anyone, though I've met an employee—a young man with a master's degree in education and a photographic memory; he commented and proceeded to attempt to praise me on my kitchen shelving rearrangement and disposal of out-of-date foodstuffs; I changed the subject and commented on how word and deed travel fast in this microcosmic community.

"Yes," said the man; he laughed. "We really are our own little biome... Is that Huxley?"

"I'm surprised you could tell by the back cover."

"I read the same edition... and I have a photographic memory so that helps."

"In relation to books, do you photographically recall arrangements of words or images, or do you recall the information connotated with each arrangement of words or images?"

"I recall the words as they're arranged on pages, though *it* takes an effort. High school was a breeze for me; I could remember the chalkboard or sheets of paper."

"So you had an imbued cheat sheet."

The man laughed and said, "Yeah, essentially."

"Do you find a photographic memory to be a blessing and a curse?"

"Yes, if I see something I didn't want to see-"

"Like something haunting, or grotesque-"

"Yeah, exactly—I'll never forget *it*."

Earlier today, a man named Leon sighed and frowned, seated at a terminal behind me, while I stood and read; I offered assistance and asked if he worked on a project; he refused my help and insisted on showing me the full extent of his project:

An hour later, while I mopped the conference room and adjoining hall, Leon returned with a large, five-foot, rectangular, translucent tub. "Come here, I want to show you," he affirmed, tramped over my cleaned floor (in dress shoes), and began to unfasten the clamps."

"Alright." I approached from Leon's left and watched as he unveiled an enormous collection of framed prints and hieroglyphic and symbolic prayers derived from Japanese and Egyptian culture. Christian and catholic depictions of allegorical themes were arranged in neat piles—all framed with silver-studded wooden frames. Leon explained each image in elaborate detail while I asked questions; he has dedicated his life to prayer... for the sake of fortune... to *become* a djinn... a *djinn!*

"You wish to *become* a *djinn?*"

"Yes, I've been poor all my life and I'm following signs and omens given by god. Do you understand?"

"Yes. Now—just a moment, a djinn is a malevolent being that punishes men by fulfilling their avaricious wishes; you are avaricious yourself and desire to become rich so that you may bestow the same torment you seek—with the acquirement of great wealth—upon others?"

"I do right by the signs I'm following." Leon explained to me shampoos of varied colors that match the diverse collection of his prints: Beautiful illustrations of Anubis, Ra, the "Goddess of Fortune," voluptuous Roman beauties, bare-breasted and scantily-clad, Noah's Ark, darkened and desolate landscapes...

I said, "But to become a djinn, shouldn't you perform what is *wrong* instead of right—to *be* the malevolent entity you aspire to emulate; I believe your fortune awaits you through that strait."

Leon surveyed his artwork and braced both hands on the corner of the desk as though he had just now seen the arrangement for what *it* is. "Prayer for fortune," he said, and repeated to say.

"You come off as a religious man, but not spiritual in the slightest."

Leon smiled. "I intend to arrange the artwork all around my new apartment and live my life in accordance with my prayers."

A man who wishes to become rich to bestow his riches upon others who wish for riches; Leon denied aspirations of being a philanthropist and reiterated on the conception of a djinn. I shook his hand. "Thank you Leon; you are by far the most interesting man I've met in a long while... The way we spend our time, each of us, is incredible. To see your meaning of life condensed within a plastic tub is awe-inspiring."

"Yeah, these are my prayers. You must have faith and be devoted to a cause to be able to pray."

I averted my eyes from his and admired the beauty of the collection.

May 15th, 2019

7:53 AM

I finished Huxley's *Brave New World* two days ago and resonated with the "Savage" character, for he exemplifies the least of what defines the character of a literal savage. A point of importance—for *you*, self, not a damnable reader:

While the helicopters flew over the lighthouse and encouraged the savage to self-flagellate—"The whip! The whip!" You thought of your treks back and forth across bridges and main roads of your hometown and over the country roads of the *Peaceorama* and *Magical Woody Farmstead!*, pack strapped to your back... while the vehicles passed you by, and even now, while they converge and line up along the highway on your way to and from the city you occupy, you reckon those within each vehicle, those who acknowledge you with beeps of a horn, a rolled down window and venomous shout, a sudden verbal lashing; you identified with the man—the *savage*—who found civilized life too easy, mundane, and conducive to happiness, for happiness is not a state to maintain, *it* is an activity (in Aristotle's definition) to be pursued for the sake of virtue... and what is virtue, in accordance with your "self," other than an affection to be displayed and flaunted for the benefit of your position within a society, with your fellow man, determined by culture. The savage is ostracized and returned to his origins, only, without a tribe; he endures alone, repents, and is to be mocked and denigrated.

Now, while I sat at a kitchen table of a "homeless" shelter, I am enmeshed with people who indeed have a home—a veritable microcosmic utopia, cloistered from the outer world, where those who have failed to be a productive member of society are permitted to thrive, to consume an inexhaustible supply of food, to sleep, sit, and lounge to their heart's content. The people here are of the basest character I've ever mingled with, and there is an *enormous* causality between this domain and the intentional communities I've visited in the frequent past.

An inquiry I've pressed against the multitudes here is, "Would you rather live an easy life or a hard life?"

James, the so-called retired marine corps veteran of twenty years claims that he has "earned" the right to an easy life, to leech and flounder, to fill a spot among those who experience true desperation. "You choose," James expressed to me in the kitchen while I mopped, "to live an easy life or a hard life; you know what they taught me in the service?" James contemplated for a moment, his gaze downcast, vacant... he lifted his head with a renewed conviction expressed through his bleary and despondent eyes, "Only work to make life easier."

Several young men are here on parole; each has no meaning in life and have resided on the establishment for over a year. "Do you have any intention of leaving soon?" I ask them both; "No," in essence, is the answer.

The older women are the worst, there is a trinity—archetypes; I list each unabashed, a testament of my truth:

She stands before me now: alone, frazzled, blonde, beauty-obsessed and nearing the point of obesity; aged in her upper forties, she complains and consumes. I imagine she excretes, but only ever in secret, and the image of her excreting is unsavory: dejected, frowning, with wide-eyes staring straight forward at a wall, a bitter consternation of how to reap her next copulation session... she finishes wipes, stands, and returns to the kitchen table where she sits in the corner, where she may observe all activity, all passersby—ah, she *sits* right this moment! She has seated herself right where I expected her to be based on my observations of her previous behavior and she proceeds to produce guttural sounds of pain; she moans, and waits for me to validate her. She stares at me, sidelong—*through* me, while I type, and persists—*damn her*—with her muted expressions of pain equivalent to an anguished animal on the verge of death, only the death throes are transmogrified through her pitiable expression of desire. When any man speaks to her, she giggles and laughs no matter the content. Slunk up against the wall, she leans, and idles on her phone, engaged with vacuous activities… all… day… into the night, and scrutinizes her potential to copulate, which is forbidden in this institution, though the majority of the homeless women here try nonetheless. Despicable boyfriends visit and provide the few "lucky" sluts suitable distractions.

The most volatile woman, who now sits adjacent from me with a cup of coffee, to offer an initial glimpse into her mind and the nexus of her character: she *just now* spoke, "I was watching this video on *Facebook* last night, of old people dancing, but I was distracted by a video on baking when you just put the dough in the oven and walk away from it—will you watch my coffee for me while I go downstairs cuz' people be comin' in here and I don't know who be takin' and touchin'"

This miserable woman is the nexus of drama; nothing may transpire in the kitchen, living room, and laundry room without her knowledge of the activity. Her hair is combed and framed around her head in an impeccable bun. Her ill-fitted clothes hang around her saggy body, accustomed to a life of office work and intemperate consumption. Ignorance is her paramount aura; she is an idiot, on the verge of imbecility (I am the perfect judge of this, being, as I am, among these characters by choice). The complaints seep with an incessant force from her mouth in regards to the activity of others. Who did laundry when; who flubbed on "this" chore or "that," who said "this," who began drinking or threatened a fellow resident? Who, *who—who!* I wonder! I-

I… digress… For my desire to finish the encapsulation of these ~~three~~ two characters is an undue fancy… For each, along with myself, is a grotesque manifestation of society.

I volunteer for labor at the shelter to fill the void between bouts of reading my new interest, in contrast to Huxley's narrative: Joseph Conrad's *Heart of Darkness,* and trek to town for the sake of the gym and an escape from the stagnant souls of the shelter, followed by brief visits to my recruiters at the nearby station (who occupy most of their time sitting at their desks, phones in-hand, sharing sexual jokes and pornographic videos with one another); I repose on their couch for half-an-hour and listen, eyes closed, to their banter.

6:11 PM

I spoke to the primary manager of the shelter(s) today about my societal observations in regards to particular people who overindulge in the providence provided: parasites and leeches. She agreed with me on my statements of how those who have been around for a year and longer (even three months is excessive, though I refrained from exploring this spectrum of the conversation), are a burden and a drain.

The manager relayed to me her grandiose plans to revamp both buildings and to purchase a nearby hotel to expand on the design.

May 16th, 2019

7:12 AM

I'm treated as a guest of honor here and eat my fill of a plethora of free foods. A five egg omelette every morning with all my usual spices, a sliced apple or banana sprinkled with cinnamon and sided with a tablespoon of peanut butter. I'm allotted a spacious (conference) room. There is no dwelling above or below me. The other residents here live with three to four roommates. I retire to the floor at my determination, undisturbed. At 6:30 AM, the receptionist undergoes a "wake-up call" and alerts the residents of each room that we are allowed to cook breakfast from 6:30 AM until 7:30 AM and to partake in two pots of coffee.

The conference room is occupied at intervals throughout 9:00 AM to 5:00 PM; I spend these hours away from the shelter, in the midst of the city, where I stroll through *Central Park* and read, strength train at the city gym, observe the sights (I have yet to visit the nearby *War History Museum*), and return "home" later in the afternoon where I experience no stimulus other than to exist, and, by extension of my existence, observe others who exist around me.

A television drones from sunrise to sunset and the many cushioned seats in the common room are compressed by the listless, lethargic, torpid, and stuporous. Men sleep upright, both hands clasped to the arms of a browned sofa or chair, garbed in sweaty, soiled sweaters and jeans.

Throughout the day, the hollowed vestiges of personalities stand, smooth a hand over their unkempt hair, loll a pair of darkened eyes, and either resubsume with the cushion after a brief contemplation, or meander out the front door to a respective location of work, or venture to the outdoor gazebo to partake in a ritualistic cigarette smoking session.

Medications are distributed by 7:30 AM. The most afflicted with "unmanageable" neurosis/psychosis attend the kitchen by method of informal jumble; they trickle in every few minutes to receive a dosage. By 8:00 AM, the majority have lapsed into routines of entertainment consumption (I'm no exception, by means of a book) and pursue venues to seek labor or housing *only* when enforced by an authority on their "case."

Each resident is assigned a chore to fulfill: a simple mundane labor of cleaning and maintenance. The ~~trinity~~ duo of women mentioned in the above entry complain and slough their labors upon others at any opportunity available.

The surrounding housing is a dilapidated collective of slums, though this demographic is limited to a small circumference a few blocks away from the city's robust and economically inclined tourist center.

Day by day, new faces arrive and others depart; there are those who are fated *by choice* to travel from shelter to shelter—a process comparable to "osmosis," in their case.

If not for the prospect of my entry into the U.S. Navy, I would be on the road, en route southwest, as originally intended a year ago, only now, the perpetual haven of my father's residence has been severed on account of my audacious disrespect and judgment of his character. Though, I believe my father would *still* accept me if I "crawled" back to him—with a jovial "love" expressed on behalf of my endeavor and resultant failure, only to shift, yet again, to a state of pity and resentment for himself, and by extension, me, for doing so—yes, to be condemned by your own son; who am *I* to be so brazen other than a fool? My mother and father are bygone entities: providers and stiflers, life-givers and regressors.

May 17th, 2019

7:02 AM

I've dressed down to a basic pair of black trousers and a cross-hatched white casual dress shirt—untucked, with intent to study the demeanor and reactions of people engaged with me; the results have been to my anticipated expectations:

I'm no longer perceived to be "psychopathic" by the few cognizant enough here to cultivate a suspicion or to be "educated" of the terminology: namely, two of the social workers and several of the homeless next door in the adjacent house. I'm also no longer perceived to be an undercover police officer (yes, I've been accused of being an undercover "cop" and have been asked to display my badge [deridingly and seriously] by a few of the younger rogues and rapscallions who reside in the alternative building). I am no longer (disgustingly) ogled by women. Men no longer regard me with a disdain connoted in the belief that I am desperate for female attention. Soon the experimentation of garb will cease once I am assigned a strict regimen and uniform when part of the Navy—*thankfully*—for this dance of fabric is an exhaustion of the psyche. Instead, projected personality will be stymied and supplanted with variegated stripes and symbols to judge another's worth.

Last night I overheard a conversation outside the conference room between the avaricious man who believes he is fated to become a djinn: Leon, and a social worker. Leon attempts to secure a job and printed handfuls of his resume: a thirty-four-year-old man with no credentials, a criminal history, in occupancy within a homeless shelter… he refuses to work in a kitchen due to the "intensity" and wage ratio; he refuses to work in a factory due to the "intensity"; in essence, he disclosed to the social worker (and myself, when I approached him an hour later on the subject) that he refuses to work in any position except a "low-intensity" position. The preceding sentences of this paragraph are the reasons why this man is homeless.

I confronted Leon on his avoidance of labor—most notably an open dishwasher position the social worker had suggested due to Leon's claim that he had worked a dishwashing position at the age of seventeen. Leon stated that the labor is now beneath him while he reheated two (free) beef patties in the kitchen. He asserts that, above all, he would prefer to obtain a disability check each month due to a metal plate in his neck rather than work—a blatant, pathetic excuse—if I am in any position to cast judgment… of course I am; we *all* are—even *you*, reader; you read *to* judge, for the sheer pleasure of *it*.

Leon said, "I'm sick of the shit."

I said, "Sick of what shit?"

"The bullshit."

"That never ends. Life is work."

"Doesn't mean life needs to be painful, you know what I'm saying?" he leered at me with bloodshot eyes.

"Life is work and suffering; there is an exchange for the energy you-"

"No, I don't believe that... I started to experience envy and jealousy to the extremes a while ago; I never used to before; I was diagnosed with schizophrenia-"

I listened with a newfound thought-pattern at the forefront of my process and said, "At what age were you diagnosed?"

"Twenty-seven."

"Ah, so my age then."

"Yeah, what I experienced was something I still can't explain; I was being assaulted by something out there, something wrathful."

"Your own ego."

"No, no, I assure you *it* wasn't; this thing wanted to torment me and *it* took me years of therapy to clear whatever the manifestation was."

"Your ego externalized and manifested as malevolent, and hateful—what you may have interpreted as spirits, or something supernatural-"

"Yes."

"-to preserve your ego, you externalized your self-doubt which is construed through the social realm in which we compare ourselves. You're a quiet type. I can tell you're intuitive. You-"

"No man, no, I'm telling you, whatever *it* was, *it* was nothing I could ever imagine on my own; I had conversations with this thing and was at the lowest point of my life."

At this point, I imagined myself speaking to myself, for indeed, our condition of suffering is universal; yet, this man, Leon, aspires to become a *djinn* and hopes for delusions of future fortune... estranged from the reality of the mundane futility and superficiality of all human endeavors... I attempted to continue the conversation, and Leon departed with intent to meet with his drug dealer.

I stood for a moment at the counter and closed my eyes. The social worker at the reception desk watched me through the wall-mounted corner camera and seven others sat by, silent. The television broadcasted a Thursday night soap opera. Three residents slept on the couch, passed out, sidelong; heads lolled against an armrest.

"I don't like work—no man does—but I like what is in the work—the chance to find yourself. Your own reality—for yourself not for

others—what no other man can ever know. They can only see the mere show, and never can tell what *it* really means."

- Joseph Conrad's The Heart of Darkness

11:28 PM

My experience at the shelter and my associations, especially my lighthearted relationship with an ex cocaine dealer—an African American man named Marcus, have alleviated me of all vanity beyond the essentials of civil hygiene. I wear a motley of donated clothing, conduct myself in accordance with the truth of my "self," i.e., virtue, partake and contribute to community life, and repose alone; I am powerless and free—the most content I've *ever* been...

This ends in seven days.

May 18th, 2019

10:48 AM

There is an extreme lack of self-knowledge among the community here. A woman prescribed mass amounts of antidepressants sulks all day around the outdoor gazebo and within the kitchen—one of the aforementioned ~~trinity~~ duo of women. I've spoken to each woman now on an individual basis and have experienced a harrowing—an extreme depression, projected outward from the group; they enable each other. This community of the homeless *is* a quintessential home unto *it*self for not only those residents who live within the walls on a short-term basis, but for those who have found the life of this regimented microcosm a veritable providence: an escape from themselves, to stagnate amongst the complacent despondency of those around them... to identify with a lack of meaning. Most who I've asked here, "What is your self-assigned meaning of life?" are at an abject loss. I'm doleful—*not* hateful, scornful, or disdainful... no: a wistful sadness. A stepping stone to some, a limbo to others.

1:25 PM

This life is a strange, ephemeral affair; to sit, listen, and think while others pass you by; the thoughts are prominent forces for one who is willing to listen; one who wishes to glean the innermost secrets of others may know at a glance: the violent repudiations, the yearnful remembering, the suppressed secrets.

The people here know of my activities due to my disclosure—this writing, though the extent of the (current) content is veiled in a lack of disclosure. My thoughts are unsettling, and once again I'm named to be a freak—in my mind, though always, the damnable condemnation of "intelligence" is spoken to me, to which I refute the grandiosity of the blessing/curse with a confirmation of my self-chosen idiocy, for I wouldn't be among these folks if not for my ill-suited will; this, I affirm; however, where I am this moment, is where I've chosen. I've arranged to repay my debts by financial donation once I graduate from boot camp. This location serves as a mini-vacation and a case study of the destitute—where the downtrodden converge to break bread, share their woes, and reap the comfort of a sympathetic hammock.

The more I speak and associate with my comrades, the more unsettled those around me become. To understand the immediate effect of discipline and order, and to project yourself with an air of confidence in a realm of vacuous chaos, is *godlike*. To grapple with the idea of death and "know" nothing of the matter is to glean the essence of an immortal.

7:40 PM

Oh, the despair welt in my breast... I spoke with one of the social workers: an intelligent man who works at the front desk; his piercing gaze, similar to my own, gave way to his nature. I pressed him with the question, "Do you believe that all virtue is pretentious?" The man, Matt, believed I had read such an inquiry on the internet—as many people infer, due to the absurdity and spontaneous nature of my inquiries.

Our conversation elapsed over an hour; we divulged our similar sociological and psychological interests—a greater commonality than I ever established with someone; therefore, I shared with Matt my full, written, unpublished "theory" in my second manuscript of "thoughts beings objects," to which he expressed extreme agreement. Hunched over my writing device, engrossed with the material, Matt finished reading, and while our exchange elapsed, I began to notice a marked change in our mutual observations. We saw a mirror in each other, and each instance in which I moved my lips to utter a question, he seemed to know the nature of *it*, and proceeded to alter the conversation's direction to a convenient diversion. The question being, "Due to your experience of constant travel across the country and your similar interests of 'why' and 'how,' do you experience projections of energy where you intuit that others perceive you to be a 'sociopath' or 'psychopath?'"

Matt lowered his forehead and skewed his eyebrows to a downward slant; we leaned closer to each other across the desk; others around us sat by, engaged with the television and their respective phones. "Between you and I," he asserted, "you could say that I'm on a few lists."

"Ah, I ask this of you, because I know you are an intelligent man and could safely commit a murder; my greatest fear and hope is that I will one day be brutally tortured until death by my fellow man."

We shared a smirk: a simple, dark, acknowledgment.

Matt said, "I would never kill someone; *it*'s counterproductive to unity and progress, to eliminate a consciousness rather than to alter *it*."

I agreed, despite my opinion of progress, though there is merit in unity. The conversation ebbed due to constant inquiries from residents and visitors; thereafter Matt stood to assist with kitchen affairs.

May 19th, 2019

9:49 AM

I begin to write and reckon the date: four days until deployment; this homeless establishment is of no consequence, even at Navy boot camp, those who will surround me in bunks, on fields, and eventually on ships, supposedly at brothels, at bars, engaged in comradeship and brotherhood, there will be a void, a continual chasm of nothingness.

I've bonded with other "sociopaths": intelligent men who acknowledge and dismiss the label applied by the DSM(4/5) and the APA. I walk with Marcus, a man of extreme intellect and empathy, though his demeanor is a complete antithesis of mine, and still, we bond through our disillusionment. Marcus desires power and attainment of status—in his *own* reality. He is an ex-social worker and a psychological major, aware of the pitiable state of not only those around us, but also for *ourselves* for choosing to *care*.

I sit at a kitchen table after an hour walk with Marcus; we discussed how much we loathe and despise the women (the ~~trinity~~ duo of harridans mentioned in previous entries) he now bonds and banters with before me; I listen, and he continues to indulge and discourse sweet nothings with all three women. I observe and write of *it;* he has attempted to reform those who are too uninspired and unambitious to help themselves. Now Marcus despairs, and will be pitied by those he had strived to "help."

The dissimulation practiced by all parties is palpable, a constant presence; those who pretend—literal pretentiousness manifest through the practice of enforced virtue—even in homeless shelters. I'm appalled. This is incredible to me—I compare to my imaginings of primeval man and wonder at the raw ineptitude: Those hoarded around a nightly fire, tucked away in a cavern, each and every one of them striving to subjugate each other, copulating with the women—and the women, prized and awe-inspiring, subjugate the men, *unbeknownst* to the men. A mental and emotional chess match—each ego in harmony; a horrible, terrible— *beautiful, dance...* oh, the dance of men and women, in wonderment and awe of each other. Even myself, an outsider among them, is *only* one of them.

My rant, tirade, and utter grievances over the conditions of humanity know no bounds; there is a lamentable state in all affairs, and I am unable to extricate myself, for *I am* what I "know."

3:11 PM

I stand, silent, and listen from the conference room; Marcus calls for me, for the sake of companionship, an outlet for entertainment. He begins to discuss my intelligence with others; by the result, my teeth start to grate: a reactionary impulse... my head downcast, I am appalled, again, much as Marcus is appalled, yet what he believes is a boon (intelligence) is my detriment. He repeats to the women, "My father told me: The moment people stop talking about you, you're dead." He's taken to calling me by nicknames: terms of endearment. "Baethan has a dark intelligence," he *shouts*, "Baethan sees things differently than others in a way that most can't understand, but *I* can; he's my parallel."

I have failed to remain silent and *spoke,* to the loss of myself, for the benefit of temporary validation, a *reciprocating* loss to all parties.

Earlier this morning, after Marcus and I returned from a morning constitutional, I idled with seven other ~~key~~ prominent residents of the shelter at the gazebo and listened to vacuous dialogue on topics varied from the weather, food, drugs, and *complaints of other people*... I engaged, and confronted the most base, brutish, and unintelligent man on the premises, and ordered him to file a grievance (shelter policy) if he experiences issues with other people rather than threatening others with physical violence and proceeding to complain for the sake of himself. He backstepped away from me—this gargantuan moron, closed his eyes, and slurred, "You're going to make me hit you!"

In essence, he made an ass of himself, hobbled away, and I condemned everyone, in both houses, and those who sat around me at the gazebo, by means of a verbose, uninterrupted outburst of dialogue, to which the people studied me with astonishment, their sheepish countenances receptive, and for the first time in my life, I experienced what *it* is to be a tyrant: feared and respected. This is no delusion; this is the observation of an *illusion:* power. I'm sickened.

Hail! Lord of the destitute!

"The art of being wise is the ability to know what should be overlooked."

- William James

"Droll thing, life is—that mysterious arrangement of merciless logic for a futile purpose. The most you can hope from *it* is some knowledge of yourself—that comes too late—a crop of inextinguishable regrets. I have wrestled with death. *It* is the most unexciting contest you can imagine. *It* takes place in an impalpable grayness, with nothing underfoot, nothing around, without spectators, without clamor, without glory, without the great desire of victory, without the great fear of defeat, in a sickly atmosphere of tepid skepticism, without much belief in your own right, and still less in that of your adversary. If such is the form of ultimate wisdom, then life is a greater riddle than some of us think *it* to be."

- Joseph Conrad's Heart of Darkness

May 20th, 2019

7:27 AM

I visited many homeless and drunks around town two days ago—to their extreme dissatisfaction; I encountered a trio of men and women in their mid-fifties: a toothless African American man, a rugged Caucasian (biker) man (who hailed me from a streetside bench), and a mid-fifties Caucasian woman. They drank a bottle of vodka passed between them and we engaged in philosophical banter spurred on by me. The interaction ended with overt hostility, to which I implored the rugged biker—who had stood and threatened to punch me in the face—to *do* so. The biker backed down on my conviction that his act of violence will be punished due to law and order (we stood on a busy side-street during the evening).

The woman and I began to discuss my theories, to which she "poo-pooed" my suggestion of total anarchy and absurdity as the ideal "utopia." She claimed to have attended college and acquired a master's degree in philosophy.

"You wouldn't even begin to believe the circumstances that occurred throughout my life that led me to the situation I'm in now," she disclosed to me prior. As a retort to my theory, she shook her head: "What comes after?" she inquired, lips tight, arms folded. Beady brown eyes peered out from below the brim of a dirtied blue ball cap.

"What comes after what?"

"Anarchy and absurdity."

"Chaos, and whatever spawns thereafter is a product of a cycle."

The woman eyed me, lowered the brim of the end of her hat over her face, glowered, and said, "Have you read Hegel?"

My countenance lit with interest. "No."

"You *haven't* read *Hegel* and you consider yourself a philosopher?" She laughed.

"We're all philosophers."

"No we're not; have you read Spinoza?"

"No."

"Aristotle?"

"Yes, I read his Nicomachean-"

"Ethics—yes, alright, how about Hobbes?"

"No."

"Leibniz?"

"No."

The woman scoffed, "Humes, Rousseau, Stuart?"

"No—and what manner of evaluation is *it* to judge the merit of my *own* thought—which is worth, to me, more than the combined product of every lecture you've attended and every assigned excerpt from a book you've read?"

The woman regressed to her seat and proceeded to glare at me from beneath her hat; at that point, the men reengaged me with initial implied threats of violence, to which I reacted with warmth and candor. Each implored me to leave them, especially the woman, who became infuriated at my mention of Aleister Crowley; she snapped, "You do know he was high and drunk when he wrote that horrible *The Book of the Law,* correct?

"Well, you're intoxicated now and you lecture me on precepts and doctrines you've studied at a bygone time, what of *it?*"

"Alright," she sighed and slumped in her seat, only to regain a semblance of self-assured posture a moment after, "You need to go before I become angry."

"You choose to become angry-"

And so the men redoubled their frivolous threats; after diffusion of the situation, I spared each of them the insufferable sight of my existence and strut back to the homeless shelter.

10:32 AM

I've removed myself from the shelter and sit at a quiet table at the local public library. I've encountered two other residents from the shelter within the library. The energy here is neutralized: a stimulation to allow me to think with a clarity I haven't known for weeks.

At the shelter, while I sit at the kitchen table, vagrants, the destitute, the sick, and the idiotic pass me by. Sloven, obese, malnourished, gimped, idle, and afflicted with gross self-absorption to the point of paralysis—similar to a state I experienced two years ago within the confines of my father's home—the souls and energies dispersed around the establishment are a loathsome acculturation of the surrounding slums: the lowest convergence point.

Outside, between both buildings, the literal scumbags of society—the invalids of the shelter, hobble and wobble to sit beneath the domed roof of a wooden gazebo to partake in their communal ritual of chain-smoking cigarettes, incessant gripes, and bemoaning of a perpetual "victimization." Those who are "renowned" around the establishment are the epitome of vermin, for they have overstayed their presence to become "known": infamous for their lack of exploits.

New folks arrive and I greet them, eager to learn of the ineptitude. Each shares their tragedy with great relief expressed in their visage. Many expect pity, relish *it;* I don't provide, and instead, probe, to the baseness of the behavior, to the core of the character, to the soul of a demon. I partake in communal meals and observe. I engage in chores and *observe*—all the while, *I'm* observed, and by consequence I observe the outcome *of* my observations, which I have expressed to the residents and employees. I'm hated by the majority for my *choice* to reside at the shelter for the sake of an experience—a case study. I've crossed the threshold of working alongside those capable of maintaining a wage for their survival, to *residing* with those unable (the majority by damnable choice).

Perpetual children, prescription-addicted dependants, alcoholic (secret) loafers, scoundrels and cretins. The nomads drift in for handouts and depart back to their "self-reliant" lifestyle. Each social worker employed as a monitor between shifts expresses their qualms with the conditions of society—to the *residents*—often to the people which they outright condemn!

Judgments are cruel and unrestrained, for the thoughts are energy expressed and felt by perceivers—this "knowledge" is now second-nature to me; I have incorporated the sensations into my self-understanding and reckon the impact of every conscious thought, moment to moment. I've reckoned those who entered the shelter within a similar timeframe as myself and noted a downward spiral of confidence. The longer one situates themself and identifies as "homeless," with no labor or creative expression to provide a value or warrant positive recognition, the greater the disparity between their personal truth, and therefore happiness, due to a lack of virtue.

"To write" is my mission.

At my present position, I sit and scowl while I write of this experience; a woman my age sits diagonal to me and deems me as an intolerable and remarkable sight. Her energy rebounds off me as a byproduct of my recording.

3:28 PM

I've delved into the content of Spinoza's *Ethics* by recommendation of the homeless woman. Fascinated, I've begun with a preface by the editor in which he summarizes the precepts, and I have experienced a feedback dissonance upon reading the following, derived from the text:

"Spinoza will try to convince you that thoughts do not cause actions, that most of your knowledge is imaginary, that inanimate objects have minds and that you have no inner 'self'."

In conjunction with this, I've begun to read a text I've found on the shelter bookshelves: *Conversations with God,* by Neale Donald Walsch, recommended to me by Robert, a spiritual maintenance worker who stops by the shelter periodically. I have noted an extreme causality between the two texts: "God" is everything observable and everything that *is* existence and *being*, independent from the concept of a divine and supernatural entity propagated from a theological source.

I've concluded, in the briefness that I've read these two texts simultaneously, and with the retained knowledge of every book I've read in the past which attempts to "explain" the systematic processes of the universe through word instead of mathematics, is that true knowledge has been known since the dawn of man—prior, before knowledge was to be "known," and that each iteration is a preposterous presentation from what exists: the purity of thought in every moment experienced by the unity of "God."

My being is a mote within a mote, a microcosm within a microcosm... I reckon everything I am, and "know" of my *freedom* to be ordered within a self(less)-contained design of progress with the *purpose* of entropy.

May 21st, 2019

8:28 PM

I've established a strong bond with the man, Marcus. His history is nothing to me, as mine as to him; we validate ourselves; therefore, we empower each other; two facets of "God" in awe with each other's acts of pretension. We've discussed "sociopathy" and "psychopathy" at length. Despite our characters being antithetical, we are compelled by strong passions that intrigue one another. Marcus strives to entertain others through an extension of compassion—his *passion,* to validate himself. In contrast with my process of writing, our juxtaposition of character is remarkable, and our immutable energies—compelled by our passions, create an immediate impact. Marcus and I sense this in each other; we interact, and thrive off the validation of one another, regardless of the sinister mechanism.

Marcus' being is reminiscent of an Egyptian god, with a large, squarish, shaved head, wide-brimmed nose, small fiendish eyes spaced far apart, and a wicked smile; his astute features are battered and scarred from age, which bestows him with a grizzled countenance, and his boisterous voice overpowers all who attempt to speak—yet his demeanor is subdued. His observable intelligence is blunted for he yearns to project his personality; however, when Marcus focuses, there is a soulful fire expressed in his iris'. We "break bread" together, as he dubs the act of consumption, and indulge each other in conversation… Marcus desires me to write of him; his will has indeed triumphed in this regard. I chose Marcus' alternative name on a commonality we share for respect of the dead emperor, Marcus Aurelius.

I'm at a loss… I've read an abundance of material to "enjoy the moment," written a plethora of nonsense to fulfill my "god-given" *self-assigned purpose,* and reclined to think, a glass of milk in-hand…

I signed on for a $10.00/hr job to clean a bouncy house today alongside three other residents of the shelter and pocketed twenty-five dollars in my front right pocket… This lesson is important—an acknowledgment of wisdom gleaned: You *hated* to work for the charlatan who owned the bouncy house; the labor symbolized every dairy cooler you ever scrubbed, every toilet you ever rubbed, and every broom you've ever pushed. Stay the course.

One of my recruiters uplifts me from this damnable sanctuary of the uninspired tomorrow at 9:30 AM to stay overnight at a hotel before my morning plane departure to Illinois. My next entry of this document will be the first of a series of copying from a set of journals over a two-month timespan.

Lo-

THE SAILOR'S CREED

"I am a United States Sailor.
"I will support and defend the
"Constitution of the United States of

"America and I will obey the orders
"Of those appointed over me.

"I represent the fighting spirit of
"The Navy and those who have gone
"Before me to defend freedom and
"Democracy around the world.

"I proudly serve my country's Navy
"Combat team with Honor, Courage,
"And Commitment.

"I am committed to excellence and
"The fair treatment of all."

May 25th, 2019

5:38 AM (Day 2)

The first prolonged, sleep-deprived experience of psychological acculturation has enlightened me on many facets of the lifestyle I've chosen to attain. Although my conduct is of absolute militarism and seriousness, there is an undertone of indifference in whether I pass or fail which my superiors no doubt glean. Myself, and 70-80 other recruits are treated as quasi prisoners; this treatment is most notable during our feeding sessions. Silence is enforced, though many whisper regardless. Communication by countenance and gesture encourages the masses to stare down at empty trays or into the folds of a training manual: our single permitted literature.

We've been equalized across the board of appearance. For the totality of the entire division, there are few "intelligent" men (to my dismay) with the exception of a few "nukes" and those rated for the aviation or electronics fields. The majority of recruits are young adults between the ages of 18-25.

We've endured tests within the first forty-eight hours consisting of one forced sleepless night in conjunction with constant stimulation, two-hour-long instances of standing at "attention" heel to toe, and sitting cross-legged on a hard floor (the worst of my pains). I'm eager to endure, though I was certain that on account of several purposeful blunders and

318

disregard for conduct that I would receive the literal boot and take to the streets of Chicago.

When we first arrived and departed from the bus, we were greeted with an incessant onslaught of petty officers and chiefs who berated and cursed our entire group with a lackadaisical conviction. The orders we are instructed to follow are often obtuse and serve to test the integrity of our compliance. Standing watch is an exercise of patience.

The gauntlet of the cafeteria is of my utmost interest; the manner that we are treated is abhorrent and perpetuates the notion of recruits being subhuman at specific intervals throughout processing and being served our assortment of wholesome foodstuffs. The propaganda proliferated around the establishment is a constant trickle of stimulation to crystallize the values being taught. Due to my discussion with the younger recruits and the consultation of a book titled *The Bluejacket's Manual*, by Thomas J. Cutter, I've learned that this station is temporary and that our division will transition to a new "Ship" (building) in a little over a week.

Marches at formation around the base is a test of our stride, the clench of our hand, the alignment of our spines everything is accounted for.

The best instance of psychological conditioning I've experienced has been the visit to the barbers, where eighty men, myself included, lined up in four files, toe-to-heel, and awaited for our heads to be shaved. On a far wall to our left, a quote:

"Far better is *it* to dare mighty things, to win glorious triumphs, even though checkered by failure... than to rank with those poor spirits who neither enjoy nor suffer much, because they live in a gray twilight that knows not victory nor defeat."

– Theodore Roosevelt

Adjacent to the quote, pictures of past women recruits, circa 1980, lined up and seated at the barber: vacuous enormity expressed on their countenances, seated in *chairs*. The lot of us sweltered, groaned, shuffled, and humped against each other's asses. A faint jazz tune from the '80s played and undertoned our scenario with a hint of comical joviality. I unleashed a few suppressed sniggers while those around me wiped their brows, scowled, and glowered at the back of another's head.

JUNE

June 4th, 2019

8:19 AM (Day 12)

"These are your brothers and sisters to help you put warheads on foreheads," said our chief RDC (Recruit Division Commander) while he discoursed a topic: Sexual Assault and Harassment. "I've had family members attend court with fear in their eyes." The chief paced in front of our seated congregation of over eighty young men and women seated cross-legged on a discolored white floor. A painful silence lingered while we waited for a follow-up: "You are not here to make friends. You want to do cool shit out there and put warheads on foreheads. You are not here to make friends."

To sit on (in) a cramped school desk chair slanted plastic conjoined with a wooden top while sleep-deprived, in a room over-filled with dozens of people, ten files, seven ranks deep, dressed in PT (Physical Training) clothing, while we wait for the processing of our personal payment information, followed by an immediate PT test, is of great concern to me, for I desire meet the standard to qualify for a pay grade/rank advancement to "E-2."

There are those around me who suffer great pain from being seated due to a medical shot we received, dubbed, the "Peanut Butter Shot." We received this shot in our left ass cheek after being corralled akin to cattle into a foray of needles and disgruntled government corpsman.

I stood to use the "Head" (bathroom), and on my return, I passed a fellow recruit who I internally regard as "The Imp" due to his incredibly short stature and pudgy, rounded face; he slid across his chair, winced his facial features compressed into a tight red bundle, and dared to express a muffled exhalation of pain. I'll be surprised if he passes the initial PT test.

I wonder, what sensations and feelings are to be booted from boot camp, more so as time progresses. No matter my lethargy and diminished strength due to strength training restrictions, I know I will project and push myself to the nth, that I may stimulate and invigorate my body.

I write this entry in the note section of our issued study book with the intent to copy the entry to typed word months afterward. My self-assigned meaning is a device to suppress my consciousness of afflictions and environmental conditions. A belly full of three hard-boiled eggs, cantaloupe, peaches, cheesy home fries, oatmeal, blueberries, and yogurt... there is only victory.

I reiterate, my greatest challenge at boot camp is to sit for these prolonged sessions; to succumb to exhaustion before "Taps" (lights out) is a surefire method to be booted from boot camp.

Despite the routine warnings of our RDCs for the penalties of fraternization, wherever I may be in this facility with a female recruit present, conversations are attempted by these desperate sods in the desire of an emotional outlet, and are rejected by means of my silent disdain.

Yes, yes... a hum of an oversized fan in the small cloister of this cramped den. Akin to cattle we inhale and expel a mechanized union of industrial militarization; obey, obey, and we are served in return, anything we may desire, within reason, *of course*; I've no doubt I'll be broken and reformed as my superiors wish. To consume, yes, consume and place *warheads on foreheads*. I'm inspired:

There was a man who could not obey simple orders.

"Stand at attention eyes forward," screamed a belligerent little man garbed in an ensemble of pleated khaki attire: a chief.

"But my ass sir, please—"

"Shut the fuck up and drag your ass to medical if *it* hurts."

"No sir, err pett *chief*, I don't need medical please!"

Forty-two male counterparts stood by and watched, eyes glazed in the direction of the spectacle in the large chamber room: Arms straight, fingers clenched into a fist, thumbs aligned with the seams of (navy) blue sweatpants, posture erect; a single bead of sweat on the hairline of one tall, lanky man with lips too big and eyes too small for his face; he shivered, blinked twice, and stared through the forehead of an enraged face and listened to the reverberated screams of an infuriated khaki-garbed officer echo throughout the cavernous living quarters.

11:23 AM

Two notable events transpired after the submission of processing: A young boy of a careless demeanor was called on by the chief. We are required to speak "moving chief" as a response, to which the boy *did*, though he went unheard. The chief "corrected" the boy with a verbal dictation; the boy snapped back, "I *did* say 'moving chief,'" to which both the present chief and petty officer accepted *without* issuing disciplinary action to the surprise of all the recruits, myself included. I suspect this mouth-breathing child's intelligence is far above average, though he suffers from what the psychiatric establishment would define as "autism," which in actuality is a blatant disregard or care, i.e., general indifference towards others due to intelligence, which grants the boy a quasi immunity from the jurisdiction of our superiors.

A girl behind me muttered, "Wow, ballsy," on the utterance of the boy's comment; she is the chief's daughter, I overheard her state aloud a moment prior... to my dismay, for this is the same girl who attempts to fraternize with me. I've marked this "chief's daughter" as a bane, a scourge to be avoided.

June 5th, 2019

1:03 PM (Day 13)

For the swim qualification test, I elected to take lessons to brush up on the skillset, whereby a harridan proceeded to scream and chastise myself and the group (in *need* of lessons) for being incompetent children unable to handle or comprehend the waves of the ocean, *before* our lessons even began. We were instructed to sit, stand, and lean forward and backward in a small training pool by this old crone paid to attack the confidence of young men and women for the sake of her own satisfaction.

I was informed, *after* our brief lesson, that our group will be set back and unable to graduate with our initial division due to the extra swim training; this matter upset me, and when I requested to undergo the swim test immediately following the degrading swim lesson, my wistful countenance was screamed at for insubordinate behavior by a tattooed man twice my size and with half of my intellect.

June 6th, 2019

7:09 AM (Day 14)

Last night I volunteered for roving sentry and waited in line two floors below to report the (immutable) conditions of my compartment to the OOD (Officer of the Deck: a bored chief sitting in an office). I stood over the chief's head by a wall-mounted print of the American flag enshrouded with the wings of a bald eagle and failed to conduct physical and spoken orders four consecutive times. At that moment, and for many days prior, I had decided to quit... resign... terminate my employment. The nameless chief behind the desk sensed my resolute indifference to his insults and began to display his humanity. After my fifth and *finally* successful attempt to knock, advance three measured 30-inch steps, recite the exact jargon, and acquire a signature on my form, the chief said, "Where are you from, Balor?"

"[Town Name], chief."

"Hot damn, I'm from ([Aforementioned] Town Name), small world, huh Balor?"

"Yes, chief."

"How old are you, Balor?"

"Twenty-seven, chief."

"What's your rating?"

"Culinary specialist, chief."

"Why did you join?"

"I joined the U.S. Navy for the sake of my writing, chief."

"Your what?"

"My *writing*, and on this account, I believe I've made a grievous error, and I will be resigning tomorrow."

The chief leaned back, both forearms flat, fingers interlaced; he said, "*Resigning*, what do you mean?"

"I'm quitting my service for the U.S. military, chief."

"No, you aren't." I locked eyes with the man. "No, you most certainly are not," he reiterated. We stared at each other, our gazes soft.

"Why do you want to quit, Balor?"

"My philosophy, chief."

"And what's that?" he grinned.

I inexactly quoted Epictetus: "*It*'s better to be in poverty and free than to be a slave among many."

The chief leaned back, straightened his posture for a moment, tilted his head at a 150° angle, raised his eyebrows, and said, "That's very interesting," and resumed his hunched forward position of forearms flat against the desk. My stoic countenance skewed down at a "*superior*" man, yet what he saw at that moment was an equal of flesh and consciousness. "Let me tell you something Balor I'm humanizing with you right now; this is something I never do hardly ever. You want to write; that's why you joined; well, this is a great job with medical, dental, pay, opportunities, travel, and you're going to write. You're going to write about all your experiences and do great things in the Navy. You aren't going to quit." My face strained and I looked down at the upside-down print of one piece of assorted paperwork on the desk. He continued, "What rating did you want?"

"Yeoman on a submarine. My recruiters wanted me in nuke, though I admitted to using CBD oil and disqualified myself."

"CBD oil... You didn't get that waived?"

"No chief, I attempted."

"I can tell you're a nuke; you can always tell a nuke. I want you to go down to classifications and request the rating you want, Balor, you understand?"

"I'm content with my current assignment if I were to stay, chief."

"You're staying Balor; this is a good job."

I closed my eyes for several seconds and imagined everything I've ever been and will be: whimsical, fleeting pains and joyful recollections and imaginings of what manner of change will usher unto the illusion of my control. I said, "Aye aye, chief."

"Good, get back to your compartment, recruit, stay strong."

"Aye aye, chief."

On return to my compartment, I spoke with the roving and starboard watchmen about my whereabouts on account of my extended observance. The watchmen inquired about my discussion with the chief and expounded their opinions that the chief had no right to contribute his thoughts on my decisions. Both watchmen asserted my will to choose is my own and that the chief assesses us as numbers.

The starboard watchman, Williams, requested to speak with me within the port hold (janitorial closet). We discussed our feelings of disillusionment on my conveyance of the quote by Epictetus that I spoke to the chief. Thereby the conversation evolved to a matter I recorded several days prior:

Williams said, "Why did you stand that one day when we were all waiting..."

"At the dental line for our X-Rays?"

"Yeah, we were all being punished and—"

I said, "I stood to join you."

"I thought so, and that's what makes you so cool, man."

"I stood for selfish reasons and sat before you were relieved, mostly to empower your group, with having to face that crowd of jeering brutes from the seal division wannabe killers."

"Yeah that's what I thought you stood for, I sensed that."

"I'm surprised you did; I didn't expect anyone to understand, perhaps a few of the RDCs who reacted to my behavior with circumspection, though no one else."

Williams said a line I'll never understand: "You're an essential part of the division; I don't care who else does or doesn't think so. I know *I* want you here."

Our banter persisted for fifteen minutes; a few of the seaman recruits peeked their heads into the doorway of the closet and demanded us to vacate on account of their fear of the RDCs discovering Williams and myself together in a closed closet space before reverie.[28]

The military life is *beyond* far removed from my personal paradigms of conduct. I'm tempted to quit the day of, or the day before graduation; five years is a long time to obey.

I sit in a dental office with half of my division. We've waited for two hours, corralled and confined to multiple seats. I'm due to have four teeth extracted: three wisdom teeth and one fractured tooth.

I've been injected, evaluated, garbed, fed, and provided for. I hear the sound of three to four drills in tandem and await first-class treatment. Yes, this particular slavery is grand and beautiful. I acknowledge my foolishness and ingratitude; all the metaphorical hoops I've jumped through for the previous six months to sit where I am now is nothing but a memory copied to a book. I speak my sentiments to few: those who inquire of me, and the ripples of regret pulse from each individual for doing so; they doubt themselves. Is this lifestyle worth the "benefits?" Perhaps for a month or two, as per usual. My uncertainty is paramount in all my dealings. I amble through "processing" with the conviction of a fool, indifferent to my "fate," yet, I'm at odds with myself, for my behavior, if unattended, will elicit negative marks on the division... the consciousness... "voices," the "madness" informs me, and incites an immediate reaction to my reality. I'm unsettled when I unsettle others by thought alone.

---

[28] A wakeup time, when an officer enters the compartment and screams the first command of the day: "Get the fuck out of your racks! Why the fuck are there people still in the fucking racks! Get the fuck out of your fucking racks! Get the fuck out of your rack! Make your rack! You have five minutes to make your rack or you're all going to get beat! *You*—get the fuck out of your rack!"

2:45 PM

On my return to the "ship," my bloodied and distorted maw is a beautiful sight for my peers. The RDCs have been informed by the Officer of the Deck that I desire to go "home," wherever "home" is. I realize the fantastic opportunity to abuse the system in this domain; the dentist encouraged me to utilize the services throughout my stay at boot camp. There is, in fact, a plethora of skills to learn. If I am to graduate, the feat will be on account of a miracle.

Seated up high on my second level rack, situated in the corner of the enormous quarters, I've been bestowed with "SIQ" (Sick in Quarters) status for two days. This time permits me to be a veritable fly on the wall, estranged *and* involved with the oath-signers of this culture.

June 8th, 2019

12:21 PM (Day 16)

Military culture represents the philosophy I've taken to as a unity of consciousness; I gaze around from the back of a classroom and feel the energies of each individual as my own. "Voices" are now guideposts, representations of the understanding of my social standing among others per the amalgamate of individuals I'm surrounded by. I've removed myself from all central locus' of operations and perform best when alone. The faces across from me shift and contort along toe lines and aligned in formation, each of us trained to behave akin to dogs and respond as parrots.

Men's confidence fluctuates in accordance with their accumulated mass (fat and muscle tissue) the imbeciles at least, though I'm no paragon of intelligence or aptitude, I reckon the transient opinions of envy and pity much like anywhere I've ever been, even subsumed by a culture of "no identity," humanity clings to the ego; in this manner, the teachings of *A Course in Miracles* and many other religious dogmas go hand-in-hand… to relinquish the self in favor of the *entity, i.e., god.*

I entered this establishment with a vibrant ego; this facet remains intact, yet always suppressed. If not for the outlet of the meaning I've chosen for my life, I would excel and climb the ephemeral ladder of power. There is nothing for me here, or anywhere, only myself and the natural world of consciousness via written word.

1:06 PM

"Bend over and touch your eyelids with your pinky finger just the tip."

"Aye aye chief," said a nineteen-year-old boy; he touched his eyelids with the flats of his pinky fingers.

"What the fuck is wrong with you! I said *tips!*"

"Aye aye chief."

"Sit down and shut the fuck up. Now think about why you're here."

"Yes aye aye chief."

"Shut up; stand up."

"Aye aye chief."

"What's your eleventh general order?"

"My eleventh-"

"No it's 'Chief, my eleventh general order is...'"

"Yes chief. Belay my last chief. Chief, my eleventh general order is... to be especially watchful at night, and during the time for challenging, and..."

"Shut the fuck up."

"Aye aye chief."

"Sit down."

"Aye aye chief."

"Study."

"Aye aye chief."

June 9th, 2019

1:02 PM (Day 17)

On my way out of the galley (cafeteria), I observed the first RPOC (Recruit Chief Petty Officer) assigned to our division: Jackson seated, hunched forward, wide-eyed and despondent; his hollowed eyes and mechanical mastication while he stared straight forward were proof of a recent social fumble with the RDCs, witnessed by the entire division.

I'll never forget Jackson's face at that moment: Haunted.

June 11th, 2019

9:11 PM (Day 19)

Instructors employed for ten years with wearied, forlorn visages. Marches progress, divisions sync, systematic pride.

There is a married man by the name of Rowan; when I first met him, he was a gregarious, optimistic, altruistic man. Over the past two weeks, he has assumed the role of head laundry PO and mulls around, enforcing silence with severe intent. He is harsh and abrasive, with shouts that boom and a formidable presence on account of a large body, yet his casual demeanor laid up in a bunk, for instance, is often effeminate, and the content of his speech is whispered complaints, or (unheeded) commands to fellow recruits beyond the realm of his desired authority.

The man who I arrived with at the airport, Brown, is no longer with the division for reasons unknown to me. Dozens have dropped out throughout these two introductory weeks: many who I didn't expect.

This experience has shaped those most affirmed with their personas into uncertain templates. Each person yearns to blend, to assimilate with the standard and expectations of our "superiors."

I suffer from boredom... extreme lethargy, in the least of all expected places. My writing suffers on account of information hijacking. The policed perusal of a single formulaic book throughout all granted hours of leisure has arrested my retention.

June 12th, 2019

9:36 AM (Day 20)

There is a general consensus among those in the division that a lack of activity constitutes a "good" day. To sit on our "2-packs" (as dubbed by our RDC's), for over six hours of accumulated time from sunrise to sunset, is *magnificent* by my peers' cumulative judgment to be paid for the matter too...

Well, "How grand, this dream is," shouts a man named Stone with aspirations to be a successful orator for the sake of "manipulating people," as he disclosed to me my first week with the division. Stone requested the titles of my books. I refused.

An excerpt from a speech he shouted between the middle of our ranks: "I've already been separated; I've already had this dream taken away from me, and now I come back to this division and hear all these people talking about how willing they are to throw away the dream!"

While he spoke, I thought of one of the closing statements to a chapter of a book I read three years ago:

"The communist world and America, in their being persuaded of having a universal mission to accomplish, represent a reality to be reckoned with. An eventual conflict between them will be, on the plane of world subversion, the last of the violent operations and will require the beastly holocaust of millions of human lives; and so, the last phase of the involution and shift of power through all four traditional castes and the advent of a collectivized humanity will eventually be achieved. And even if the feared catastrophe of a nuclear holocaust is averted, this civilization of titans, iron, crystal, and cement metropolises, of swarming masses, statistics, and technology that keeps the forces of matter at the leash will appear as a world that wobbles in orbit; one day *it* will wrest *it*self free and lose *it*self in a space in which there is no light other than the sinister glow cast by the acceleration of *it*s own fall."

– Julius Evola's Revolt Against the Modern World

I'd be content with this "American dream" if not for the trials of sleep deprivation and the straits on personal education. Alas, these conditions won't change when a recruit emerges from boot camp into the force if one wishes to *aspire*, to *become* this "American dream!"

2:09 PM

A new, unfamiliar chief stepped into a classroom after a chaplain's lesson and chastised our division of sleep-deprived and sick men and women: "You must *own* boot camp."

The chaplain reinitiated his lesson and asked the division, "Who has ever been on a Navy ship?" A young girl answered and confirmed she has.

The chaplain said, "What was the occasion?"

"My brother was in the Navy."

"What was his rating?"

"He was a seal, but then he dropped out as an undesignated and became a boatmate's swain."

The chaplain smirked and said, "Excellent." (I.e., the chaplain said, *"Your brother is an idiot."*) I observed the chaplain's expressions, for this man is an officer, expected to be revered and acknowledged as a man of supreme eminence. I reckoned a disheartened glower and intuited, further, the chaplain's thoughts:

"This division is full of truly lost souls. This class is lifeless."

A young man stood and disclosed, "My mother bore me at the age of sixteen and she only loved me when I had money. I joined the Navy for... unity."

The chaplain assumed an equipoised smile, dissimulated a series of empathetic head nods, steepled his hands together in front of his flat abdomen, and said, "Physical, mental, spiritual... This young man has much spirit for making the decision he did. You never thought you could sleep three to five hours each night and still be productive but we do *it* out of love for our country."

3:13 PM

Corralled between classrooms, aligned in marches, constrained in behavior and prohibited from physical training outside of the prescribed regimen, I am lethargic, apathetic, on the verge of angered for what?

There is no outlet for expression; the work is *too* easy; therefore I struggle to obey... you must obey the most absurd of orders, instructions, and accept fallout elicited by your superiors. We sit for extensive periods engaged with nothing but the idle thoughts of our imaginations. Suffering *is* illusory in this domain; the duress is of impatience: to sit, sleep-deprived, and *not* succumb to the misery of a self-imposed stasis, to submit to the system, to drink what our chief dubs the "Kool-Aid."

Countless moments, I've made a supreme ass of myself, with no care or regard for my peers' opinions, nor for the overblown infractions designed to be a penalty to my self-esteem, *if* I choose to accept the conditions as detrimental. Before me, I see men and women dressed in attire with little pins and flared colors obey. *Respect*, for the experience those *above* you have accrued based on rank to *recognize* those worth more than yourself. "You will no longer identify with civilian life; *it* is now us and them," said the chief RDC of our division one lazy afternoon.

We the people.

June 13th, 2019

10:03 AM (Day 21)

Boredom is anguish.

I'm between wonder and desolation, for what reality is. I often stand, march, sit, observe, and fascinate over my surroundings, the immediate sensory perceptions, the habitation of my flesh and physical functions, the whiff of scented flowers on a march past a well-kept row of gardens juxtaposed by the stench of a sewer grate overfilled with rainwater, the consciousness expressed on each human face, tangible through generations of hominid forms.

We train for war and behave akin to undisciplined children officer and enlisted alike, for war is a game best played by children; the soul never ages; there is only a temperance of doubt and fear. The wisest child slaughters with glee expressed in the constricted blackness of their eyes.

Idle chatter and dissipated glances. Stupefied grins and whimsical stares. Beeps of watches and flashes of LED lights. Despair undertones each interaction, subverted by the will to thrive while our instructors deliberate. I'm astonished and jaded, weary and attentive; society never alters, only the manifestation of culture. All we know is the book we've been prescribed as a creed. This station is a temporary rift between life elsewhere, where all who *want* to be *elsewhere* choose to be...

10:43 AM

Our division visited a barbershop for our second out of four scheduled haircuts on a march to a different "ship" adjacent to our division's "ship."

Another division formed a line to the galley and precluded entry to the barber shop; this unanticipated circumstance infuriated our RDCs. Our division entered and arranged ourselves for an intense, expedited process of hair removal. After three weeks of music deprivation (excluding nationalistic fanfare and cadence), Michael Jackson's *Billy Jean* began to blare from surround sound speakers nestled in the corners of the shop. Recruit heads started to bob; shocked smiles transposed out of chiseled frowns.

The moment the recruits of our division donned NWU's (Navy Working Uniform), I recall the throngs of grown men engrossed and prideful with the idea of their garbed image among the "civilian world." Now, we wear, fold, stow, and wash the fabric each day; glamor faded a day later. Parkas, blouses, boots, caps the entire wardrobe is lusterless, yet the characters of those fixated on vainglorious pursuits shone bright within the span of that dark, systematic moment, corralled in a quasi retail outlet when we first acquired our uniforms.

June 14th, 2019

9:36 AM (Day 22)

I want out, trapped, akin to a hamster in a cage with no wheel. My RDCs respect me for my character and conduct; they abhor me for my flagrant indifference to whether I pass or fail this series of instruction-based tasks of rack assembly and clothes folding. I've memorized all the jargon and live with a suppressed mode of ego exhibition which grants me forbearance among my peers.

There is one recruit I've nicknamed, "The Skulking Corrector," to his face, for he scrambles around our compartment and performs minor adjustments to other's racks and shoe placements... *all* day; he pouts, mopes, and his feeble admonitions are tinged with fear.

Most of these men are desperate for their egos to be validated by this systematic process. There is no failure unless you are incompetent or throw yourself under the proverbial march, trampled by the division *and* the jurisdiction of your superiors, connoting penalties within the "Civilian World." As government property, we are locked into ill-fitting holes and turn right-face; left-face; about-face; parade rest; attention!

"Yes petty office."

"Aye aye petty officer."

"Good afternoon petty officer."

"Yes petty officer."

"Yes petty officer."

"Aye aye petty officer."

"Good evening chief."

"Aye aye chief."

"Aye aye petty officer."

The musings of monotonous, automatic greetings are an exceptional representation of the relinquishment of personal autonomy and autocracy. Each moment with my posture erect, knuckles flat against the seam of my trousers, I stare forward and wonder, awed by the divinity of perspective, of the body, and personal will.

The key players of the division have been assigned insignias: replicas of officer pins, clasped to the center of their respective uniforms, which serve to symbolize the distinction between "them" and "us." Now, the power plays have manifested three-fold; those once arrogant and restrained are now haughty and disdainful; insignia-wearers are a step above the normal division "law," and are permitted! Corruption is encouraged! Each unites in a flock and converges in groups reminiscent of high school cliques. Insignia-wearers' visages of patronizing scorn acknowledge the depressed and dejected miens of the unadorned recruits those who arrived on the same bus! Equalized and bonded in hardship and trials, divided due to competence in the management of resources *allocated* to us by our "superiors": A microcosmic society! governed by individuals who claim to be unified with the masses, yet elevated by a badge of distinction and the performance of extra duties. However, the ~~peasants~~ recruits work, each in a way conducive with their aptitude: some skate by with the performance of the bare minimum (I designated myself to this bracket for the sake of the steady continuation of writing throughout daylight hours and copying from federal-issued notebooks and the textbook margins of a training guide to my personal journal), and there are those who grovel and worm through the course of each "evolution" (training event). Most of those who fail to comply, despite their *worming,* have been separated by this point.

I've drawn the ire of the RDCs; a spoken reputation of being intelligent, foolish, stern, and indifferent, is assigned to me. Often my instructor's nightmare, my infractions are minor enough to be an annoyance and frequent enough to be a nonpunitive disruption.

I've been assigned a new rack centered in the middle of the compartment, bottom-level, with a new rackmate: an overweight ex-wrestler African American man, Williams the man I spoke with in the broom closet about my desire to resign. "Demoted" from the "Starboard Watch" position, Williams has been condemned to bunk with me in the center of the compartment (high surveillance) to exacerbate his punishment. Williams rejoins with the throngs of plebs and acclimates with the relief of his extracurricular duties. My new placement is similar to my first rack, only now I'm opposite to and across from the RPOC (Recruit Chief Petty Officer) of the division.

I'm the least depressed and the most *miserable* I've ever been in my life. I yearn for a walk through a boneyard, Bach, Vivaldi, Haydn, Corelli, mornings of solitude, alone with the maelstrom of my fruitless thoughts, free to perform labors of the body, to read, to write, to consume free to terminate slavedom at my discretion, free to *will*.

Property! I've signed a contract; bewitched by my benefactor, I commit through highs and lows.

I've determined that my life is an act of permanent self-malice and wayward desolation. Solitude is attainable at brief moments while behind the closed curtain of a toilet cubicle, though many stalls around ~~base~~ the ship are devoid of privacy augmentations due to recruit vandalism, to my curious delight. I prefer the rare moments alone; there is no indecent exposure when showering daily with throngs of men.

A girl seated next to me nods her head ad nauseam in an effort to stay awake. This girl stood adjacent to me in line at a swim qualification class where I saw that she has a semi-colon tattooed on the nape of her neck. After the test, while we donned our equipment, I said, "Why do you have a semi-colon tattooed on your neck?" on our way out of the establishment.

"*It*'s personal," she moaned. "C'mon, I don't want to get in trouble if we take too long."

I said, "We won't take too long nor will we '*get in trouble*' if we did."

"C'mon! We need to go!"

We exited the building together; I sped ahead of the girl and ran the mile back to our ~~base~~ ship. The girl reverted to a walk three minutes into the mile and arrived after me, eight minutes late.

8:15 PM

My attitude has shifted; our RDCs have begun to mark "hard cards" (permanent records): Three strikes and you're out. Enforced physical exercise for the incorrect answer to questions, incompetence, and failure to follow instructions has resurged; the authentic boot camp oppression has been reinstated. I thrive off the pressure and renew my social ostracism in the spirit of the challenge indifferent to success or failure; my composure and esteem is assured on account of my life's purpose, no matter my "fate." However, my "fate" may be the outcome *of* my self-assigned life's purpose: So shall *it* be.

I've reverted to my mode of silence, favored by my superiors and disdained by my peers.

"Mama mama look at me,
"What the Navy's done to me.
"Used to drive a Cadillac;
"Now a sea bags' on my back.
"Just a little ho a little ho-
"A little rock n' roll,
"The kind that soothes the soul.
"Oh you betta'-get-outta-my-way-now,
"Before I walk right over you.
"I knew a girl, she wore a yellow ribbon,
"In the early month of May.
"She wore *it* in the springtime,
"In the early month of May."

June 16th, 2019

4:25 PM (Day 24)

There is an inspection we train for titled "Fold N' Stow," whereby the division removes two brown shirts, a pair of NWU's, two "skivvies" (slack, absorptive underwear), a black turtleneck, and a towel from our respective bunk compartments; these items are to be unbuttoned, turned inside out, and assembled in a particular order atop our racks within five minutes.

I and twenty-three other recruits received "hits": errors accrued on an inspection, detrimental to the RDC's division score,[29] i.e., shit trickles downhill. Three hits amount to one "demerit chit": a permanent negative impact on a division's score. This pseudo competition gauge with other

---

[29] A division score reflects the competence of the RDCs who train and command the recruits to become qualified Seamen. Inspections range from the integrity of one's uniform, exact clothes folding specifications and placement inside one's rack (a large rectangular cubby beneath a mattress), PFAs (physical fitness assessments), march formation, the parroting of spoken commands, and the exact recitation of Navy jargon. The chiefs and petty officers glut their egos on a division score under the pretense of a grandiose nationistic pride, i.e., the defense and preservation of the country and "putting warheads on foreheads." Indeed, hope is an ideal all these men and women have.

divisions is an effective method to assist in the enforcement of team-based learning and cooperation.

Upon the inspection phase, once the division completes each phase of "Prepare, Destroy, Rebuild" ("Rebuild" being the phase when we turn our clothes right-side out, rebutton, fold, and stow away to the proper location within fifteen minutes), our individual racks are scrutinized while we (recruits) are ordered to stand stoic and at "attention" while an inspector performs the presupposed "dreaded" inspection around the compartment, to check each button, crease, and seam after the "Rebuild" phase. Likewise, each article of clothing atop a rack and every button is inspected after the "Destroy" phase.

I and the twenty-three other recruits were ordered to the center of the room for more mediocre PT (jumping jacks, squats, 'tens') as a "punishment" to "break" us. After the session, while my comrades sweated and panted around me, the female petty officer out of the trinity of our RDCs implored those who "don't want to be 'here' to go 'home,'" throughout a long-winded tirade over an hour-long, meant to demoralize us while the division stood at "attention":

"Everyone who fucked up is a waste of time for those who actually want to be here. For anyone that doesn't want to be here go, get the *fuck* out of my division; we won't miss you."

I broke my stance of "attention" and moved towards the door of the compartment.

"*Balor*, what the fuck where the fuck do you think you're going?" the chief shouted. Every man in the division and all three RDCs fixated on me; I had the limelight, center stage of the comedy.

I said, "I was commanded to walk out the door if I didn't want to be here, chief."

"No you're not walking out of my fucking door; you do realize that'd be an infraction on the UDMC and I'd have security called on your ass and you'd be in jail?"

"No chief."

"Yeah you've signed a contract, you ain't getting out that easy. What the fuck are you smiling what the *fuck* is funny?"

"I signed a contract, chief."

A dozen recruits chuckled, to my amazement. The male petty officer stepped towards me and said, "Balor, you want to leave, huh? You want to get out of here? Well, we're going to get you out our way, after a whole lot of sweat, breaking you."

I affirmed with a head nod, hopeful, eager, and said, "Yes petty officer."

All people lie.

June 17th, 2019

2:03 PM (Day 25)

There is no permanence in the attitudes and demeanors amongst this motley group of individuals desperate to prove their self-worth by a method of arbitrary instructions set for a glorified career path. All enforcements and chastisements issued by RDCs are insignificant prattles that exacerbate the prisonesque environment and quasi cultural conditions. This cult of sleep deprivation, book study, jargon recital, and clothes folding/bed making parameters, is a pylon for the "American Dream."

We train to kill "evil" terrorists, to defend our country by putting warheads on foreheads. "This ain't no fucking summer camp," spews an officer of inconsequential rank and grade, yet, I feel reminiscent to an adolescent trapped at a gigantic middle school sleepover with three strict relatives of an acquaintance I've known for only three weeks.

4:08 PM

I stand after an inspection I exerted no effort for; my rack mate, Williams, has also failed; I am able to discern before the results due to his poor time management, the sweat on his brow, and defeated mien. I *know I've* failed, and expected to be either removed from the division to join a division earlier in training, or to be sent "home," i.e., nowhere, with the liberation of my body and mind manifested through the disavowal of my pledged oath: "Honor, courage, commitment."

I retain a single hope; due to the severity of my infractions on the inspection on account of misplaced clothing and careless folding, I expect to be reprimanded, and when the inquiry arises as to why I failed in the grand manner I did, I will answer: "I failed to care, petty officer/chief."

To be set back, I will be a burden on taxpayer dollars and will be paid to consume; there is nothing more than this fact. I've determined my life is of extraordinary proportions. There is an understanding: I will have no time to pursue a personal education or hone my writing if I were to graduate boot camp and achieve the "dream"; there would be only an education prescribed to me, to perform my duties, by *oath*. There would be no time to venture into domains of thought at leisure. This culture does not end at boot camp.

The employees stationed at RTC (Recruit Training Command) represent the denizens aboard a ship, only the demeanors of those on a ship would be affected with a stricter severity due to the nature of imminent "warfare."

I know I won't be out of this place soon. I'm told getting out of the military is more difficult than getting in; I'll explore the route for the sake of my ego, individuality, and consciousness... *my* divinity.

For now we fold clothes and assemble racks to exact specifications, march to the cadence of a sorrowful female African American recruit, revise jargon ad nauseam, perform mediocre acts of fitness training, and consume... the highlight of each and every one of our waking hours... consume.

June 18th, 2019

8:36 AM (Day 26)

Seated at the middle-school cafeteria themed tables of the galley, rows of men raise a training guide to their faces with one hand and a small cup of coffee in the other. Lo! these refined and cultured people, how they may as well be reading the morning paper delivered onto their manicured dew-covered lawns! The weathered books, frayed and torn after less than a month of use, crease at numerous locations and pop with vibrant highlighter colors. A sip over the remnants of grapefruit and banana peels esteemed scholars verily! Ah, the clatter of a fallen plastic cup incites the rows of accusatory heads to gawk! "Who hath transgressed upon the equanimity of our stupor!"

I sit on a plastic chair positioned at the front row of a chaplain's classroom with a wad of tissue stuffed into my left nostril to stymie the flow of blood onset from a recurrent nosebleed on account of my perpetual sickness due to being surrounded by a contagion of foreign matter proliferated by my fellow human beings, i.e., I blow my nose too often. I listen to a lecture on integrity and long for release. I'll take a dish pit over dictated behavior, alone, with the annals of my mind.

June 19th, 2019

4:18 PM (Day 27)

A chaplain boasts that he utilizes fear to wake our sleep-deprived division seated at classroom desks by solely the aspect of his rank and authority.

Restroom facilities in all non-compartment sectors are deplorable; all are devoid of soap, paper towels, and clean surfaces. Urinals overflow. Toilets are spattered with urine and encrusted with splotches of feces. Toilet paper and paper towels litter the grimy tiled floors. The conditions are atrocious, on par with a carnival outhouse managed by degenerates, i.e., recruits.

June 21st, 2019

1:11 PM (Day 29)

A chief screams at a room filled with men dressed in NWUs (Navy Working Uniforms) aligned with a "toe line" (a crease in the floor where two tiles meet), "Division! Who is the NETC Force Master Chief Petty Officer?"

I, and a few dozen men standing at attention roar in unsynchronized unity, **"Chief, the NETC Force Master Chief petty officer is, Force Master Chief Cole, chief!"**

"Division! What does Force Master Chief Cole wear as a collar device?"

"Chief, Force Master Chief Cole wears as a collar device, two gold stars, three chevrons, a rocker, a perched eagle, and a single gold star in place of a specialty mark, chief!"

"Division! Who is the Master Chief Petty Officer of the Navy?"

"Chief, the Master Chief Petty Officer of the Navy is MCPOW Smith, chief!"

"Division, what does the military training director wear as a collar device?"

"Chief, the military training director wears as a collar device, one silver maple leaf, chief!"

The division answers questions in this manner for up to three to five instances a day for twenty to forty-minute intervals.

June 23rd, 2019

4:53 PM (Day 31)

"Aye aye Chief!" said thirty-four male voices and twenty-five female voices.

"On your feet!" commanded our chief RDC (Recruit Division Commander).

"Feet!" Our group shouted in unison, unified in purpose by the manner of our subordination.

"Division! What does the commander of RTC wear as a collar device?"

An overweight, boisterous, twenty-seven-year-old female petty office of eleven years of service screamed of her future retirement at the anticipated age of thirty-six and referred to her wife with the pronoun "He" throughout several medical discourses.

The Best of First Aid Class

"Hopefully you've worked out before you arrived at RTC so you know what your body feels like."

"How many of you know that your lungs have two sacs? How many of you raised your hand because other people did and you didn't want to look stupid?"

"Sucking chest wound is my favorite and abdominal evisceration is the favorite of my partner here."

"All I do after teaching you recruits all day is go home, kick my feet up, and watch Disney movies."

"Boot camp is great; I was in the best shape of my life; I was fed three
square meals a day and I was told what to do and when to do *it!*"

Oh yes, we're paid throughout our due course in training and education:
benefits at the cost of time and years of personal autocracy. This attitude
I exhibit toxifies those who associate with me. I choose to retain my
demeanor, for the fool's path is my sole recourse and guiding light through
this murk of boons.

"Division, who is the NETC Force Master Chief Petty Officer?"
**"Chief, the NETC Force Master Chief Petty Officer is, Force
Master Chief Cole, Chief!"**
"Division, what does Force Master Chief Cole wear as a collar device?"
**"Chief, Force Master Chief Cole wears as a collar device, two gold
stars, three chevrons, a rocker, a perched eagle, and a single gold star in
place of a specialty mark, Chief!"**
"Division, who is the Master Chief Petty Officer of the Navy?"
**"Chief, the Master Chief Petty Officer of the Navy is MCPON
Smith, Chief!"**
"Division, what does the Military Training Director wear as a collar
device?"
**"Chief, the Military Training Director wears as a collar device, one
silver maple leaf, Chief!"**

June 24th, 2019

4:01 PM (Day 32)

My personal journal that contains the entirety of my written content, at
and before boot camp, has been confiscated by a senior chief. I'm uncertain
what will transpire on account of this unforeseen circumstance at the
authentic mercy of my superiors, I'm rendered crestfallen, for I experience
true *fear* for my loss... my creation, that which exceeds me in spirit, in *its*
initial conception.
The last I viewed a fragment of my life's meaning (my journal), I stood
at the fishbowl and observed two chiefs and two petty officers play with
the pages. The senior chief clenched both edges of the journal and walked
past me; our circumspect gazes met.

June 25th, 2019

8:31 PM (Day 33)

I said, "Senior Chief, respectfully request permission to ask a question, Senior Chief."

"What."

"When will my religious text be returned to me, Senior Chief?"

"When whoever has received *it* up the chain of command decides to return *it*."

I stared through the Senior Chief's forehead and said, "Aye aye Senior Chief." Two hours later, While I finished packing my three bags for transfer to another division on account of a failed jargon remembrance test and a failed Fold N' Stow inspection, the Senior Chief reached down while I squatted and held my journal inches away from my face.

I looked up, astonished, and said, "Thank you," omitting the "Senior Chief," title intentionally out of genuine respect.

The Senior Chief turned, began to walk away from me, and said, "Yeah."

Mercy... *mercy*, I thought relieved from the fear of loss! Lo! I first noticed the reduced weight of the journal; second, the gap between the front and back pages; third, I opened *it*.

Sleep-deprived and forlorn, I expressed an acute glumness and despondency; my journal had been returned to me, with the entire thirty-three pages worth of recorded boot camp content torn out from the centerfolds: missing.

I had returned from a nine-hour wait since 7:00 AM in the lobby of a mental health facility; I requested permission to visit the facility when my desecrated journal had been returned to me. While being consulted by a psychologist, I listed and acted premeditated conditions which I knew would qualify me for a schizotypal and/or schizoaffective diagnosis; this warranted my permanent separation from the military, yet, I am spared the record of an official (civilian) diagnosis.

I sought out the man in power over my new division with the faint resolve to reacquire my journal pages before being ushered to SEPS

(Separations) and said, "Senior Chief, respectfully request permission to ask a question."

"No. Put your seabag on your back and carry both your backpack and all your clothes in your left hand. Let's go."

"Aye aye, Senior Chief."

I went, and arrived at an enormous, extended compartment full of two-hundred men: one of the two male separation divisions, Alpha SEPS.

Sleep deprivation; I can write no longer.

June 26th, 2019

4:06 AM (Day 34)

"What is your self-assigned meaning in life?" I said to an eighteen-year-old-man assigned watch duty for the two-hundred man compartment my new home.

The watchstander stared at me, bleary-eyed and confounded for six seconds. "I don't understand your question."

"What is the purpose you have chosen for your life?"

"That's a good question; I've never thought about *it* before." The watchman's timid gaze locked on my genuine visage. "I mean, I guess this place isn't for me after all, at least I think so. I don't know."

I said, "This establishment validates people."

"I've noticed that, and *it* frightens me, I'm... Well, I'll be going home as a failure to my friends and family, but I don't want to stay here any longer than I have. I don't want to become like them and change into something other than what I know I want for myself. *It's* just... going home as a failure..."

I said, "You may be surprised."

"Surprised how?" The watchman inclined his head.

"With the reception you receive back home, more so if you tell your family members what you just told me."

"Thank you; I needed that."

I presented a fist to "bump." The man reciprocated with a feeble tap. I said, "Enjoy the rest of your night."

"You too."

5:38 PM

Limbo, funded by taxpayers, for hundreds of other men (and women in segregated compartments).

Another seven-hour wait in the medical facility for a five-minute session with a psychologist. I await confirmation for a session with a chaplain and a legal representative in an attempt to recover my severed journal pages.

7:59 PM

I'm appalled by the benevolent wastefulness in regards to "failed" recruits. A plethora of books and board games have been provided to us. Unkempt bathroom facilities are stocked to a bare minimum enough for tolerable sanitation: a few rolls of toilet paper scattered throughout four out of every twelve stalls. We are allotted an abundance of free time to live as we please. Many idle and congregate in cliques. Former recruits with a fallacious "alpha" disposition assume roles in accordance with previous division life, e.g., Yeoman, Master at Arms, RPOC, laundry PO, Head PO; however, the roles aren't practiced with the enforcement of an officer.

The petty officers and chiefs on this "ship" are lenient and behave as social workers. At three intervals a day we march a half-mile to and from a galley utilized to serve marine trainees [30] and gorge ourselves on an unrestrained buffet (limited to the capacity of our trays) of wholesome food. We *failures:* treated with such indifferent *magnanimity!* For being the residual byproduct of wasted effort, we are treated akin to privileged prisoners, veritable celebrities en mass. The *failures* are the true *victors;* assigned to this separated "ship" for an average of two to three weeks, each individual may continue to utilize health and dental benefits, are paid, provided entertainment, exercise opportunities, and still, there are those with the audacity to complain! On the contrary, there are those who transgressed "the system" and have extended their own sentence by up to forty-five days paid all-the-while!

I'm overjoyed to be here! Hope has been renewed within my nexus of thought on account of a phone conversation with a chaplain; I informed the officer of my duress in regards to my confiscated journal pages and

---

[30] The most suppressed, and consequently depressed lot of silent adolescents I've ever witnessed—statuesque and vacuous, seated at long rectangular cafeteria tables.

requested information. Investigations conducted on base last an average of one week. When I visit the legal department (one to two weeks from today), I will be *permitted* the opportunity to request my fragmented creation to be restored to the rightful owner.

Failure to practice my oldest personal discipline [31] has condemned me. The vendetta against my resolve perpetuated by the female petty officer who discovered my journal when she emptied the contents of my backpack onto a compartment floor in a fit of rage has been exacted.

"*It* is better to remain silent at the risk of being thought a fool, than to talk and remove all doubt of *it*."

- Maurice Switzer

This acculturated motley of variegated young men intrigues me. I've been afforded no greater opportunity to observe, consume, and be paid to do *just* this. The potential permanent loss of my initial writings of the first thirty-two days, while being enmeshed with this cultish culture, bestows me with a reason to hope. If unattained, and what I have written is withheld, I have retained an alternate notebook and one-third of the original entries written in the margins of the pages of my "Recruit Training Guide" which will serve as waypoints: fragments to be copied with renewed fervor, to expound on the detestable social and political miasma that is U.S. Navy boot camp.

"Giants are not what we think they are. The same qualities that appear to give them strength are often the sources of great weakness. And the fact of being an underdog can *change* people in ways that we often fail to appreciate; *it* can open doors and create opportunities and educate and enlighten and make possible what might otherwise have seemed unattainable."

- Malcolm Gladwell's David and Goliath

---

[31] Do not speak unless spoken to or any more than necessary.

June 27th, 2019

1:22 PM (Day 35)

I'm impressed by those who earned the uniform, for their unique despondency and estrangement from anything other than the world in which they operate. This blip of space where I stand, in the corner of a massive compartment, is naught a relic of inconsequential memoirs. I stand by an unauthorized open window and listen to the steady hum of a summer breeze, bird songs, the rustle of leaves, a distant cadence of a proud male: *"One two one two... two... two one two... two..."*

Indoors, with the compartment denizens, the men either enjoy or suffer free time, engaged with each other in trivial banter. Many read and keep to themselves. Some languish on the floors: a stasis of the body, attempts to sleep, pondering and brooding.

An action-gangster movie lulls a majority into a subdued convergence, mesmerized and enraptured by the video displayed on an old wall-mounted "box" television suspended from the ceiling.

People live, despite their lot; this quasi jail is beneficial, though slaves are never paid for their incarceration... I'm affected by profound gratitude.

This institution has taught me to lie and obey; there is no sanction from the implausible: karma, reincarnation, cyclic soul rebirth within the confines of an alternate universe... I gaze out to the grass and scoff.

"We strive for the best and attach great importance to getting into the finest institutions we can. But rarely do we stop and consider—as the Impressionists did—whether the most prestigious of institutions is always in our best interests."

- Malcolm Gladwell's David and Goliath

I believe in pain, and by extension, the inherent suffering. If I were to throw myself from this three-story window and break most of the bones in my body, I wonder if the remainder of this morning's phlegm would expunge from my lungs.

All people lie, regardless of the spoken word. If you're a virile man and meet eyes with a beautiful woman, does your averted gaze constitute a lie? If your child studies you for approval after committing a dreadful yet necessary deed, does your smile lie?

If the "truth" you've been taught is a lie, does chaos reign, and by casualty, is order a fickle human construct equivalent to time and mathematics?

"One plus one equals two," lies a schoolteacher, for the "truth" is inconceivable; the material world is an absurd representation of a supreme "order" unbeknownst to us.

Ah, but the songs of birds–

"Are you good?" a passing (useless) roving sentry on duty inquired and interrupted my stream of consciousness.

I said, "I'm *well*. Are you *good?*"

"No I'm fuckin' crazy man."

"So you're *bad*."

"Are you good?" he repeated, eager to resume his pointless patrol and hassle others.

"Do you believe all people lie?"

"Yes of course *it*'s a natural human instinct," spat the man in a single hurried breath that connoted precognition for my question.

I nodded and smiled.

"You good?" he uttered for a third instance; warped and yellowed teeth grinned at me from behind two brown lips at the bottom of a round, acne-pocketed face.

I flashed a thumbs up and he left me with my pen and paper by the ajar window. Some sentry, he is.

"One... one... two three four, three four, one-a two-a three-a four oonnee!... A-one... a-one... a-one two three four, three four, a-one a-two a-three-a-four oonnee!... ohha-onne! A-one... a-one two three four!"

"One two three four... three four, three four-oh-one two-a-three-a-four oonnee... oh-a-oonnee, ah-one, ah-one two three four, three four ah-one two-ah-three-ah-four oonnee... oha-oonnee, ya-one, ya-one, ya-one two three four!"

2:14 PM

The men are expected to clean the compartment throughout several intervals of the day. Over half of the men always perform no function and prefer to idle, read, or banter. An "MA" (Master-at-Arms) are volunteer "enforcers" who ensure others perform their assigned roles. The most common MA is of a teenage authority: quintessential high school bullies.

The compartment functions of boot camp are upheld. Cadence is sung by vacuous individuals who rue on being seperated. I, and three others relieve ourselves within a bathroom stall and an assertive young man shouts from behind the curtain: "If you're using the toilet during hygiene, you're *wrong!*" I persist with defecation and ignore the nameless voice.

The men seated in stalls around me bantered:

"I'd eat the corn out of someone's shit to go home today bro."

"I'd straight-up pay for an Uber three states away just to leave here today; bro, I'm not even joking."

I listened to the incessant chatter and closed my eyes.

"When I get home I'm fuckin' manscapin' boys! *Oh, daddy!*"

New arrivals await appointments with a legal man for a departure date; I'm among the ranks.

"Ears!" screams an MA.

"Open, mouths shut!" responds a few.

"Ears!"

"Open, mouths shut!" retorts several dozen more.

"Ears!"

"Open! Mouths shut!" roars an annoyed hoard.

"Unbutton your NWUs, turn them inside out, and turn them in!"

9:36 PM

To secure a positive reputation within this enlarged, disreputable clan, I've volunteered as a primary head (bathroom) cleaner. I never volunteered for any role with my division.

There is a formation titled "Forward I.G." When invoked by a petty officer or chief on duty, the entirety of the compartment's denizens are to convene and sit near the front entry point of the compartment to listen to announcements in regards to activities, e.g., appointments, legal, developments, muster (alphabetical headcount), cleaning directives, and, *of course,* chow.

This quasi society unifies and cooperates for entertainment, to stave boredom away and enrich each instance between Chow: Three files

351

of over two-hundred men march, three abroad, to a cafeteria manned by government social workers. From the back of the line I peer over an unauthorized book while we saunter at ease and reckon what is nicknamed, "The Fleet," for this "ship" of recruit failures is a ~~pitiful~~ wondrous marvel to behold. Our numbers stretch at length equal to one-tenth of the base. The beautiful June skies and a sunny horizon is underlined by rows of degenerate scum, cretins, traitors, incompetents, husbands, *children,* and the few men with authentic reasons for their separation, all dressed in NWUs, fed, paid, and *housed* by the American government; whereas, if otherwise, mutiny would develop and the legions of detained would riot.

We are prohibited from naps and to lay on our racks or the floor, and must assemble six to eight instances daily for Forward I.G., to sit and listen to commands and comments issued by a sleep-deprived petty officer or chief.

"Taps": the time when we are granted liberty to sleep, is precious; the severity of the compartment's resistance to comply determines the time which we spend seated, prohibited from the sweet relinquishment of consciousness.

June 28th, 2019

8:03 AM ~~(Day 36)~~

There is no necessity for sadness or happiness in this domain, yet there are many who lament, bemoan, and complain of the present:

"I can't wait to get the fuck out of here"; "I miss my family"; "I got shit to do and I'm stuck here"; "I hate this fuckin' place I fuckin' hate all this shit." Each grieves and pities themselves in a unique method, congruent with previous life experience and the assets one anticipates to return to on departure from the base.

Yes, a return "home," where the attitudes of woe will flare with a different color! Disinterested girlfriends, spouses, and wives who decided in the brief two months of their partner's absence, that their substitute lover is preferred indeed she hadn't the few years of anticipated time to elope, and now, a *failure* of a man returns to her, unable to provide resources!

"Ah, but our love is of the essence of diamonds; there is *no end* to us!" Fool!

"I've got a job lined up; I'll be makin' one-seventy-grand as soon as I get outta' here." Fool!

"My girl loves me; we'll do anything for each other. She'll be surprised to see me, but she'll be happy." Fool!

Lies, to oneself, the strongest of all, for when these men depart from their positions amongst this quasi clan, their realities, with the oculus of the ego within their flesh as an expression, will exhibit the inherent energy of their characters and continue to be wrathful, to grieve, to *be* a perpetual victim!

Those who assume enforcer (MA) roles are often uneducated individuals who desire to assert an influence unto those around them; young and belligerent, whereas, the rare, educated MA volunteers are often compassionate and empathetic, thereby overpowered by their peers and exploited by subordinates men on the same level as them. What differentiates men of power: Intelligence, ambition, lust, or, despite natural inclinations, *desires.*

"How are you doing today Baethan?" An eighteen-year-old African American man who knows my first name interrupted my writing.

"I'm well, yourself?"

"One more day closer to getting out of here."

"If you're not content here, what makes you think you'll be content when you're out of here?"

"I'm just sick of being controlled all the time."

"Freedom is in your mind."

"Well, we're stuck here, so..."

"I understand; to be told to enter our racks for sleep only to be told to change out of our black socks into our white ones and stand at the toe-line ten minutes later..."

The man laughed. "Yeah that's some bullshit!"

Ah, the confinement of the physical body! Rejoice in pain, no matter how slight. This temporary limbo delights and disheartens.

10:14 AM

"I was given a thorn in my flesh, a messenger of Satan, to torment me. Three times I pleaded with the Lord to take *it* away from me. But he said to me, 'My grace is sufficient for you, for my power is made

perfect in weakness.' Therefore I will boast all the more gladly about my weaknesses, so that Christ's power may rest on me. That is why, for Christ's sake, I delight in weaknesses, in insults, in hardship, in persecutions, in difficulties. For when I am weak, then I am strong."

- 2 Corinthians 12: 7-10

There are no thorns in this domain, only stripped brambles dipped in honey.

Always slaves to ourselves. I listen to thunder and watch the rain. What worth is a thought? Consume. Akin to waterdrops, we fall and are subsumed.

7:51 PM

For our subservience and compliance, we have been "awarded" (scheduled) time at the "Lounge": an area within another compartment of this "ship" converted into a room for recruit leisure.

After a day of three buffet meals, reading, a (prohibited) nap on the floor at the far end of our compartment, and the cleaning of two dozen toilets, the compartment denizens and myself stampeded to the lounge a floor below us, replete with arcade games, vending machines, pay-for-use computer terminals, telephones, sofas, a jukebox, a pool table, and a (restricted) gym area stocked with cable machines and dumbbells.

I marveled at the scene of men who behave with bombast and masculine callousness within our compartment lapse into chocolate-lipped children engaged with arcade games. Men jaunt, hop, "shoot baskets," "grab-ass," "horse-play," and laugh on behalf of each other's folly. I meandered among them, observed, idled, and on the verge of revulsion, I found a small pamphlet among a small stockpile of books, titled, *Bless All Who Serve: Sources of Hope, Courage, and Faith for Military Personnel and their Families.* I stood by a closed opaque window and read while a cacophony of human antics elapsed behind me for over forty minutes.

I've been assigned a two-hour watch from 2:00 AM to 4:00 AM: to pace a compartment for nonexistent threats, a walker among sleepers, while a petty officer works at a computer terminal nearest to the point of entry.

We're taught to feel guilt for the providence and resources provided to us on account of necessary time to process each recruit's separation from the armed forces.

"You guys are paid to sit on your ass and eat all day long; shut the fuck up!" screamed a petty officer to a group of surly youth.

Amen.

June 29th, 2019

2:06 PM ~~(Day 37)~~

Another scheduled "reward" has been allotted to our compartment: an area titled, "Recruit Heaven," an outlet adjacent to the commercial exchange. Our hoard of men marched across base and over three-hundred bodies surged into the cramped spaces and fought for the utilization of pool tables, dozens of arcade games, eight computer terminals, one ATM, and a single female bartender serving exorbitant, non-alcoholic drinks. For two hours, men occupied themselves with degrees of superfluous spending and consumption. I meandered into a large area filled with chairs and sofas, sat, and lulled in and out of consciousness, neither there nor anywhere. Accompanied by many slumberers, I gazed around on six instances of being jarred awake by shouts and reckless movement and observed rows of lolled heads skewed over the edges of cushioned armrests and bodies strewn out on the floor with rolled parkas propped underhead for a pillow and a cap placed over the eyes.

We departed, a half-mile "at ease" march back, to stand and await muster, compartment cleaning, and another assembly for a grotesque feeding session.

Earlier this morning our numbers were put to labor; corralled in a compartment filled with hundreds of used *Recruit Training Guide*s and *The Blue Jacket's Manual*s used uniforms, seabags, equipment: everything a new recruit is issued. We organized, hauled, stacked, and disposed of materials: a great team effort, supervised and enacted by our own autonomy.

Lapses into lethargy and social disinterest inhibit any purpose I have for this writing endeavor. Everyone has a story to tell, lies to express, fortunes to envy, lovers to covet. I contempt those who attempt to speak with me, yet I "know," if not for this journalistic outlet of expression, I *would* reciprocate. Few are persistent despite my disclosure of contempt.

"I really don't care if you contempt me," one who has asked to read my journal's recent entries proclaims, "I think you're an intelligent, super-cool dude."

"Why, when I want nothing to do with you and know myself to be an asshole?"

"You're interesting and fun to talk to."

Sorrow, for those.

8:16 PM

Perturbations of the mind; does this ill-bestowed professional diagnosis of schizoaffective/schizotypal, elicited by my own recital of DSM-5 criteria, discredit my persona, philosophy, theories, and creeds? Ah, no, I'd reckon the *practice* and recording of my own activities and thoughts is enough on *it*s own to discredit myself. Yet, I'm an *intelligent* man speak other men who I fail to define, for I am careless. They are motes of consciousness, amalgamates of flesh held taut with sinew and bone; beautiful blood-filled empathetic synaptic-compelled creatures of stardust! I gaze around and marvel at my comrades: fellow graceless inmates, confined to a life of temporary mediocrity, a stasis to define "limbo," where no man regresses or advances in spirit lo, to the wayward men *and* boys of this little compartment located in the middle of a Naval base built on a tract of land on the border of a lake a reservoir within the continental terrain on the northern quadrant of this planet betwixt the orbit of innumerable spherical masses across the convoluted expanse of inconceivable galaxies proliferated throughout the infinite unknown of our *known* universe...

"You guys are doin' great." A no-name failure breaks the silence and interrupts my stream of consciousness a recurrent theme here. "Keep stayin' quiet and we'll get our phone call for sure!"

Irritated failures respond to the praise with Navy jargon:

"Yo lock *it* up!"

"Lock *it* the fuck up!"

"Yo, please lock *it* up!"

June 30th, 2019

5:46 AM ~~(Day 38)~~

We awaken each morning to a throng of shouts and coughs.
"Yo wake the fuck up!"
There is unrest; those who yearn for liberty rebel against the authority of petty officers with petty protests. There is nothing to lose for many. An equal proportion hopes to "control" through the exertion of power over fellow failed recruits, manifested through the attempt to command another to "Step one pace to the left" or "Look forward" during circumstances which amount to nothing.

9:27 AM

A division of sea cadets passes our compartment while we wait in line for the galley; dressed in white and black, the young and malleable group of boys no older than the age of twenty (average age of seventeen) files by. One by one, the rows of faces pass, the majority overwrought with intense emotion: agitated happiness, pompous pride, fearful uncertainty, disdain, hateful trepidation, sorrowful joy, eager serenity, and contempt; all these faces and more... onward, young minds, to pledge allegiance, fidelity as fickle as the will wavers per personal desire.

4:22 PM

Thinking the Twentieth Century, by Tony Judt, is an ostentatious, intellectual exposition, a narration of the author's life and a summation of accrued cultural/historical knowledge, formatted in an armchair dialogue: Better if left wedged in the drawer where I found *it.*

I'm astounded by my own inclinations. The previous critique of Tony Judt's work may apply to myself, yet I have no credentials or professional history. The desire to thrive is my sole interest. My vested interest in humanity is null. I cycle through memories of my past and understand that I find myself right where I should be: at the precipice of an open third-story window after a heavy rainstorm.
"My meaning of life is to feel the full spectrum of human emotion

and to help those I meet to cope with their physical and mental ailments," said a man named Llyod.

"My self-assigned meaning for life? Oh, man... to make people smile and laugh as often as I can. You can consider me an entertainer," said a man named Thomas.

"Fuck bitches; make money, what else?" said a man named Whorton.

Men laze, read, nap, play Chess, Uno, "cards," write letters to loved ones... speak mundane banalities; I'm comforted by the triviality.

Outside, we converge on the expansive lawns beneath the shadow of trees; I see chimps, meerkats, and parasitic clusters in all of us. I see the world through a lens of faded luster; inherent beauty is lost in the sweep of my darkened gaze.

"Line up for chow!" repeats an array of maudlin male voices.

8:49 PM

"The loneliness here is the hardest part for me to deal with," said a spry, glasses-wearing, red-headed young man while he played with a pair of unnecessary crutches.

I said, "I'm surprised you say so with the condition of being surrounded, or rather, stuck with people. Do you mean that despite constant interaction, you feel as though nobody understands you?"

"Yeah, that's exactly *it.*"

"How has the experience of being here changed you?"

"The loneliness; I really don't like the feeling of being isolated, no matter how many of us there are."

"I prefer the loneliness, though I crave isolation; here, I believe the contrary of what you believe. When you look around, we're unified in uniformity; material wealth is equalized, and we are all subjected to the same stimulus; flesh is the single distinction, though our consciousnesses are integrated."

"I suppose you're right, though *it*'s just the same thing over and over again; I think that's why I feel lonely."

JULY

July 1st, 2019

7:48 PM ~~(Day 39)~~

There is no loss or gain; society and the phenomenological study of all inherent facets of consciousness and being in relation to the human creature is a wearisome travesty.

History, memories, reality: the lies of nations and men who have spent the majority of their ephemeral lives engaged with the perpetual consideration of what *was* in reference to what is *now* ever-changing absurdity: scholars, historians, acolytes, sages pretenders!

I continue to read and near the end of *Thinking the Twentieth Century,* despite my revulsion of the egotistical, autobiographical exposition of an intellectual obsessed with being known and remembered as an intellectual. There is no envy for the factoids, literature studied, and concepts cross-referenced. The opinionated, flowery text stifles what would be a tome of interest!

Yes, what is my journal but an intellectual obsession with phenomenology, a self-proclaimed foolish savant of my own reality? the master of nothing: a ~~disturbed~~ intelligent man when judged by contemporaries, who thinks his life purpose is justified by means of this loathsome expulsion-

I've an appointment with legal tomorrow to determine my departure date from this stasis and to discover whether my stolen journal pages will be returned to me, by my *"rights!"* ha!

My attention is divided; therefore my will is fragmented. I yearn for nothing but isolation, food, a writing tool and the autocracy to exert my body.

All the "isms," "ists," and "pathys" of society are a product of disillusioned people, fearful of themselves an unknown void death; we strive against death for the sake of each other and recoup in the essence of another's "(mis)understanding" *more* lies, for, the only man or woman one may "know" is themself.

"Hello!"

"Hi-uh, I'll take the fried chicken, the biscuit and uh, the corn-on-the-cob please."

"Is that all?"

"Yeah."

"Enjoy," said a disabled food service worker; she slid a five-compartment lunch tray beneath a wall of steel-rimmed plastic. A nineteen-year-old-man took the tray, turned to a twenty-two-year-old man behind him, and said, "I hope this chicken doesn't taste like last time."

The man behind the nineteen-year-old said, "Even pussy doesn't taste that bad."

Both men laughed.

The food service worker listened to the banter, turned to me, and said, "Hello!"

July 2nd, 2019

2:04 PM (Day 40)

"First thing I'm going to do when I get out of here is smoke a cigarette, *and* watch porn."

"Me too, I-"

"Well I'll do both at the same time."

"That's what I was thinking."

A third interjected, "Yo, my girls' at home and she's wicked pissed off right; she spends all her time with my parents and she's going to have a baby in a month and nine days."

"Shit bro," said a man occupied with the consumption of a peanut butter and jelly sandwich and an entree of mozzarella sticks. The other men, seated in rows, side by side, along the edges of several long, conjoined, cafeteria tables, listened, their visages vacuous, mouths slackened, eyes deadened; a few foreheads pressed against sweaty palms.

"I hope she takes me back or I'll kill myself yo."

"Bro..."

"Naw, I mean, I'll definitely hang myself or at least cut myself."

"Seriously bro?"

"Naw I'm no pussy faggot, but f'real though."

"That's fucked up."

Two food service employees strolled between two tables; smiles expressed whimsical happiness despite the overt negativity projected by a collection of malcontent youth.

"Yeah, first thing I'm doin is smokin' that cigarette and watching some brunettes give head."

"I haven't been able to get *it* up in a month ever since I came here."

"You can't even get hard?"

"No bro."

"Wow."

Writing provides no joy, satisfaction, or *meaning;* my self-assigned purpose is to rot.

Aspirations are nullified in this domain. Creativity has been sapped from my vital essence.

The Nameless

A newborn golem, forged of blood,
Bends backward: a reaction to an
Evening sun; boil, golem, your flesh is
Raw and supple, reactionary to the touch
Of a human hand. You wonder why you
Thrive when you only wish to die.
"Truth," you say; if you knew the word's
Meaning inscribed upon your head, which grants
Life at the stead of a creator, you'd be
Maddened; no difference, between I or you.
A scourge, a blight, a tumult of a
Mind confined to a vessel born to
Serve a nebulous master: form
Rendered clear in a reflection of still-water.
Golem, we are one, in action and will;
Share the pain of consciousness
Disparate by body, holistic in purpose.
A void supplants each act of consumption,
Yet the golem abstains and becomes what is now:
Perpetual being, resolute envy.

7:09 PM

Literature has been prohibited on our walks to and from the galley. I, and upwards of three-hundred other men across both the "Alpha" (my compartment) and "Bravo" compartment, must carry our parkas (regardless of weather conditions) and "hydration tools" (water bottles) for an average of two hours each day while being suppressed by jejune volunteer enforcers assigned to control and discipline our mass of bodies mouths to feed, in and out of the grinder; clockwork cogs: we consume and return, fed on "taxpayer money."

A return to the compartment invokes immediate "ABC Muster" (alphabetical attendance). The Head (restroom facilities) are blockaded by volunteer MAs and the entire compartment of men is circumvented and corralled, front and center, to listen to an extensive list of last names, whereby each individual must respond with the last four digits of their social security number. Between three instances of "Chow" and "ABC Muster," the compartment denizens resume quasi prison life and engage in a variety of leisure, e.g., an assembly in front of a VHS television display, chess matches, book reading, letter-writing, veritable chest-thumping, cards, general "horseplay," outbursts of song, complaints, impersonations of the female orgasm, and ceaseless outcries of asinine ululations.

July 3rd, 2019

4:56 AM (Day 41)

The legal man offered no assistance with my stolen journal pages; I have resorted to scheduling another appointment with a chaplain.

Two men of a boyish age snickered beneath a noon sun. Their place, 278th in line out of 321 individuals, unphased them. Sweat poured down from beneath blue ball caps onto every feature of their faces. One began to hum a six-tone tune and the other snapped a thumb against an index finger.

A man two rows back said, "Hey, shut the fuck *up*."

The boys ignored the order and the one who snapped said, "This nigga back there be a bitch man, pickin' on the little people. Pick on someone your own size."

"*Hey,*" said the man two rows back, positioned behind seven hunch-backed boot-draggers, "*Shut* the fuck up."

"Hey man, hey man," the finger snapper opined; he skewed his neck and gazed over his left shoulder, "You ain't gotta' bring on the heat; we got nuff' o' that already man. Hear me man?"

"*Ohhh now, I wanna'-go-home now,*" sang the tune-hummer with a sudden variation from his cadence.

The rear-most man blurted, "There are petty officers all over! Shut the-"

A petty officer encroached from the back of the line and shouted at the rear-most man, "Hey! Shut the fuck up guy! The fuck you have to talk about while walking down the fuckin' street?"

The two performers ceased the song, stifled laughter, and the one who had hummed whispered to the one who had snapped, "*This guy behind us, this guy behind us,*" and shook his head.

11:48 AM

I flip through the pages of my journal and stop at the excised segment; my thumb glides over the sharp paper edges and I wonder what course my life's meaning is. I'm surrounded by those in the same position as myself, each of us with our woes, sorrows, and manners in which we entertain ourselves to occupy our time. Lethargy and vapidness are pervasive.

"Line up for chow!"

1:24 PM

A stark white-washed twelve-by-eight cell reflected two rectangles of fluorescent lighting into a prisoner's eyes. A slot in the cell door opened. The prisoner scrambled to his feet and gazed into the darkness beyond.

A demure voice behind a thick steel door said, "Hello, Frank. I'm Suzanna, an apostle of the local sisterhood."

Frank wiped at the corners of his eyelids with the knuckles of both thumbs and said, "Who are you?"

"Suzanna." The door swung open and the apostle stepped through; her complete black ensemble of a silken robe with cowl and curvaceous figure contrasted the sharp outline of the brightened metallic cell.

Frank stood, fumbled with the frayed edge of a weathered shirt-jacket, and stumbled forward into the embrace of Suzanna's suspended arms; his emaciated face rested against her breasts. "I've been through hell and returned more times than I can count!" Frank blubbered and gripped hold of Suzanna's waist with a fearful manner akin to how a toddler clings to a mother's dress.

"Oh..." Suzanna held Frank firm; one of her hands clasped around the long frayed hairs of Frank's bald head; the other pried at the skeletal fingers laid flat against her bosom and worked to wrestle their four palms together: hers against his. "The sweetest of hells rests dormant in your mind."

"Don't give me that *bullshit* now not *now*, you... just what are you!" Frank screeched a cry: a feral reverberation.

The cell door, still ajar, crashed open against the inner metal wall. Two guards armed with batons and kevlar vests layered over green uniforms entered and separated Frank from Suzanna.

Suzanna screamed a single listless plea while the guards beat Frank into a senseless submission. "Beasts! Beasts!" Suzanna's feeble hands grazed both armored backs. The guards persisted. Each feverous swing resonated with a hollow thud. Suzanna lifted both of her arms over her head, tilted her neck back, wailed a dispassionate cry, lowered both arms, covered her face with two fists, and backstepped against one of the cell walls.

The guards relented, fatigued. Both moved aside and gazed down at the product of their labor. Frank's crumpled body, unrecognizable, glistened in a misshapen spread of blood. Satisfied, the guards turned, synchronized in demeanor and movement towards Suzanna; both acknowledged her addled visage. Two tears streamed away from Suzanna's feckless eyes in solid vertical lines and blemished her austere beauty; she droned, "Get out."

The guards ignored her. Soft thuds of boots against concrete and the rustle of heavy fabric faded from behind the heavy steel door.

Suzanna stooped down and addressed Frank's shattered countenance, "Reckon what you've become." A hushed whisper expulsed from her mouth in one prolonged exhale: "Is this the hell you condescend to; is there mercy, do you feel the wrath imposed by you throughout your wicked life retributed unto your soul in this incarnation of your mangled body?"

Frank shifted a broken forearm and retracted his lips to reveal a maw full of disfigured and reddened teeth.

Suzanna knelt closer to Frank and dipped her knees into the edge of a warm expansion of blood. "You see what happens; you see what happens now," Suzanna's voice trembled. Frank gazed, terrified, at her apathetic glower. She mewled, "I want your last thoughts to be of everything you ever were, and what sweet hell you invent will be your infinite heaven, forever onward, beyond death; you will obey your psychic design of self-wrought liberations and limitations you..." Suzanna lowered her eyes to the fresh corpse of Frank; she lingered for several seconds, stood, and departed the cell into the narrow corridor beyond.

July 4th, 2019

5:33 PM (Day 42)

One two, two, two-a-three-a-four one two, two, two-a-three-a-four, one two, two, two-a-three-a-four, one two... two three four... three fourrrr, three four-aa-ya-one-two-a-three-a-four, two-a-three-a-four oonnee-yaa-oonnee... ya-one, ya-one, ya-one two three four.

July 5th, 2019

5:49 PM (Day 43)

"In socialist countries one of the most irritating sources of alienation is the necessity to spend much of one's free time in line for food, for clothing, for entertainment, or for endless bureaucratic clearances."

- Mihaly Csikszentmihalyi's Flow

We begin on a formation of earth: a beach, a jagged outcrop of rock, an expansive plain. The ocean represents the expanse and depth of human consciousness. There are those who never venture further than the safe familiarity of the low tide on the white sands of the beach they've always known, or the violent crash of waves over an assembly of weathered stones at the base of a peninsula. There are those who wade out and test the water's temperature and retreat to the comfort of knee-deep lappings of the tide. There are those who learn to swim, dive, to cross and traverse the great berths of shallow water along coastlines beyond the territories of what each name "home." There are those who construct vessels, apparatus, and equipment to voyage out to regions on the surface and to the depths below. There are those who dedicate their lives to the exploration, study, and documentation of secret fathoms and the unknown nethers comparable to the horizon which rims every facet of our perception.

And the *horizon,* the nebulous infinitude above, represents all knowledge and experience inconceivable by our limited human faculties. Despite the immensity and profundity of the ocean's parameters, the tides occloud reality. How the horizon is perceived by man is an indecipherable riddle.

For "*it* is what *it* is."

Each of us yearns to make *it;* I wonder what *it* is. I sit at a galley table with my "division," the mass of men in due course out of this institution, and reckon the "active training" divisions file in against cafeteria walls, in line for chow. Each man grips their ~~bible~~ training guide and hunches towards the wall, as instructed: to read scan stare... at the *words,* all day, though... Lo! Some dare to glimpse away from the prescribed doctrine and look to the sea of liberated faces to their rear: The men of my compartment rabble and behave as what we are: children! *Laughter, conversation,* boisterous *enjoyment* despite being ordered to remain silent, for the inconsequential ramblings of those *already* designated for departure (us) amount to *nothing.*

The *men* in-training gape the wonder, intrigue, *envy* and *pity* exposed on each face betrays the aspiration, the paramount desire to *be* subjugated, to *become* an ideal, a beneficiary of an institution, to become a singular entity provided for *by* **the** entity. The frowns and grimaces account for the present, what each endures; doubts and questions resurface. I smiled and nodded my head at their training manuals as if to suggest they should refrain from peeking to return to their read for none of those in training should *ever* desist from studying! Aye aye Chief! Aye aye Chief! Aye aye Chief!

Alas! There is hope on the horizon! For the sake of strife, there will be peace, inward, outward, *oh* my country 'tis of thee, sweet land of liberty... my providence, so long as each submits to the order imposed by the future chaos of *guaranteed* war: This is our freedom!

July 6th, 2019

9:22 AM ~~(Day 44)~~

I've determined, when I depart from this institution, to utilize the option for flight by plane to a new location equal to or less than the distance from the address I flew in from. To return to the town of my youth would devastate my psyche; to be among the company of ill-gotten comrades once more... to return to my father... my "self" would succumb to abject ruin.

There are pay-per-hour terminals at the recruit commissary; I will utilize this service to continue my publishing process by email correspondence. My recruiters retained my writing device and I intend to have *it* shipped to me once I secure a residence in a state with the lowest average cost of living: Information I will research via aforementioned computer terminal.

2:01 PM

We assemble in "Forward I.G." daily, often, for each transgression by an individual is a transferable punishment against all (now one-hundred and seventy-four men). Literature has been prohibited throughout our days except for allocated free time.

The unrest and lack of discipline affects all members of the community. There are those who outright refuse to remain silent; these individuals *must* speak; their ego depends on the validation negative or positive, to be reassured of an identity, of an *existence*. I'm amazed and appalled by the noncompliance of these individuals.

A petty officer allowed us to raise our hands and to inquire about discrepancies on behalf of the group during a Forward I.G. session. While others struggled to formulate coherent rhetoric, or focused on personal problems, I raised my hand, compelled the petty officer to call on me, and said, from the back of the assembly the first instance of me ever speaking amongst our assemblies, "Petty officer, to regress to the primary issue, as an amalgamate of over 150 men on average of varied creeds and cultures, there is a lack of a sense of unity and discipline in regards to the Navy ethos despite the efforts of each petty officer and chief who passes through our compartment day by day. How would you propose we, as individuals, should manage those within our unit who toxify and provoke others, thereby reaping punishment for us all?"

A few men began to clap; one cheered; one whistled, and a dozen screamed for silence and order. I stood, disheartened with the unruly, albeit, upbeat response, and felt crestfallen, for I had resorted to speech in an attempt to benefit those who only hate.

The petty officer said, "The rules in place are the jurisdiction of the UCMJ and you all are to be held accountable for the behavior of those who fail to comply."

I stepped two paces forward and said, "Is there a possibility for a system we may implement to enforce that the individuals who refuse to comply are punished while the remainder of us are spared?"

The petty officer shook her head and parroted, "If you have issues with the system in place then you're going to have issues in the future."

An uproar transpired; many shouted again, for silence. The petty officer proceeded to listen to various outbursts of recruits who felt their rights were violated due to minor personal matters. I said, "I believe that's why I'm in separations, on account of the enforcement of arbitral rules and standards which-"

"-What? I couldn't hear you," said the petty officer, and she returned her attention to me.

I said, "Nevermind, thank you," and resumed my place behind a row of men. The histrionics persisted and the men continued to be punished (if punishment may be the applicable terminology) by being forced to remain in a seated position with television privileges suspended.

Why I attempt to intervene with this silly sect of cultural deviations is, yet, another foolish prospect.

4:36 PM

Thoughts aren't objects. There is no objective reality. No philosophy, creed, dogma, script, or mode of existence is worth a thought. All notions and power plans are foolish. There is no true intelligence, only an applied mastery acquired through the application of the body and mental processes constrained to this material existence. All thoughts lead to death, and death, too, is but a thought a whimsical fancy, a mote of intangible byproduct wrought by life.

July 7th, 2019

10:02 AM (Day 45)

A ceaseless approach of individuals who desire to speak to me has garnered me an acclaimed reputation of, "That writer guy who is writing a book about boot camp." I've passed at least twenty index cards to those who inquire of my work and the reasons for why I'm at SEPS (Separations) detailing the titles of my books and my pen name. I expect all the cards to be discarded or destroyed.

The poor fools all of them; there is no "boot camp experience," there is only humanity comprised of producers and consumers. Thy will be ever-consummate. I've nothing to offer damn me, if you will.

Entities pass through and are supplanted with similar flesh-embodied consciousnesses which desire to be manipulated and/or entertained. From all walks of life, each converges as a failed recruit and emerges from this threshold with new impressions and sensory stimulus... *thoughts,* a unified Godliness; praise the insatiable appetites for *knowledge* the pinnacle of madness!

Oh, validate me!

3:22 PM

Forward I.G.

Tap my feet, twirl a chain,
Flip a coin, fold my legs.
Stretch my back, hold my head,
Shuffle cards, brace the floor.
"Forward I.G.," screamed a man:
A nameless face amongst the mass.
Forced to sit, I ponder:
Frowns abundant, sighs galore.
Smiles are a scourge to be ignored.
Stomach full, a place to sleep, to sit
Compels men to think-
An intolerable condition-
The mind rebels and one

Must speak!
"Forward I.G.," screamed a man;
Return to the floor and belay your last.

July 8th, 2019

2:16 PM (Day 46)

In Mihaly Csikszentmihalyi's *Flow*, he proposes a few theories with the basis of entropy as the fundamental propulsion of life.

Alas, entropy, my God and nullifier, what becomes of my recorded thoughts, of my observations, "insights," "revelations," and theories. There is only absurdity... yes, I *believe;* therefore, I am. Statistics, history, mathematics, geology, astronomy, theology, philosophy, phenomenology, and all ideas under the umbrella of consciousness are moot snippets of superficial understanding within the limited scope of the human creature!

Why, I submit myself to this nebulous meaning, disinterested in any singular facet or study... *oh,* the *consciousness,* I claim to obsess over and believe each face and fleshy body I interact with (or ignore often) is a reflection of *my* humanity and what... of... *it!* By the god of Being, I wonder while I begin to read *Sapiens: A Brief History of Humankind,* by Yuval Noah Harari, what remarkable nothings I'll glean.

July 9th, 2019

11:04 AM (Day 47)

I sit on the floor of a bank with two dozen other failed recruits in expectancy of a new debit card with $1,179 on balance. This money will be the extent of my funds when I arrive at [City Name], Arkansas; this amount is about $600 less than I had anticipated after initial clothing and food is accounted for. $350 of this figure must be allocated to my publisher to ensure the production and distribution of hardcover copies for "(Year Two)" of this documentation.

This foolish endeavor will ensure the severance between everything I once was and all relationships. My father raised me well; he is an exceptional man despite the conflict of our humanities.

Preposterous: My callous disregard for my welfare and for the bestowment of my father's lifelong providence; he deserved better treatment from me; I grieve and pity no longer *ever*, for myself again. My fate, by my determination, is sealed. Lo may I die today, for what *it's* worth!

A dwarfish man, half my weight, with spectacles that magnified his eyes, stood behind me in our long line out from our compartment on our way to a breakfast chow. He said, "Hey pal, my guy, my man."

I said, "I am none of those in relation to you or anyone."

"Ah well," the dwarf grinned from ear to ear, shrugged, and said, "That's alright."

"Your spirit seems uplifted."

"What do you mean?"

"You aren't crestfallen and dejected as per the usual disposition."

"Oh I am though," the dwarf stepped back and forth, side to side, and leaned his weight onto each respective foot; he laughed.

"So *it's* a ruse, then?" I smiled.

"Yeah, I'm on antidepressants right now!"

I glanced away, unable to maintain eye contact. We marched out, single file, at the end of the line. The dwarf attempted to walk alongside me a few paces for the sake of continued conversation; what he expected from me is beyond my realm of competence.

July 10th, 2019

10:54 AM ~~(Day 48)~~

"Shut the fuck up! Get in your racks!" mocked a nubile man behind me in the chow line.

Three other nubiles and one middle-aged man giggled and sweated beneath a morning sun. The largest patted the ass of the smallest; the smallest turned to an uninvolved bystander in line to the left of him and said, "Bro, you're gay."

Another said, "He's gay for me," and five more men began to snigger, banter, and gesture.

One shouted from two rows ahead of me, "Shut the fuck up!"

"Shut the fuck up! Get in your racks!" repeated the aforementioned nubile man; his back-turned head and smug grin infuriated rows of powerless observers.

"Lock *it* up!" commanded a man standing 6'5 tall.

"You... *shut the, fuck up,*" sang a debonair voice from seven rows forward.

"The dudes' a little bitch, ain't got balls," said a square-faced man situated in the file to the left of me; he twirled his ball cap.

"Don't let me pull your chest hairs or anything," said a husky African American voice from the back of the line.

"There isn't shit to do but talk."

"Lock *it* the fuck up!"

"Suck my dick bitch."

"Yo, yo, yo, why you gotta be like that man?"

"You guys petty officer you guys is coming I think."

"Lock *it* the fuck up!"

And the sun shone on the cracked sidewalks. Trimmed branches of trees aligned along the exterior of plain red brick walls patterned with rectangular white windows. Birds chirped.

"Will I be in your book?" said a fleshy no-name to me after being introduced to me by a fifth-party rumor spoken by a man who spoke to me only once throughout our dual reality.

"No."

"Why not? C'mon Baethan, we're cool right?"

"No. You're my enemy; I speak to you now out of respect."

"Oh, what? I don't want to be your enemy."

"That's my choice."

"You talk smart. What's the name of your book?"

"*Outbursts of a Welfarist; Thoughts of a Newfound Charlatan.*"

"Yo... what the fuck?"

Alas, everyone wishes to be an actor in the play, this theatrical stage of men hoarded into a single chamber, forced to *eat, stand,* and *sit!* Condemned to indolence! The injustice of being paid to do so resounds from the mouths of taxpayers nationwide; *I* consume with glee: a *successful* sociopath. I perform my role as I would anywhere, with the instruments of thought: pen and paper. Books produced from the minds of others grant me a reprieve from the intangible mass of entropic consciousnesses around me, each disillusioned, vexed, and damned by their own verdict!

"I can't wait to go *home!*" shouted an ingratiate.

And what is "home" but another platform to suffer and continue to be disillusioned, vexed, and damned by your own verdict!

374

"Forward I.G.!"

"Get in forward I.G. now!"

"Are you fucking serious again?"

"Forward I.G.!"

"Forward I.G.!"

"C'mon the *fuck*."

"Forward I.G.! Face forward!"

12:12 PM

"Line up for chow!"

A stout mongrel of a petty officer said, "The next person I catch not wearing a belt... all of you will be sitting in Forward I.G."

These imagined and imposed societal conditions are comical, even beyond the confines of this particular building estranged from the authentic boot camp experience as I and my peers are where a veritable centrifuge filters the manner of citizen the military accepts, grooms, and refines into subservient pawns, entrenched with the benefits of their service. The ego becomes dependant on the ~~corporate~~ government entity a unified banner of nationalism and patriotism that self-accredited superiors may command to harvest the resources of foreign powers-

Bah, old, stale, foul! My social placement among the hierarchy of these men is a product of my own subjective opinion, to which we choose to accept due to the underlying belief of virtues, ethics, and morality... lo-

A champion entered a spherical chamber; a small television screen resonated at the zenith of the room's domed ceiling. The stark colors on the screen rippled with power. The champion, naked and pearlesque before a crowd, knelt before a throng of desperate faces. An animalistic cacophony resounded: immutable, ceaseless; the faces remained resolute in their despair; each gazed upwards and fixated on the screen.

4:02 PM

There are two occasions that warrant a celebration among my peers: A legal appointment and a departure date. I celebrated neither and instead sat in solemn contemplation about the infinite options and opportunities at my disposal.

To be a *scumbag of society*... ah, how the title soothes: a sweet balm slathered onto one's entire body, greased-up a slippery nincompoop.

A reiteration on the men who celebrate departure from one confinement to a larger one: They're all fools. The high-fives, fist bumps, back-slaps, outbursts of glee and jovial tirades condemning the establishment of which each of us signed a contract to join, is literal monkey shenannigans histrionical, egotistical business.

Many intend to return six months later for another attempt. Some proclaim an interest in a different branch of service (the Army being most common), yet everyone shares a condition of restlessness and boredom. I veer between book, to book, to journal soon-to-be miniature notepad, often interrupted by individuals in want of conversation to distract themselves from the wretchedness of their existence. I escape the crowds and alleviate stress with the performance of (prohibited) simple calisthenics in a vacant shower room.

8:05 PM

Two-thirds of the way back in the line of 333 men in wait for chow, I gazed at the pane glass window of the double doors where our formation stands and waits before and after service: A long stretch of gray sidewalk between two well-kept lawns, rows of pine and maple trees, two beds of white stones at the base of both compartment buildings, and the forest beyond at the opposite end of a football-length-field, illuminated beneath the expanse of a cloud-arrayed blue sky.

I turned my head forward and observed the men: frowns, heads leaned against walls, arms flat against sides, eager grimaces, ponderous stares of defeat. Each moment suggested a repressed agony unique and secret to each individual. The few who smiled and chatted with an adjacent person represented the tenacity of the human spirit against-

An hour-long wait.

Oh, woe, woe, betwixt despair and despondency, there are those overwrought with woe, woe-

To wait to be served a full course buffet three instances a day is an insufferable injustice to be endured no matter your race or age, *it* would seem.

I'm awed by the necessity of my peers to speak; the wills of others overlap and produce a veritable bloodbath of mental energies expelled for naught a cause other than an ephemeral remedy to aforementioned woe, woe, etc.

376

July 11th, 2019

"When we get back to the compartment, I'm going to take a fat shit," muttered a man with a broad, distended, overhung, bony brow; he hunched forward, head slumped diagonally off his shoulders while we walked side by side on a return from chow.

I said nothing and stared straight ahead at clumps of dandruff ensnared by knotted black hair.

Each day is the same: Awakened by, "Good morning Alpha SEPS!" shouted fifteen to twenty times by the separation division's volunteer RPOC. Rows of large overhead fluorescent lighting flick on; red lights are flicked off. An immediate cacophony of coughs, throat-clearing, toilet flushes, and the gush of running tap water accompanies the sight of NWUs and the glare of spotless achromatic floors. "I fucking hate this place," "Shut the fuck up," and "Fuck SEPS," are typical dialogue. Over a hundred men flow in and out of the bathrooms to brush their teeth, shave, and relieve bowels.

"Why are you in SEPS?" is a substitution for, "Beautiful weather today, ain't *it?*"

"When do you get out?" is equivalent to, "You working today?"

"What time is chow?" is synonymous with, "How are you?"

We assemble for chow, wait to wait outside for chow, wait outside to depart for chow, wait an hour marching and in line to eat chow, eat within 8 to 14 minutes dependant on the mood of our assigned petty officer, wait to deposit our dirty dishware, wait outside to return to the compartment, and return to wait during a 20-minute "ABC Muster."

After muster, volunteers assemble to "clean house" in a similar manner that individuals volunteer in an authentic division. I have assumed the role of toilet cleaner, my favorite task, for toilets should be cleaned to the highest standards, especially when you live with over 150 men.

After cleaning, we are allowed "free time" or are summoned to "Forward I.G." dependent on overall performance. Those with appointments assemble to depart either before or after morning chow. Opportunities to visit the recruit commissary are permitted Tuesday and Thursday.

Time elapses; men drone, read, write, play games, and speak.

"Line up for chow!"

Time elapses in an aforementioned manner.

"Line up for chow!"

Hygiene commences. Taps (lights out) proceeds.

"Good morning Alpha SEPS!"

Men continue to seek me out for a conversation on behalf of a perceived judgment of my intelligence, despite my taciturn disposition. I reiterate: there is no true intelligence, only a study and mastery of a narrow strait of "understanding" compounded by the combined efforts of our species. Advancements and breakthroughs in all fields are *inevitable*. For one to claim success or progress in any domain is an illusory projection of the ego.

From the dawn of "knowledge," thoughts manifest in reality as action, a shared experience an exchange of the observations of consciousness. One may concentrate attention on a concept and utilize previous observable elements of authenticity to build on what is already "known."

Every moment of despondency is a result of heightened awareness.

7:36 PM

I waver between self-understanding and cognitive dissonance in relation to what I desire of being human and my communication with others; I'm sought out, for the interest in my behavior; there is no *self*-interest for me to reciprocate, to *feed* into the void of others who wish for something more than what they "know." An example:

"How are you faring?" said a man who earlier today had discussed with me his neurosis and ambition for a return to boot camp.

I turned away from my writing and said, "Why, and in what manner: my mind or physicality?"

"Uh," he began, repelled by my standoffish regard. "Anything really."

"I'm well."

"You tired?"

"No."

The man gestured towards a book he held, "Ah, I am. I've been reading, figured I'd come over to see how you are."

I nodded and said nothing, my eyes fixed on his.

"Well," he bowed out," I see I interrupted something."

I thought to reassure him and speak, *"No,"* and instead remained silent.

The man said, "Alright, well," he began to walk away from me towards his rack. "Goodnight. I'll talk to you later, or tomorrow."

"Goodnight."

I think sinister thoughts and suppress passive desires to speak out against misguided, stupid, debased, and the vitriolic word spoken and action committed within my vicinity. There is no lack thereof, yet, I remain silent and am perceived as stoic, well-composed, and unaffected, whereas, my contempt festers at the forefront of my mind... The pursuit of life among others is damnation and a liberation. There is sadness and a lack of want: a causal relation.

To refrain from verbal communication by choice is committal to a reality of self-imposed ostracization to forsake oneself from the pleasures and pains of friendship. Spiritualists worldwide, is *this* method how you achieve "Nirvana," a sublimity of the consciousness, to train yourself to be content with the ill-conceived indictments of society, to be one with the squalor and abandonment? To exude compassion despite the weakness to profess yourself powerful on account of *virtue?* What joy is there without suffering? There is no meta to my self-chosen sanctified path; my *divinity* is reposed on every word: the worthless labor of a man, a man *only!*

"Please touch me where I yearn to be touched," said an overfed prostitute to a grizzled wretch, haggard by years of logging and late-night intoxication.

"Your desperation disgusts me."

"I don't care." The prostitute pressed her overwrought breasts against the wretch' chin scruff. "Take what you paid for."

"No, this is really too much."

"Take *it.*"

"You stink of cat piss."

"Take *it.*"

The wretch gripped the prostitute's left breast with a limp hand and said, "You're a rotten bitch."

"I know *it.*" The prostitute moaned.

July 12, 2019

7:45 AM (~~Day 50~~)

"Line up for chow!"

154 men meandered down three flights of stairs and assembled three-a-breast outside a facility beneath a morning sun and waited ten minutes.

"Get the fuck back up to the compartment!" commanded a petty officer. "About face!"

The men processed the command, and one by one, began to obey; bodies turned and marched back up three flights of stairs, and idled, uncertain for five minutes. The petty officer entered and bellowed, "There's been a change of plans no chow for twenty minutes so clean the compartment or some shit for fifteen minutes then line back up."

Supplies were distributed, mops were filled, and the men assumed their self-assigned roles, myself among them.

The petty officer shouted fifty seconds later, "Change of plans! We're going to chow now!" Groans and sighed resounded throughout the compartment. "I know, I know, I'm just as pissed off as you are, but I'm not going to lose my career over this so hurry the *fuck* up!"

Men scrambled to stow supplies, empty mop buckets, retrieve their gear, and resumed their position in line. We filed down the stairwell, one by one, and waited on the road outside for our scheduled meal. A prime example of daily military affairs: cut the losses, forget the rest. Efficiency is critical, even if the byproduct kills men under your command.

"Hark!" yells a general, "Lo! Heed me; forward up the hill towards the battlements!"

The infantry obeyed, ran up a grassy gnoll, and was blown to pieces scattered into bloodied chunks by a few well-aimed mortars deployed from a hidden bunker.

"Hark lo lo," the general called. "Retreat! Retreat! Retreat!"

The six survivors scrambled back down the gnoll, uniforms smeared with their comrades viscerals and dirt; all converged around the general and one man stuttered, "What time is chow?"

Absurd. What general says "Lo," or "Hark"?

"If you laughed, you're wrong," said a petty officer. "The television is unsecured. Shut the fuck up sit down and shut the fuck up!"

Chiefs and petty officers pass through the halls and acknowledge (failed) recruits with scorn. One said to a stout nineteen-year-old, "Aren't you going to say 'good morning,' recruit?"

"Good morning Chief," spat the shocked and stupefied recruit.

"That's 'Senior Chief'; good morning *'Senior* Chief'."

"Sorry Senior Chief."

"I'm not a *'Sorry* Senior Chief,' I'm a *'Senior Chief,'* say it fuckin' right!"

"Aye aye Senior Chief sorry Senior belay my last aye aye... Senior Chief."

"Unfuck yourself recruit."

"Aye aye Chief."

10:40 AM

"What are you separating for Balor?" said a chief from behind a traditional office worker desk; he prepared to sign the digital documentation for my departure.

"Seven-eleven, Chief."

"Depression? Anxiety?" His face scrunched inward; he had no business to know, nor any right, though I sensed that the inquisition of a constant stream of no-name failures in and out of his office is the single source of entertainment to delight him throughout twelve-hour shifts.

"Schizotypal or schizoaffective."

"Or? What the fuck do either of those mean?"

"That I don't care, Chief."

The Chief stared at a computer screen. "You're good. Enjoy the rest of your day."

"Thank you. You too, Chief."

2:33 PM

A decorated third-class Petty Officer briefed me and thirty-two others on our departure: Four minutes of necessary information and an hour and twenty minutes of personal anecdotes of his career. Out of the stories, while

I sat at the front row of desks and stared through a glass pane at an influx of fresh-off-the-bus, culture-shocked recruits, the Petty Officer conferred a gem to my ears:

"You guys should've seen SEPS years ago; you think you hate *it* now, oh man... A few years ago, the average wait time to get out was six to eight months and there were one-thousand recruits on the third floor alone on average." Aghast exhalations of recruits accentuated skeptical chuckles. "No you guys think I'm fucking with you right? No that's how things were not too long ago. I don't condone *it* and I sure as fuck don't agree with *it*. There were rampant diseases spread, male to female contact was an issue, gangs, Navy police visits each day three to four gangs within each compartment... yeah, SEPs is a *whole* lot better than *it* used to be."

The RCU (Recruit Core Unit) is considered to be a more hellish deviation of boot camp due to recruits who have broken limbs, or have succumbed to a debilitating illness, confined to their racks, while undergoing the boot camp "training" experience, i.e., enforced reading of the training manual while bedbound.

Separations from "A School" are comparable to those in SEPS on account of blatant stupidity, e.g., a group of thirteen students constructed a meth lab.

7:05 PM

I'm grateful for chow.

July 13th, 2019

6:32 AM ~~(Day 51)~~

I'm fated by my determination to regress through the Hindu ideology of soul ascension if there is, in fact, a transient essence of consciousness which I doubt.

My thoughts are foul and my actions dissimulate the wicked humor of my concealed motive. To refrain from speaking is to prevent the proliferation of personal chaos rather than to perpetuate the aspect of sagacity, wisdom, and reservation, which many fools assume me to vitalize.

Forward I.G.
Instills men with glee.
One knows fun while
Staring at the floor.

5:39 PM

I've finished reading *Sapiens* by Yuval Noah Harari and have noted four quotations from the text that is pertinent to my current condition and previous thoughts from yesteryear up to the present.

The first: The average quantity of men in a SEPs division fluctuates between 130-200 depending on the dropout rate and the efficiency of legal processing.

"Sociological research has shown that the maximum 'natural' size of a group bonded by gossip is about 150 individuals. Most people can neither intimately know, nor gossip effectively about, more than 150 human beings.
"Even today, a critical threshold in human organization falls somewhere around this magic number. Below this threshold, communities, businesses, social networks, and *military units* can maintain themselves based mainly on intimate acquaintance and rumor-mongering. There is no need for formal ranks, titles, and law books to keep order." [32]

As our division numbers fluctuate, so does the chaos, rebellion, and unrest whenever new masses overtake the absence of departed members. There are brief intervals of order, compliance, and calm, between the moment "veteran" members depart and new "failures" are indoctrinated.

Second: On the synchronization of thoughts which I commented on the date of April 13th, 2019, there is an affirmation of my thought on this matter, which further reinforces my ~~belief~~ notion of a "collective consciousness," or rather, the inevitable progress of humanity, regardless of an individual's contribution:

---

[32] Yuval Noah Harari's *Sapiens: A Brief History of Humankind*

"During the past 500 years modern science has achieved wonders, thanks largely to the willingness of government, businesses, foundations and private donors to channel billions of dollars into scientific research. These billions have done much more to chart the universe, map the planet and catalog the animal kingdom than did Galilei, Christopher Columbus, and Charles Darwin. *If these particular geniuses had never been born, their insights would probably have occurred to others.* But if the proper funding were unavailable, no intellectual brilliance could have been compensated for that. If Darwin had never been born, for example, we'd today attribute the theory of evolution to Alfred Russel Wallace, who came up with the idea of evolution via natural selection independently of Darwin and just a few years later. But if the European powers had not financed geographical, zoological, and botanical research around the world, neither Darwin nor Wallace would have had the necessary empirical data to develop the theory of evolution. *It is likely that they would not even have tried."* [33]

Indeed I often wonder why I even try, for, to quote the closing sentence of *Sapiens:* "**What do I want to become?**" this is the question of an age in which we may soon be able to manipulate our base desires.

Third: To deviate from the core problem of our existence (homogenized meaning), a particular passage resonated on what modern psychosis and neurosis may be, with the lens of a "liberal humanist":

"**According to liberals, the sacred nature of humanity resides with each and every individual Homo Sapiens. The inner core of individual humans gives meaning to the world, and is the source for all ethical and political authority. If we encounter an ethical or political dilemma, we should look inside and listen to our inner voice—the voice of humanity."** [34]

Harari published these conceptions years before I even began to write (with intent to publish), though these ideas were dormant in my youth, and, I presume, in the consciousness of others as well; a veil beneath a veil. A stimulus and catalyst prompted Hararia to commit to the deed (the written book) of what may have been at the forefront of the attention of

---

[33] Ibid.
[34] Ibid.

researchers, scientists, gurus, yogis, sages, politicians, theologians, and fools around the world.

Egoism is altruism no profound conception, being the basis of capitalism; thereby, I'm enlightened on how outdated in quality my daily musings are.

To encounter the gem that *Sapiens* is within a book drawer in a compartment designated for Navy rejects is unexpected and delightful. The number of anti-establishment books, e.g., *David and Goliath*, are also worth a comment; I presume these books were mailed in by family or friends of failed recruits and bypassed the (indifferent) jurisdiction of federal drones.

One day remains, i.e., "Hoo-yah three more chows!" [35]

July 14th, 2019

6:03 AM (Day 52)

A group of E1 and E2 seamen apprentices sat at a table adjacent to the line for SEPs' morning chow. The men behaved the same as the failed recruits I'm accustomed to: An invariant distribution of frowns, smiles, scowls, consternations, and vacuous stares. Uniforms served as the only distinction between "us" and "them."

2:11 PM

"I" identify with "my" writing. The experience of stolen journal pages by a force of authority incurred a lesser reaction within myself than expected. There is no injustice. There is no indignation. The loss I once perceived has been identified as the material product of my labor. I'm grateful for the opportunity provided by the nameless Senior Chief to reflect on what "was," to acknowledge the source of my pride as the ability to express, communicate, and manipulate the power of language.

I've no desire to relinquish my ego: to become a tranquil stump. The ability to experience loss validates me. Spiritual "masters" are damned,

---

[35] Reject recruits are fond of shouting their time remaining until departure by the amount of "chows" remaining, opposed to days. After "taps" men announce the number from their respective racks in the manner of "Hooyah (#) more chows!" In response, envious and tired men holler, "Shut the fuck up!"

for the human being is bound to mortal flesh. I own nothing but my expressions, i.e., "Energy, strength, and will." [36]

7:21 PM

On the route to my final chow, my first (genuine) division passed by our ranks, a week away from graduation. The RPOC still the same young Caucasian man, shouted pristine commands, and the AROC still the same young African American woman, sang a cadence with a melancholic voice... "One two, two, two-a-three-a-four-a-one two, two a-three-a-four-"

I heard my former chief scream from a distance while we entered the front doors of our assigned galley building, *"Get in step!"* as the cadence commands faded. Chow ensued:

A typical wait in line, staring through the backs of heads and ignoring those who speak to me. A sit down at the cafeteria table with my smallest meal yet (personal penance) of chicken, tuna, mixed steamed vegetables, and a small cup of milk. I consumed and endured the ceaseless expulsion of mutterings, inane conversation, and insults fit for a ~~high school~~ middle school cafeteria lo this is, in fact, the esteem worthy of the ~~men~~ boys; even those who graduate remain in a stasis of maturity, indoctrinated into an institution of limited educational scope and preset creeds. There is no time for those beset with an onslaught of work for the sake of security to pursue a secondary education between instances of vulgar entertainment and socialization.

Men around me celebrate a proximate return home to everything they hoped to escape; each man expects their families to receive them with the same energy conferred on their initial departure for a now broken dream.

I sleep on a tract of Arkansas tomorrow, liberated from all but the bittersweet providence of my mind and the straits of my body.

July 15th, 2019

12:11 PM (Departure Day)

I sit between two women engaged with multimedia devices while seated on a plane destined for Dallas, Texas, for two hours and twenty-five

---

[36] - Johann Wolfgang Von Goethe

minutes. Both are preoccupied, yet, there is an air of malcontent and misery emanating from both.

I've been sent off with a yellow "Navy" t-shirt and *navy* blue "Navy" sweatpants. At the airport, I purchased $240 worth of two black name-brand polos and a pair of cross-hatched gray dress pants at the first department store I encountered (at the airport): A superb, superfluous expense, my first since being released.

On initial arrival at the airport I purchased an overpriced garden salad for nine dollars and a latte for four dollars, seated myself by a far corner window, and enjoyed a prolonged "chow" with a vast wall-window before me, exposed to the illumination of a morning sun, contrary to being seated adjacent, opposite, and diagonally to five children for the past two months and gazing forward at a face of equal dissatisfaction.

The utilization of a military terminal at the airport allowed me to plan for my arrival at Arkansas. I've planned routes to the library and post office, secured a P.O. box, informed my recruiter of where to ship my writing device/phone/birth certificate, and contacted several establishments for employment. Two studio apartment options are available. Tonight I'll seek shelter outdoors in the ninety-degree rain.

3:29 PM

Some books I encounter in this life are marvelous "coincidences." Before departure from SEPs, I secured Eckhart Tolle's *A New Earth: Awakening to Your Life's Purpose,* from the bottom left drawer of a metal bookshelf. Before I transitioned to the second airport terminal where I now sit, I ambled through an airport gift shop and purchased a recent work, *How to Change your Mind: What Science Teaches Us About Consciousness, Dying, Addiction, Depression, and Transcendence,* by Michael Pollan. These two books complement each other and distract me from the reality of my desire for immediate death.

The instantaneous shift of being cloistered with boys within a military institution in a quasi jail environment to being garbed in mismatched designer clothing while sipping a gourmet coffee has shocked my sensibilities. These dress pants are to be substituted with contemporary khaki shorts the moment I stumble upon a clothes retail outlet along my jaunt through the streets of Arkansas. I'm reminiscent of an ignorant spoiled rich boy suckling off daddies' haired teat—the manifestation of the *exact* physical projection I sought to avoid via an excursion into the nothingness of a foreign realm, deprived of all social and financial support.

Unemployment benefits and homeless shelters are anathemas; I'll forge my own path under the care of a new slave owner or die from heat exposure in the process. Life is made fun once more by the constraints of *my* design. Lo—to the power of word. I sneer at the thought of my reader; behold the foolishness of my "insanity" and reflect on what feelings you may regard of my intangible *self* back upon *you;* as you would leer at a mirror, so too, do you read.

5:22 PM

There is a small woman from the female SEPs division aboard the aircraft to Arkansas; this woman, by chance, attracted me the most throughout my duration at SEPs whenever the male divisions crossed paths or integrated with the female division. My energy is overtaken by curiosity, lust, and a desire to seize the opportunity to obtain information about boot camp/SEPs life from a first-hand female perspective. This woman has seated ten rows ahead of me; the delay at which we depart from the aircraft may impede me from an interaction. I sit and direct thoughts to my inner ego towards communication with her in hopes that my will may override chaos and impact her consciousness with reciprocal thoughts, i.e., an energy exchange madness.

I gazed at the woman and smiled while we boarded, twice; she averted her gaze: a visage of uncertainty and abject worthlessness. If this woman is present and within my field of vision the moment I emerge from the shuttle, she will be my first objective.

5:49 PM

She's gone. There is nothing more of *it.*

6:13 PM

Lo! I found the woman and secured her email.

It is a declaration of freedom to sit on the stoop of an apartment leasing office, sweaty and surrounded by mosquitoes. Night falls and I know I must obtain insect repellent for a restful sleep within a secluded area of the city—yet to be determined.

To walk streets again, mantled with my Navy-issued backpack, feels *almost* preposterous, for to be holed away for two months with no control over my activity or outlet for physical exertion has dampened my psyche. I'm intoxicated with contentment, liberated by reckless abandonment... I'm surrounded by limitless opportunity with a belly full of a rotisserie chicken, two bananas, and several tablespoons of peanut butter. Two sets of unsullied clothes and necessary hygienic items maintain my pretentious image. Blessed be the damned.

July 17th, 2019

8:24 AM

Action—*action* abound, perhaps a paltry version of what certifiable/ qualified/socially indoctrinated men live, yet, despite my absurdity and moronic behavior, I live a life of great satisfaction thus far since airport departure.

I sleep in the outdoor interior of an elevated loading dock atop metal grating. The top section of a dumpster conceals me throughout the night. Insect repellent is my blanket; a backpack is my pillow. The temperature drops from an average of 99 °F - 93 °F at sunset to a comfortable 78 °F - 72 °F overnight. The location I've selected is adjacent to the main street of the city. Opposite the road, at the front of the structure where I've chosen to sleep, is the city's only shopping mall. A few blocks away are two all-you-can-eat buffets ($11.99 lunch) where I gorge myself after strength training at a similar fitness corporation I utilized at my hometown for a $10 a month membership fee. Despite all the monetary savings, I spent an additional $160 on two "bamboo" material shorts, one shirt, one pair of briefs, and two pairs of socks. I donated the $240 worth of name-brand airport clothes I purchased to a gregarious service clerk; he assured me that a few college students who work for him will be grateful. The "bamboo" material is odor/microbial resistant and lightweight. I dress in a similar style that a seventy-year-old-man would wear on vacation, or to Sunday mass. I'm comfortable with this modest garb.

A walk to and from downtown has secured me a mailing address. I await my writing device and phone to be mailed to me posthaste by one of my three disappointed and astonished recruiters.

To rove in search of work is difficult beneath the southern sun. My pasty white skin burns despite sunscreen and care to seek shade whenever possible. Life is too simple; I scrutinize the industry and commercial venues around me which I depend on for survival and laugh.

Seated on a bench outside a library, I wait for 9:00 AM in the shade of a monolithic stone water fountain positioned at the center of a small circular garden. I hope to find a computer terminal within, and to establish access to my email prior to the arrival of my writing device (damn my negligence to record the [forgotten] password of my secondary email to bypass security). Without my previous cellular phone number and access to my primary email, I'm unable to contact my publisher or to be contacted by employees with job offers. I must revisit establishments in-person several days later for updates. There are no payphones *anywhere* in this city and I refuse to plead with a stranger.

And my book-in-progress… cursed—my life's meaning!

8:56 PM

This silly game of life...

Another eventful day of consumerism and job hunting yields $44 worth of multivitamins, creatine, and aloe vera burn gel. Another $204 has been spent on an "ultra-light-weight," compact, outdoor-ready, durable, inflatable mattress (repair kit included). The location I've chosen to sleep is occupied by laborers; I hear the activity through the ventilation of an overhead door. My mattress is aligned against the door where cold air seeps out and wafts over me. I imagine I'll be discovered (soon), and when I am, a relocation will be a simple transition.

"And I love my little pig hog, and my pig hog loves me.
"I'm gonna cherish that pig 'neath the green bay tree.
"My little pig goes ump, ump,
"My little guinea goes paderack,
"My little hen goes cluck cluck,

"**My little rooster goes cock-a-doodle-doo,**
"**doodle-doo, doodle-doo.**"

- Almeda Riddle

July 18th, 2019

8:06 AM

I wake to a barren and desolate panorama of darkened concrete and variegated lights. What is fiction when *this* is reality? What fantasies could my mind concoct that would compare to twenty-four hours of *anyone's* life? Behold:

I rise, put shoes on my feet, deflate and store an air mattress, don my pack, and run to the gym at 4:00 AM where I strength train and shower until 7:00 AM. The sun peeks over flat commercial structures, shines onto one of many empty parking lots, and tingles the burned skin of my calves. I veer left and enter a breakfast establishment to check the status of my application for employment; there is no dishwasher position open. I depart for the nearby market and purchase my first breakfast: A can of tuna and two bananas (I carry a jar of peanut butter). I depart the market and cross the calm six-lane street towards the shopping mall, enter before any of the shops are open, sit on a metal chair within a large food court chamber replete with roof windows and Romanesque columns, and observe a spectacle:

At least a dozen men and women circuit the mall perimeters: a power walk for one is a slow amble to me. Each individual has dedicated a segment of time to *walk*… albeit, the mall is air-conditioned, features music, and provides ample space to roam in the comfort of a consumer's dream.

Enter "I," seated upright, back braced against the aforementioned seat, with aforementioned food items set before me on a simple square table, engaged with lackadaisical and *poignant* consumption. My eyes follow the feet and bobbing heads of overweight mothers, grandmothers, and, well, the majority are women on the verge of obesity—and a few men, each who surmise the fundamental activity a hominid *should* engage in for the majority of their conscious life—*walking*—as *exercise*. Yes, you've planned a route for minimal exertions… I wonder what daily life these people lead, while I *sit* for a stint, backpack by my wayside, to enjoy a snack.

Oh... how censorious and haughty I am; who are *you* to judge *my* judgment, reader, i.e., future self?

The absurdity of life is how convoluted our delusions become; the substitution of simplicity and chaos with complexity and order toxifies and distracts from the moment-

Ah, spiritualistic postulations again? This must be the result of my two current distractions: the words of Eckhart Tolle and Michael Pollan. Thoughts are objects; I am but a vessel for the "unified/collective consciousness"... for lack of a better explanation for the intuitive reasoning of feelings we harbor when subjected to the observation of *others observing*.

A cave! A cave! I am my own culture! Leave me to my ~~equanimity~~ (in)sanity! There is no god, only the "I" we "know" ourselves to *be*.

9:16 AM

"'I felt a little like an archaeologist, unearthing a completely buried body of knowledge. Beginning in the early fifties, psychedelics had been used to treat a whole host of conditions,' including addiction, depression, obsessive-compulsive disorder, schizophrenia, autism, and end-of-life anxiety. 'There had been forty thousand research participants and more than a thousand clinical papers! The American Psychiatric Association had whole meetings centered around LSD, this new wonder drug.' In fact, there were six international scientific meetings devoted to psychedelics between 1950 and 1965. 'Some of the best minds in psychiatry had seriously studied these compounds in therapeutic models, with government funding.' But after the culture and the psychiatric establishment turned against psychedelics in the mid-1960s, an entire body of knowledge was effectively erased from the field, as if all that research and clinical experience had never happened. 'By the time I got to medical school in the 1990s, no one even talked about *it*.'"

- Michael Pollan's How to Change your Mind

From the mall's overhead speakers, benevolent ambient music is accentuated by male singers reminiscent of a Christian Pop band and intermittent children's laughter: reverberations of whimsical giggles. I'm compelled to purchase a latte.

2:30 PM

A perusal over the library's shelves, I decided by the deterministic volition of my fate, to enter the "Philosophy" section and pulled the first book to harness my attention: a "mystical" force of extraneous will: Mortimer J. Adler's *Ten Philosophical Mistakes*. I scanned the contents and flipped to chapter three: *Words and Meanings*. After five minutes I experienced cognitive dissonance.

"Two of the three mistakes that I will report in this chapter and shall try to correct are consequences of the mistakes discussed in the two preceding chapters: one the mistake of treating our ideas—our perceptions, memories, imaginations, and conceptions or thoughts— as objects of which we are directly aware or conscious; the other the mistake of reducing all our cognitive powers to that of our senses and failing to distinguish between the senses and the intellect as quite distinct, though interdependent, ways of apprehending objects." [37]

There is much to read, and for why I happened to procure this book first out of the multitudinous *thousands* in this library and flip to the aforementioned passage connotes the wonder of a fairytale.

July 19th, 2019

3:33 PM

There is a framed drawing at the back of the room on the second level of the library:

Sharp lines and angled features. A crowd of villagers attacked by two armed assailants. A mother clutches her child; the assailant grabs for the terrified youth's leg and aims a rapier at a naked bosom. The women behind the scene gather close, their faces darkened with dismay, grief, and incredulous despair. Beneath where the two assailants stand, piles of children's bodies lay contorted and mangled by fatal sword wounds. There is no hope rendered in the pencil strokes.

The librarians are unable to identify the artist for me, though my

---

[37] Mortimer J. Adler's, *Ten Philosophical Mistakes*

interest revitalized previous controversy (unbeknownst to me) of whether the work should remain on the wall of a public library.

"Innocence," and all deviations of the word, should be eliminated from all human languages.

People are nefarious, saints most of all. Saints, by consequence of their existence, provoke the worst out of the human creature. I *feel* too much and suffer too little.

This morning I woke to the cacophonous thunder of a 5:00 AM garbage truck emptying the dumpster beside the dock where I sleep. Never again. I wake at 4:00 AM and run to the gym henceforth—no later.

July 20th, 2019

12:34 PM

Sunburned Scalp

Wake from an industrial grave.
Scratch reddened skin flakes;
Sniff a sweat-soaked shirt:
Smells syrupy, redolent of a past
Lover's saccharine perfume.

July 21st, 2019

4:19 PM

Adler's work, *Ten Philosophical Mistakes,* evoked new insights, though *not* in the realm of thought I consider to be constructive to my own theory: Thoughts are objects—the human and/or animal body being the vessel, a veritable transmitter for thoughts. Rather, Adler skimped around the ideas comprising my theory; I feel insular, isolated in thought as one would on a deserted island would feel, with too much beach and too little shade.

"We appear compelled to admit that, for any one individual, the ideas in the minds of other individuals are not objects of which he or she can be conscious. Their subjectivity puts them beyond the reach of his or

her immediate awareness. In other words, the ideas in a given person's mind are objects for that person alone. They are beyond immediate apprehension for everyone else." [38]

Yes, *yes...* cognitive dissonance; *ideas* are objects, and what is an idea but an amalgamation of thoughts, and when these thoughts—tangible *only* to the sole thinker, arise, the energy impacts the physiology of the human body and elicits change, whether the thought of a profound computation in nuclear physics, or the somber remembrance of a departed loved one— or the contemplation of grape or raspberry jam between two slices of *Wonderbread.*

"Whatever can be properly called an idea has an object."

On several rereads of the aforementioned sentence, I realized the philosophical postulates of Adler and myself diverged into unrelated fields of metaphilosophy. I digress.

Alas, three pages later:

"For John Locke, the awareness we have of our own ideas is entirely a private experience, exclusively our own. This holds for all those who, in one way or another, adopt his view of ideas as the objects of our minds when we are conscious—objects of which we are immediately aware and that we directly apprehend. They are in effect saying that all the ideas that an individual has in his mind when he is conscious result in private experiences for him, experiences no one else can share. To say this is the philosophical mistake that has such serious consequences in modern thought." [39]

I agree, and for that, I relapse to the reality of existence and the inter-relational effects of all thought, no matter how minor, for the energy of humanity sifts through us all by a power unnameable, indescribable— *Lovecraftian* consciousness! God? Is that you?

5:59 PM

The library closed before I could finish copying one final passage. Lack of established residency prohibits me from a library card to borrow

---

[38] Ibid.

[39] Ibid.

books (I'd return the book damaged anyway). I trekked towards the buffet restaurant for a read outside in the shade until 7:00 PM and decided on a whim to check the local movie theatre in the mall for a list of distractions. A young man in an empty room behind a counter greeted me with the worst forced smile I've *ever* witnessed, even beyond the wickedness of those flashed to me by my disgruntled teenage girlfriends—oh, *so* long ago: before I chose ~~contentment~~ madness.

"How can I help you today?" said the boy with the reversed inflection of one who had no desire to help.

I said, "I don't know," and shrugged.

"Um, well-"

"I stopped in to see what movies are playing; do you have a comprehensive list for me to read?"

The boy's head snapped down towards a boxy terminal; he recited three innocuous films and regarded me with glazed eyes.

"I don't believe you can help me." I smiled.

"Yeah we need better movies."

"What is your self-assigned meaning in life?"

"... Contentment."

"Yes," I nodded; the boy's face twisted to a *genuine* grin. "How do you achieve contentment?"

Another employee of similar age and gender and greater confidence and grooming standards waltzed out of an adjacent darkened theatre and sat at a round table to my far left.

"Comfort in living," said the boy behind the counter.

"Are you comfortable now in this environment?"

"Yeah, *it* isn't so bad."

I addressed the other employee: "Hello."

"Hello."

"What is your self-assigned meaning in life?"

This boy repeated my question and said, "To provoke a reaction from people."

I lifted both hands from my sides and revealed my palms. "You have elicited my reaction by your presence alone; here I am; therefore, I believe you have fulfilled your meaning in life—for the moment." I chuckled; the two boys humored me with entertained smiles.

"What's your meaning in life?" said the seated boy.

"My meaning is to write."

"Ah," the boy entwined his fingers on the tabletop. I exchanged glances from both youthful visages and said, "Well, I'll be going then."

The seated boy said with a goading snidery expressed in his voice, "Write about this moment." We locked eyes and nodded.

"I will."

"Good. *It* was nice to meet you man."

"You too." I pushed a glass door open to the blaze of an afternoon sun and contemplated if I *would* write of that moment.

Seated on a bench in an underground parking lot, I wrote of that moment, and on completion, pondered the validity of my self-assigned meaning and understood at once the fragility of my exposed ego. Death would be justice.

July 22nd, 2019

6:56 AM

I've chosen to undergo a thirty-six-hour fast; zero expenses on food equates to zero expenses for the day.

A violent wind and rainstorm startled me awake last night due to a din of thunder. Inside the loading dock, I enjoyed the cool lashings of gusts and considered myself lucky to have located a shelter which has protected and concealed my body for a week… a week already.

Three job interviews are scheduled for today and I hope to receive my writing device soon. The library is spacious and quiet; I pace between the bookshelves, book-in-hand, and throughout unfocused spans of conscious efforts, wonder how long each dull moment will last until the next. There is no anxiety or worry; a rather uncomfortable state of being supplants the throes of want and desire.

After an hour pace along a vacant store-front reading the final chapter of *How to Change your Mind*, I reflect on my ego and the uncertain course of life, seated alone on a chair within the confines of a stately eatery area outside the city mall: wallflowers, hanging bulbs, double lanterns, giant potted ferns. Rain pours from a plain gray sky. There is nothing to hear but the flow of water.

I tire of this notepad and hope to soon retire *it* alongside my eviscerated journal.

The library is open; I resume yesterday's *idea:*

"When ideas are treated as the only things with which we have direct acquaintance by our immediate awareness of them as objects apprehended, we are compelled to live in two worlds without any bridge between them. One is the world of physical reality, in which our own bodies occupy space, move about, and interact with other bodies. Our belief in the existence of this world is a *blind and irrational faith.* **The other is the completely private world in which each of us is enclosed— the world in which our only experience is the experience constituted by consciousness of our own ideas. The** *assumption* **that individuals other than ourselves also and similarly live in the private worlds of their own conscious experience is as** *blind a faith* **as the belief that we all live together in the one world of external physical reality."** [40]

Faith! The intellect is grounded in faith! From mathematics, to phenomenology, all ideas are faith-based derived from the *limited* sensory faculties of the human creature. Our hominid brains may as well be a gnats-worth of comprehending "power" relative to the greater unknown rifts of reality—that of which, as a collective race, we would no doubt fear—if we *knew* of the unknown's existence!

Escapist entertainment and the comfort of our delusional ego is far more enjoyable.

Faith—in the ego!

"To believe that life has any meaning at all is of course a large presumption, requiring in some a leap of faith, but surely *it* **is a helpful one, and never more so than at the approach of death. To situate the self in a larger context of meaning, whatever** *it* **is—a sense of oneness with nature or universal love—can make extinction of the self somewhat easier to contemplate. Religion has always understood this wager, but why should religion enjoy a monopoly? Bertrand Russell wrote that the best way to overcome one's fear of death 'is to make your interests gradually wider and more impersonal, until bit by bit the walls of the**

---

[40] Ibid.

ego recede, and your life becomes increasingly merged in the universal life.'" [41]

Pollan also cites Albert Einstein, [42] *also* quoted in my first installment of this senseless yearly trite.

The pieces of the egoic puzzle draw together with my accumulated "knowledge," yet despite the grasp on the intangible, there is nothing to *truly* know; there is only choice in each moment, as cliche as *it* is; so choose, enlightened self, to "know" what you've "known" all along!

5:41 PM

Despite what ~~you~~ I know, ~~you're~~ I'm a loathsome wretch with no prospects other than an illusory meaning ~~you've~~ I've chosen for an ephemeral existence.

I read a small, golden, hand-sized book titled *On Truth,* by Harry Frankfurt: more expositions on the inherent meaninglessness of life, and how "love" may be described as the joy one experiences when around a being or entity which grants you an opportunity to learn of your "self." [43]

I've read a portion of the editor's introduction to Jean-Paul Satre's *Being and Nothingness* and am enthralled, propelled down an abysmal channel of existential passages written by a dead man.

Stand, pace, run, walk, each domain is an otherwise temporary reprieve from a greater mass; there is no personal sanctuary from the acute sensation of observing and being observed.

Women abound, I reckon each with a stony glare and think instead of what I've read, and my own and other theories of mind, of consciousness— now dissonant unravelings when confronted with thoughts of similar yet disparate caliber by (dead) men far more learned than myself. *This* is my life's meaning: The ego disperses, voided by a lukewarm flow of

---

[41] Michael Pollan's *How to Change Your Mind*

[42] "A human being is a part of the whole called by us universe, a part limited in time and space. He experiences himself, his thoughts and feeling as something separated from the rest, a kind of optical delusion of his consciousness. This delusion is a kind of prison for us, restricting us to our personal desires and to affection for a few persons nearest to us. Our task must be to free ourselves from this prison by widening our circle of compassion to embrace all living creatures and the whole of nature in its beauty."

[43] Pelagia described her attraction for me as this; these fickles feelings of validation are now a bygone memory.

nothingness. A new form manifests, one leveled into flatter plains where I may now reckon a greater horizon than the mountainous vistas my enlivened ego ever offered.

To be destitute and dissonant, there is hope after all, for the manner of man I had been transmuted: None shall miss him.

9:02 PM

I've lost a fragment of my humanity somewhere along the way. All I speak to regard me as a foreigner and question my ethnicity and origin. Even in my hometown I inhibited my oratory abilities by purposeful negation for a comical effect. My pretenses of forced *lack* of affectation have nothing to do with my origins, but the *journey*.

July 23rd, 2019

11:53 AM

I'm a quintessential (no longer picturesque or eclectic) case of "mental illness" in accordance with the DSM-5, yet I think and feel saner than most I encounter. "Homelessness" is a choice; I maintain and improve my health daily since being released from captivity, and the search for employment ends soon—I hope… and hope is all we have.

Three hours at the gym for strength training and hygiene. An hour read (and completion) of Pollan's *How to Change Your Mind*. Five minutes until I end my fast with a buffet. The results of job interviews await my inquiry, and for the remainder of eight to ten hours afterward, I will indulge myself at the library with Sartre's *Being and Nothingness*.

6:56 PM

"I"—the vicious imaginings of "I." Repulsed by humanity, I *must* be ill to write of *it*.

At the mall:

"*Oh* look at the pumpkin in the window!" mewled a pregnant mother of two stroller-bound toddlers to a friend. Two shopping bags hung slack from a feeble forearm; a limp wrist hung forward.

"He just texted me," said a young, slender blonde-haired girl amongst a throng of nubiles.

I passed a convergence of nubile girls and evaluated *my* body—the piece of flesh *to be* assessed that *it* is. The girl's hearts palpitated, salivary glands innervated, and vaginal canals lubricated. I stared straight over each of the girl's pampered heads and surged past, close to their group, and wafted the foul stench of my week-unwashed pair of boxers and shorts into each of their nostrils.

Eyelids drooped, foreheads crinkled, and one corner of a pair of lips upturned.

I purchased another article of bamboo briefs and intend to wash my sullied pair with hand soap in a gym sink tomorrow before training.

This is my life story.

8:49 PM

Deviations of "I've decided to go an alternate route," is a phrase I heard thrice today regarding employment: coincidence? No—a product of my actions.

I have an interview one week from today as a sales associate for the office supply retailer whose loading dock I sleep on each night. I write this memoir now, on one of the last five pages of my notepad, after a dinner of canned tuna, sardines, two bananas and forkfuls of peanut butter.

The *abject absurdity...* if I am to be hired where I have claimed my reprieve at night... to don the uniform by day, and to round out to the loading dock at my shift's end for slumber, to invigorate and shower at the nearby gym, consume at the nearby buffet... I may *laugh* if I am to achieve employment where I have chosen as a hub.

July 24th, 2019

3:38 PM

Four-Dollar Latte

Foam of milk atop darkened water
Colored a brighter luster beneath frothy bubbles.
Diminished: opaque reflection evokes sentiments of
Days squandered longing for tomorrow.
Each four-dollar latte deducted from a
Bank account elicits new numbers of
Inconsequential meaning—for now:
Sip foam from the rim
And long for another tomorrow.

A street-side idler allowed me to borrow his phone to contact (one of) my recruiters for an update on the status of my package containing my phone, writing device, and birth certificate: In transit. My recruiter also informed me that my father is desperate for information in regards to my whereabouts and activities; I declined to allow my recruiter to disclose the information.

I miss my old man for his guaranteed validation, all the more reason to remain destitute and ostracized from his resolute bestowment of love. The world has much to teach me of humanity; my father and mother: no longer.

July 25th, 2019

5:10 PM

I should be joyful to have discovered a hidden hardcover volume on the shelves of the library psychology section containing work of three of my all-time favorite thinkers of antiquated history: Plato, Epictetus, and Marcus Aurelius. I've verified my temporary postal address, borrowed the book for two weeks, and stow *it* in my pack for the long stints of reclusion I enjoy at various public facilities, e.g., bathroom stalls, vacant parking lots, empty construction sites, and benches among park copses.

I read a small book titled *On Art and Life,* by John Ruskins: a quaint expression of appreciation for the Gothic architectural style, of iron (plowshares, fetters, swords), of an artist's ply with base materials, and of militaristic training for a society's youth.

Each day I return to the grotesque drawing at the back of the second floor of the library and revel in the superb depiction of human cruelty. There is a nobility of the honesty, the forthrightness of the dark lines interjected amongst each other to create a thing unwholesome to the eye, yet spirited in the crudeness: the *naturalism;* I ponder the anguish depicted on the women's faces and the scorn on the men's.

A woman sits down near me; I reckon only her face staring straight ahead; she is aware of my awareness: Soulful eyes rendered bleak and a thin mouth.

The stasis of terror captured on the visages of dead infants: this is no feature of the aforementioned drawing, but of my mind.

"Oh," commented a sack of flesh and bone, "but you're *so* intelligent."

Yes! Tell me, arbiter of men, if I am this intelligent creature, why do I dine on sardines and bananas in bathroom stalls? Why do I sleep atop a loading dock and wonder why my fellow men yearn for the company of a woman… or a man… or a dog, or perhaps a nubile adolescent? Why does my mind fester with illogical thoughts of intuitions and *nothing* else worth merit to the advancement of society? Is this expression the extent of my gift to mankind—my vile expulsion: "my," being a condition of society. Alas… I am *"yours."*

7:08 PM

"*It* is in anguish that man gets the consciousness of his freedom, or if you prefer, anguish is the mode of being of freedom as consciousness of being; *it* is in anguish that freedom is, in *its* being, in question for *it*self."

- Jean-Paul Satre's Being and Nothingness

8:43 PM

The consumption of one can of sardines, a banana, and 32 ounces of Greek Yogurt behind a grocery store dumpster has introduced an immediate 116g of protein and a gratuitous surge of uncustomary probiotics to my digestive system.

July 26th, 2019

12:38 PM

"Hello, hello there, oh my-" said a middle-aged woman with bright, sympathetic eyes while I finished a seated shoulder press set at the gym. Three young men stood behind her switching turns on a leg press machine and watched my disinterested countenance move:

"Hello."

"My husband and I see you walking all the time, my... with your backpack on, this morning too... my... Are you alright?"

I attempted to stare through the woman's forehead and instead met her fixated gaze with a stupefied smile. "Yes, I'm alright. Are you alright?"

"Yeah—I'm alright, *it*'s just we see you all the time, and now I see you *here* working out and..." The woman's self-righteous altruistic "intentions" overshadowed each of her other characteristics.

I said, "So you saw me and figured you'd initiate a conversation to establish a connection?"

"Well, yeah, but, are you *sure* you're alright?"

"Yes. What do you mean?"

The woman pondered her next words and said, "Whenever I see people I know, I ask them if they're doing okay, just checking."

"Ah." The eager saint didn't want to offend me and rendered herself a liar.

"Well, *it* was nice to actually meet you; God bless you and good luck!"

"Thanks. You too."

I sit on a park bench opposite the library and observe many diverse women dedicate a segment of their life to the sole act of walking, not for long, either.

My *life* is a walk *in the park!*

6:46 PM

I've no idea of the man—no, *creature,* that I am. Social interactions err—to my benefit, yet I strut from pseudo caves to hidden nooks, concealed alcoves and obscured paths. I desire nothing but strength and health for my body and the will to write of my disjointed and dispirited will... to live—for I live to write, and write of nothing; what else is there?

Homeless, friendless, jobless, on the verge of true destitution, I'm *grateful*, for each solace and ephemeral moment of inspired happiness. Perpetual anguish accentuates my contentment. I dwell on the potentialities of "evil" and refrain on account of acquired virtues... for the "good" I "know," inherent within my*self*; therefore, to the same degree, my fellow man. I'd rather rot in tepid squalor, emaciated and imprisoned, than to injure another for my own gain: Noble or foolish? There may be nobility in "evil" and ignobility in "good."

July 27th, 2019

8:19 PM

The events of today are outrageous upon review; to a judgmental human: a comedic accomplishment.

I've trekked fourteen miles for naught other than the expenditure of energy; one direction to downtown for the sake of a post office visit after a rising sun read of Plato in the park, opposite of the library. I discovered that the post office is closed on Saturday... I *could've* inquired of this, yet—no! My demeanor prohibits me. Back—towards my hub, for a breakfast buffet: Fish, chicken, egg, guacamole, spinach, olives, jalapenos, broccoli, turnips, brussel sprouts, green beans, yellow peppers, liver and onions, cabbage, pineapple, cantaloupe, cranberries, raisins, pickles, and *sweet potatoes...*

Every morning I glut in this manner and think, *"What is this absurdity of life"*—the ease: I yearn for a catastrophe to my health!

A venture to the eastern edge of the city to check on applications for pending employment yielded *nothing;* therefore I stopped at a nearby coffee shop to reward myself for the nothing I reaped where I sat in a cushioned black chair and attempted to read Plato while three twenty-something-year-old college-bound employees spieled about television shows, giggled on the utterance of recent memes, and shared leads on the latest cat videos (I *wish* I exaggerate or lie to you, self [and bored reader]).

I trekked back to my hub where I trained at the gym for three hours until the onset of sundown, purchased another 35.2 oz container of unflavored Greek yogurt, three bananas, and a can of sardines. I backpacked these items to a secluded cubby adjacent to the mall and squatted on the filthy cement to consume my meal. A nearby porta-potty serves me well. I'm vexed by two drops of fish oil spilled on the collar of my shirt.

July 28th, 2019

9:09 AM

Born, out of a maelstrom of nothing, a mote of ephemeral essences flickered into existence and faded; one remained and lingered on a precipice of silver light, outlined by an opaque abyss comprised of absolute black: darkness wrought from the void of God.

"What is?" said the mote, though the voice resounded only as an intangible thought devoid of language and substance.

God responded, **"I."**

The mote pulsed with striations of ethereal energy and said, "What else?"

"Nothing."

The mote quaked: a tempest, a convalescent nebula, a resurgence of what never was; *it* said, "What is 'I'?"

"*You,*" commanded God, and the mote ushered in an existence of *it*self:

"I'm *so* tired of shopping all the time. I can't wait until like, I can like, in the future, buy something to do the shopping for me," said Deborah over a large cappuccino.

Sarah wiped translucent yellow grit away from the cheek side corner of her left eye and said, "A clone, they have those now."

"They do? I bet they're *super* expensive."

"Yeah. I'd clone my husband so one could stay at the office all day and fuck his dumb office skanks while the other could stay with me all day to raise the kids with me, go shopping—with me, and *fuck me* instead of those dumb *fucking office skanks.*" Sarah sipped a frappuccino.

"Oh my God that's the best idea I've ever heard but I'm too poor to ever do that and Mark is too… I don't want to say 'incompetent' to earn a raise or be promoted but like, I don't know, I can't think of a better word for him, oh Mark…"

Sarah snorted and said, *"Mark."*

3:35 PM

The simultaneous read of Plato (Socrates) and Sartre is often too much to process in harmony, for one subscribes to virtue and the salvation of one's soul; the other, to a dissonant self, always in flux (anguish) and relatable to oneself only through reflections of others.

"Lest we become misologists, he replied: no worse thing can happen to a man than this. For as there are misanthropists or haters of men, there are also misologists or haters of ideas, and both spring from the same cause, which is ignorance of the world."

- The Dialogues of Plato

A supersized man sat in the second row of a movie theatre with a supersized popcorn braced against his skewed left arm; he held his phone, crooked, to the right of his face, and texted his wife offhandedly while a *Coca-Cola* commercial featured interracial couples "in love," engaged in variations of the "American Dream," e.g., sunbathing on the hood of a car, cookouts with an extended family, holding hands while pacing a sunlit nature trail, and playing chess with a joyful grandchild inside of a vaulted living room. Socrates believed the earth is suspended in the heavens, and of an immortal soul. The aforementioned pictorials are a snippet of humanity's designs. Where is the love, in truth? Is there *"wrong?"*

July 29th, 2019

9:06 PM

The ego exists for others.

Due to the tacit contemplation of my behavior, I've determined my lunacy—yet, people esteem me as a "gentleman," even beyond the thresholds of establishments where those who are paid to ingratiate themselves with customers speak thus.

I gaze through those who are innocuous or serve me no function. I awaken to strength train, feed on a glorious buffet of nutrition, march across the city in search of labor and visit the post office in expectancy of my phone and writing device (I've purchased my third pocket journal; there are dots where lines should be printed on the pages), and read *Being and Nothingness* at the library, which has crystallized my ego's insane values. I *am* perturbed by the nothing that I am. I consume two cans of sardines, one with olive oil, one in water, a 35.3 oz container of 0% fat Greek yogurt, three bananas, and 6 ozs of raspberries, at the rear end of a shopping complex behind a dumpster—seated on a stoop, surrounded by mosquitoes held at bay by an application of insect repellent.

I value the assimilation of the flesh; my God loves me, and I *it*.

July 30th, 2019

3:40 PM

A naked man charged over a meadow proliferated with lilacs and daffodils. Feverous exhalations muted the palpitations of an overwrought heart. "I'm going to die!" said the man, his head cocked skyward, voice strained.

"Who is going to die?" said a maiden from a hut fifty paces away; she emerged from a doorway, bare-chested and supple.

"I'm going to die—if I… continue running… at this length… and pace!" said the man.

"Stop at once!"

The man skewed his head and acknowledged voluptuous breasts first, sharp lines of a contoured face second, and elegant calves third; he slowed, stopped, and stood for a moment to scratch the mesh of brown hairs below the slight protrusion of his abdomen; he said, "Is *it* just you who lives in that hut?"

"No."

"Who else?"

"I won't say."

The man panted, advanced one pace toward the maiden with his right foot and back-stepped half a pace with his left. "Why won't you say?"

"You're a hooligan with foul intentions."

"Miss, if I am correct in titling you thus, a man's lust is no treason against God or a crime against humanity. Your attractive options rouse me and I desire to act."

"And what of my mind?"

"What of your mind?"

The woman cleared her throat, shook several long strands of golden-brown hair away from her face, and stepped out from the shadow cast by a colossal oak tree into the rays of a cloud-concealed midday sun. "The contents of my mind: what care do you have for that matter?"

"None at all."

"I thought so; therefore, begone from this place and never return, for the sight of *your* body is loathsome and the contents of what you've revealed of your mind—irredeemable."

The man advanced two paces towards the maiden and said, "Who is in that hut?"

"A man."

"Man in the hut!" the naked man shouted, "approach at once, lest you admit to your lady and to myself of your cowardice!"

"He's out for a hunt and will-" The maiden truncated her speech and screamed; the naked man sprinted towards her; she turned to retreat and grasped at the edges of a flimsy wooden door. One clammy hand gripped her forehead, another hand of equal dampness braced against her belly. The maiden unleashed a fitful cry and failed to conceal her terror. The naked man laid his weight upon the maiden's back, toppled her, and pressed her face into stiffened blades of yellowed shrubbery. The naked man proceeded to grasp for the maiden's wrists and stymied the panicked thrashings of her body; he pressed his chin against the nape of her neck, stared forward at the slight opening of the wooden door, and said, "What animals do you own?" The maiden wailed and the naked man applied greater pressure. "*What* animals do you own?"

"… One pig," the maiden gasped and wriggled against an earthen floor.

"What else?"

"Two—two *horses*… ah, two goats—a sheep, and-"

"What sex is the sheep?"

The maiden's efforts lessened and she spoke with newfound revulsion, "Female."

"Where?"

"In… in the barn… out back."

"Out back?"

The maiden stammered, "Yes?" and on her quizzical affirmation, the naked man retracted his right hand, formed a fist, and battered the back of the maiden's skull with three, swift, forceful strikes; he leapt up from the unresponsive body and bounded around the hut between rows of unkempt shrubs and layers of fallen tree branches, to a barn, whereupon the naked man flung the heavy set double doors open, surveyed the downtrodden squalor, located a lone, despondent sheep engaged with the consumption of a small thatch of wheat, and tackled the animal.

The horses neighed.

"Of pleasures, those which occur most rarely give the most delight."

- Fragments of Epictetus

I am the antithesis of a "godly" man. No matter how much I read of virtue being the salvation of the "soul," I regard all with derision; the grotesqueries of belief and understanding are abhorrent; as a species we strive to ascend our humanity and thereby become *subhuman,* less than optimal for life *now,* no matter the pursuit to occupy one's time until the inevitable leveler of death—and even *that* is speculation. Whether my consciousness is shared by all life or is inherent within the universe makes no difference to anything at all; even if a profound revelation to the meaning of existence were to be illuminated—even a shred of insight, nothing would change except for the change which "nothing" already is and undergoes ad infinitum.

July 31st, 2019

7:33 PM

Denied loans and jobs, I'm a lucky man.

Epictetus contradicts himself in matters concerned with the body and consumption: fast and despise food whenever on offer to ascend yourself with the "Gods," yet, there is praise for health, robust, and muscular bodies, such as what Diogenes exhibited. Epictetus'—nay, *stoicism,* in general, is a fit philosophy for what ~~contemporary America~~ any society would deem a lousy, self-preserving egotist if you examine the mind becoming of the man, and the internal discourses of the man which is produced: one whose ego is sanctified and safeguarded with the delusional belief that one is best to contend with every matter and circumstance indifferent, preoccupied with thoughts of "God"—defined as an all-pervasive essence—an inhabitant within oneself. Epictetus and Marcus Aurellius alike are egotists in the *name* of God—*however,* both claim to *not* know, so what are they then but madmen if *not* faithful to the precepts of their own determined virtues established through a hopeful solidarity that what their *culture defines* as a virtue, and their practice of defined virtue, will increase the chances of an agreeable death: the unknowable.

"The gods, who are free from death, do not resent their need throughout all the length of eternity to tolerate in such numbers such worthless creatures as men: what is more, they even care for them in all sorts of ways. And do you, with the merest time before your own exit, refuse to make the effort—and that when you are one of the worthless creatures yourself?"

- Marcus Aurelius' Meditations

"Or what reason hast thou (tell me) for desiring to read? For if thou aim at nothing beyond the mere delight of *it,* or gaining some scrap of knowledge, thou art but a poor, spiritless knave. But if thou desirest to study to *it*s proper end, what else is this than a life that flows on tranquil and serene? And if thy reading secures thee not serenity, what profits *it?*—'Nay, but *it* doth secure *it,*' quoth he, 'and that is why I repine at being deprived of *it.*'—And what serenity is this that lies at the mercy of every passer-by? I say not at the mercy of the Emperor or Emperor's favorite, but such as trembles at a raven's croak and piper's din, a fever's touch or a thousand things of like sort! Whereas the life serene has no more certain mark than this, that *it* ever moves with constant unimpeded flow."

- The Golden Sayings of Epictetus: Verse CXLV

-What I've written all along, poor, eager reader, forget these words and what I am; let this sentence be your last; forget the "I" for which I claim to be and love yourself for your own.

No? Reading and writing are marks of an unsettled mind; there is no equanimity, and whatever one mistakes as the fickle feeling one has when reading or writing *as* equanimity, delusion prevails. Void words of a crippled slave or a Roman emperor, deluded *and* corrupt *with* virtue.

AUGUST

August 1st, 2019

3:13 PM

The mirror's reflection is a farce, a concealment of the consciousness within the mask of flesh.

No labor permits me excess time to consume, exert, and observe. I've lost my sensibilities to the roil of nothingness, the pretensions, false enigmas, images and portrayals of grandeur. Many don't bother. Some care too much. Either end of the spectrum, of the care-*not*-to-care, and of the care-*to*-care, produces the same human being equivalent in their respective extremes of falsehoods.

"Throw away your books; stop letting yourself be distracted."

- Marcus Aureillus' Meditations

Marcus wrote for himself with no intent to be published. An emperor had no time for distractions according to his own jurisdiction. What man has any authority to know what is best for another man, yet a reader persists in reading words I write for myself *and* choose to publish to indict myself by *my* jurisdiction—my delusional meaning of life suspended in doubt. Marcus wrote for himself for he had an empire to govern, and what have I but the will of my flesh and bones?

3:47 PM

Seated on a third-floor bench inside a mall, I listen to the wails of children, the shake of a plastic garbage bag, the beep of arcade games, the laughter of adolescent girls, the patter of footsteps, and the dull reverb of a mall movie.

Wealthy or destitute, my immediate interpretations of sensory stimuli, no matter where I resign my body for moments of respite against the weariness of being, would remain constant.

I'm aware of my awareness. What am I aware of other than greater disparities between my own lack of knowledge for *what* knowledge is worth?

One, big, happy family bumbled side by side through the annals of a shopping mall: A mature man and woman studied the behavior of their two beautiful children. Cheerfulness and joy emanated from the group and compelled men and women, alone on their shopping trips, to feel envy and frustration with their lots in life.

"Daddy," said the son of the mature man.

"Yes, son?"

"What's for dinner?"

"Pork chops and cheesy potatoes."

"Yummy!"

The expressions of quintessential American family affairs overpowered overhead mall music.

"Daddy."

"Yes—son?"

"I want hotdogs and hamburgers or hot pockets instead."

"Not tonight."

"When?"

"Tomorrow."

"Tomorrow is so far away."

"Exercise patience my son."

The mature woman said, "I want hotdogs and hamburgers too, that means *you* cook tonight."

The mature man said, "Okay."

8:49 PM

After a session at the gym I cleaned my body and idled in a vacant locker room. A large television affixed to the ceiling broadcasted the United States president: Donald Trump, and his "reaction" to a state rally "against the government." Behind a podium, Trump's head uplifted at a thirty-degree angle while a crowd appraised and applauded each sentence he spoke—each sentence of sentimental, nationalistic tripe, void of substance and humility, e.g.:

"-And in honor of our proud nations military families-"

"-No matter what you believe we are all united in obeying and upholding the Constitution of the United States of American-"

"Above all, in the name of the God we trust."

Thunderous applause. A cacophonous turnabout of sweet nothings spoken to a vacuous *people*, whether accepted or rejected, to turn your attention to windbag histrionics (politics) renders you confused and inert. For what do you grieve and gripe at other than a rehearsal of actors engaged with play on behalf of the *people's* demands for show? *You*—among them, do you feel shame, or is there enjoyment reaped from the shared sense of interactivity within your narrow-minded community when you watch officials babble about what is cyclic, and *you* too mimic these aforementioned charlatans with "informed" and "knowledgeable" discourses of what you *know* of how ~~this nation~~ the world operates, of who commands, who *obeys,* by the light of a screen which tells you so?

I'd rather hear your comments on the weather, or what passage you think is interesting from a silly book you read.

August 2nd, 2019

9:14 PM

My ego is a diluted moral fiber represented by a man and woman; I yearn for *both* to cease to exist and allow me to consume in peace! I may have lost my fevered mind though a substitution is always readied after each slough of outdated credos!

If only my parents could see me now, isolated among many, seated behind a desolate grocery store dumpster plaza on a concrete stoop with the trash of a meal beside me… four to eight days of projected food remains dependent on my purchases, after which, I will have no money.

Hark, to the desolate hermit—desperate for work. More loans denied, social services avoided, credit cards pending for approval, verdicts of job interviews to be decided, and my writing device, birth certificate, and phone—essentials for communication and progress, have been "lost in the mail" by my recruiter's hand. Instead, I carry three journals and scraps of the Navy Recruit Training Manual containing what remains of my original documentation and continue to hope for nothing. I sleep on the writings of the last four months beneath my torso and yearn for a thief in the night to steal *it* all away; thereby, I'll be freed, to suffer anew.

9:51 PM

A light rain falls and sprinkles against the concrete road beyond the loading dock. I sweat from every pore in my body and am hesitant to dream. I don't remember the last time I cried.

August 3rd, 2019

4:18 PM

My character is juvenile, from my affectations to manner of dress, in contrast with the mind of one who believes himself to have lived far too long.

Sartre's work is equivalent to reading a Stephen King novel of philosophy: descriptions of existence to the minute detail of existential dread.

7:15 PM

To return to the methodology of one meal a day for nourishment and nutrition is the way I've chosen in these straits, for a body laden with excess tissue and encumbered bone is useless. The self-imposed lifestyle I live is the greatest teacher of humility and modesty, more so than any institution or teacher could ever strive to instill in a man. The obsession with the strength and constitution of my flesh must end if I am to be free, for my thoughts are entangled and prevent true contentment.

August 4th, 2019

6:11 PM

Out of the innumerable ways I may die, I hope I am never burned by hot iron plates, flayed, stretched on a rack, torn by beasts, or roasted on an iron seat. This hope leaves enough variance to be rendered null, though the imagery of my imagined body in regards to the aforementioned events amounts to a pleasant present by respect, for which I am thankful to sit in a shopping mall bathroom stall and listen… smell, the suffering of a man engaged with explosive diarrhea in the stall adjacent to me.

A boy entered the bathroom and shouted, "God damn!" My ears rang from the reverberance. "Are you alright?"

The African American man in the adjacent stall said, "Yeah—yeah!"

"You fucking stink!"

"Yeah—yeah!" the man guffawed.

The boy exited the restroom and the man's laughter continued for twenty seconds.

"Yeah—yeah!

"Yeah—yeah!

"Yeah… yeah!

"Yeah I fuckin' stink—yeah!"

6:46 PM

I've visited both nature trails this city offers and repose at each often. The mind is numb, how *it* yearns to be. My ego pities the direction of my writing: I'm a loser in full acceptance of the fact. My poised walk and upraised head is no act—a pretension of confidence—of what? Being alive? What is there *not* to be confident of? I'm no scumbag, urchin, thief, drug dealer, parasite, or scoundrel; I may write of myself in jest—these confessions of a failure and this series of books are doomed to fail from the onset… my self-assigned meaning: a martyr to my ego.

What *good* is a story, a man—the stories of men or the man who writes of non-man, of *his* mind and the terrible thoughts wrought, for all fiction is tripe; thus, I write:

Seated on the edge of a three-foot-high and five-foot-wide circular stone monument composed of bricks cut into ovoid fixtures, a man slumped naked; his chin rested on the knuckles of a curled fist. "I've nothing to say to you, begone," the man said to a cloaked maiden who passed by, unaware of his presence.

The maiden said, *"Well*—you startled me, and I must admit your lithe body and princely face pique my interests, even with your flea-bitten skin, but your attitude is enough to dismay a whole village of ever wanting to bear the sight of you again."

"I care not for what you think or of the innate allure of your body which compels my flesh to covet yours. Leave me."

419

"I was never *with* you. You're pathetic." The woman strut away, proud and robust in her gait.

Minutes elapsed and a man of great stature and virility approached; he acknowledged the naked man seated at the edge of the monument and said, "What are you doing there, exposed as you are?"

"I recline into my mind away from men, though wherever I go there is only another man to greet me."

"You talk a riddle and speak nonsense. What do you do?"

"I act in accordance with my will."

"What skills do you employ?"

"None."

"What of your family?"

"Abandoned."

"Who is your master?"

"No one."

The virile man swaggered away and said, "You're a disgrace."

The naked man remained equipoised in the callousness of his thoughts: a temporal serenity; a moribund wish.

"Live with the gods. And he does live with the gods who constantly shows to them, his own soul is satisfied with that which is assigned to him, and that *it* does all that the daemon wishes, which Zeus hath given to every man for his guardian and guide, a portion of himself. And this is every man's understanding and reason."

- Marcus Aureillus' Meditations

Marcus would've been judged schizo-something by the DSM-5.

August 6th, 2019

6:40 PM

I've fulfilled the predestination of this year's epigraph by a coincidental meeting with an aged African American man on my route away from the mall parking lot; he called out to me, "Well, aren't you a fine, young, tall, sexy man!"

To ease my future mind and cut straight to the grit: I stand in an old schoolhouse converted into apartments, engaged with this journal, a cup of coffee, and volume 35 of *Great Books of the Western World: Locke; Berkely; Hume,* dressed in black panties, i.e., women's lingerie.

Last night I performed fellatio on the aforementioned African American man and experienced anal penetration for the first time in my life, in exchange for a shower, (properly) cleaned clothes, a room to sleep in, walls to keep the elements and mosquitoes at bay, and the enjoyment of J.S. Bach.

I've become a literal slave, of sex, to a domineering fifty-nine-year-old African American male, in exchange for providence, whereby I *could* have reaped unemployment benefits, food stamps, and continued to sleep on the loading dock… I *chose* this route, for ~~my ego~~ I knew destitution and hunger was imminent. There will always be a master: this man, Lewis, lives a simple life and has included me in his design while I continue to seek employment and *wait.* Hurry up and wait—I may as well be in the military, only, my rectum would be retained if that were so.

I lay awake in an unfamiliar bed this morning, stared at an unusually high ceiling of this new abode, and recalled my proclamation of how I'd rather die of starvation than to continue as a slave… yet, here I stand, content.

The lingerie is of no consequence and I embrace my newfound feminine role for the time I necessitate the act.

August 7th, 2019

6:59 AM

Lewis and I walked back to his apartment after a visit to a corner-side convenience store and crossed paths with a decrepit old man accompanied by his starry-eyed wife. The man pushed a two-handed support cane on wheels, equipped with a basket; inside this basket: *a caged parakeet.* The bird's perches rattled and jostled over sidewalk cracks and the cage slid across the unsecured bottom of the basket.

The old man said, "Well hello you two!"

Lewis laughed and said, "Well, hello!" and suppressed his thoughts until we passed; thereby, Lewis expressed the disgust he experienced: "That man was *walking* his bird… Birds *fly*—he's torturing *it;* men like him are in congress, walking their damn birds. What the hell man." Lewis shook his head while I marveled at the symbolism of what we beheld. Indeed, to *walk* the bird.

Racism is a prevalent subject with my new companion, Lewis. Ah, the "injustices" we trouble ourselves with. I think Lewis' outlet for racial inequality and discrimination at the forefront of his mental processes is the acquisition of indigent white males to sexually dominate in his bedroom.

8:10 PM

I've secured employment at the one university within the city as a food service worker on campus; paid orientation begins the 13th of this month.

On my return "home" after fifteen miles of walking through the city's main streets, from banks, to the gym, to the library, and back to Lewis' apartment, I entered a dark and empty abode; Joseph Haydn played from the sound system and I inspected two pairs of black lingerie and two spiked choker collars left out for me on the bed. I undressed, showered, and garbed myself in a spiked red collar connected by a silver heart at the front of the neck, and a lacy black thong.

I've no money, yet tonight, I dine on baked fish and asparagus.

August 8th, 2019

7:12 PM

I awoke this morning to the jovial banter of Lewis and his AA (Alcoholics Anonymous) acquaintance on how both men abuse the state and federal government for monetary assistance. I languished for a moment between two pillows and reflected on my foolish pride to forgo such aid, for if I *hadn't,* I would be in an entirely different financial, living, aye—life scenario, and the chance circumstances of Lewis hailing me in the mall parking lot would have never come to fruition, and my anus would be preserved.

Lewis and I pass the time with conversation, chess, and consumption throughout the day. The roles we play as humans fascinate and perplex: the reciprocal utilization of other human beings under the pretense of virtue. There is no true justice; justice is an opinion, and justice, being the foundation on which all other virtues depend, renders all other subsets of virtues an *opinion*.

The absurdity of being alive is agonizing; humans are nothing but adaptable, egoic, flesh-bound parasites upon a terrestrial plane.

"I confess, we find among the Jews, as well as other nations, that men did sell themselves; but *it* is plain this was only to drudgery, not to slavery; for *it* is evident the person sold was not under an absolute, arbitrary, despotical power, for the master could not have power to kill him at any time, whom at a certain time he was obliged to let go free out of his service; and the master of such a servant was so far from having an arbitrary power over his life that he could not at pleasure so much as maim him, but the loss of an eye or tooth set him free."

– John Locke's Of Slavery

The title of this book is null sensationalism, though I retain the title of "Hypocrite" (and "Sociopath," and "Fool," from the two preceding titles): **Outbursts of a Hypocritical Sociopath; Thoughts of a Contented Fool**. I'll leave the jurisdiction to the DSM-5.

August 10th, 2019

7:02 AM

On my route out of a gas station with a bag of ice in-hand for Lewis, I encountered a deplorable demographic sample of downtown's homeless, converged beneath a tree, and scattered around adjacent sidewalks; each held a rectangular cardboard cut-out written on with bold black font. Each of these signs may be interpreted in meaning as: "Give me money."

I approached a young African American boy spinning a sign: "Please help. God bless." An old man with a mop of disheveled, mottled grey hair strewn over his face, and an obese bug-eyed woman (the old man's companion) seated on a broken stone curb, stood when they saw me approach. The woman clenched her fuzzed jaw and appraised my bag of ice. "I want some of 'dat."

I stopped and said, "What?"

"Somar'dat." She pointed at my slackened bag; the blaze of a ninety-degree afternoon expedited the rate which a basin of water accumulated at the bottom.

"Some of what?"

The old man grumbled, "She wants some of your ice."

My eyes shifted between both greasy visages. "I have no intention of opening this bag."

"No ice?" gummed the woman.

"No."

The old man said, "Hey, that's alright, friend. You got any change? Spare change?"

I stood stalwart, ignored the question, and looked around. A dozen men and women sat cross-legged beneath an old oak tree, dressed in basic weathered clothes, e.g., blue jeans, khakis, and discolored short sleeve t-shirts, though most were shirtless… tanned, flaccid bodies, some covered in sores and blemishes. Most faced a middle-aged man near the tree's trunk; he waved both hands and guffawed through an unintelligible dialect. The group seated before the man gazed and gaped in random directions. I wiped sweat from my neck.

The old man in front of me said, "Hey, uh, yeah we're doin' our best— get by ya' know what so you got spare change cuz'—could really use some."

"For what purpose?"

The old man waved a hand behind him towards a vacant street and said, "I gotta family, uncle and his kids and my wife here and I gotta eat and we could use spare change."

A black van pulled up in an adjacent parking lot. The bug-eyed woman, who had reseated herself on the curb, lurched to a stand and stumbled toward the vehicle. The old man diverted his attention away from me, to the woman, and shouted, "There he is again! Go see if he has any!" A man with a large fast-food drink cup and a furled grease-stained bag emerged from the driver's seat of the vehicle, reckoned the old woman hobbling towards him, slammed the driver's side door, hurried across the street, glanced over his shoulder thrice, and shook his head between each intermittent acknowledgment of his pursuer.

"Yeah—get em', get em'!" said the old man. He chuckled, stepped one pace towards me, and said, "So you got any spare change?"

"No."

"Thank you sir; well, God bless you sir; if you ever have spare change stop by again—ya' know, I mean, you don't need to but thank you."

"You're welcome." I walked away from the scene and prodded the extent of the large reservoir of water at the bottom of the ice bag with my alternate hand.

11:22 AM

I sit in the lobby of an information research facility within the city mall in wait of training for my first day of a recruiter/interviewer employment role to supplement my full-time employment position at the university. I've secured many masters at once.

3:53 PM

One moment I'm dressed to impress, reading surveys aloud at 170 words-per-minute; the next, I'm at a gym—dressed for the road, and after that—"home," where I strip down into lingerie and perform fellatio for a man twice my age. I consider my life circumstances from an objective viewpoint and marvel at the duplicity of human presentations: what we project ourselves to be, and what we are—an illusory contrast between real and unreal designed by the ego to delude others.

Awe and nausea. I knew myself best in solitude, on the road, behind dumpsters, amongst forest glades, atop the concrete of a loading dock.

August 13th, 2019

1:07 PM

A train horn blows from beyond the interior of a performing arts building, the setting for a mass employee ~~indoctrination~~ orientation I attend for a food service role.

"I hate when people cry," states a high-power woman in high-heels and a black dress. "When in doubt, shout *it* out," this woman proclaims as her motto... Pizza and fried chicken is rolled out on carts to feed the flock. "When in doubt, shout *it* out," the woman repeats this self-affirmation, a commandment. "I want you all to adopt this philosophy." The woman gestures a full circle with both hands in front of her. Several heads nod; a few sets of eyes glisten; one jaw slackens.

5:06 PM

Malaise and fever; I suffer from an anal fissure or abscess. I experience no pleasure in any sexual act performed for or received from a man. Lewis is openly gay and proud. My subservient state is the primary source of pleasure for him. He performs fellatio on me for his own enjoyment at increased frequencies as our relationship develops; however, I've yet to ejaculate through this stimulation and must resort to masturbation to satisfy him.

I lie in convalescence between walks from my newest employment at the university, where I learn the ~~obscure art~~ process of frying pre-cut chicken filets.

The gross depravity that is my life has amounted to everything I could have ever hoped or expected; I achieve a record personal low point monthly.

I defecate malformed feces coated with a milky, translucent mucus, and discharge an involuntary pus expulsion from my anus with a discomfited frequency throughout my days. I've researched the potentialities of an STD, though my symptoms are of an infection.

My anus is barred from foreign entry henceforth until my death. Only a necrophiliac(s) may reap my body for the sake of lust. Lewis believes I jest or lie as a means to circumvent sexual servitude. My resolve is adamant.

Life is well, I have a roof over my head, a well-nourished body, two jobs—one of which authorizes to feed me straight from the kitchen cooler for free, and I have this exquisite little novelty of word-play.

Lewis is an excellent companion and I have no qualms with his character; on the contrary, he cares for me, albeit, to fill the void within himself, though why else do we care? The *care* to *aspire:* the fool's path, or rather, an unhappy man. I'm grateful for the genuine goodwill of my fellow human beings—I must reiterate to believe *it*. Lewis purchases antibiotics for my devastated pus-filled rectum, and I lay in a warm bed each night. I've no idea what I am every moment. I consider no ethnicity, gender, sexuality, or individuality; I've abandoned all niceties, all pretenses, and ponder on what remains. I lay with a man or woman: There is no difference in the consciousness relatable by empathy, only the temperament, the shape, and the odor (pheromones/hormones), serve to distinguish. *All* is repugnant.

August 16th, 2019

10:16 PM

I glanced at an open bookstore display at the college campus bookstore and read *"Higher Education."* A few bullets down: "Functionalist: A functionalist believes that everything in a society exists to serve a function-"; I stopped reading, for the category struck me with immediate notions of absurdity—as do all categories and labels. What function does a child rapist serve, beneficial *or* detrimental? And if a child rapist is considered out of the realm of a functionalist's consideration, I instead wonder why there is a name for a philosophical state of mind that is self-evident.

"Things exist to serve a function."

"No," said a buffoon, "You function to exist!"

Or is *it* self-evident?

What would a child rapist think of the matter?

"Yeah, yeah, the ones with raw, red asses are the best. Don't mind any sores down there."

"Should I use protection?"

"Why would you need to protect yourself? How could these little ones possibly be of any threat?"

"I meant from communicable diseases."

"I wouldn't be eating them if they were diseased."

"Oh… Well…"

"Are you good?"

"Yeah. Yeah, I guess I'm good."

"Alright, now remember, don't give 'em any leeway, no matter how loud they scream or cry. Besides, when they tremble while you're in 'em you get that extra vibratory sensation, so look for one that already seems like they're suffering, for the superior ride—you know what I mean? Also, if any of 'em look like they're on the verge of death, let Carl know when you're finished."

"Okay."

The statuesque body of a four-year-old-boy wept beneath the sweaty palm of Ren. A glossy mane of sweat sheened on the spotless back of the child, illuminated by four eight-foot long fluorescent rectangular fixtures separated by five inches of unfinished concrete ceiling. Ren cupped his other hand around the boy's left buttock, squeezed, and dropped his hand by his thigh. Ren raised his hand with intent to clutch the buttock again, tighter, though he refrained, and instead allowed his hand to linger millimeters away. His immaculate fingernails contoured against the radiant edges of damp flesh highlighted by the glare of overhead light. Ren's fingers trembled; his heart palpitated, and he retracted—shimmied away from the boy, and braced both palms on a purple mattress embossed with teal patterns of lilacs and long-stemmed thorny roses. Ren swallowed air and stared down at his abdomen, at his moistened, unkempt pubic triangle, at his five-inch flaccid penis, blemished by a membranous squiggle of blood beneath a circumcised head. Ren lowered his body and stopped when the tip of his penis grazed an off-centered divet in the mattress. He breathed hoarse inhalations through his nose and quiet exhalations through a crease between two chapped lips that he licked with a compressed tongue. The supple body of the boy enshrouded by Ren's shadow convulsed with intermittent spasms.

August 17th, 2019

9:04 AM

"We live by faith, not by sight!" said St. Boniface; a handaxe swung by his velveted hands sundered the first of one of the hundreds of ancient trees considered sacred by a pagan sect of the village locale.

Thongs of pagans—blasphemers and heathens, by the decree of this holy man: Boniface, and his disciples… yes… *throngs* of pagans gazed at the maimed trunk of a three-hundred-year-old oak and murmured anguished cries with each weighty strike of iron on wood. St. Boniface paused and said, "God's love will not tolerate your worship of all things begotten by the lord of evil. Look to the sky and close your eyes! Feel *our* Lord's love!" Bursts of splintered wood resumed and resonated throughout an undisturbed wilderness. Fanatical peasants armed with cudgel and spear stood by to bulwark St. Boniface, to advocate the quest of God's love—proliferated, endowed—nay, *bestowed* upon their wayward fellow men misaligned by the influence of evil.

"What're the options on the menu tonight?" said one tree branch-wielding peasant to a nearby priest.

The priest glowered and said, "What?"

"What we be havin' back at the church tonight, to eat?"

"You have interrupted my incantation."

The peasant scratched his nose, licked his lips, stepped forward, backward, stood idle for four seconds, and said, "What's for dinner?"

The priest leered at the peasant and said, "Sheep and sugar loaves."

"Aye." The peasant smiled.

August 18th, 2019

5:11 PM

Two raccoons scurried out from the shadows of a twilit shanty and stood on their hind haunches; both sniffed the air, gazed in my direction, and hastened back to the narrow space between two garbage cans each emerged from.

"Damn, I tell ya', sometimes I forget I ever was human—hell, I often think I still am sometimes, with situations like that," said a disease-ridden raccoon to a malnourished raccoon.

"I don't remember any of *it*, or if I ever even was human, like you keep going on about."

"I'm *sure* of *it;* I don't remember my life or my body, but I remember the sensations, the feelings... I ended up as this creature when I died because of some unknowable universal schematic."

"That's interesting."

"Yeah—I'm tellin' ya', I see these humans and I wanna shout out to 'em, but I'm in *this* body now, yet, everything is familiar, only now... *It*'s more than that; it's... *it*'s indescribable; I can't even begin to convey... I mean..."

"Are you going to eat those eggshells?"

"No."

"Ah, well, alright then."

Around the city, on the main street, at three to four street intervals, there are signposts: small, white backgrounds, bold black text, adhered to two wires embedded in the dirt. On one side reads, **"Don't Give Up,"** and on the other, **"You Matter."** An apartment complex courtyard features a large billboard that reads, "Welcome to [City Name]. Your life matters here. Don't give up!"

On my arrival from the airport and along my walk to the city center, I figured myself to have selected a city with the highest suicide rates nationwide. A few days ago I deduced the origin of the signs (not a bored and benevolent individual that I hypothesized) are from a Presbyterian church. Out front, on the church grounds, a digital sign cycled through proverbial phrases and marketing jingles. "You Matter," and "Don't Give Up," flicked across the screen, accompanied by a flash of pixelated sparkles.

6:49 PM

"Lo, vermin, creature of rot and waste, destroyer of the immaculate, what principles hast thou defiled by thy presence! Enough! Roll out the corpses of baked children, O, Venerable One! Indulge in the nutrition of the Gods, bestowed upon your brethren—by the womb! Exalted being, you are *chosen!*"

And so, the priests appraised the majordomo with muffled claps of pink fingers against white palms, for the boys were well-spiced, and the men, satiated.

"I wish to be instructed in your mastery of the culinary arts!" said an enamored priest.

"Inquire with the demiurge," said the majordomo. A hush fell throughout the cathedral cloister.

"You are but a majordomo," said a nameless priest, "For one of your status to defer another to the will of the demiurge is forbidden—nay… impossible!"

The majordomo forced a wry grin and said, "The demiurge is responsible for the flesh; *it,* above all, appreciates fine cuisine."

"Heathen!" said a priest; "Blasphemer!" said another. The ensemble encircled the majordomo and assaulted him with verbal lashings; to no effect of this attack, several priests synchronized vehement ululations. Four of the priests unsheathed five-and-a-half-inch crescent ceremonial daggers from sash-bound holsters and disemboweled the majordomo.

August 19th, 2019

9:13 AM

A flash of a pan on a stark-white stovetop accentuated the click of a dial to heat setting "6," a tab higher than "medium." A small incandescent bulb illuminated an adjacent blue-grey counter on both sides of the stovetop. Opposite of the stovetop, behind a home kitchen work area, a man sat on a simple cushioned wooden chair at an expanse of identical blue-grey countertop constructed a foot lower than the kitchen area. The seated man said to the cook in the kitchen, "What is that?"

"Peanut butter and honey." Smoke rose from an overheated section of bubbled peanut butter at the pan's center.

"What are you making?"

"Peanut butter and honey," repeated the cook.

The seated man observed the stoic countenance of the cook engaged with cookware, two open jars of peanut butter, and one jar of honey on the counter. The seated man said, "That's really all you're making?"

The cook disengaged from the pan, turned to the fridge, procured a twenty-two-ounce container, opened the lid, slid a spoon along the edge of the container, and plopped two tablespoons worth of margarine onto a heap of smoking browned peanut butter and honey amalgamate in the pan.

August 20th, 2019

8:31 PM

Sorrowful remorse. I desire nothing: the antithesis of being, to subsume with a void. Each day is routine, senseless, nonsense. I've no satisfaction in any of *it*. There is listless treason of my mind against my body; both are unsubstantial vessels for a life of no desire.

The will compels me to persist, whereby I feed, exert, and work. Life is an extemporaneous gift from a disillusioned god.

9:42 PM

I've been heckled by a total of four intoxicated men, each of whom have preached to me the existence of "God" since my landing in this no-name city of Arkansas until now. There is a definite causality between spirituality and *being* "poor in spirit," in the manner in which the lack of spirit promotes the desire *for* spirit, i.e., spirituality. Alcohol is a superb catalyst.

August 21st, 2019

10:07 AM

Each day is a pass of moot, inconsequential progress encapsulated within a limited realm of individual understandings. I play at war (Lewis' favorite game is chess) in substituion of assplay, and consume a modest quantity of food to sustain me for each day of labor to enable me to return home to play at more war.

I'm sickened by the pall of life. Antibiotics and fiber supplements have remedied the condition of my colon. I've enforced prohibition of my anus from further usage and have restricted the sexual satisfaction of Lewis to oral "play," though there is no "play" for me, even when I'm the receiver, for the engagement disgusts me and I desire to be engrossed with solitude. However, Lewis treats me with respect and by consequence I owe him my company—indebted, for a time... two... three months, perhaps less... I must play at war.

11:04 PM

A shepherd's lantern flickered. Out of the darkness, a wolf arose from slumber and said, "This hunger kills me."

The shepherd scratched his brow and said, "I hear the wind lash at my ears."

The wolf growled, began a patrol along the shade of a grove, and said, "You despicable man."

"That wind again," said the shepherd. "That *damnable* wind."

August 24th, 2019

3:11 PM

Each day I think of death, and what *that* is, *exactly,* is nothing. I'm haunted by reality, what *it* is, the culture, the people, the populace, the inane endeavors. I shine the "looking glass" onto the metaphorical waters of my mind and grovel before the reflection. Self-assigned meanings in life are routes to personal damnation.

The wolf said, "I hunger, yet you would ignore my plight?"

The shepherd said, "If I were to feed you, I'd be at a loss; what gain would I attain from the satisfaction of your desire?"

"A compatriot, an ally." The wolf barred two rows of browned teeth.

August 25th, 2019

1:09 PM

The shepherd said, "I've no necessity to be affiliated with any of those titles, especially by one of your ilk."

"Oh?"

"*Yes*—you fiendish beast, incapable of devotion and steadfastness of character. Begone!"

The wolf paced an eight-foot semi-circle over blades of beaten grass and snarled. "We could accomplish so much together," the wolf's voice went unspoken; no syllable had been uttered throughout; the entirety of the conversation elapsed within the shepherd's internal egoic rhetoric. The wolf leaped at the shepherd's throat. The shepherd hammered at the wolf's head with a closed fist and shouted a pained cry, for another pair of wolves emerged from nearby overgrowth to tear at the top of the shepherd's head and at the wrist of his left hand.

4:36 PM

A sharp spike of anguished pain channeled through the shepherd's synapses. An intolerable duress wrought upon his consciousness by a slew of panicked thoughts elicited an inundation of guilt, subverting his faculties with primal terror. A surge of blood erupted from a gash at the base of his exposed neck. Serrated canines lacerated a mesh of tendons and striated muscle amongst a network of bones converged at his wrist. "Just what am I?" he pleaded in silence; the pitiful, unspoken thought resonated. The wolves feasted on a desolate tundra. The sun set below a white-lined horizon and life thrived into the morning hours.

Set fire to paper.

5:08 PM

From an objective viewpoint, my life is now set in such conditions that I begin to thrive.

Beetle on the window—little god, tell me of your desires.

Uplifting jazz music mutes the cries of a moribund baby bird outside an apartment window.

6:16 PM

Whimsical flute music plays on the death of a moribund baby bird.

August 27th, 2019

10:37 PM

"Baethan, you are the most important person in my life right now," said Lewis.

Lewis is an astute, fifty-nine-year-old, 6'0, stocky, African American man, with a keen creative mode expressed through dance and music, and an amateur acoustic guitar player. Lewis is a recent ex-convict, sentenced to jail for eighteen months on account of a failed drug sale. Throughout his duration of incarceration, Lewis experienced four months in solitary confinement due to battering a cellmate on account of the cellmate's refusal to shower.

Lewis occupies his time with other gay men and corresponds with men who desire to be "saved" from their bondage (sexual enslavement) with other men, i.e., mate poaching.

Affirmations are abundant from my companion despite a lack of my reciprocation; I am indifferent to circumstances and enjoy the companionship provided by each other's company which permits us to thrive.

I've liberated myself from sexual "expectancy." Instead, I am enjoyed for conversational intimacy and mental stimulation. Lewis invites other willing men to his home in my absence to fulfill his desires.

To sit on Lewis' lap and caress and kiss his short, compact, salt and pepper hair is a natural outcome of shared humanity. To lay beside Lewis in bed and grasp each other's hands, nuzzle our heads against one another, is a blip of nothing, a recurrent necessity of the human creature, a bitter longing—never to be satisfied, primal and object to failure.

I said, "You are the only person in my life and therefore the most important."

August 28th, 2019

8:33 AM

Lewis' mind is overwrought with perceived social injustice, i.e., African Americans (or blacks) are subjugated, marginalized, and prosecuted. I consider each element of Lewis' chosen conviction daily, how he allocates time each morning, afternoon, and evening to the consumption of media displayed on his phone that is pertinent to racial injustice. I witness a perpetual victim—an ex-convict, once immersed in a lavish lifestyle rife with young, troubled, wayward (white) men—to *control, dominate, and manipulate* under a sexual dominion. Now, removed and estranged from the financial amplitude that preceded him before being jailed on account of a failed lucrative drug trade, Lewis lives in the studio schoolhouse apartment that he now shares with me and is supported by the welfare system utilizing a (fraudulent) disability claim. Once the remainder of Lewis' eighteen months of probation has elapsed, he intends to move to Seattle, Washington… and has suggested that I travel with him under the hopeful expectation that we will still be affiliated with each other by then.

I have no love for any man, myself most of all—this fleshy vessel of delicate growth and decay.

A train whistle blows; steel wheels rattle onward. Every schism of the mind is an illusion.

I owe Lewis a debt which he perceives to be null; my companionship is enough repayment, he claims. I disagree, and arrange to reimburse and pay my dues of rent, bills, food, hygienic and medical amenities provided to me—not out of benevolence, but on account of the experience I have to know what veiled entrapment is. My repayment will render us equals and negate the pseudo-dominate role perpetuated by Lewis upon my initial entry into his home with nothing of material value—except my *body*—to provide. A slave to a slave… I think back on the quote by Epictetus I chose when I first began this installment in November: the epigraph of this discharge of inconsequential thoughts written on paper with a pen, to what

435

will be digital documentation, to a published book for a wastrel, finalized, moot and valueless unless otherwise assigned a value by a consumer.

Reflect on the validity of Epictetus' timeless words, reaffirmed by my actions, a testament to the consistent cycles of humanity throughout the ages. I am a veritable *Concubinus* of ancient Rome; however, I serve a pleb.

August 30th, 2019

7:21 AM

A rotunda of spinal columns reflected dull rays of moonlight and bedazzled a clan of wayward warriors midway on a quest—a mission from God, to spread the love of their faith.

"Behold," said a bishop garbed in gold-embossed white robes, elegant scepter in-hand—raised to a rift in dark clouds converged amidst a pale sky. "Observe what our brothers have left behind."

Throngs of warriors stood, statuesque, transfixed by the massive monument of bone.

"You may not fall while prostrated before God!" shouted the bishop. Red silk tassels ruffled from a stagnant wind beneath two outstretched arms. The bishop grimaced and back stepped onto a mound of dust: a reaction to furious roars produced by the bowed heads of a platoon under his command.

August 31st, 2019

7:23 PM

"When two men sit in silence… you don't want that to happen with another man," said Lewis.

A speaker blares either classical or jazz music while we work together to survive; what is the theme of life?

Is the meaning of life enjoyment and contentment? What else is there to care or aspire to? When hunched over this crucible of memories, observed by my delusional convictions of self-directed thought, I wonder— the pathetic clown that I am.

SEPTEMBER

September 1st, 2019

1:26 PM

"You may not fall while prostrated before God," muttered a deacon to the shepherd.

The shepherd lay mangled in a pool of cold blood and stared up at a cloudless orange sky streaked with subtle blue hints of an evening come to a close: a finale to what the shepherd knew as life. A crowd of peasants cheered and feasted on clumps of rye and watery beer.

Dogs tore into limp chunks of flesh held taut by the bloodied torso of the shepherd.

"How dare I transgress against your word," the shepherd strained to speak through agonized breaths.

"There is no word," retorted the deacon. "Action compels. If you are to continue with this mode of being, you are to be devastated."

"I-"

"There is *only* devastation; your life is a tragic comedy. I am elated to see you die."

"I perish in your name, my lord."

The deacon's eyes narrowed.

I am desired for my body and intellectual capacity; this submissive life I live as my chosen act is sustained through will and vitality.

3:02 PM

I've transposed from a militaristic clockwork enterprise to a salubrious vacation of homelessness—on the verge of destitution, to being made a slave of once more, the slave I *desired* to be and have become. My sexual arousal is null concerning men *and* women. There would be a severance of the ego to commit to another human being to fulfill any personal void. I am bound by another man and relinquish my masculinity with the expectancy of a favorable incremental gain.

5:46 PM

Wishes are equivalent to wet dreams.

6:46 PM

There is an emptiness in one's repose, a sentiment of heroic failure. I wonder what all my work is and find myself distracted by want. The anguish imposed on oneself is a palpable substance felt among the synapses of one's mind as pain. If one's body is crippled and/or shackled to a bedpost, confined, etc., what else is there but repose? The mind revolts and seeks stimulus.

"Hail, Satan, commander Rakishuka reporting."
"Speak."
"News from the overworld: St. Boniface fell the Pagan's trees at quadrant three-fourteen north, one-bound, westward."
"Ah… *Boniface,*" Satan laughed.

September 2nd, 2019

9:02 PM

These are the last vestiges of thought I experience. What is a motley expulsion of stories and poems but an escape to squander my reality?

September 3rd, 2019

10:35 PM

Worms on sunlit pavement: a writhing of pink tissue on heated cement.

September 4th, 2019

9:07 PM

Up and down the tarnished concrete avenues, up and down, the slouched vagabond roamed, eyes set to the brightened slates of heated roads. A noon sun highlighted the scene: clay huts and squalor, stacks of timber, and windowless openings in each abode revealed a haggard mother, grizzled father, forlorn child, or darkened space rife with dust.

Dogs howled, yelped, barked, and whined; a cacophonous reverb of labor muffled the beasts: Men engaged with strenuous manual work groaned, shouted... and scowled at the vagabond hunched over a wide concrete road.

Worms writhed at the vagabond's rag-encased feet; he knelt low and plucked scorched remnants of pink bodies rendered an ashy black by an overhead star.

"That's a supreme undertaking," whispered an old maid into the left ear of her preoccupied daughter. The old maid pointed a gnarled finger two inches beyond a paneless window threshold at the vagabond and sighed a rueful whistle through a gap in her top row of marred teeth.

The daughter gazed out the windows, disinterested, listless, and said, "What is he doing?"

The old maid inhaled through two hairy nostrils and shook her head.

A burlap sack filled with the corpses of dead and moribund worms hung slack from the vagabond's limp wrist. Carts driven by emboldened asses and malnourished horses rattled past either side of the vagabond; he hunched low and squeezed a plump, dry, and blackened specimen between index and middle finger, sniffed twice, and slipped the worm into the sack.

"He's searching for worms to eat—poor old man; look at him there. You understand what I'm saying girl?"

The daughter cringed and said, "Why would anyone ever eat worms?"

"When you've no other options, you eat what you can. Decent rain this morning draws the creatures out and then they cook on the roads by noon... my, look at him, just look at how he's dressed. Despicable, really."

September 5th, 2019

9:47 PM

My life is a jungle fetish orgy of exertion and consumption.

September 6th, 2019

7:38 PM

I theorize that my senior chief from the division I attended while at Navy boot camp—the man who excised the contents of my original journal and confiscated the pages with no chance of redemption, is responsible for the withholdment of my writing device, phone, and birth certificate.

Yes, my life is a pathetic comedy; a fifty-nine-year-old African American man lusts for my body; my mind tantalizes him; we strength train together with a bench, pull-up bar, and a configurable set of 52 lb dumbbells I've purchased.

To write in several small journals for the last five months has been an extreme impediment to efficient thoughts... in a way, a rueful, agonized way, I remember with fondness my time endured while embroiled with the Navy.

I've been blessed—in all *truth*.

September 7th, 2019

9:40 PM

Asceticism results in physical weakness and vulnerability: a downside of the practice. As a result, one *must* adopt a stoic philosophy to endure the judgment of one's peers when one's diminished physique is perceived.

Consumption results in lust, the ultimate sin, second to wrath, yet is this *so* "bad"?

September 8th, 2019

3:01 PM

A repository of filthy thoughts accentuates strength training while listening to J.S. Bach.

Consumption and rest this productive Sunday afternoon. I regained control of my life with the purchase of a new phone and laptop, due to arrive in two days. What else is there but the exposition?

September 9th, 2019

8:27 AM

When you stand to kiss another man you may glimpse a twinge of humanity: another consciousness trapped in a cage.

September 11th, 2019

10:26 AM

I've acquired a new writing device and phone; authority and control over my technological life and writing venture are reinstated with the full force of my sensible faculties applied.

Lewis and I live a romantic, sensual (sexless, to Lewis' dissatisfaction and my contentment), and amiable life together. I've decided to abandon our mutual, reciprocal venture more than thrice—in personal theory and conversation between us, though I've reconsidered on account of the good we provide to each other. Both of us fulfill a meaningful role that benefits the other; our symbiosis is remarkable considering our disparate traits.

For the moment, I relish the use of my new system's keyboard, in retrospect of the months affiliated with the Navy—my journal pages ripped from the folds of my metaphorical ego… Alas, I am becoming once more, by the grace of Taiwanese factory ~~workers~~ slaves.

9:28 PM

"He looks ragged, and cold, and miserable," said the girl to the old woman; both gazed out a paneless clay window and watched the vagabond bend over a cluster of worms strewn over a cracked segment of the concrete road.

"Yes, well," said the old woman, "That's all there is to *it*. Whenever you recognize *it*, look in the mirror, young girl, and tell me what you see."

"That's not nice to say."

"Now now, don't you worry; just watch," the woman pointed out the window.

The woman and the girl watched the vagabond depart the small Noname village, whereby he clambered up a mountain peak to an ovoid entry of a hidden recess weathered out of a stone cliffside. On arrival, the vagabond descended into a cavernous alcove and met with a wretch.

The wretch said, "I'll give you three of these," and held out a handful of black beetles, each the size of his thumb's fingernail.

"That won't do; you'll have to do far better than that." The vagabond squeezed the bloated abdomen of an enormous pink worm. Both scrutinized the worm's flesh by a candlelight positioned on a narrow rectangular wooden table between the two of them.

"This is all you'll get," the wretch inhaled a sharp spike of air into his flared nostrils, "and if you attempt to barter, I'll sever your spine and consume your heart and liver."

Silence lingered between both men for twenty-six seconds.

The vagabond said, "You don't have the gall, nor the conviction."

"You're right."

"You've got a deal, then."

The wretch whispered, "Really?"

"Of course."

"Well, alright then."

Both shook hands and exchanged three beetles and a worm.

September 14th, 2019

11:45 PM

My desolation of the mind is paramount.

Lewis' lifestyle is reminiscent of my father's. I'm intrigued, for both are at the extreme opposite ends of the political and ethnic spectrum, yet both have adopted a lifestyle of leisure. My father survives on a pension; Lewis survives on fraudulent welfare checks for a fallacious leg disability.

Both men consume coffee from dawn till dusk, prepare food with equal flair, have a history of alcoholism and drug abuse—though Lewis is thirty-three-years sober of alcohol and marijuana.

Don't you understand what this is, reader, who has endured me thus far to care?

I have found refuge in the providence of a man of similar intellect, wisdom, and self-prescribed psychoticism comparable to the effect of my father's demeanor. I'm disturbed by my thoughts.

There is an abundance of women at both establishments where I work who express interest in sexual relations and offer me contact information; I accept, with suppressed remorse, for I injure all who I associate with on account of my self-invoked martyrdom perpetuated by my self-prescribed meaning of life. Every conversation and romantic pass of the body is a distraction to the mind's labors.

I pay for the behavior I practice with derision expressed on my countenance all-the-while.

A young woman named Amethyst longs for me after a few exchanges of dialogue. I'm disturbed by an e-mail message she composed for me after three days of knowing each other (conducting movie surveys as co-workers at a mall). The last proclamation she yelled at me while parting today, "Love is a philosophy!" amplifies my suspicion of Amethyst's character: a sycophantic vixen.

Yes, disturbed and perturbed... titillated too. I remain indifferent to the matter and play the act; Amethyst had been disappointed and "mad" at my initial rejection of her, yet I professed my attraction for her to alleviate her self-doubt and have condemned myself to wantonness.

September 15th, 2019

2:28 PM

A demagogue leered at a crowd of plebian consumers and said, "I endorse all to eat bananas at sunrise and sunset."

The crowd roared a boisterous shout of approval.

"I'm humbled by your approbation," said the demagogue; he lowered himself to one knee and bent a crowned head towards a speckled marble floor.

One pleb upraised a furrowed eyebrow, lifted a hand, and said, "Aye, aye, I'm struck with consternation, for what need is there for bananas when we've barrels full o' oats to feed on at leisure, at whatever hour we please already?"

"Yes," a young girl with two brown and braided locks chimed in, "bananas are a weird shaped fruit—and so *yellow.*"

"Aye," decried an old woman, "and they only taste pleasant after being afflicted with the black rot of Sheol; a damned fruit deserves banishment!"

Half the crowd resounded with a declamatory lamentation.

The demagogue shed a tear onto a marble floor and whispered, "My people."

September 17th, 2019

10:12 PM

It's all fun and games until I'm gone.

September 18th, 2019

7:35 AM

"Don't treat me like a bitch," I said to Lewis after returning from work while we stood in the kitchen. I wore a red spiked heart collar around my neck, black-laced lingerie hiked up between my ass cheeks, and new furry bootstraps around my ankles.

"You're all up on me right now Baethan, back up—back up."

I repeated myself to a man who perceives himself as a victim of the situation, who considered me to lack respect for him. Indeed, *it*'s difficult to *not* be a bitch when one is dressed for the role.

This morning Lewis and I grappled with one another after I attempted to walk away from his command to sit on the bed next to him. An arm wrapped around my waist and laid me on my back, whereby, on account of adrenaline and survival instinct, I rebounded and maneuvered myself towards the kitchen, both of us locked in a grapple. Several attempts to restrain and immobilize me were countered due to my greater total strength of the body and the agileness of my reactions. I knocked Lewis' grapple attempts away twice with the classic "palms against the shoulders" move.

A few more sentences were exchanged, coffee brewed, and life ebbed on… I rebel against my self-assigned slavery, weary of the slavish lifestyle: commutes to and from a designated money-reaping activity, back to exert the body for the sake of growth, to consume—and to have these activities dictated in *time*—my most valuable commodity—by external beings! Always! If I am a cog in this gross human empire, I desire to be lubed and extracted from the comical machine and discarded amongst a colossal heap of dregs, for lack of suitable words, i.e., I serve fried chicken and waffle fries on a college campus, conduct movie trailer opinion surveys on weekends, strength train, write, and read. Trials and tribulations enhance life; conflict breeds strife and change.

I pass a homeless man by a bus stop on my walk to Lewis' apartment each night. A few other homeless men lay on abandoned scaffolds to rest while the sun sets and casts a somber twilight over stark terrain, though this man in particular, with his detritus and belongings littered in front of him each night, catches my attention. Conversations with this homeless man revealed his convictions of once being a major influence on the decrease of the city's crime rate, of owning clothing warehouses and a brothel in the past, and to have killed people if he deemed the act "just."

September 21st, 2019

7:31 AM

On my hour walk to and from the university, I pass a locale populated by peculiar denizens who congregate on the back porch of a low-income backroad; these persons: haggard, boisterous, dressed in loose-fitted t-shirts and ratty pants… despicable cretins, to describe characters of esteem worthy of adjectives to denote baseness and vicious behavior.

"Left, left… left, right, left…" a man called out from the convergence on the back porch. The stifled harmonics evoked nostalgic feelings of dread. I refrained from a head turn, or to grimace, or to flaunt a gesture of disapproval towards the direction of the jeerer and his compatriots; no, instead, I assumed the rigidity of one on the march: Fists clenched, knees upraised, posture stiffened, I stepped along sidewalk cracks and stared straight ahead while those on the porch to my distant right observed and laughed.

Later, after a Friday shift, early in the evening, I passed the house on my route and again reckoned the half-dozen men idling on the porch. I turned my head and smiled; the man who had previously sung cadence began anew: "Left, left… left, right, left."

Instead of his anticipated reaction of me performing as before, I turned on a heel, ninety degrees, and walked my "natural" march towards the group, who, as a combined conglomeration of consciousnesses, focused on me in a manner equivalent to a great television broadcast. Each balanced their individual weight on a rickety wooden rail and smirked. I said, "What are you all doing out here?"

No response—from any stupefied countenance. The one who sang cadence said, "What?"

I said, "I see all of you out here each day; what are you doing?"

"We're in rehab," said the cadence singer. He grinned.

I said, *"Oh*—alright," delighted.

Another scrawny, wiry man, dressed in a stained white t-shirt three sizes too large, said, "Yeah *oh!*" A few of the others shifted stances and cocked their heads.

I said, "I've been recently separated from the U.S. Navy, so to hear that cadence caught my-"

"Oh, you were in the Navy huh?" The cadence singer leaned forward on the rail.

"The Navy eh?" said another nameless face, dark and haggard.

"Yes," I said, "I was in boot camp for about a month and a half, then I was sep-"

"Where are you from?" shouted the oversized shirt wearer.

"I'm from upstate New York."

The cadence singer said, with a mock northerner accent, "You're from New *York*," and forced a fake laugh, which incited a few others to utter several affected chuckles.

I said, "Why are you in rehab?"

"For drugs," said the cadence singer; he shrugged.

"But all of life is a drug, from the food we eat to the oxygen we breathe."

The men shifted on my proclamation and voiced several affirmations of my words: "Amen brother"; "Aye"; "You said *it.*"

The cadence singer gazed at me with amiable circumspection expressed in his eyes and said, "You may want to get going before the boss sees you."

I said, "Is this private property?"

"No, but *we* shouldn't be talking to anyone; we're all straight from prison, or jail."

On cue, the proprietor of the establishment stepped out of the back door and pushed his way between the small crowd. The man's compressed facial features scrutinized me for a moment; he frowned and said, "Can I help you?"

I said, "No."

Silence overtook the group; heads turned to acknowledge the unwanted presence of power and authority. The newcomer man retreated a step, skewed his body sideways, and waved at me: a farewell gesture.

I waved, nodded, and resumed my journey back to Lewis' apartment; not a word was spoken by any man on my disengagement, though I felt sets of eyes affixed to my back before I rounded the corner of a filthy blue dumpster.

9:12 AM

My second book is scheduled for publication. After I signed the documentation for approval, I studied the cover art once more and realized, to my dissatisfaction, that I had overlooked a supreme error (in my judgment): The word "Sociopath" lacks a semicolon. On this recognition, I lapsed into a moment of intense consternation, though the thoughts abated, and what was extreme dissatisfaction metamorphosed into contented acceptance. The front cover error is a testament to my care and competence.

10:38 PM

Languishment of thought and the retreat to the comforts of flesh and material entitlements bestows me with a newfound woe. I've done well for myself, thrust amongst this new land, and find myself surrounded by pursuers. What else is there but an incredible torment, self-inflicted by a mind wracked with guilt—taught unto-*it*self, damn *it* all; there is no retreat or withdrawal from reality—fool; take a long look at yourself and wonder, be awed by the self-examination.

A man coughs amongst a crowd of orchestra observers. All men and women seated among rows of thirty-six bleachers turn their heads and shout, "Quiet your sullen mouth, *fiend!*"

Now *that's* an escape from reality—*fools!*

"I've sinned! I've sinned," cried the damned, condemned to a life of eternal torment. Lewis observes me while he lays strewn over a bed, enraptured by my visage at work, the transition of thoughts to objects. Watch me, fool, for what I am, and my manner of being; there is a creepiness in my arched over pose, focused on the dexterity of a few digits against a template.

"Oh, you have such a straight posture!" said an upright pleb.

11:02 PM

Crickets chirp.

I live in an alternate reality of my father's home.

Except, a fifty-nine-year-old African American man has claimed me as a "bitch"; I rebelled, and order had been shattered. Lewis cried into my arms as a result of his "ego," he proclaimed.

I apologized thereafter for the withdrawal of my trust.

For my self-chosen burden and design, I am vindictive of myself; therefore I am vindictive of others due to my projections—manifest by my thoughts, this consciousness, constrained to this body; there is nothing else but ~~hell~~ perdition or ~~heaven~~ sanctum; make your choice and consume the poison of a self-prescribed equanimity.

September 22nd, 2019

1:04 PM

With accumulation of over $2,000 in credit card debt with intent to accrue at least $200 more in a security deposit for a new apartment and $405 for a month's rent, I have become a slave among many.

September 24th, 2019

9:36 AM

None are to be trusted. All I encounter on the streets and on porches desire to speak—*only* to bemoan of issues, to gripe, to lament, to *complain,* in a manner equivalent to this vile documentation I maintain; what better am I? I am fit for damnation, for having squandered my faculties in favor of gross consumption and aversion of my fellow men and women.

"Intelligent" and "smart" are the two words employed to describe my character that I hear uttered by others more than any other adjective, yet if the utterers of these inconsequential labels were aware of my *viciousness...* of my unadulterated malevolence of thought, I would be judged despicable and pathetic; therefore, *I* know *myself,* and judge my own character with the precognition of one who lives and acts by personal truth.

I'm maligned and envied in secret by those I associate with, my closest comrades, most of all. Envy is an atrocious feeling to suffer on account of another's doubt. I'm disgusted with myself to feel the slightest twinge of envy, for those who have exerted their physical bodies and consumed more than myself, for their girth, for the base behavior of being a creature of excessive consumption, yet, I yearn for muscle mass, to intimidate and repel the feeble-minded and those who see only the flesh for flesh, and not the intellect inherit—a folly, on my behalf.

I'm devastated by my relations—disappointed, disillusioned, and confounded by the complexity of the machinations perpetrated by *every* human being I encounter; by this mode of observation, I determine the synchronicity of consciousness, of the sameness retained, of *our* parasitic egoism. The individual is a lie.

10:24 PM

A cleric said, "I wish to enjoy a good life without being judged by others."

A villain said, "You vile pig, God damn you."

"Which one?"

"The *only* God."

"This sounds familiar."

"How so?" said the villain, spiked cudgel in-hand.

"Familiar to the moment a few hours ago when I clubbed a man to death for his variant expression of faith," said the cleric. He stepped forward; a flourish of a gauntleted hand revealed a large, imposing mace, gilded in silver plating.

"Oh… " said the villain, "What do you profess?"

"I profess that *I* am God," said the cleric.

The villain conceded: "Alright."

And God was good.

September 26th, 2019

9:13 PM

The second installment of this valueless trite has been produced and published for purchase on online venues at an inordinate price.

Dealings with the homeless to and from the establishment where I work ends soon on account of the acquisition of a new apartment on the east side of the city which allows me a twelve-minute walk to and from the university where I'm employed.

The extent of my reserves of gratitude is depleted:

"Oh, oh, hey man… I've been on my feet all day long, had a donut to eat this morning, yeah, ain't knowin' where I'll be eatin' next. Man," said a hunched African American man dressed in fine clothing. I reckoned the round sticker of a sixty-dollar ballcap and the aged lines of a mature face. I thought of the new slogan posted in bold black lettering within the plastic encasement of a cross-shaped bulletin on the streetside of a Presbyterian church: **"JESUS IS THE PASSWORD TO A BETTER LIFE."**

The man said, "What's the time?"

I lowered the chicken wrap I ate while I walked, pressed a button to illuminate a digital watch on my left wrist that I purchased at the Navy boot camp commissary, and said, "Eight-thirty-five."

"Aw shit—man I hope they're open, I be so hungry—on my feet all day ya—know—wha'—I'm sayin'?"

I walked alongside the beggar for several seconds and scrutinized my chicken wrap with a twinge of modest guilt expressed in my visage; this I knew, despite being unable to view the features of my countenance at that moment, for my thoughts disinclined me from any notion of care— for every homeless man I ever aided… I recollected the vacuous stares, parasitic gratitude, verminous postures, demeanors, mannerisms…. The guilt I felt had been taught; this man attempted to *teach* me.

I said, "I wish you luck," and crossed the road.

The man muttered, "Thanks brother," and acknowledged me with a sidelong glance of crestfallen contempt; he sped ahead, shoulders slumped forward, head bowed low, and faded amongst an umbra of shadows cast from a row of enormous oak trees by the opposite roadside.

September 27th, 2019

5:18 PM

Unhappiness. I exist in the "castle" of another man who reminds me of this often, whenever I express thoughts incompatible with his current state. Lewis has a particular arrogance of character and attempts—and fails—to assert his masculinity and dominance over me in a pseudo-relationship only he is an actor and participant of.

Lewis and I now cohabitate as my father and I did, as silent combatants of the mind. There is no love. There is no romance. There is no relationship; I have invoked this outcome.

I move into my new apartment by no later than October 1st to become a slave of my own dictation.

September 28th, 2019

8:40 AM

Last night a rotund dwarfish man with putrescent teeth and a flabby visage called out to me on the city's busiest street while I strode past a bar.

"Hey—hey, ain't that a real shame. Ain't that a shame! Got them guys in there! Hey!"

I stopped, turned, and said, "What?"

The quasi rocker/biker wobbled towards me. He wore a *"Queen"* band shirt. "They won't let me play yet they got those guys in there playing their music and they think they're somebody." I smelled the pungent stench of alcohol emitted from his uncouth maw: Hard liquor.

I said, "Everybody is nobody."

"Hey man, I like you," he outstretched his hand for an (unwarranted) upraised shake of the hand; I accepted and embraced the classic *dead fish* delivered by his doughy appendage.

We proceeded to banter while I sought to terminate the interaction; he followed me, shook my hand on *five more* instances, accused me of being a robot or affected by mushrooms due to my behavior, proclaimed his disdain for the crowded streets of New York City, and on his parting statement, said, "Hey man… Everybody is somebody."

"GOD'S RETIREMENT PROGRAM FOR CHRISTIANS IS OUT OF THIS WORLD."

- Unsubstantiated Presbyterian Church Sign Post

September 29th, 2019

7:36 AM

Prelude to a terrific day:

I lay in bed awake adjacent to a man who has lived his life as a rogue. We disgust each other; the feelings are tantamount in our idleness. Lewis… Yes, he longs for companionship, a yearning for the flesh, and I, enraptured by the futile delusions of humankind, lie next to him, distanced by several feet between us, and stare at the high ceiling of an old schoolhouse room converted into an apartment.

Empowered—by the inconsequential nothings of humanity and the strivings of each individual to become something *more*—by greater designs, we align ourselves with subjective expectations: an elysian dream of our egotistical machinations distracts us with moot purposes, null and void—to validate a senseless voyage, locked in our bodies… We may *only* compare the ambition, achievements, and aspirations of one another: therein, is the hatred—the envy—the loathing, despising, the *love*—yes! For what is love without the foundation of hatred to elicit the feeling? When the veil of our own illusory beliefs unravels in light of another consciousness fit to judge us as an equal—for what we *are*—there is a reciprocal distancing from our gravest fear: Death.

And what is death?

"Ah, she no longer moves or responds to my touch. A maggot lingers in her left ear, and her abdomen bloats… I am grieved," said a hapless man aside from his three-day-dead wife. He's yet to inform local authorities of his catastrophe: The man loved his wife more than he ever has, for she has become nothing—a *true* absence, and he is free to become as he desires, liberated from her judgments, and may now be with the memories of his choice, manufactured, altered, revised—ah! How beautiful!

"How beautiful she is!" The man lamented by his dead wife's side; propped onto his right elbow, he caressed her forehead and grazed four fingers through a tuft of her black hair, down to her neck. "I miss her now more than ever; I wish she could be at my side to witness my grief for my loss… of her." A cold tear fell from the man's chin into his dead wife's slackened mouth. "There is joy in this torment!" The man blubbered and slipped a pinky finger behind the lobe of his dead wife's right ear. "I wish I could lie with her forever, at this moment, for eternity."

My Beautiful Dead Wife

The way she feels moves me
To tears; cold against the warm
Flesh of my groping hands, I wonder:
Why couldn't she have left me
Sooner than now. For fate, whimsical
And callous to a man's desires,
Laughs at the throes of my
Grief—to be alone with her—
Stiff and discolored, I wonder:
What did she believe as a child?
My beautiful dead wife, alas,
If you were here by my side
To reckon my passion, for what
I've lost, by the loss of you,
You'd be enamored by my
Conviction of woe, and be
Mine again, in love.

OCTOBER

October 1st, 2019

9:40 PM

After two-and-a-half months of slavery, destitution, and bondage, in that order, I've secured a home for myself once again, liberated, and sanctioned in a private space I may call my own—yet, the light of god (consciousness) permeates all and continues to observe *it*self; therefore, a wretched character manifests, one engrossed with the idle enchantment of the self in solitude. I am at leisure in my labor.

Infatuated, with the twenty-year-old vixen, Amethyst, my mind is subverted into the dark subterranean chasms of passion. Wicked she-devils pair well with self-engrossed scumbags. We met for a date at a local family-owned Thai restaurant and stared into each other's eyes. The lighthearted conversation and homely environment enchanted me, whereby we spent brief moments enthralled by each other's gaze. A delicate, resolute smile beneath a pair of bright, youthful eyes delighted me. *"There she is,"* I thought, *"And here I am."* Our first moments spent together outside of an establishment of work elicited feelings of the classical rendition of man and woman, overjoyed, for the simplicity of the companionship of the other. We consumed flesh, and the psychic energy of each other, seated opposite to one another... the polarity of unification—what I began to acknowledge with hatred festered, metamorphosed, and apexed into the vague aspect, a cheery sentiment, a fatuous hope, of what one may name, "love."

October 3rd, 2019

9:38 PM

What am I but a creature of gratuitous consumption, whereby I consume—*information;* engrossed, with the body, lowly pleasures—*enraptured,* by insecure little girls yet to blossom, who look to me for a foundation: An unstable foothold upon the pinnacle of a rocky outcrop suspended over tumultuous waves!

Lewis is a bygone memory whose machinations and perpetual viewing of liberal news stations broadcasted through a near-maximum volume portable Bluetooth speaker is a distant relic I wish to obliterate from my memory… recorded on this odious manuscript instead. *Manuscript*… the audacity, the nerve, the arrogance of my words!

Mother! Father! Imagine me, oh dear begetters, spreadeagled, subjugated, and emasculated upon a bed—naked, with a spiked collar strapped tight around my neck: A deliverer of the throes of passion for a man twice my age. My desecrated anus is a testament to ancient wisdom… Never again will I be at the (voluntary) mercy of a sexual deviant. An embarrassment? A shame? No—the mere course of events transpired is a product of the inexorable forces of nature, for the paths I've chosen and the man I've become.

Lo—on the nature of man, *mother* and *father,* heed these words, for only you will, out of embittered curiosity for what *has* become of your precious miscreant amidst foreign lands:

A hater of men, one who wishes to repel, to revile, to intimidate and threaten by sheer force of will and mass: a despicable lowlife, a petty thief, a remorseless offender. *A vicious man,* to the detriment of all who I engage with. I love to hate and hate to love. Your rotten seed surges forth—*strewn* over a blank template. Remember, I was never yours; to grieve of my depravity is a selfish act… this much I expect from you both.

October 5th, 2019

7:42 AM

Darkness: the idleness of one's mind prompts new engrossments.

Flies, centipedes, and spiders are a scourge of my living space; this occupancy has been devoid of human activity for a long while. Flies suffer an erratic, prolonged death when sprayed with vinegar-based cleaning liquid. The convulsions satisfy my curiosity. I wonder, if I am to be punished in the afterlife for my transgressions against ~~inferior~~ disadvantaged creatures, yet I think of each instance in which I apply soap to my body and murder innumerable microbes, or the moments when I indulge in any act of consumption on behalf of the denizens of this world that have been slain in a foreign county—packaged, and shipped to a megalomaniac corporation, whereby I purchase the flesh of plant and animal alike… By this logic, I conclude my sacrosanct behavior, alone, with my mind, while I observe an arrangement of supine flies rub at their multifaceted eyes after being engulfed by a toxic mist.

I sliced a centipede in half with a steak knife; the creature enacted the involuntary defense mechanism of curling into *it*self and uncurled immediately after the head touched the severed end of a middle-body.

"Ah! I am defeated," thought the centipede. *"Out of all the incalculable ways I might succumb to the cruel hand of death, I have failed to foresee this fate; alas, I will lie here to die, for I am nothing without the lower half of myself."*

October 6th, 2019

5:14 PM

A man I work alongside at the center of the city's only mall is endowed with a dreary freckled face, yellowed teeth, a frazzled brown ponytail, and a physique which speaks volumes of his inactivity; this man approaches me often with mundane topics to conversate on—all subjects I am indifferent and/or adverse to; albeit, between his forced giggles and chuckles, the man touched on a matter of intrigue: Depression, and his ~~concern~~ fear of people misunderstanding him.

"Why would you write about what I say?" he asked me, perplexed with my stoic reaction to his divulgence of suffering chronic states of depression. We stood dead center at the cross-section of the busiest quadrant in the mall, clipboards in-hand. Name tags connected to a blue fabric hung around our necks and dangled over our abdomens.

I said, "The projection of your depression onto others intrigues me; your character is one to inspect."

"Oh… *no…* " he said, and paused to recollect his bearing. "I don't like where this is going. I *really* don't like where this is going. I've had people misinterpret what I say in the past and *it* didn't end well for me."

"If you fear being misunderstood, I pity you."

"Why?"

"Nobody ever fully understands one another."

"Well… I mean… I just don't want something I say to be… misconstrued—and then something happens where I'll lose something."

"Has that happened to you in the past?"

"Way too many times."

The man continued to discuss his chronic depression, extreme anti-personality disorder, and a slew of other learned DSM-5 jargon—a throng of mental labels and categories in an effort to establish order and reason to one's incoherent thought processes manifested from an untamed ego.

Praise be the egotists, every one of us, glorified with the personal expressions and expositions of our minute, pissant lives. The lowliest street wretch exemplifies equal mental chaos as the human whose esteem is the highest among us, from the wealthiest, to the most powerful, spiritual, virile, magnanimous… there is nothing in wait but a ruinous recycle.

October 7th, 2019

8:40 AM

I walked the span of the city to visit the vixen who I've become involved with: the twenty-year-old self-labeled alcoholic that I have enjoyed the last two weekends with each other's company. The first instance: A date at a Thai restaurant with a follow-up of a walk through a park. The second: I visited her new apartment where she lives with her nineteen-year-old sister and her sister's "baby daddy."

On entry to the barren apartment, Amethyst lay prone on her sister's mattress and played an old *Playstation 2* videogame *(Jak and Daxter: The Precursor Legacy)* on a miniature square television. Cigarette smoke toxified the air, and an open styrofoam container containing an assortment of sliced fruits (gifted by a sixty-year-old Arabian next door neighbor who desires to "marry her") rested on top of a furled blanket. I stepped onto the coverless mattress and seated myself on a black, fuzzy body pillow, and aligned my spine against the wall behind Amethyst, whereby I watched her play the aforementioned game for ten minutes.

Amethyst paused the game, inserted an old *Loony Toons* VHS, and snuggled up next to me. The infantile innocence of the scene, an escape from my own wretched reality of day-to-day labor and constant review of what *it* is to be a meager hunk of flesh, captivated me, and elicited great joy. Amethyst wore a soft red Christmas tree-themed long-sleeve shirt and pajamas printed with *Day of the Dead* skulls. The supple, petite body, 2/3rds the size of my own, curled against me, and an angelic face peered up at me on my occasional outburst of unrestrained laughter at moments of *Looney Toons,* to the astonishment of Amethyst *and* myself… I *laughed*—pure

462

and jovial, at a moment when the character Marvin the Martian shot a "Ultimatum Response" in the form of a bullet as a peace request to the character Daffy Duck. The bullet halted and floated in a stasis a few feet away from the circumspect Daffy Duck; the bullet's point lifted on a hinge... a second of anticipation, and an explosion erupted from within to engulf Daffy Duck... Alas, the ingenious dialogue of the stuttering Porky Pig prompted a few chuckles as well.

Amethyst gazed up at me, wide-eyed and concerned, for she had not known me to be one to *laugh*. I looked down at her... nuzzled up against my left leg, head pressed against my waist; I shook my head.

A rush of nostalgia overtook me, back to the bygone days when I enjoyed life—for what *it* is, and nothing more, when I never thought of the moments in passing which will cease to be. At the tender age of six, seven, and eight, I enjoyed *Looney Toons* to the utmost, and never thought of the cartoon again, and *now then*, I laid with Amethyst in my arms for a fleeting hour-and-a-half and listened to the low-quality audio comprised of a whimsical soundtrack and intelligent dialogue and shed two selfish tears onto the back of the beautiful girl's long, unwashed, and tangled black hair. My hands caressed and traced the contours of her body; thereby, she reacted with subtle shifts and pleasurable exhalations-

Lo! The human creature! Reckon what we are and *wonder,* for what *it* is that we strive and yearn for! Everything I could ever desire lay within my arms, and I could do nothing but grieve for *it*'s inevitable passing! This little girl braced against my body and veered in and out of slumber. Her delicate, slender form began to show the subtle onset of years of maltreatment—of entropy... I envisioned us dead, and moved away from her, callous, cold—dejected by my own ruinous conceptions of reality, and sensed the pity of God—the self-awareness bestowed to me.

The *Looney Toons* VHS ended and cut to a vivid black and white swarm of shifting patterns overlaid on the screen. I sat and stared at the nothingless displayed on the old television and laid a hand on Amethyst's back. The VHS began to rewind and replayed the same cartoons of yesteryears, forgotten by many, and remembered with fondness often by the girl who lay beside me, and myself, for that moment.

I stood, rounded off the bed, woke Amethyst from a quasi sleep, and said, "I'm going to go."

Amethyst yawned, assumed a cat stretch pose, rubbed her face, and said, "I'm sorry I fell asleep. I'll show you to the door."

I experienced anguish while I tied my shoes, donned my pack, and gripped Amethyst in my arms. I had purchased condoms prior to the visit in anticipation of the unknown, yet her nose rubbing against mine, and the few brief kisses shared between us while we stood by her closed front door exceeded my expectations. I said, "I'll see you next week," and nodded myself out, down a rusted stairwell, and trekked the hour and fifteen-minute walk back to my apartment. A recent rain colored the empty streets with a translucent sheen. The cold air of night invigorated me.

October 8th, 2019

7:52 PM

Haunted, by my own designs. I think of the night with Amethyst, in her new unfurnished apartment: an impoverished young girl… the *Looney Toons*—the night lingers with me, for the symbolism, while she lay curled in my arms, I listened to the forlorn sound of ~~my~~ *her* childhood emanate through an antiquated television.

The vixen desires sexual intercourse and I am apathetic to the *idea* of *it*. The entire basis of her advancements has been thus. I am but a mere wanderer in the robust arms of a miniature world I now meander back and forth through: A perpetual stasis of my own becoming. Yes, we want *it* all, everything there is to be, everything we could become, yet, what we choose are distractions… alas…

The *Looney Toons;* I replay the theme song opening in my mind throughout the day and envision the girl, her past of prostitution, gang involvement, drug abuse, and the dozens of men who influenced her, who taught her what ~~men~~ boys are. I'm entrapped by my *own* impassioning, for the concern of Amethyst's welfare, yet I rebel against myself and therefore wish to repel her for the sake of my self-preservation with the knowledge that my efforts *will* be for naught, that she will continue to deprive herself of a state of well-being by a resolute and indifferent volition equivalent to my own.

My supervisor, Kim, a despicable old crone (for she despises others), threatened to fire me today for utilizing two "clicks" (dispenses) of a small hand-held apparatus to salt waffle fries instead of one "click." I spoke with an auditor a week ago and confirmed the company standard is two "clicks."

Kim's enforced policy is one "click," for she believes our student clientele prefers the waffle fries to be less salty due to *two* complaints she received.

"How many clicks was that?" Kim said over my shoulder.

I turned to her, already weary of the admonishment I anticipated, and said, "Two clicks."

"*Only one* click of salt for a basket of fries," she commanded; we held gazes for four seconds.

I said, "Alright."

"You *will* perform the way I expect in *my* unit."

To my surprise, I unleashed a hearty chuckle and dribbled a strand of spittle onto the floor.

Kim said, "You think this is funny? You can *not* come in anymore if you don't want to."

I turned back to her, sincere, indulgent, and said, "I like to come here."

Kim addressed me with a final grimace of dismayed disgust and walked away. We spoke no more of any matter for the remaining fifty minutes of her shift.

October 9th, 2019

8:50 AM

A low sun shining amidst a thin sheet of gray opaque clouds illuminated a narrow and sandy path along a beach a salt miner's wife walked on. A fervent stride accented the seriousness of her stiff posture with a tenacious zeal which alerted the salt miner—who sat idly by the shoreline; he expected no company, and had been alone for many months with gulls, waves, and grains of sand between his blistered toes.

"You *damnable bastard*," said the salt miner's wife, and she shrieked a miserable wail fit for a newfound banshee.

The salt miner's head snapped to attention and turned towards the horrific sight of the skeletal humanoid bounding towards him with demonic haste expressed in each vicious compression against whitewashed sand. The salt miner remained on the ground, his knees skewed before him at a ninety-degree angle, palms against the side of both thighs, arms bent, chin low, eyebrows leveled; he opened his mouth to speak and instead quietened—overpowered, by the outburst of his estranged wife.

"You good-for-nothing lowlife," screamed the salt miner's wife, "After all this time, here you sit; I bet that's all you've been doing since I left, isn't *it?*"

"I've been-"

"*Shut up—shut up!* Shut! Up!" On the salt miner's wife's approach, the salt miner lifted his left hand over his face, palm out, to ward off an anticipated hail of blows. Instead, the salt miner's wife loomed over the salt miner, two feet away, legs spaced, exhausted; she leered down at the top of his matted hair and inhaled… exhaled… "Well?"

The salt miner said, "Well, Sherri, how've you been?"

"You think I'm some idiot, some bitch, some villain come again to make your life rotten and miserable?" Sherri spat an involuntary globule of salvia onto the beach between herself and her husband. "No, Henry, I've been back, back when you weren't around, and I explored the little cave you call 'home'; I found all your stinking stores of fish… and—you," she blubbered, "You *good-for-nothing* liar! You cruel, greedy man! I-"

Henry stood and faced his wife. Cold winds ruffled the fabric of a pale, ill-fitted dress. "Sherri… " Henry's wife covered her face with both of her veiny hands and began to weep; her vicious demeanor relaxed to a disconsolate state, her maleficent aspect now dire and innocent. Henry advanced a step and outstretched a hand; the hesitant touch of his fingers against Sherri's right shoulder blade incited her to recoil and amplified the woe expressed in her outburst of grief. "Sherri," Henry repeated, and advanced the second and final step to enjoin with his wife, body to body, in a rigid embrace.

"I've despised you for months."

"I understand," Henry whispered.

Sherri shook her head against his chest and said, "I still despise you. The fact that I stand here in your arms…"

Henry pulled his wife closer; her feet remained fixed while her body leaned into his. Henry sniffed his wife's hair and traced the lobe of her ear; he closed his eyes and despaired. "I'm so happy you're back," he said.

Both stood for two minutes, inflexible and engrossed by the individual sufferings of one shared by the other, yet both knew the full extent of the other's thoughts and feelings were incomprehensible, intangible motes of irrelevant fodder compared to the far more pertinent anguish of the moment as a whole.

Sherri shivered and drew back; she spat in her husband's face, though the spittle flew southbound into the sea's foamy waves. Henry stared at her; his hand, settled at the nape of her neck, withdrew, and fell limp.

"I'm not back," Sherri whispered, "I'm already gone. If you were to kill me now, I'd be gone. If you were to restrain me, haul me back to your salt cave, and torture me until the end of my days, I'd be gone, but I know you won't do any of that, for you're a coward, Henry. I came back one last time to hurt you, though I've only hurt myself. I'm already gone, for I know when I go again and never return, you'll resume what you've always done and become a miserly man as you've always been… " Sherri paused and looked up at Henry; he acknowledged her with a stony gaze and said nothing; thereby, she proclaimed with renewed purpose: "I'm gone, Henry."

The woman severed herself from the man's lifeless gaze and turned. The man watched her go and pondered what he felt. Pondement abated to wonderment as her figure shrunk and distanced against a bright horizon. Befuddlement overtook wonderment, and the man scratched his head; he stood for eighteen minutes and listened to overhead gulls. Fear supplanted befuddlement. The man reacted to the onset of tremendous terror with a fishing rod and tackle box.

11:15 PM

I applaud you, reader, for your investment, even if you are to view only this particular sentence at random; you reckon the senseless proportions of my unilateral mind. No matter the day, month, or year, I am dead.

October 10th, 2019

10:11 AM

I read *Self-Reliance and Other Essays* during my idle times before work, between periods of exertion and engorgement.

"Or, do men desire the more substantial and permanent grandeur of genius? Neither has this an immunity. He who by force of will or of thought, is great, and overlooks thousands, has the charges of that eminence. With every influx of light comes new danger. Has he light? He must bear witness to the light, and always outrun that sympathy which gives him such keen satisfaction, by his fidelity to new revelations of the incessant soul. He must hate father and mother, wife and child.

Has he all that the world loves and admires and covets?—he must cast behind him their admiration, and afflict them by faithfulness to his truth, and become a by-word and a hissing."

- Ralph Waldo Emerson

October 11th, 2019

8:16 PM

Looney Toons. I reflect, and lament my damnable foolishness. Pity?—no, I have wrought upon myself a mirror of my own heinous persona. The young girl, Amethyst, is cold and callous to my unguarded interest. Why do I vie to reciprocate the fraudulent affections of one who wheedled her way into my arms and made our newfound intimacy a spectacle for mall-goers and co-workers? I'm a pawn, a dupe, a moron… for what I know to be the pretended tenderness of a *vixen;* her, desperate for me to fill the physical void, to sate her lust and dominate the flesh; and I, desperate for an emotional release—a bond, a rapport, the touch of femininity. Who is the greater demon? We are unable to satisfy each other. I will terminate my relationship with Amethyst on the eve of a final meeting, no doubt invigorated with wine and food, primed for the sexual appetites; the relationship will instead be severed, the planes leveled, and justice rendered to us both through a mutual, ephemeral, misery.

Love: How may I fear the impalpable?—what began with bilateral, unconscious hatred from both parties. We shall end with an outcry of unrequited love, for the ego, once validated, deprived of the validator, is tormented, and yearns to reconcile at the expense of *it*self.

I desired to write of topics of intrigue I've recorded on a new voice recorder, and of the many notes I've jotted down throughout the past few days; instead, I scribe my romantic afflictions so that if I am ever old and grayed, I may, on nights of mourning, return to my bygone days of advanced youth and resent everything I ever was.

*"Oh why didn't I just screw the girl as she had wanted—as we **both** wanted?"* decries my elder 'self.' *"I had all these damnable philosophies, principles, and my faculty of **reason** to hold me back! I had to make* it *all more than* it *was in my mind, and for what? What-"*

"Oh, shut up Baethan," commands a fifty-three-year-old woman from an adjacent kitchen. "If you're so unhappy about your past and your present with me, down your entire bottle of painkillers and be done with *it*."

"*No, I love the pain too much to quit.*"

"Then please shut up. Your oats are ready."

October 13th, 2019

7:46 PM

Amethyst (a [unqualified] supervisor of the survey job at the mall where I'm employed) called me in for work; I accepted, clothed myself in the routine all-black dress clothes, donned my military-issued pack, and walked the mile and a half to my destination.

Throughout my brief shift, I recruited one jovial twenty-year-old man for two movie trailer surveys, and another desperate thirty-two-year-old man for one movie trailer survey. Meanwhile, Amethyst's vacuous behavior was more pronounced to me than ever before, and her indifferent regard to my genuine amiability dissuaded me from holding out until our planned "date" on Monday.

Amethyst rambled to herself all-the-while, her expressions of thought banal and snide.

I said, "What is my directive?"

Amethyst stared at a computer screen, widened her eyes, assumed a wicked frown, and said, "What does that mean?"

"What should I do?"

"Well, we're about to close... so... You can wipe the windows down."

I proceeded to clean the pane glass windows serving as a barrier between the rented establishment space and the totality of the mall, returned within, brought the trash out back to the dumpster, returned indoors, walked down a long narrow hall, powered on my voice recorder, and said, "Before I go, I would like to say that I think you and I should stop seeing each other."

Amethyst gazed up at me with prior expectancy that I would say something pleasant or cordial; on the pronouncement of the last syllable of my sentence, her head snapped back towards the monitor and she said, "Okay," without processing my words. Seated on a wheeled office chair, she rolled backward, floundered with a few papers, avoided eye contact with me, consternated for four seconds, and said, "I feel the same. Nothing against you but I feel the same. I feel like *it*'s going to end in tragedy… so…"

I raised an eyebrow; she looked at me, reassured by her statement.

"Tragedy," I thought, and turned from her to procure my belongings without speaking a word. On my way out, I stopped to stow my water bottle in my pack's proper compartment.

Amethyst spoke with aloof disengagement in her tonality and said, "Baethan, what's two-hundred-and-seven minus seventy-seven?"

I said, "I don't know," with ambivalent sincerity expressed in my precise response and pushed my way out of one of the two glass doors.

October 15th, 2019

9:00 AM

A square indoor mall intersection upheld by four massive white columns. An overhead, vaulted sunroof, seventy feet above. A drone of mall denizens and the faint resonance of upbeat music underlaid with soundbites of children's laughter and parental guffaws. I walk erect, clipboard in-hand, garbed in slim-fitted all-black dress clothes, my form distinguished by the line of a brown belt at my waist. Rows of kiosks for *National Hiring Day* form a smaller square within the square at the center of the intersection. My jaunt around the perimeter draws the attention of shoppers and shop attendants, restless that I am, agitated, and *hateful,* though this latter feeling is suppressed—my visage rendered unwholesome, unpleasant, and *attractive,* for I exemplify the mien of a (pretentious) psychopath.

A new employee saunters alongside me and enjoins me for a non-formal introduction; his name is Bob: 5'8, skinny build, he wears a white and tan checkered dress shirt tucked into black dress pants; a pair of brown and black formal shoes complete the image: One of impeccable exactitude of proportion and coloration. His soft face is round and framed with an apish mat of head and facial hair. He's an aspiring musician. His eyes exude a starry intelligence. On our introduction to each other, after three farcical comments on the sleazy nature of our job, Bob said, "You're very serious."

I said, "You're very human."

"I can't argue with that."

We were comrades, from that moment until the end of our employment. Bob orbited me and observed my over-rehearsed, undeviating pitch:

"Excuse me (evaluate potential sucker's/sap's/mark's interest and social cues), would you be interested in being paid to watch a trailer for a film that hasn't been released yet?"

Bob practiced his own pitch, and due to my interjection, I happened to capture the most novel conversation I've experienced since I arrived at the city airport on account of the voice recorder situated in my left pocket:

"Hey," Bob began at a passing middle-aged couple, "Would you like to take a survey?" The couple shook their heads. "Are you sure—free money! *It*'s free money!" Bob cooed and swaggered past both.

I waited several seconds for his satisfied countenance to meet with mine and yelled to him from several meters away, "*It*'s not free, *it* costs them their time."

"Yeah *it* costs them way too much time for like what little—like, *it*'s definitely not worth like, the *time,* you know what I mean?"

With haste, I said, "Two dollars for twenty-five minutes of your time?"

"I think more than that-"

I affirmed, "You need to pitch the experience."

Bob smirked all-the-while, good-humored, despite my somberness, and spoke with wryness, "Come into a dingy little room, and hang out with *me,* and watch movies—and get harassed with redundant questions... *it*'s an experience," he chuckled between words, "You can write about *it*—you could write a novel about how much you hate me after. Like *it*'s that much, like, information."

"You dictate the experience though."

"See there you go, 'dictate'—that immediately has like a negative connotation come to mind, everything about this."

"*It*'s a dictation."

"Yeah *it*'s absolutely negative."

I had been unable to resist the negativity: "From the get-go *it*'s all pretentious."

"Yeah, right? I mean maybe. I mean *it* could be."

"I think *it* is. Do you believe that all human interaction is an act of pretension?"

"Ah, maybe."

"How we dress, how we behave-"

"I've met some guys who aren't pretentious, I've met a handful of people, but they're also scumbags so... " Bob giggled. "They're like 'sociopaths.' But I mean, you could say-"

My attention honed, focus realigned; I said, "Did you say they 'are' or 'aren't'?"

"They aren't pretentious but they're scumbags."

"Yes."

"They're like total assholes, just like—like I don't know if you're familiar with G.G. Allen? Punk rocker-"

"I consider myself to be a pretentious scumbag 'sociopath.'"

Bob beamed and said, "... Well, that's good!" and laughed, his first unpretentious laugh of our interaction thus far.

"Well, *it*'s about knowing myself." My tonality softened.

"Definitely—well you got to uh… uh… work with what you got man."

"We all are though. The label of 'sociopath' is a 1920-1930 jargon… *It*'s an umbrella term for antisocial traits that aren't beneficial to society."

Bob said, "But we all operate on a spectrum of antisocial behaviors."

"Exactly."

"*It* just depends on how 'sociopathic' you are."

"Yes," I affirmed. "We're all human. There is no difference between us. We all understand each other through the basic tenets of suffering: The tenets of suffering-"

"You really sound—you're starting to sound more and more like a movie villain—that's where we're going, when like, you're like," Bob's voice shifted to a poor impersonation of a nefarious character: *"We must all empathize through suffering! And pain!* … I mean I get *it*, trust me, I get *it*… I don't know uh if you've ever read of the Dharma Sangha or anything like that but *it*'s something the Buddha laid out thous- A *long* time ago, a very *long* time ago. Basically he said that everything is relief from suffering: That food is uh, that *eating* is uh relief from the pain of hunger, that sex is relief from the pain of sexual frustration—I mean *everything* is relief from pain."

"That's interesting how that contrasts with the Christian sense of sin: How eating and sex for satisfaction… is a conduit for shame and guilt—how that's all taught to us."

"Uh—*it*'s not taught to me. Never believed in *it*, no offense if anybody does but—I mean I look at all religion and everything from just like an objective standpoint; I don't try to involve myself with any of *it*."

"I've read the *Bhagavad-Gita*, *it*'s the only religious doctrine that I've fully-"

"The *Bhagavad-Gita* is pretty—pretty good, I mean I really like all the Hindu, uh, myths, honestly, like uh, you should definitely—if you like the *Bhagavad-Gita* try to read the *Upanishads* sometime, because those are like the Hindu *classic* classics you-know-what-I-mean?—or the Vitas I guess are the classics too-"

"Based on Taoism?"

"Umm, Taoism I think, I honestly think that everything precluded Taoism because that's actually like one of the first um, uh, uh… written… uh, one of the first recorded things that we actually have…"

Frank, the man prone to fits of unwarranted laughter who also fears being misunderstood, joined our conversation for several minutes and spoke nothing; he stood by and listened, and seized the opportunity to speak on this occasion: "That's about the only thing that I ever, outside of you know… being raised in a Christian dominated state—Taoism is the only thing I've ever read into." A useless interjection.

Bob continued, "Taoism is more like—the eighty-one verses I think are pretty much the basis—like you think about Nietzsche's *Beyond Good and Evil*, like literally I went and I read—I love Nietzsche, I think he's like the first philosopher I've read that I really love, and uh, pretty much everything that he laid out in *Beyond Good and Evil*, Lao Tzu simplified in the Tao, thousands of years before—like he's (Nietzsche) is basically just expanding upon these ideas that are thousands of years old, you-know-what-I-mean—good and evil are just constructs of the human mind, blah blah blah, you know but—literally, Lao Tzu said all that before anybody else, and he wrote *it* in a little tiny verse (meager size gesture with both hands), whereas Nietzsche had to write *it* out in literal volumes, ya' know, so, I like the simplicity of the Tao."

I opened my mouth to speak a postulation pertinent to Bob's sentiments and instead refrained on account of Frank's input: "Maybe *it's* because I was spending too much time around, um… stoners, but, uh… From what I remember studying the Tao Te Ching, is *it's* basically sitting on your couch and doing nothing." On cue, Frank erupted into nervous laughter and looked between Bob's jovial expression and my disgruntled one.

Bob said, "There's a lot of that in there—there's a lot of—there's a lot of 'Why do anything?' Like—why interrupt the flow of the universe, but, there's also a lot of stuff that—I can't remember exactly—the—the… like verbatim what he says but, essentially like: Put your hand in the situation, get *it* done, get whatever you're trying to do over with and then just stop thinking about *it;* there's absolutely no point; don't procrastinate, don't dwell on *it,* ya' know."

My ego could restrain *it*self no longer; I said, "*It's* the perpetual conflicts that justify all we have, for being, and becoming something else; as you said," I nodded at Frank, "You sit on the couch and do nothing; that reminds me of Eckhart Tolle, if you're familiar with him-"

Frank said, "I didn't get to uh-"

I cut Frank's admission of ignorance short: "The vacuous stare off at nothing and him (Tolle) claiming to be content; if that's contentment, then, I'd rather stay far away from that state of mind. I would rather be afflicted by turmoil and chaos constantly."

Bob said, "Well I think that some of like, some of the greatest minds in the world lived their lives in turmoil—I mean if you think about like religious classics, there's a lot of turmoil in those—and Buddha trying to find out who he was, but I think like, even like, in contemporary times, like—musicians, like some of the best musicians out there like—I—I, I really try to steep myself in as much music history as possible, and pretty much every major musician, their whole life is just tumultuous... Ya' know, like they went through a lot, trying to find like—and even if they didn't, trying to become a musician is a fucking endeavor in *it*self, you-know-what-I-mean?"

Frank said, "But on the practical side of that: Ya' know, the 'not doing anything' versus stress, if you look at—two things I can say to look at... um... Stoplights versus roundabouts. You know which is, you know, which is safer?"

Bob said, "Roundabouts?"

"Roundabouts," Frank confirmed with a hostile inflection. "You know what people are more comfortable with? Guess."

Bob repeated, "Roundabouts?"

Frank said, "Do you know why roundabouts are safer?" Before Bob could answer, Frank yelled, "Because you're not comfortable with them! Because you don't know what's going on! You *have* to pay attention. You are not allowed to become complacent in a roundabout!"

Bob turned away from Frank and asked a fellow stout female employee adorned with *Crayola* crayon glasses: "Ma'am would you like to take a survey?"

The woman stated coyly, "I work here." The irrelevant conversation between the woman and Bob persisted.

Frank abruptly addressed me and said, "Mouse utopia."

I stared at Frank.

"Do you know what the mouse utopia was?"

"Yes-"

"Okay-" Frank attempted to inhibit me.

I spoke regardless, "They were allowed free reign of sex and nourishment."

Frank spoke with a tenacious zeal, "Yes—and they all got depressed, stopped eating, and died. Like, some of them—they started *killing* each other, they started um… ult—ultimately they died off… the mice died off, but… they got really territorial, even though they shouldn't have been—like more territorial than normal. They started killing each other, eating their own babies. Eventually they stopped breeding; they stopped eating… just progressively getting worse… and they had everything that they needed. So, you know, low levels of stress kinda' seem, necessary, or else—the mind is so good at like—the big thing that separates humanity—I have to say—is our capacity for *laziness.*" Frank scrutinized my vacant face as if I hadn't heard his profound revelation; he rephrased: "But the big thing that elevates humanity from other animals is our capacity for laziness."

Bob reentered the conversation and addressed Frank, "Have you ever seen a dog before—have you ever raised a dog?"

A conversation about dogs proceeded and I wandered away.

October 16th, 2019

8:38 AM

The girl, the girl… Amethyst, how I've lost sleep over you, for what I've severed in us both; our egos, diminished in unison, at the mutual acceptance of what should never be. The desire for physicality, yet the innate knowledge of incompatibility derived from our *doubts*… Are we not, then, unified? Amethyst will come to hate me, and from there, I *fear*… for "love" may then be possible.

I wish thoughts of her to be cast out—banished—negated! The vixen spirit baffles me! A hussy! A *strumpet*—by her *own* regard… yet, I'm fascinated despite my self-inflicted solitude. The comedy is now.

"Our doubts are traitors, and make us lose the good we oft might win by fearing to attempt."

– William Shakespeare

Enough of this, I will *not* succumb to the false ideations of the mind! Twisted scoundrel that I am! Leave her be, even if she harangues you with sweet nothings and desperate sorrows! A second childhood of mutable infatuation derails every process of thought pertinent to personal growth and comprehension. Forget her, as you have the others, for the sake of yourself—you lowlife, worthy of nothing more than a segment of a worm blistered against sun-warmed pavement, or an ort of feces secreted from the boiled body of a millipede; you're mad—*crazy!* Examine yourself!

Despite Amethyst's character and self-destructive principles, she is *intelligent...* God(s) condemn(s) her; I am vexed by this, for we share a conviction of spirit, debauched and depraved.

May we never validate each other's miseries. Amen.

October 19th, 2019

9:51 PM

For the seed yearns for the minds of men and women to provide ample sustenance for newfound duress to develop between both parties and whatever progeny is sown between the two.

The wondrous trees of the backyard I once knew, of my first home: One, a tall pine tree with layers of needles spread thick at the base of a three-foot-wide trunk, and the other, a small (fruit) tree at the opposite end of the modest expanse. My mother attempted to grow a vegetable garden, though she failed to afford the time to cultivate the crops amongst her other obligations.

I remember tall glasses of whole milk and white bagels with a half-inch layer of cream cheese spread on both halves; the top half being my favorite, for the texture of the topside half of a bagel is mushier and less grainy than *it*s counterpart.

I remember the few instances when my father visited the home for dinner with my mother and half-brother. Seated at the family table, we often dined on a variation of pasta and fended two dogs away from the table: A Sheeba Enu, and a Boxer. I recall the tenuous dialogues of my father and mother, the embittered silences, and the careless laughter of myself at everything extrinsic of the moment, of what was.

Most of all I rejoice at the infinite love I received from my father and mother, siphoned to me on behest of the lack of their love for each other.

At that young and tender age, I was to be sanctioned from admonishment and reproof by my mother; and for my father, I was to be disciplined and spared the impunity of my mother's sanctuary.

October 20th, 2019

7:13 PM

Called into the survey job for three hours of work, I enjoyed the time engaged in conversation with Bob on a multitude of philosophical, metaphysical, psychological, and sociological topics—too much to record in text, even though my voice recorder captured every minute detail of our multifaceted discourses.

By the second hour, a tall, unorthodox girl caught my eye; she gazed at me, seated with a coffee, garbed in a form-fitted brown dress thatched with black patterns. A dull-colored shirt worn beneath the dress covered the skin that would have otherwise been exposed. Circular, thick, black-framed glasses vexed a supple and rounded face. Black hair pulled back into a loose-strapped bun outlined an obvious application of makeup. Neither apple nor pear-shaped, the girl's body brought to mind an oak board with pronounced double bumps, front and back, one-third of the way up and down.

The girl veered towards me, established pronounced eye contact, and looked down at her feet on my acknowledgment of her existence. She had studied me for the past hour, seated alone with her coffee and while she caroused between the kiosks arranged and operated by old collectors of trinkets and memorabilia at the mall center.

I said, "Excuse me, do you have any interest in watching a trailer for a film that hasn't been released yet and being paid for *it?*"

"Yes."

The girl's immediate response enchanted me. I said, "Oh, well, alright—how many films have you seen in theatre in the past two months?"

"Two or three," she spoke with the dialect of a foreigner, though precise.

"And what's your name?"

"Emma."

"Emma… " I reflected. "How old are you?"

"Eighteen."

"Ah, I apologize, but our criteria for today is twenty to fifty-nine-year-old females."

"That's okay." Emma smiled and stared at me.

"Well, thank you for your time."

"Thank you."

I continued my rounds alongside Bob. Our banter mellowed from metaphysical and existential matters to the more mundane topic of female dealings. All-the-while, Emma mulled around us and browsed the wares of an independent poster art creator. Our eyes met on several occasions; each instance she looked away and blushed. I became aware of my elevated testosterone.

Bob said, "Why don't you just ask her out?"

"I wouldn't want to subject anyone to myself; I'm too selfish."

Bob and I committed to our laps around the circuit, distracted by each other's words for what makes for an ideal male-female relationship, and our lackluster attempts to convince middle-aged women to follow us into a small alcove to be paid two dollars for a twenty-five-minute interview. I held Emma in my view for brief intervals to admire her exotic poise and dignified demeanor. Twenty minutes elapsed: Emma decided on a purchase and strode towards where Bob and I were headed; in her right hand, she grasped a laminated cardboard print of Van Gough's *The Scream*.

My mind fogged. I scanned the print and honed in on every slight nuance of Emma's countenance: An eyebrow raise, a fascinated smile, a joyful validation. I stopped in front of Emma; Bob moved onward, around her. I nodded at the print and said, "That is *excellent.*"

"Yes, I'm a collector of art and this piece caught my attention," Emma spoke with genuine enthusiasm and waited for my response. I addressed her with a suppressed gaze of desire transposed into the visage of a professional, said nothing, nodded my respects, and rejoined Bob by his side; while we walked, I told him, "I paid my respects to the art and let her go."

"Damn man."

"I think I'm going to run after her."

"She's quite a ways away… " Bob trailed off; I had already jaunted ahead of him, a fast walk at first, a gallop, a jog; Emma's lackadaisical maneuvers allotted me enough time to meet her before she reached the west-side mall entry/exit.

"Excuse me," I spoke with the same tonality I utilize to address potential survey dupes. Emma turned to me, shocked and interested. I closed the wide gap, maintained four feet of distance between us, and said,

"I'm not here to conduct a survey… I find you to be… alluring. May I have your phone number?"

"Sorry," she blushed. "I have a boyfriend."

I retreated a step, bowed my head, said, " I understand," and disengaged. Emma called after me, "Thank you though!"

I jogged back to the four pillars, the kiosks, the denizens of the mall, and Bob—where together, we spoke of idle inclinations, though I retained at the forefront of my thoughts the lovely aspect of Emma and imagined only of what "good" the venturesomeness of men has wrought upon themselves in dealings with women.

Pet Millipede

Slow crawl around four corners of a plastic container:
Where do you think you're going, or where you are?
Do you think at all, of your will to live,
Or of the dehydration that impels you to die?
There is no anguish or anxiety in that little mind.

October 23rd, 2019

10:12 PM

A Conversation Between a Lich and Death

A sunny vista illuminated by a spring sun. A four-person picnic table decorated with a stark white cloth bespeckled with patterns of red and yellow roses. A series of tumultuous waves crash against a craggy cliff bottom. A dozen seagulls fly overhead.

Death shrugged. "You must be weary of *it* by now."

A lich rasped, "No."

"Well," Death's concussive voice, a mere murmur, muted proximate noise, "I fancy you must at least be *tired* of your undeath, or rather, *unlife,* by this point; what's *it* been: a millennium and a few centuries? I haven't been tracking you *too* intently; why bother? Just consider, if only for a few moments, the relinquishment of your accumulated knowledge."

"No." The lich's verbal expression, spoken from a glossy jawbone, expelled as a translucent icy vapor that curled out and hovered above the tablecloth for several seconds before dissipating amongst sixty-four-degree afternoon air.

"You've outdone yourself, admit *it*—you've outdone me; I'm at a loss, for I relish in no pleasure in the observance of those who suffer, but rather, the cessation of suffering, of torment, of anguish, of the pain and duress of a body no longer fit for consciousness."

The lich gaped at Death and said nothing.

Death shifted on the table seat and adjusted an amorphous ebony hood hung slack over an ovoid vacancy. "Listen, *you*… This is the fourth instance of which you've summoned me by one of your nebulous incantations, so here I am, *bound again* in this timeless space—with *you*—again… Alas, haven't you the good sense to make use of yourself? You've diddled away amongst the fathoms of caverns to which no man has ever dared ventured; you've witnessed the turning of the ages, submerged beneath the deepest realms of ocean fathoms, while humanity limped forward, unbeknownst to you—you being preoccupied with the nether…" Death waited. The lich sat, statuesque, and neither addressed or ignored Death with two empty eye sockets.

"How long do I have?" rasped the lich.

"I will not say; if you wish to die, recover your locket from the subterranean catacomb in which you've hidden *it* and destroy *it* yourself; though I know, you fear me, after all, so why would you?"

"I enjoy your company."

Death's posture straightened; he smoothed the wrinkles of the left sleeve of an immaculate robe with three skeletal fingers. "Of course. You *enjoy my company*; we're familiar, accomplices, *acquaintances*, though we may *never* be companions."

"I know."

"Yes, what don't you know other than the date of your own demise? Not even with your infinite wisdom and precocious intellect could you surmise *that*. I pity you."

The lich uttered a vexed whisper, "Farewell," and nullified a spell with a slight gesture beneath the sleeve of a tattered robe.

Death laughed. The conjuncture ceased to be: The vista, the picnic table, the waves, the seagulls, the substance of time that bound the entities.

Within the deepest recesses of a subterranean cavity at the bedrock of the earth's primordial crust, the lich reeled from the negated sorcery and prostrated on a monolithic stone slab enveloped by abyssal darkness.

October 26th, 2019

9:55 PM

Another Saturday spent conning mall-goers to participate in a twenty-five-minute two-dollar payout movie trailer survey. I've been informed through the office gossip machine that Amethyst hasn't attended work since the day I terminated our relationship.

I surveyed a vacuous, disrespectful, belligerent man today, shut in a small eight-by-five-foot room with two toddlers. The toddlers immediately commenced with violent histrionics; both banged the walls and screamed at the apex of their capabilities while the father answered my questions, indifferent and aloof to the horrendous behavior of his ill-begotten spawn. One child begged and screamed for the use of the man's cell phone to watch videos. When denied by me due to company policy, the man became distraught and said, "Then what am I supposed to do for him (his child)?" I responded with a shrug and stared at the computer monitor in front of me.

While I speed-read the words of surveys and click buttons corresponding with the interviewee's responses, I lose regard for my body and become a mental schism involved with only the functionality of reading and clicking. I fascinate myself in the meanwhile by imagining myself in the interviewee's body—a sympathetic attempt of a stranger's perspective, seated with me, engrossed with their own opinions. I've endured a few apostles of integrity chastise me for the incorrect selection of a menial question such as, "Do you strongly agree, somewhat agree, somewhat disagree, or strongly disagree that the character in this movie portrayed by Dwanye Johnson is charismatic?"

A disgruntled seventeen-year-old-girl chides, "I said *strongly* agree, not *agree*. Trigger happy much?"

"Ah, I apologize," I utter with absolute sincerity, "You got me."

Yes, the opinions of others are the most valuable commodity: the knowledge *of* truth.

A few new, young, nubile, attractive female employees flirt with me and reveal the extent of their capacity for debauchery after the utterance of several sentences; why should I care? Each desires emotionless affection; this I may bestow with ease, though I refuse, for the only emotion I feel is pity for humanity, for the animals we are. I reflect and internalize this pity on account of my enforced estrangement from the absurd conception of love and scorn all attempts of fornication directed at me. I'm miserable and desire no company.

I intuit the subdued mental agony of an old woman seated with her lunch. I intuit the depressive relationship between the man and woman who live a cloistered life of loveless codependency above me. A man who worked at the mall as a fellow surveyor quit the job; he emerged from his apartment one week ago to greet me and to inform me of why he has been absent: "I have crazy up in my head," he disclosed from a second-floor balcony. "I'm schizoaffective," he rephrased. Ah, and who *isn't* afflicted with a perpetual malady of varying metacognitional pathologies and degrees of severity? My, oh my, my, my… Everywhere I go, I listen to the learned deficiencies of my fellow being, and here, on this unholy template, I write of my indignation of such grievances, and decry my own insanity to be on an elevated plane by unintended consequence.

October 28th, 2019

10:16 PM

An enormous cockroach crawled across my floor while I paced through the quadrants of my living room and kitchen with a plastic quart container filled with a medley of black, brown, and white rice, boiled with broccoli and red peppers. The cockroach stopped on my observance of *it:* the quantum mechanisms (whatever that is) of the world are active interplay. Though I believe the roach hadn't foreordained *it*s horrific death and my ambivalent intrigue.

I squatted low with tissue paper in-hand and scrutinized the creature's idleness and decision-making process; the miniature being shared the same consciousness as my own, only constrained by the limitations of the body.

Enthralled by the potentialities, I aimed for the grotesque head and slammed my tissue downward, though the roach sensed my anomalous overhead movement and evaded imminent death—to *it*s detriment, for I shifted upwards to stand and struck down with the flat of my foot. I heard a wet crunch, louder than the typical resonance of a cracked carapace, and retracted my limb. The roach's innards adhered to my sock and moistened the fleshy bottom of my big toe. Visceral oozed from the roach's torso and deposited in the form of long, wormesque strands. I removed my sock while the roach languished on the floor and smelled a putrid whiff of the opaque grey puss smeared along the toeline. I sniffed again: Still putrid. *"Hm,"* I thought, *"That's unpleasant,"* and sniffed one final time before discarding the sock on top of a laundry heap in my living room closet.

The roach conserved *it*s last vestiges of life and lay still on the kitchen floor, though the vitals of the creature still coursed with activity. Rendered vulnerable to my machinations, I lifted the roach by an antenna, watched six segmented legs kick and squirm, lopped the creature onto *it*s shelled wings, and observed the desperation. I imagined myself as the roach: grieved with the loss of 1/4th of my internal matter, helpless on my back, expectant of death, yet incapable of conceiving death, only abiding by the instinctual response to pain.

Pain… I retrieved my bottle of tabasco sauce and dripped four drops onto the roach's ruptured torso. The creature reacted to the slight sensation with a few feeble kicks, though once the sauce had set for four seconds, the unbridled convulsions amplified. *"Little being,"* I stood and pondered, *"One day I will suffer all the pains I've ever inflicted."* I dripped two drops of tabasco sauce onto the creature's supine head and lowered my eyes three inches away from the spectacle. The roach paused all movement. The mandibles turned inward: a consumptive impulse. The roach began to thrash, and fifteen seconds after, relaxed to vibrations. Both antennas stiffened and quivered while four out of six legs shook and gyrated. If cockroaches could scream, this one would have. Four minutes of unmistakable anguish elapsed. The roach's exclamatory vibrations diminished to a series of death throe twitches. Two yellow eyes encompassed by a veil of red stared up at a speckled white ceiling.

October 30th, 2019

9:37 PM

My human resources manager, Trixie, a woman who has attempted to establish a bond with me since my employment began at the specialized chicken fast food establishment, badgered me about entering a Halloween-themed pumpkin creation competition. Trixie bemoaned of the effort she exerts in the organization of events for the workplace community only to be ignored. I conceded to her whims and agreed to write a poem to be displayed alongside the other pumpkin-themed creations: [44]

My Beautiful Dead Pumpkin

Held snug in my arms
Despite noxious rot within,
I lay in bed with my pumpkin
And wake to a congenial sensation
Of malleable flesh against
My moistened cheek.

---

[44] An anonymous judge of the pumpkin-themed creations awarded my pumpkin poem the title: "Most artistic and heartfelt?" The inflated ~~judgment~~ guess lacked conviction. I "won" a white paper bag with two contents within: The book, *From Sand Creek*, by Simon J. Ortiz, and a mini folding book light.

NOVEMBER

November 1st, 2019

4:24 PM

A misanthropic man drives a white van equipped with a stereophonic megaphone blaring repetitive nursery rhyme music and serves sugar cones topped with ice cream laced with 70 mg of arsenic per scoop to the children of a disadvantaged neighborhood.

"You overthink," said an idiot to a liar.

"I disagree. I'm thinking of a lich I once knew."

The idiot scoffed and adjusted his tie reflected in the mirror of a small two-toilet restroom situated inside the most popular bar of a quiescent city; he said, "Oh really?"

"I met him along the shoreline of my favorite beach one evening, I almost couldn't believe *it;* entirely skeletal, shrouded in a tattered black multilayered raiment."

"Did you roll a twenty and slay him with a critical strike?"

The liar glowered at his reflection and averted his eyes to the glossy white concave basin of a sink adjacent to his waist. The idiot's laughter resounded: harsh, puerile harmonics—for a brief instant. Both men proceeded with their personal thoughts, embittered by each other's silence.

The idiot proceeded, "I'm joking, guy."

"I'm not."

"Okay, okay; tell me about this lich then."

The liar upturned his crooked neck, gazed up at the profile of the idiot's handsome face, reckoned the engrossed expression of the countenance engaged with a mirror, stifled a sigh, returned his attention to the inner contours of the sink, and said, "The lich didn't speak much, only once, though he listened to me—at least I think *it* was a 'he' due to the tonality of the voice, though... how an undead would retain a voice—I don't know *how-*—anyway..." The liar exhaled through his nostrils, inhaled through his mouth, and continued, "I remember the way his robes blew in the wind, as though there was no form beneath, though I felt no fear... and he listened to my troubles, my grief, and my concerns for my future—on and on, I rambled, and finally, after at least a half-hour, I *stopped* and stood there waiting... The lich said, 'Don't worry,' and subsumed with the ocean."

The idiot finalized the adjustment of his tie, stroked his trimmed full-bodied beard, turned towards the liar, and said, "Yeah?"

"Yes."

"'Don't worry,' huh; some profound wisdom there. *Subsumed* with the ocean?"

"Yes, the lich waded out into the waves and was gone."

"How do you know *it* was a lich?"

"You just… I sensed—*know,* he was a lich."

"If *it* were a lich, you'd be one of his mindless servants right now."

"No, this one was benevolent."

The idiot attempted to restrain a chuckle and instead spittled onto the liar's face. "I'm sorry guy, did I spit on you?"

"Yes."

"I'm so sorry guy, but uh, you should get your head checked out. I thought you'd be a good wingman for tonight, but *it* turns out that you're obviously disturbed or high on something and I play my game straight, so…"

The liar stared at the sink and said nothing.

"Well," muttered the idiot, "You'll grow up someday"; he placed his right hand on the liar's right shoulder. "Hey—I'm just *joking* guy. God. C'mon, you can make up for your lousy roleplaying story by buying me a drink."

The hand displaced from the liar's shoulder. The door to the restroom swung open, slammed against a metal doorstop, and shut with a muffled thud against a doorframe.

6:27 PM

I write on the reading level of a twelve-year-old and marvel at the stupidity of others and myself. I serve fried chicken to college students, conduct movie trailer surveys at a mall on weekends, train with adjustable dumbbells at home every morning, read the works of dead men, and write a book about *it*. Now is a swell time to stop reading.

November 5th, 2019

8:48 PM

No, I'm grave in my redundant manner: If you (non-future self) continue to read, you're indecent. I've written well past my quota for the year, even with a majority of my writing in boot camp stolen from me; I've no desire to write anyway. I've reread my last year's error-ridden publication in print form and have reflected once more on my sentiments, deeds, and dishonors, summarized in succinct, lawful truth, to the best of my cognitive capabilities, and have determined the integrity of my sanity, *then* and *now,* to be *eminent.* Hark, an egotistical fool I am, and will always admit to an enemy or stranger; the sagacity of my intuitions integrated with my understanding of the human creature renders my observational convictions absolute.

I meet the criteria for the DSM-5 "schizoaffective" diagnosis on nearly all counts; my self-chosen social ostracism *is* a defense against the wretchedness of humanity as I understand *it* (through understanding myself), though this *is* chosen; therefore, am I disordered, if I can develop interpersonal relations if I desired? Aristotle claimed that "introversion" is self-centered. "Disorders" of personality revolve around self-centeredness, whereas extraversion is hailed and praised—for that is the nature of the extraverted being thrust amongst fellow self-seeking validators! One who seeks validation from others rather than from an inward resource is a "machiavellian" epitome; these people enact the most severe social changes among civilizations, juxtaposed by the subtle influences of artistic and technological achievements wrought by reclusive and "introverted" madmen of every age—I digress... Evaluate my failed character as a whole and consider what I am. I revoke my individuality. Empathy prevails. My fellow men and women perceive me and fail to understand me, *and* vice versa; therefore, uniqueness is considered by both parties in regards to the other, yet this is a fallacy, for a human is a human as a spade is a spade. Ignorance of another's history and inner world permits perceptions of flawed difference. Genius is ~~inherent~~ integral in all of us, untapped and latent for the majority. Environment and genetics are the determinants of the expression of one's culture, from Leonardo Da Vinci, to Charles Darwin, to Genghis Khan; if these men hadn't existed, another would supplant them with a variation of their contribution to the "progress" of humanity, routed on the same linear, cyclic path of regeneracy and destruction.

Every day is a battle against the intrigue of others.

Every instance which I write, I attain transitory providence, sanctified by my own judgment.

November 6th, 2019

9:11 PM

A young man fingered waffle fries into his mouth and watched me plop chicken nuggets into a small, red, rectangular box. He said, "How are you?" between bouts of chewing.

I scrutinized him and said, "Why do you ask?"

The man smiled, shrugged, and said, "I don't know—chit chat."

I spooned the final nugget into the box, pressed the lid closed, and said, "What is your self-assigned meaning in life?"

"To die a quick death."

I raised an eyebrow and said, "Your meaning in life is to die a quick death?"

"Yeah, why not?"

"I could assist you with that after my shift if you're willing to pay."

"Well I get my next paycheck for four-hundred dollars tomorrow so…"

I provided this man my full attention and said, "I believe I could get away with murdering you if I'm allotted the proper time to premeditate; from now until my shift's end should suffice if you agree."

The man sauntered away and my two present co-workers eyed me with newfound suspicion on account of my fluent and unexpected dialogue in contrast with my customary shift-long mutism.

A cute, church-attending high school girl visiting the college requested my phone number today.

I said, "Why?"

"I don't know."

"Alright," I conceded, her answer being ample justification. The girl retrieved her phone from her pocket, eager to transcribe my phone number. I said, "I don't have my phone number memorized. Meet me in the back locker hallway." The girl obeyed and met me. I proceeded: "What is your self-assigned meaning in life?"

The girl's eyes bulged; she stared down to my right and said, "I really don't know; I'll have to think about that. What's yours?"

"To write."

"To write," she repeated. "I'm a terrible writer."

"Tell me something you're good at."

"Hmm, well, I'm really good at math."

"I'm horrible at math."

The girl's enormous smile channeled latent sexual energy; I desired to grip her and lay her down in the hall for a romp right then; she said, "Well then maybe we'll comp-"

"There's a parallel then," I truncated her words with my own and turned to stash my phone back in my locker.

The girl said, "Thank you," and beamed at me.

I nodded. We meet tomorrow on my break to "get to know each other."

November 8th, 2019

7:44 PM

"The lich waded over swaths of eons-old sediment at the bottom of the Atlantic Ocean. Enshrouded with the dire chill of tenebrous water, the lich forwent clairvoyant sorcery to navigate and instead felt the contours of ancient depositories and slates of mafic rock between fleshless toes rendered tactile by a novice enchantment he had mastered within the annals of an old castle library a millennium prior. Intense physical pain wrought with each labored step wracked his immaterial mind: an effect of nebulous sensation elicited by the arcane stimulus of long-decayed nerves. *'To feel alive once more,'* thought the lich-"

"Dad—I don't want to hear anymore about the lich."

The liar ruffled his son's comforter and pushed long brown strands of hair away from a cherubic face staring back at him. "Oh? Why not?"

"How could *you* be underwater and *know* what the lich is thinking?"

"What do you mean?"

The boy bit his lower lip and said, "You said you knew the lich."

"I did, you just have to trust me; you don't trust your father?"

"No..."

491

"*No?*"

"I mean, yes."

"Then let me finish the story."

"I don't like the *lich*." The boy sighed, wriggled away from his father's hand, and pulled the comforter over his head.

The liar sat for several seconds, admired the lump beneath the blanket with a contemptuous smirk expressed on his close-set facial features, and said, "Alright… Another time, then."

The boy said nothing and remained statuesque beneath the cover.

The liar patted the side of the bed with an incurved palm once, stood, paced to the doorway, flicked a light switch off with a thumb, and stomped down a wooden stairwell with meticulous, heavyset steps.

November 9th, 2019

8:59 PM

I have no psychosis or neurosis; I'm confident, antagonistic, reticent, and taciturn. If this is a "mental illness," I'm fated 'til death.

I've discovered that Emily, the young girl who requested my phone number for primal reasons, is sixteen-years-old.

November 12th, 2019

8:16 AM

A McDonald's restaurant ball pit.

A dull man sat with a banal woman at one of the six rectangular plastic dining tables between two trash receptacles and observed four children play at leisure amongst the collective of multicolored fist-sized spheres. The man turned his head towards the woman, sipped soda through a fountain drink cup straw, and said, "Your sister plays nice with the other kids."

The woman nodded, crossed her legs beneath the table, leaned on the table with her elbows, gazed at her sister, and said nothing.

The man said, "I am still a stranger to you, and I'm uncertain what manner of relationship you desire, though I admit that I felt intense chemistry between us in the slight interaction we had the other day."

The woman blushed, avoided eye contact, hesitated for twenty-eight seconds, and said, "What kind of relationship do you desire?"

"I desire intimacy with you with no obligatory parameters. A bit of background on me is required as not to be construed as vain or superficial: I maintain no friendships by choice. I seek no partner, though you have pursued me, and relationships between men and women are blatant in their design. I'm selfish with my time; if you desire intimacy with me, we agree, and I'm willing to be as flexible as I am able."

"So are you open to a relationship or not? Sorry—I'm just making sure I understand."

"Yes, and you would be the only relationship I'd sustain and put energy into."

The woman smiled, eased her elbows off the table, rested both hands over her groin, and effused, "Well, I'm looking forward to getting to know you!"

"Excellent. I look forward to getting to know you as well."

"Anything you'd like to know about me... Is age a big thing for you?"

The man swallowed and said, "What do you mean by age being a 'big thing' for me?"

"I'm sixteen... " The girl's infantile sister screamed from the center of the ball pit; a boy two years her senior tugged at her braided brown hair and tickled her waist. "Is that an issue?"

"As long as we have a mutual understanding and respect for each other, I personally have no qualms with your age."

"Okay." The girl's eye's glimmered. "How old are you?"

"I'm twenty-seven, soon to be twenty-eight."

"Oh shoot—okay."

The man frowned and said, "Are you certain you want to engage in a relationship of this nature with a man of my age? I admit you're far younger than I expected." The girl opened her mouth to speak; the man licked his lips and hastened, "The age of consent in Arkansas is sixteen-years-old. If you have no issue with my age, I have no issue with yours."

The girl's attention shifted to her sister, to the dusty paneled ceiling nineteen-feet overhead, to the stained, discolored, burgundy table, to the man; she said, "Let's get to know each other first."

"Agreed."

The above circumstance is a reimagined text conversation between Emily and myself. I haven't corresponded with Emily since we failed to meet on several occasions throughout the past four days; I've no desire to elope with *anyone*, especially an adolescent girl. Sexual imagings are corny and mundane. Ideals of a salubrious relationship are a detriment to my self-assigned meaning and could never meet the criteria of the word *"salubrious"* by my own expectations: A self-fulfilling prophecy of solemn isolation on account of my egoism.

Always remember a cave.

November 14th, 2019

7:45 AM

Whenever I speak beyond necessity, I exude hatred. I swear a personal oath of being a (pseudo) mute for the remainder of my one-year duration in this locale. No longer will I speak to thrive, only to survive. I forsake spoken greetings and dismissals of my fellow human being; instead: gestures and head nods. The next rendition of the book in this series is to be titled *Outbursts of a Fast Food Worker; Thoughts of a Pseudo Mute,* for my nature and designation is premeditated.

The few instances in which I relay personal information to my peers, I am penalized by gossip. My supervisor has filed a company complaint on account of an auditor I had been aroused by due to personal questions she asked me while under observation. My performance suffered due to this state of arousal and my supervisor demands "justice." I admitted this circumstance a day later with a group of my peers as witnesses when the inquiry arose. A day after the aforementioned admission, my supervisor approached and interrogated me on the matter of my conduct with the auditor, to which I responded truthfully; hence, the (unjust) company complaint being issued.

Silence, forsooth.

November 15th, 2019

8:13 PM

I'm no writer, nor an author. I'm a journalist; behold:

The sixteen-year-old-girl, Emily, scrutinized my fastidious behavior while I labored behind a fast food service counter after a week of no correspondence between us. Pretty smiles, flirtatious eyelid raises, iris glimmers… I ignored the all-too-human signals and served her a small waffle fry with two packets of dipping sauce. The girl flashed me a final wry grin; when she turned, the countenance shifted to disgruntled disappointment.

I messaged her later:

"Hello."

"Hello."

"Let us sever relations, the minimum that we've had. I believe this to be the best course of action. I thought *it* best to inform you of my thought processes rather than letting our correspondence stagnate into an offensive end due to neglect."

Three hours elapsed. Emily said, "What do you mean?"

"I mean that we should cease communications with no contention felt between us."

"Okay? So goodbye?"

"Yes. Goodbye. I wish you well with your education."

A man sat, ham-fisted, knuckles flat against the bottom of his chin, and pondered a dilemma. Time ceased in the narrow, constrained annals of his ignorant train of thought. Hunger prompted him to shift forward at an uncomfortable angle, after which he retracted his last movement and leaned back against the stiff contours of a mundane metal chair. He suffered a slight chill, shivered, displaced his hand to his side, stood, donned a winter jacket, tied a pair of shoes to his feet, and exited his apartment.

The man hastened over sidewalks illuminated by the dampened light of low-wattage street lamps for several miles. He arrived at the doorstep of his destination, afflicted with cold, exasperated by a mental pandemonium, and pressed a tiny grey doorbell. No response. He pushed the doorbell again, waited eighteen seconds, and performed six consecutive monotonous raps with a single arched knuckle of a right-hand index finger. He gazed up at the door's rectangular portico, projected his contempt onto two misaligned screws fastened to the woodwork, and waited; though he could wait no longer and extended an arm, gripped an unaffixed door handle, and pushed inward into the warm, air-conditioned comfort of a small studio apartment.

A young girl preoccupied with oral and anal sex prostrated on a twin size frameless bed, mounted on both ends by two athletic men twice her age. She met eyes with the man standing motionless in her doorway, disengaged from fellatio, and said, "Randy? What the fuck are you doing here?"

The man in the doorway scrutinized the contended visages of the two men engaged in the throes of uninvolved lust, lowered his attention to the rounded nose of the girl, and said, "Let us sever relations, the minimum that we've had. I believe this to be the best course of action. I thought *it* best to inform you of my thought processes rather than letting our correspondence stagnate into an offensive end due to neglect."

The girl wiped phlegm off her chin and said, "What do you mean?"

"I mean that we should cease communications with no contention felt between us."

"Okay? So goodbye?"

"Yes. Goodbye. I wish you well with your education."

November 17th, 2019

9:36 AM

An eighteen-year-old aspiring author approached me with a pleasant countenance at the start of my mall survey shift yesterday. "I read your book," he stated, expecting a polite response.

I raised an eyebrow and nodded.

"It's interesting, good though. I liked *it*."

I frowned, nodded once, forced a grin, and turned to seek victims to interrogate.

The young man said, "Are you okay?" and began to frown too.

I continued to nod, held out an upright thumb, and veered away.

The young man meandered and followed me around the circuit, his expression anxious and longing; the unrequited validation of his validation of me tormented him. I felt sorrow on his behalf… guilt… When he joined conversations other men and women attempted to have with me, he stood by, observed me, and *understood* the reasons for my silence. In fact, a hint of amusement accented his disappointed features while others relayed to me their activities, hopes, and pursuits, only to have me acknowledge them with simple gestures of my body and facial twinges.

496

'2 out of 5'

"Enjoyable fiction. Awful narrator.

"Baethan is a sad excuse for a man."

'5 out of 5'

"Favorite series ever!

"I hope he suffers a long life and dies before me."

'1 out of 5'

"Gay.

"The guy drops out of Navy boot camp, complains, avoids women, and is fucked in the ass by a black man. This shit is queer as fuck."

'3 out of 5'

"Tired exposition.

"I've enjoyed the series so far up until the end of the third; I see where this is going and I'm ready to spend my time with something better. He's an average writer and quite frankly I think his style of addressing the readers is a droll and crude attempt to break the fourth wall and be edgy. His stories are nice, if not a bit far-fetched, though *all* are too short, as if he had an idea for a few minutes and then stopped putting forth the effort for an authentic craft.

"The title is misleading: 1/4th of the book is about Navy boot camp and he fails to graduate for reasons he purports were by his own choice. Overall the book is valueless and depressing. The schizophrenic overtone is gone, and surprisingly, I missed that the most."

'2 out of 5'

"Dramatic little bitch.

"So I'll start by saying that his writing is entertaining but I can't stand him for who he is—which is a dramatic, spoiled, crybaby, who surmises that his limited personal experience encapsulates the objective reality everyone experiences.

"I've no respect for this guy and languished my way through the miasma of text simply because I spent money on *it*. The cheaper digital version kept me occupied in transit during many business trips (plane flights and bus rides) and raised my own self-esteem because I am a successful self-starter with healthy relationships opposed to the self-absorbed jejune twit that is *Baethan Balor*. A unique little find, comparable to a spec of fool's gold found in a handful of dirt with the use of a strainer by a child on one of those nature-themed field trips contemporary teachers are fond of. I'd give a 1 out of 5 rating if not for all the laughter provided at the expense of the author."

'1 out of 5'

"God-Tier Edgelord.

"Super fucking cringe. Less nihilistic crybaby 'look at me I'm a special snowflake millennial and I know so much about psychology even though I have zero credentials' writing and more please kill yourself tbh thanks."

'5 out of 5'

"very funny..

"i laughs and smiled!"

'3 out of 5'

"Disappointed.

"As a woman who once had sex with Baethan (I won't disclose his real name out of general respect), I can confirm that he is a piece of shit. He's an okay writer I guess, but still. He didn't bother to write about the sex we had so I obviously didn't mean anything to him, which I don't really care; I mean, fuck him, I guess."

'1 out of 5'

"Despicable.

"If there is a hell, that's where Baethan is going. His acts may be good-natured and kind, but his thoughts condemn him to an agony beyond human imagination. The guy kills insects with tabasco sauce and took *it* up the ass from a dude twice his age... just a sick and twisted freak. I'm thankful the U.S. military expelled him from service. A guy like him should be in a padded room, not a destroyer."

'2 out of 5'

"Lowlife scum.

"Balor has no respect for anyone, not even himself. A worthless, miserly example of the worst humanity could produce. I liked a few of his poems."

'4 out of 5'

"Intriguing.

"The book as a whole is worth the read with some remarkable pieces of fiction dispersed throughout, but Baethan is undoubtedly one of the biggest creeps I've ever read about. I won't spoil anything, but about 3/5ths of the way through you start to realize how disturbed the man *actually* is— presuming what's been written is true. There were many moments when I had to set the book down... *slowly*... and take a break for a few days or a week, as if the pages I held were tainted with innate foulness."

November 18th, 2019

10:00 PM

"What's wrong Baethan? You haven't been talking lately," said a young man by the name of Marvin, my closing companion at the fast-food establishment. I spoke to him for the first time in three days a moment prior: I implored him to relieve me of my portable speaker, for I derive no satisfaction from music any longer. He resisted at first, and tears welled in his eyes, for he considers me a friend despite my immediate rejections of such claims.

I said, "I've learned several lessons from speaking at work."

"Does this have to do with the auditor? Because everyone was worried and concerned for you—they care for you and you haven't been talking lately-"

"No, Hunter. Nobody *cares* for anyone but themselves here. They're three old women who delight in drama and all of them latch onto what little I speak and distort my words amongst each other." Hunter opened his mouth to speak, and instead, *listened* to me. I continued despite my better judgment, *"It* amuses me: how people yearn for validation, how each uttered syllable is intended to garner another's attention, no matter how obtuse and vapid the context is—yourself, for instance, you-"

"Hey I don't want validation. I just miss talking to you. My other friends don't even talk to me."

"I'm not your friend, Hunter."

He looked at the portable speaker I had gifted him two minutes prior, back to me, with confused, bleary eyes, and averted his visage beneath the brim of a ballcap. I spoke no more the remainder of the night.

November 19th, 2019

9:08 AM

The first few steps out of the airport after being separated from the U.S. Navy, into the blaze of a hot afternoon, surrounded by fields of barren grass, sparse forest, and several stretches of road, is the most confident I have ever been in my life. Money and time: inconsequential. Materials and vanity: unworthy. Relationships and responsibility: nonexistent. The world to me had been equatable to a flower in bloom, to be plucked, reveled, discarded before one's feet, and trodden over. The joy of the fear *of* the unknown is a bygone memory—true sentiments unretrievable, convoluted by the paltry words I jotted down concerning abstract ideas pertinent to future hopes which occluded my mind of equanimity I experienced at the moment. To have nothing and be nothing, to lay down to sleep on the frigid, unyielding cement of a loading dock attached to an office supply department store, scourged by mosquitoes and vexed by a myriad of city lights, I rejoiced.

November 20th, 2019

7:48 AM

Two nights ago, while I paced my apartment and read Arthur Schopenhauer's *Studies in Pessimism,* a mature millipede, braced against the wall and carpet of my living room, distracted me. I marked my page, set the book down, and touched the millipede, which incited the harmless creature to curl into a defensive position. I picked *it* up and dropped *it* into a small, translucent, rectangular plastic container. A drop of tabasco sauce spurted from a downward slanted bottle held by my right hand and coated the millipede with a caustic impetus. For three seconds, the millipede undertook no action, stationary, docile—and at once *it* uncurled: a vehement thrash of a reddened, elongated body which oscillated over the slicked plastic contours; hundreds of legs kicked and wavered, each stained with a scarlet sheen. Glazed eyes protruded from the crimson-colored head. The creature zigzagged, aimless, panicked, wracked with singular anguish exclusive to the unique circumstances, and lifted one-third of *it*s body into a vertical point, whereby several dozens of legs clamored at stagnant air.

I observed, my head bent inches above the afflicted. Thereby, I befell an inexplicable state of arousal and sought to satisfy this desire. I removed all articles of my clothing and stood naked in my kitchen beside the agonized millipede and gripped my genitalia with a resolute hold… How long had *it* been since I *desired* release? Before homelessness, before boot camp, there had been Pelagia, and now, a millipede writhed and struggled against an ineluctable doom before me. I closed my eyes, imagined the inconceivable torment, and stroked. Minutes elapsed; the millipede calmed; my ineffectual masturbatory attempt proved fruitless— the images distilled in my mind, fleeting—recollections of past lovers, of flesh, of petulant moans and acquiescent arms dominated by the weight of my body—the *memories*—otiose and juvenile. I powered on the video recording option of my writing device and aimed the camera at my body; the familiarity provided solace and confidence, and I resumed—a moment, and paused, for I caught the millipede at a threshold of respite—deliberate and calm with *it*s movements. Another drop of tabasco sauce and the reprieve dissipated, supplanted by hopeless desperation; the consciousness confined to the miniature body—miniature only by the account of *I* who perceived *it*—reared up and *froze…* a stasis: a statuesque embodiment of terror.

I gazed upon myself projected on the screen of my writing device and experienced a severance of the body, my consciousness expunged from the flesh, and reckoned the image of my repulsive form as a representation of a unified humanity. My chassis exemplified the beautiful, deformed, graceful, ugly, frail, strong, corpulent—the black and the white—the young and the old—*all* at once, and yet, there *was* nothing—no stimulus, no satisfaction, no pleasure; there had been a singularity of a lack of feeling: an abatement of sensation. I ejaculated into the plastic container and submersed the millipede in a pool of semen.

With incommensurable authenticity,
- Baethan

EPILOGUE

The man survived another year.

Printed in the United States
By Bookmasters